MAIN CHARACTER

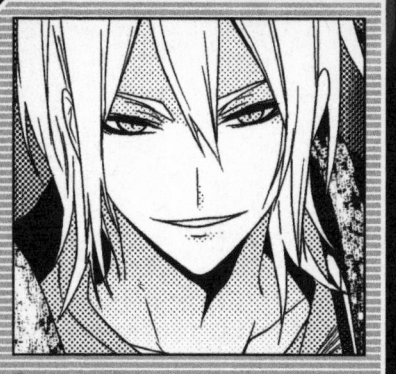

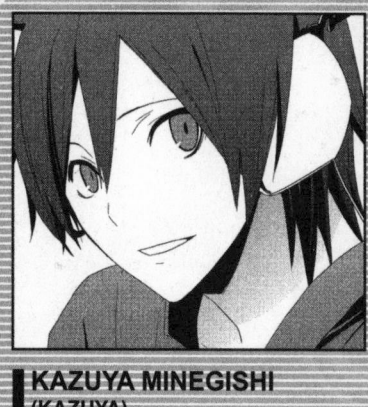

KAZUYA MINEGISHI
(KAZUYA)

Used a portable gaming device known as a COMP to make contracts with demons after gaining the power to command them. He fought off Beldr, Belial, Jezebel, and Belzaboul—contenders for the crown of the demon king—and absorbed their power.

NAOYA
(NAOYA)

Kazuya's cousin. Known as a genius programmer with staggering insight, he encourages Kazuya to follow the path to becoming the king of demons.

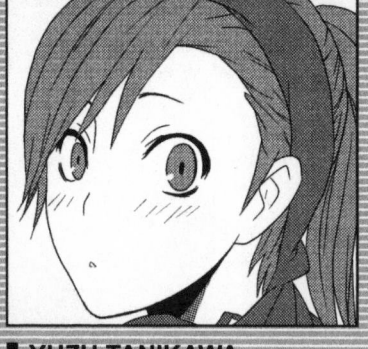

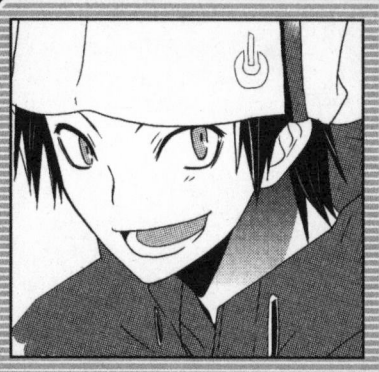

ATSURO KIHARA
(AT-LOW)

Kazuya's classmate and best friend. He's an aspiring programmer, and has been hanging with the big boys on the Internet since he was in grade school. Is currently working with Kazuya and Yuzu.

YUZU TANIKAWA
(YUZ)

Kazuya's childhood friend and high school classmate. Is currently working with Kazuya and Atsuro.

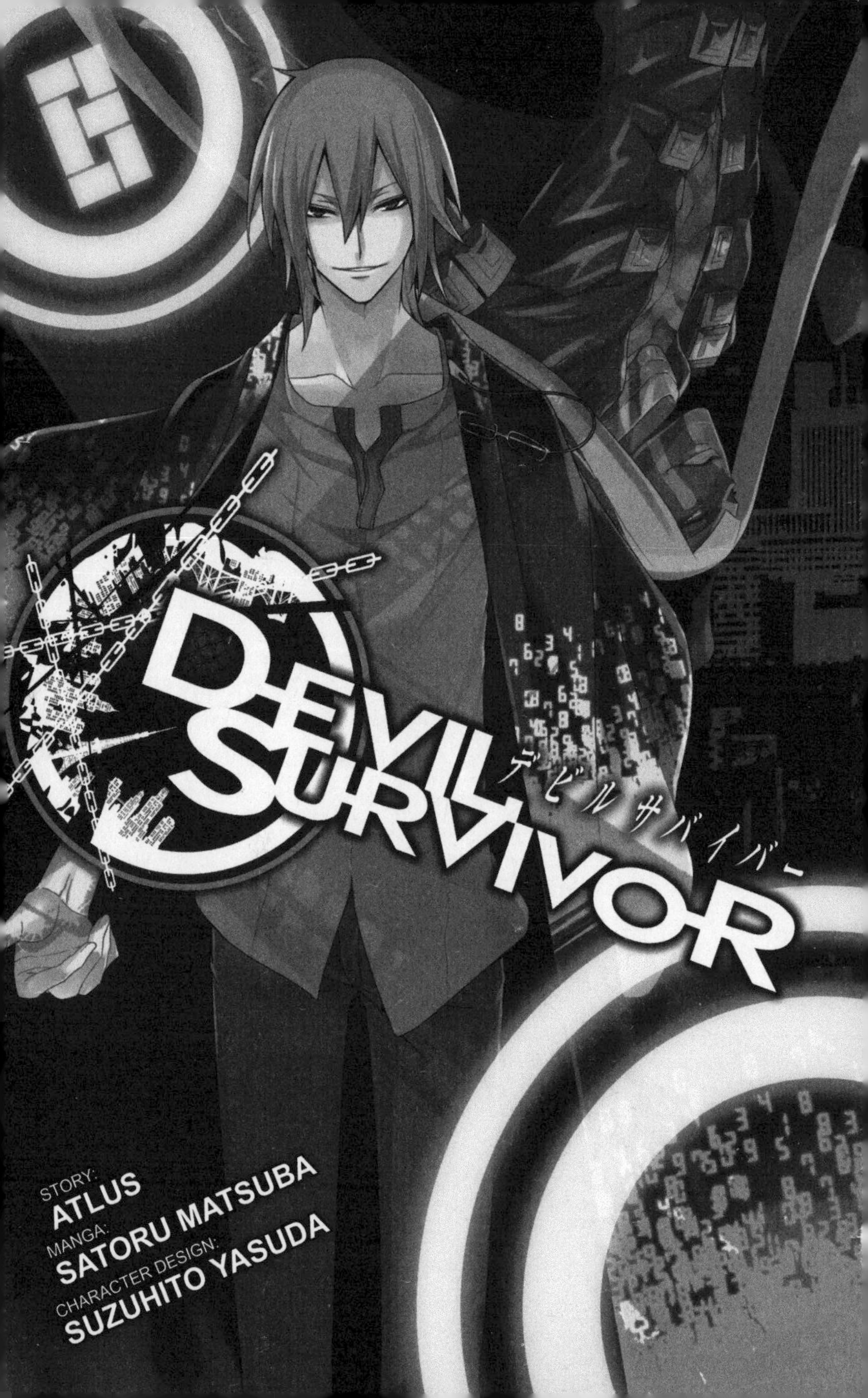
DEVIL SURVIVOR
デビルサバイバー
STORY:
ATLUS
MANGA:
SATORU MATSUBA
CHARACTER DESIGN:
SUZUHITO YASUDA

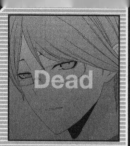

KEISUKE TAKAGI (K-T)

A middle school classmate of Atsuro's. He had a righteous streak, which led him to save Atsuro from bullying, and hated all kinds of wrongdoing. He fought Kaido as a way to stay true to his convictions, and lost his life in the process.

■ ■ ■

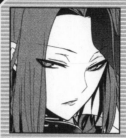

YOSHINO HARUSAWA (HARU)

Current lead vocalist of the indie band D-Va. She worries about the band's former vocalist, Aya, who was a strong influence in her career. Her singing voice seems to have the power to summon demons, and to banish them…

■ ■ ■

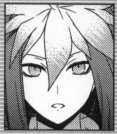

AMANE KUZURYU (AMANE)

A priestess of the Shomonkai religious organization. She had the demon Jezebel and the angel Remiel living inside her, but Jezebel was destroyed by Kazuya.

■ ■ ■

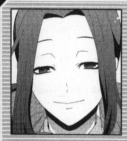

MARI MOCHIZUKI (MARI)

A nurse at an elementary school. She once worked as Atsuro's tutor. A friend of Kaido and his brother since childhood, she has an ongoing hatred for the killer who took Kaido's brother from them in the Bloodless Murders.

■ ■ ■

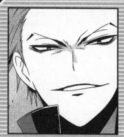

TADASHI "KAIDO" NIKAIDO (NIKAIDO)

Leader of the Daemons, a gang based in the Shibuya area. He's searching for his brother's killer so he can settle the score. He harbors a secret fondness for his childhood friend Mari.

■ ■ ■

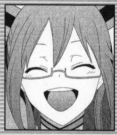

MIDORI KOMAKI (DOLLY)

An Internet idol who enjoys tremendous popularity as the cosplayer Dolly. The influence of her late father, combined with her own desire to transform herself, gives her a strong yearning to be a defender of justice.

■ ■ ■

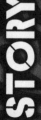

Finally, we dive into the 7TH DAY (THE LAST DAY)

Kazuya has defeated two great and powerful demons—the contenders to be the king of demons, Jezebel and Belzaboul—and absorbed their Bel powers. Our heroes head for the top floor of the Roppongi Hills Building, where they can access the demon summoning program's server and send the demons that have been running rampant across Tokyo back to the demon world. There they find the leader of the Shomonkai—the group that caused the lockdown—as well as the object of the Shomonkai's worship and the one closest to becoming king of all demons, Belberith!

CONTENTS

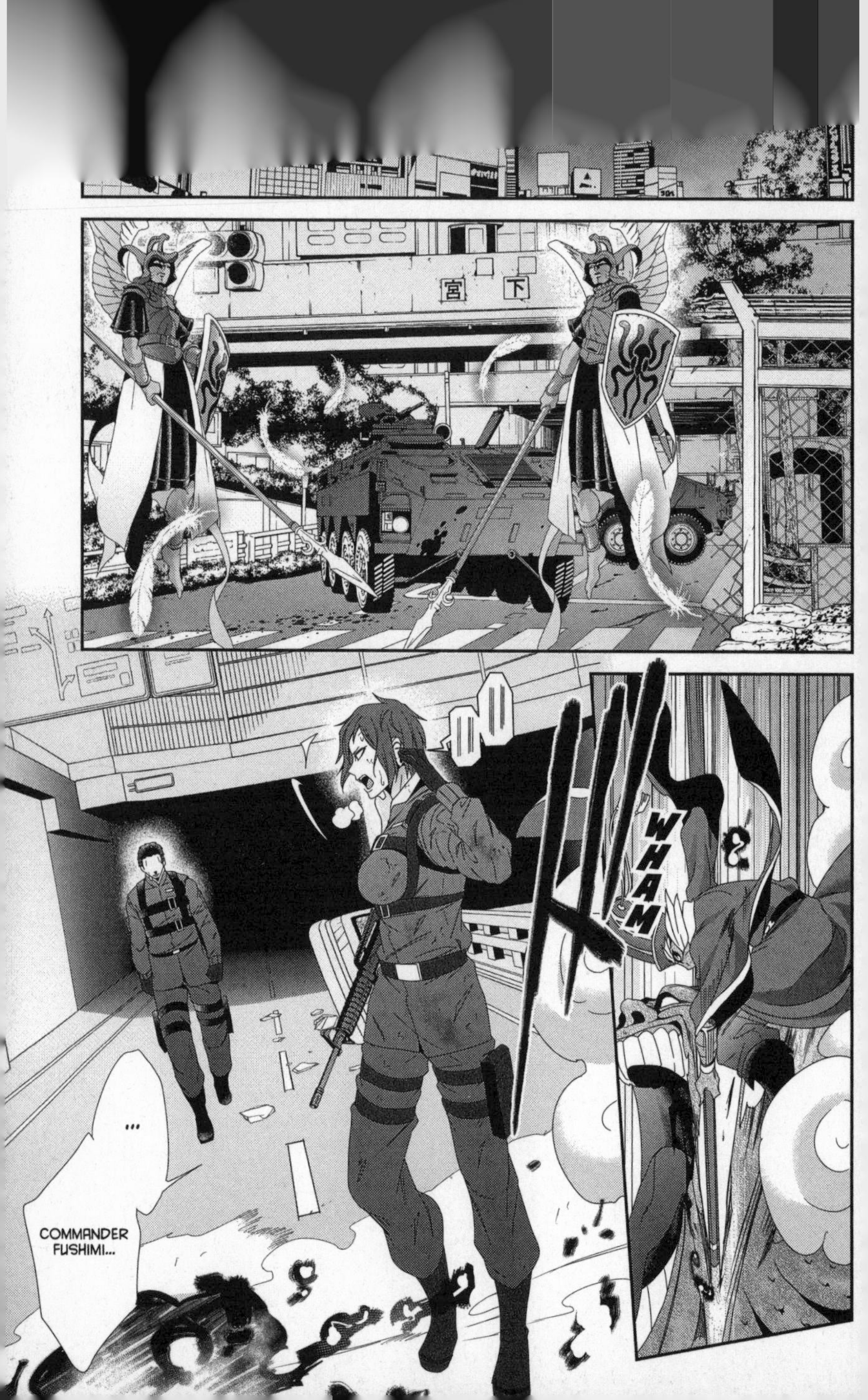
宮下
WHAM
!!
...
COMMANDER FUSHIMI...

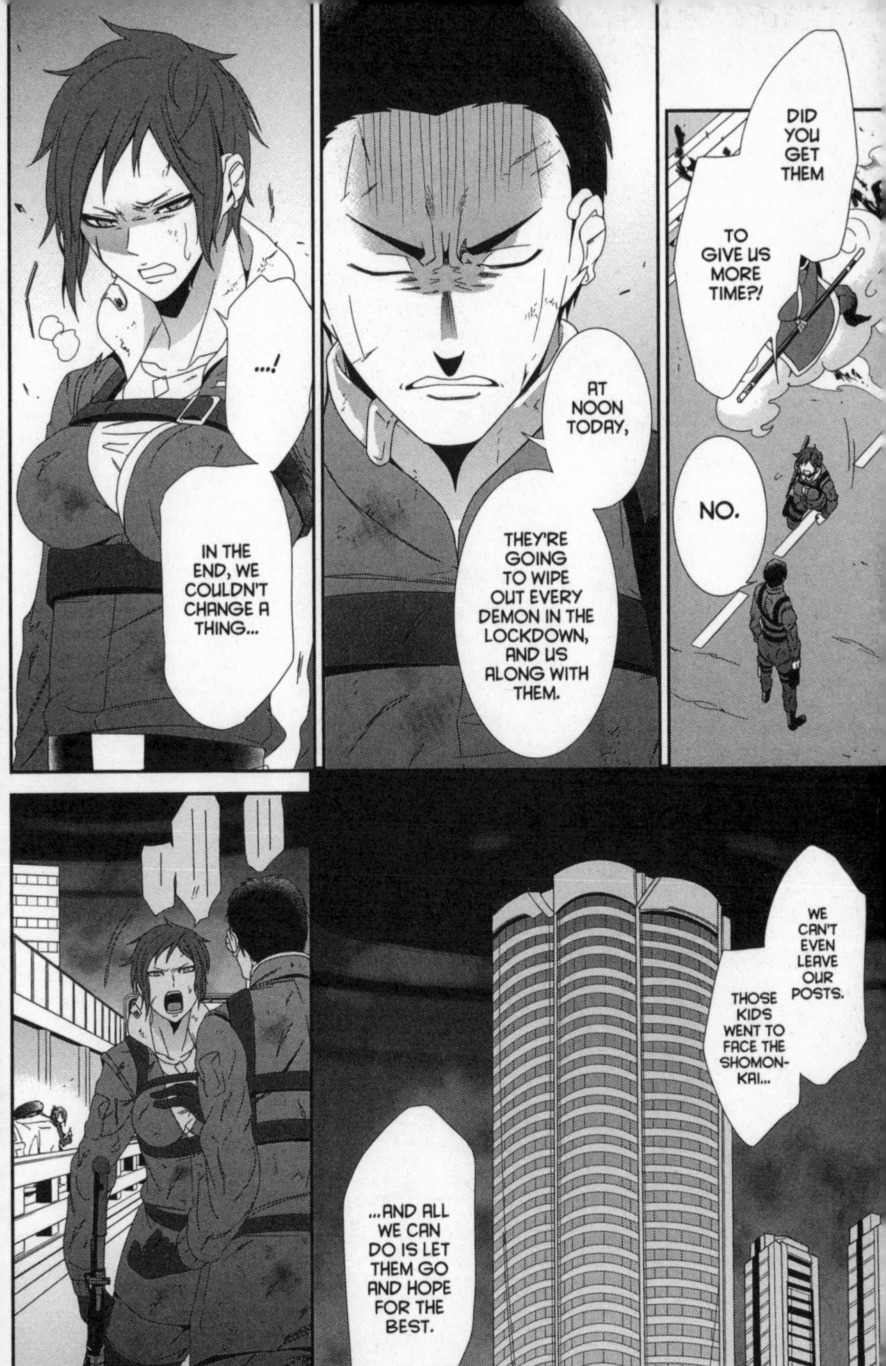
DID YOU GET THEM TO GIVE US MORE TIME?!
NO.
AT NOON TODAY,
THEY'RE GOING TO WIPE OUT EVERY DEMON IN THE LOCKDOWN, AND US ALONG WITH THEM.
...!
IN THE END, WE COULDN'T CHANGE A THING...
WE CAN'T EVEN LEAVE OUR POSTS.
THOSE KIDS WENT TO FACE THE SHOMON-KAI...
...AND ALL WE CAN DO IS LET THEM GO AND HOPE FOR THE BEST.

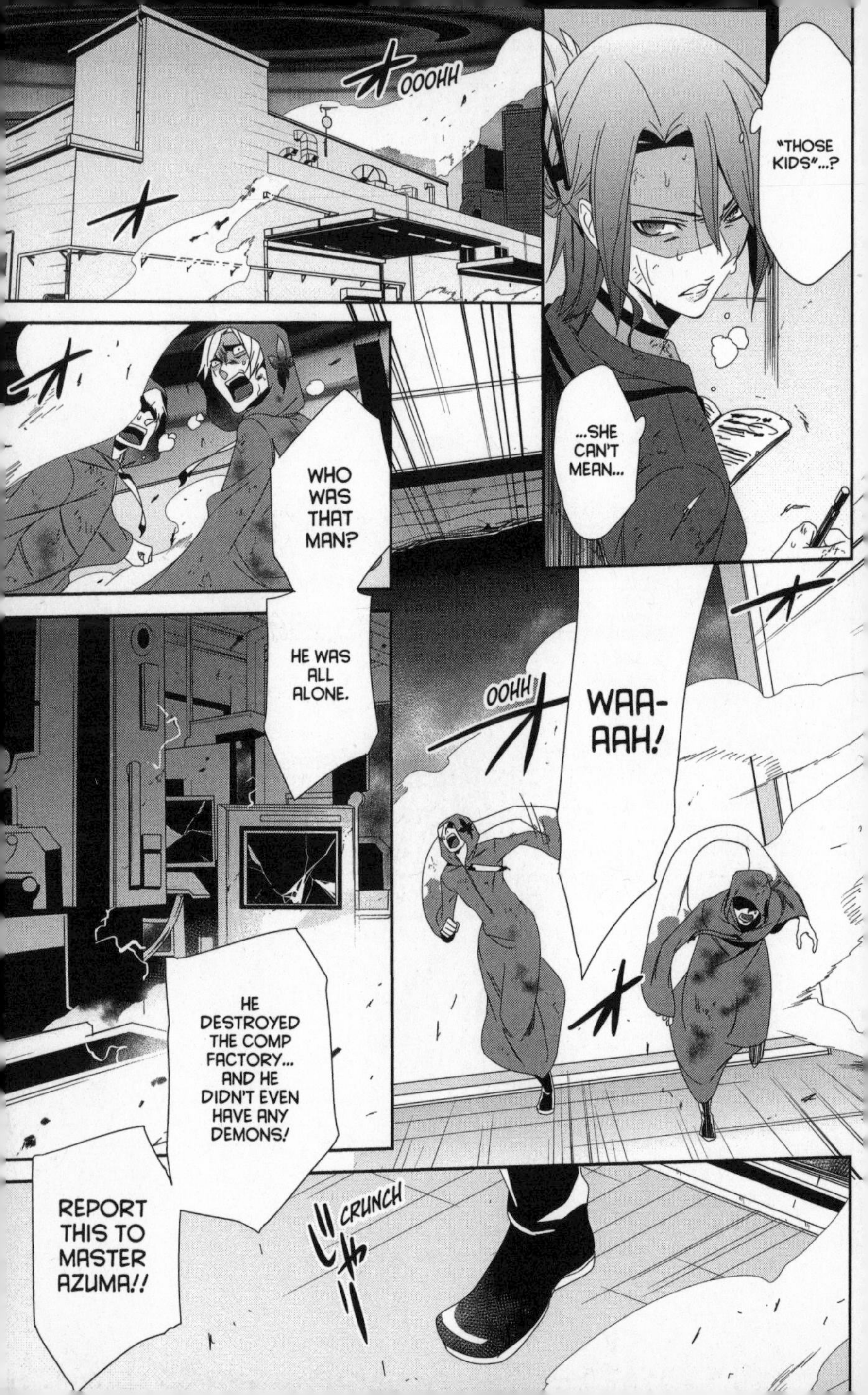
"THOSE KIDS"...?
...SHE CAN'T MEAN...
OOOHH
WHO WAS THAT MAN?
WAA-AAH!
OOHH
HE WAS ALL ALONE.
HE DESTROYED THE COMP FACTORY... AND HE DIDN'T EVEN HAVE ANY DEMONS!
CRUNCH
REPORT THIS TO MASTER AZUMA!!

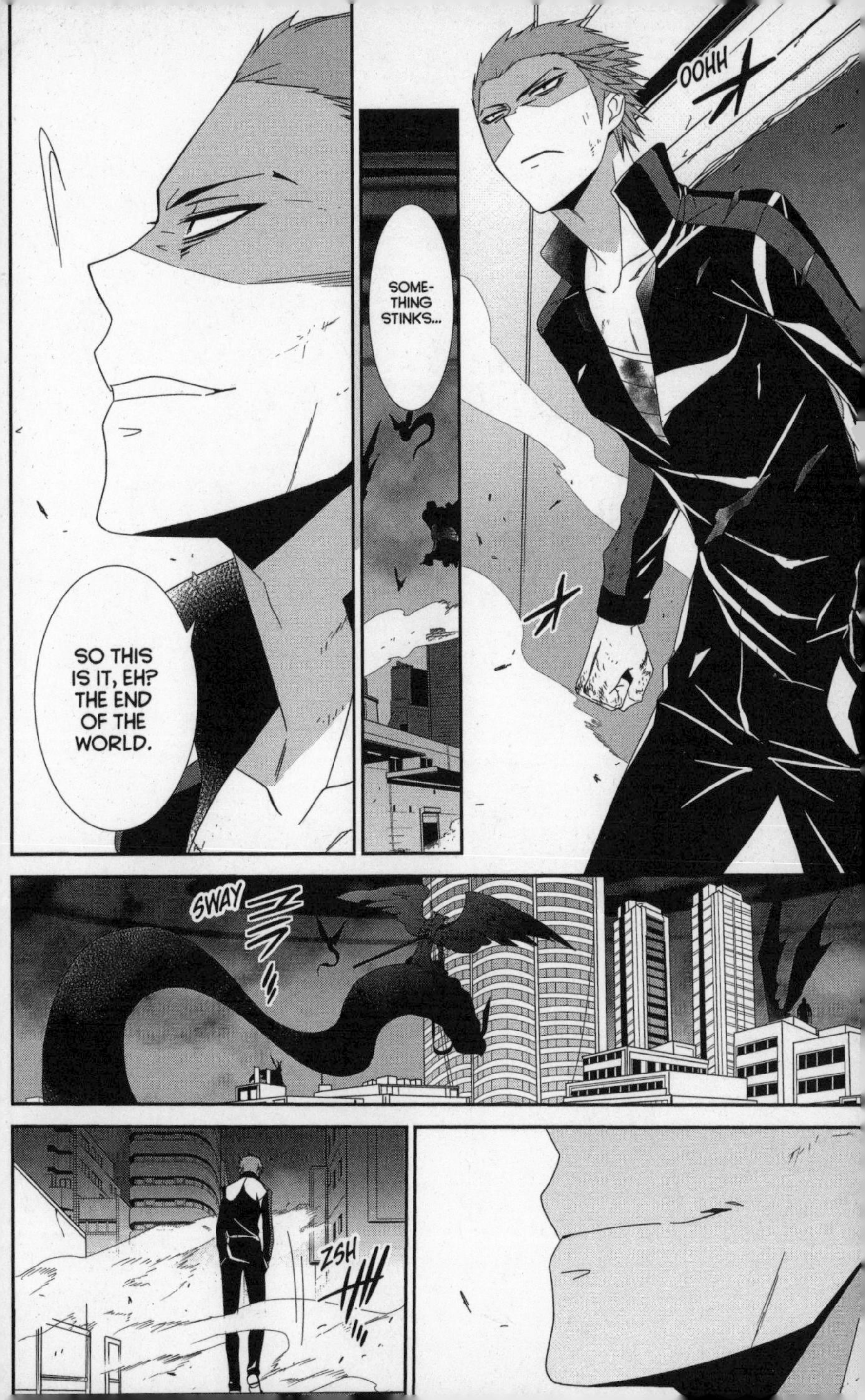
OOHH
SOME-THING STINKS...
SO THIS IS IT, EH? THE END OF THE WORLD.
SWAY
ZSH

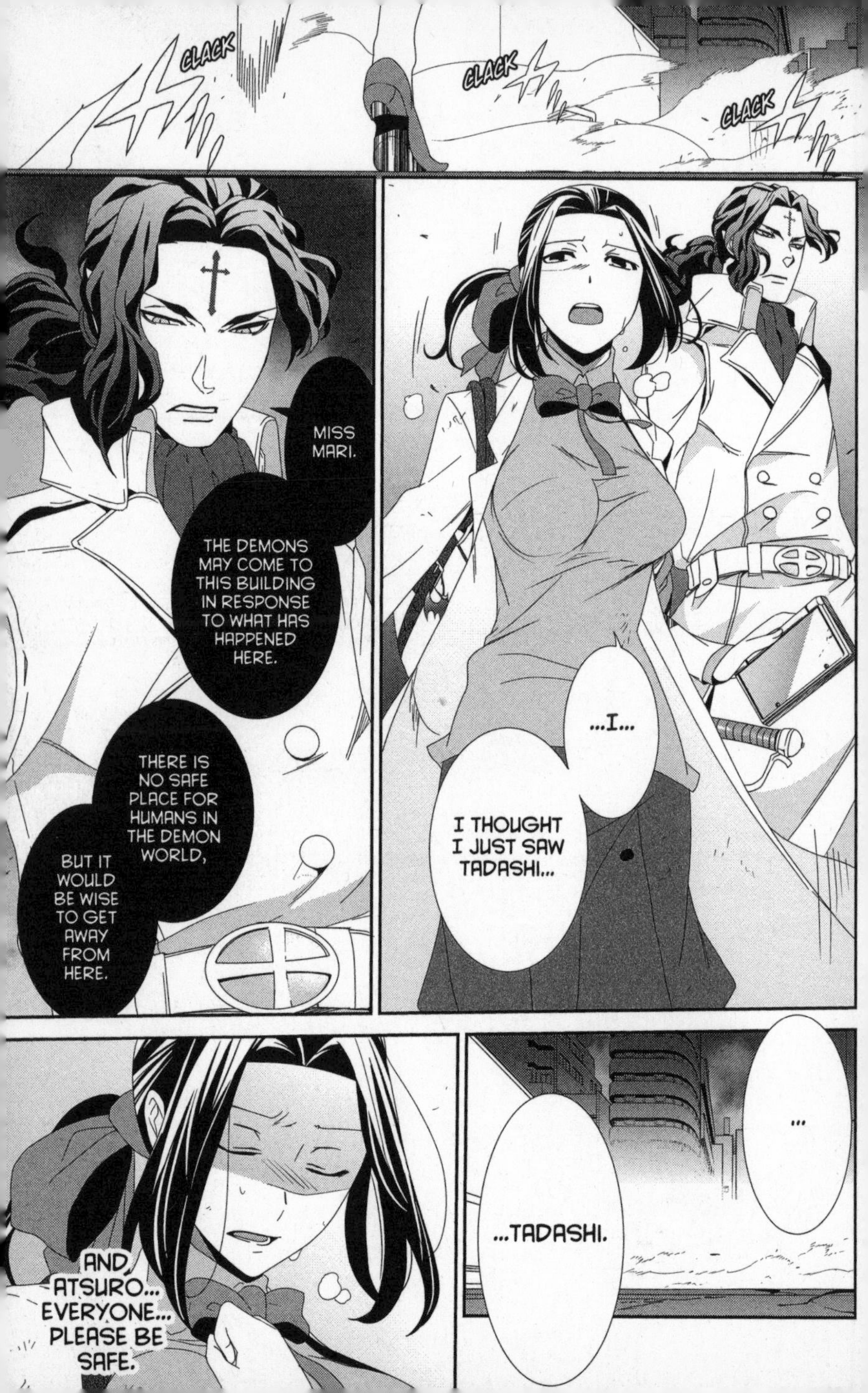
CLACK
CLACK
CLACK
...I...
I THOUGHT I JUST SAW TADASHI...
MISS MARI.
THE DEMONS MAY COME TO THIS BUILDING IN RESPONSE TO WHAT HAS HAPPENED HERE.
THERE IS NO SAFE PLACE FOR HUMANS IN THE DEMON WORLD,
BUT IT WOULD BE WISE TO GET AWAY FROM HERE.
...
...TADASHI.
AND, ATSURO... EVERYONE... PLEASE BE SAFE.

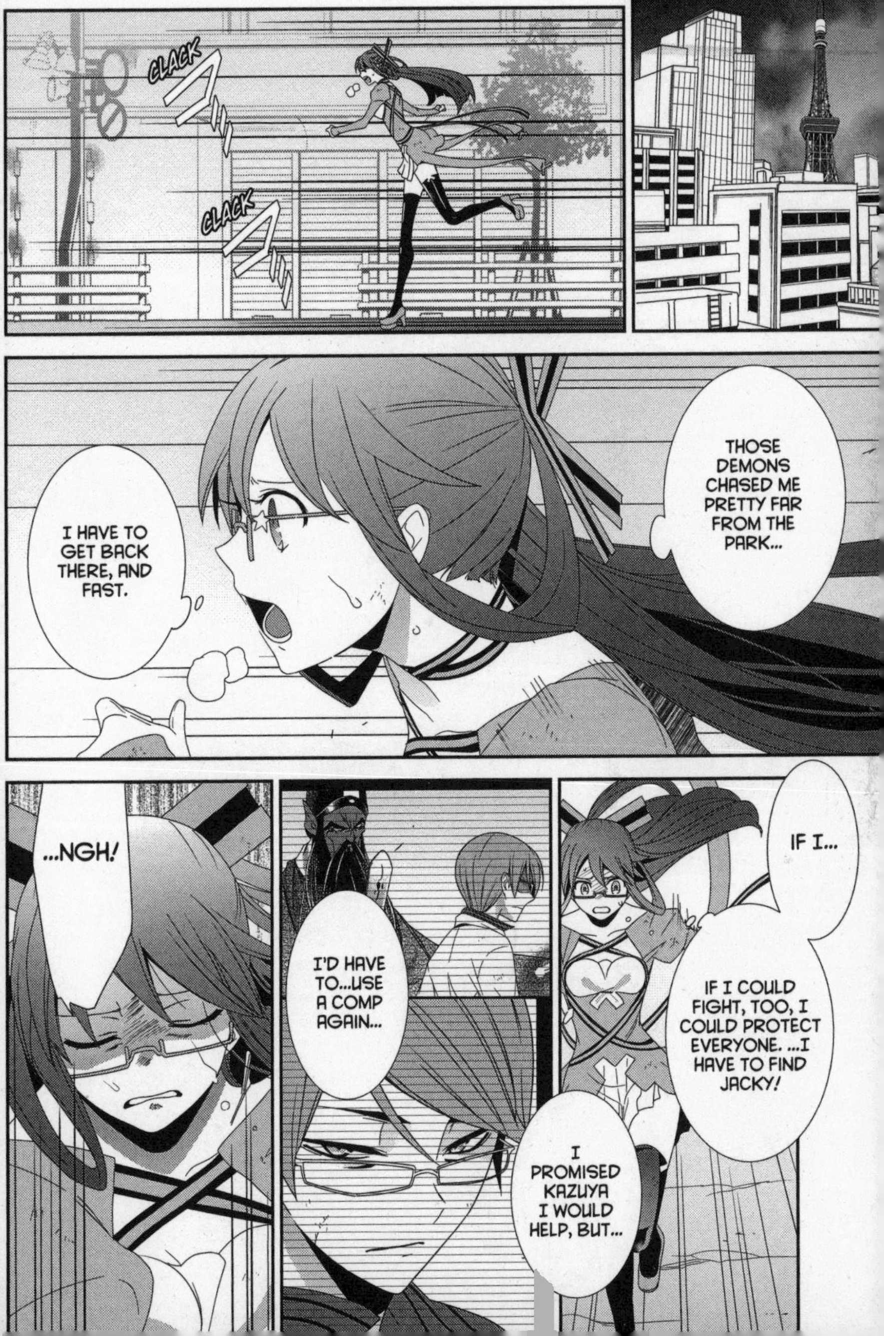
CLACK
CLACK
THOSE DEMONS CHASED ME PRETTY FAR FROM THE PARK...
I HAVE TO GET BACK THERE, AND FAST.
IF I...
IF I COULD FIGHT, TOO, I COULD PROTECT EVERYONE. ...I HAVE TO FIND JACKY!
I PROMISED KAZUYA I WOULD HELP, BUT...
I'D HAVE TO...USE A COMP AGAIN...
...NGH!

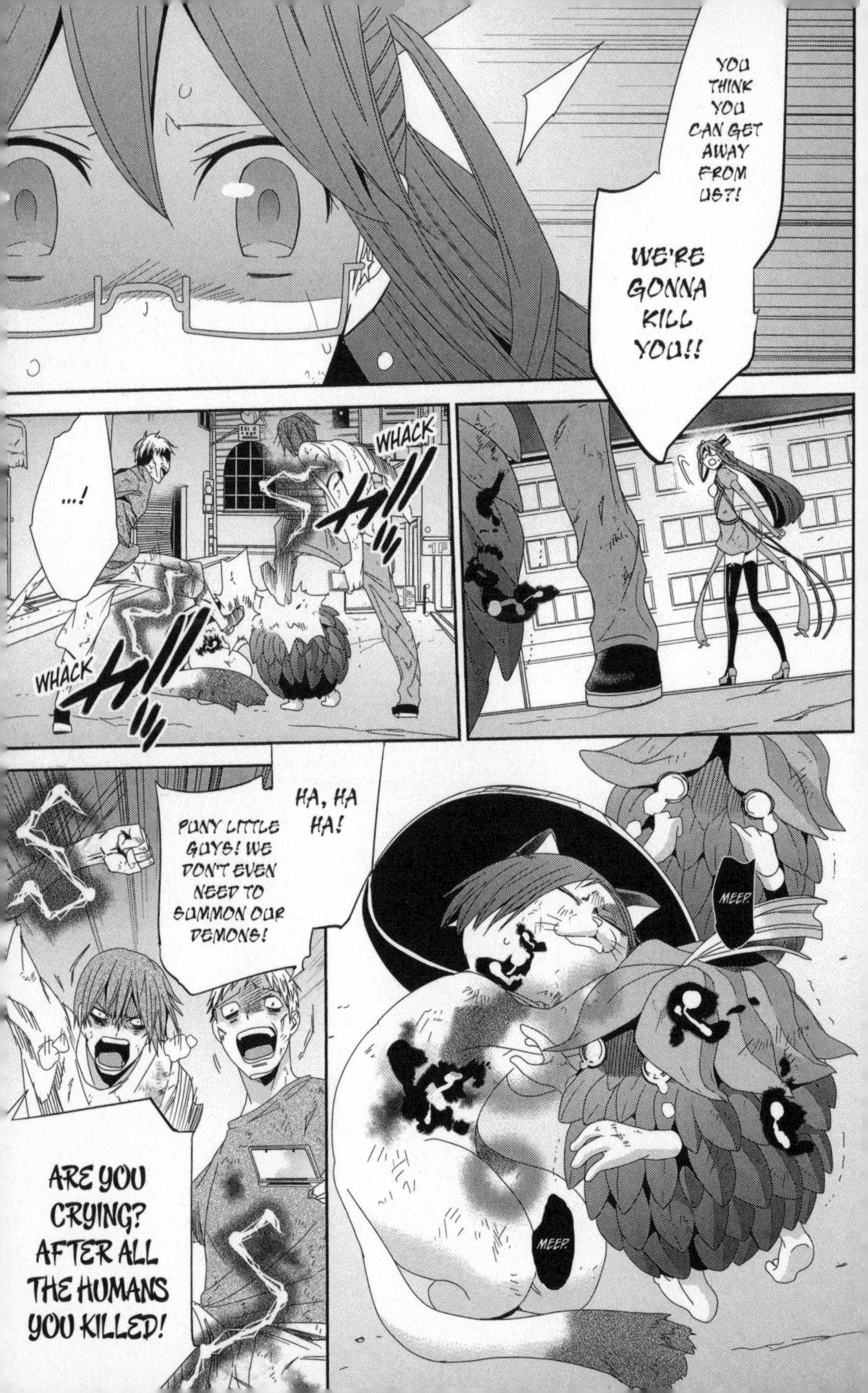
YOU THINK YOU CAN GET AWAY FROM US?!
WE'RE GONNA KILL YOU!!
WHACK
...!
WHACK
MEEP.
MEEP.
HA, HA HA!
PUNY LITTLE GUYS! WE DON'T EVEN NEED TO SUMMON OUR DEMONS!
ARE YOU CRYING? AFTER ALL THE HUMANS YOU KILLED!

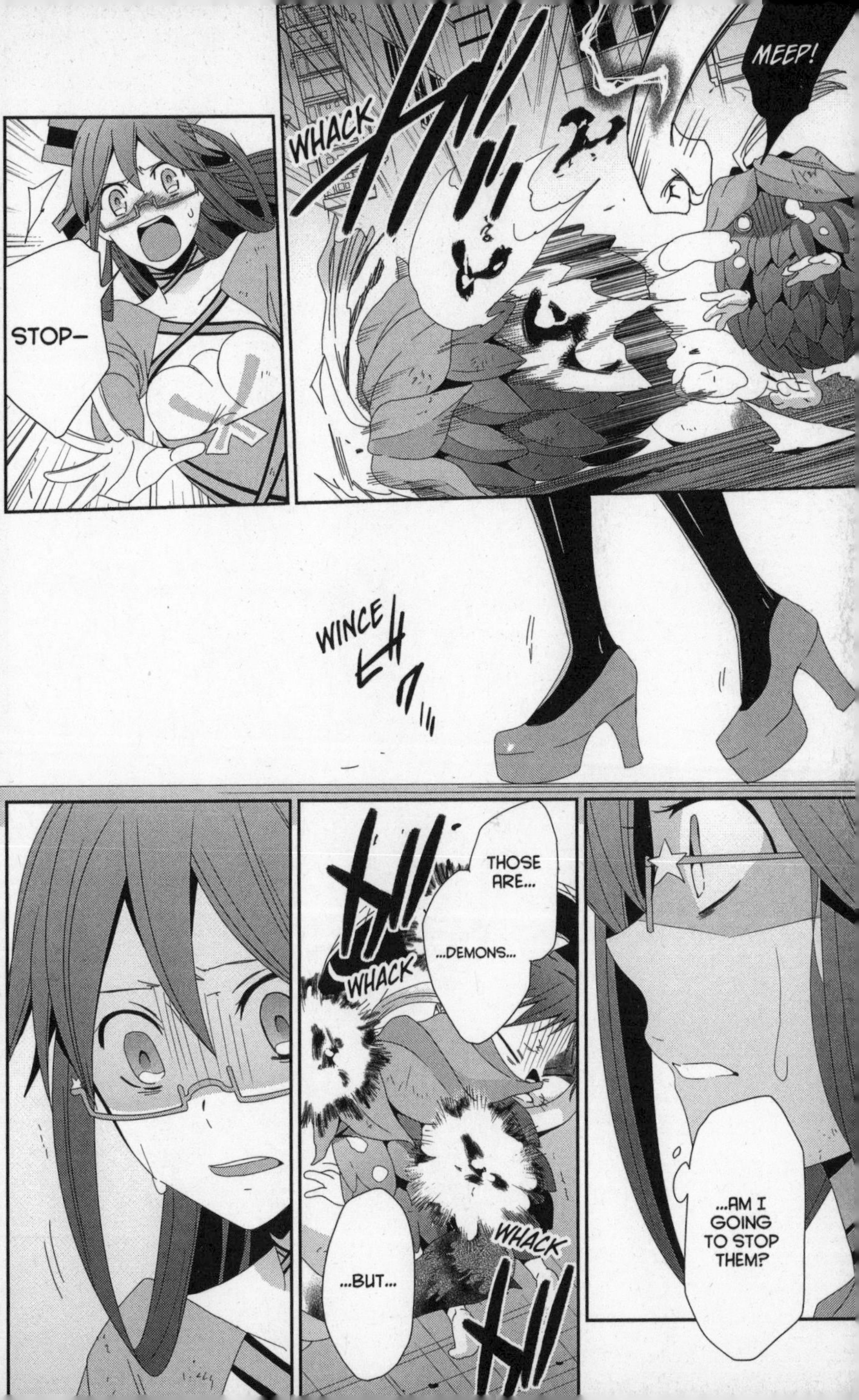
MEEP!
WHACK
STOP–
WINCE
...AM I GOING TO STOP THEM?
THOSE ARE...
...DEMONS...
WHACK
WHACK
...BUT...

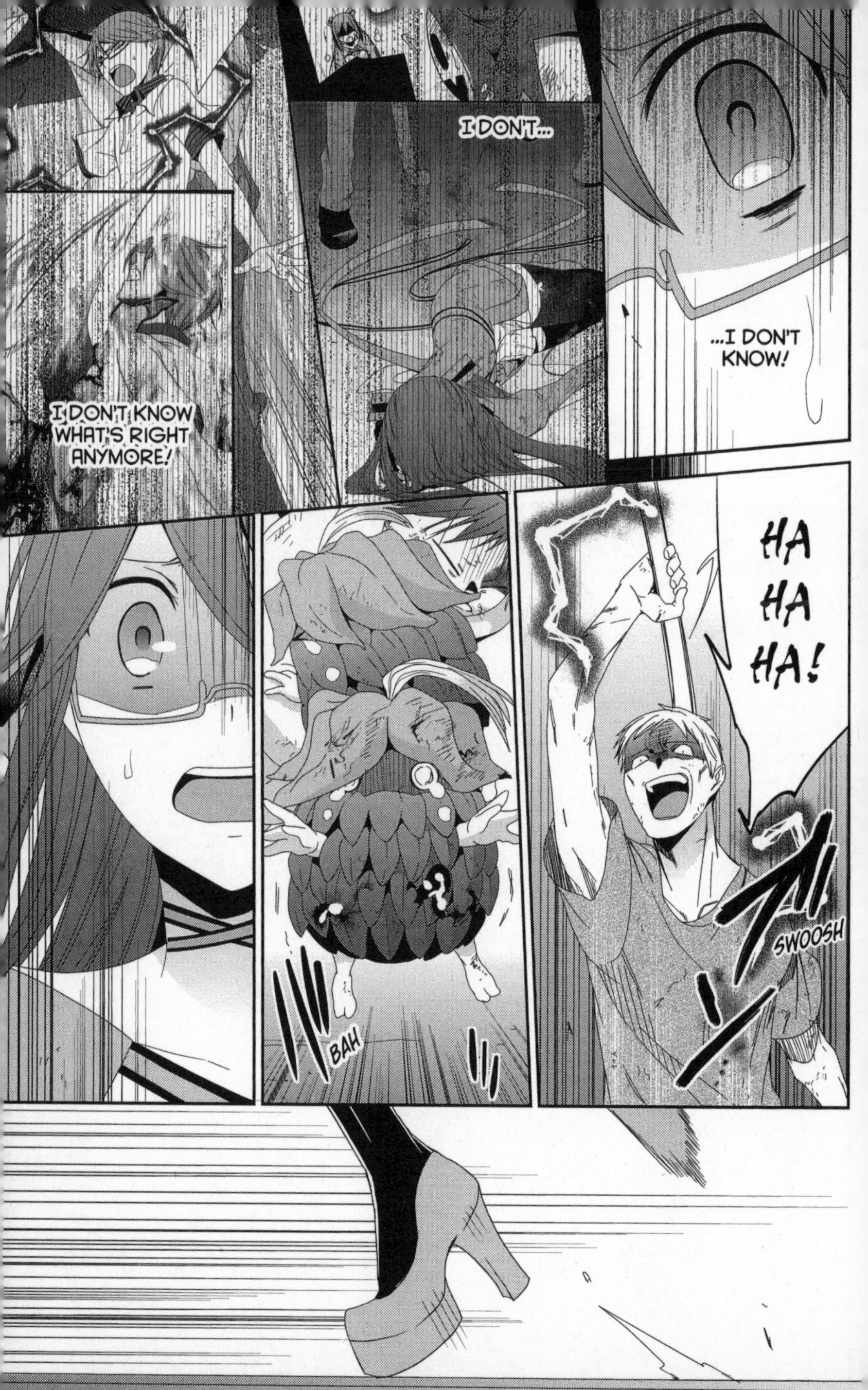
...I DON'T KNOW!
I DON'T...
I DON'T KNOW WHAT'S RIGHT ANYMORE!
HA HA HA!
SWOOSH
BAH

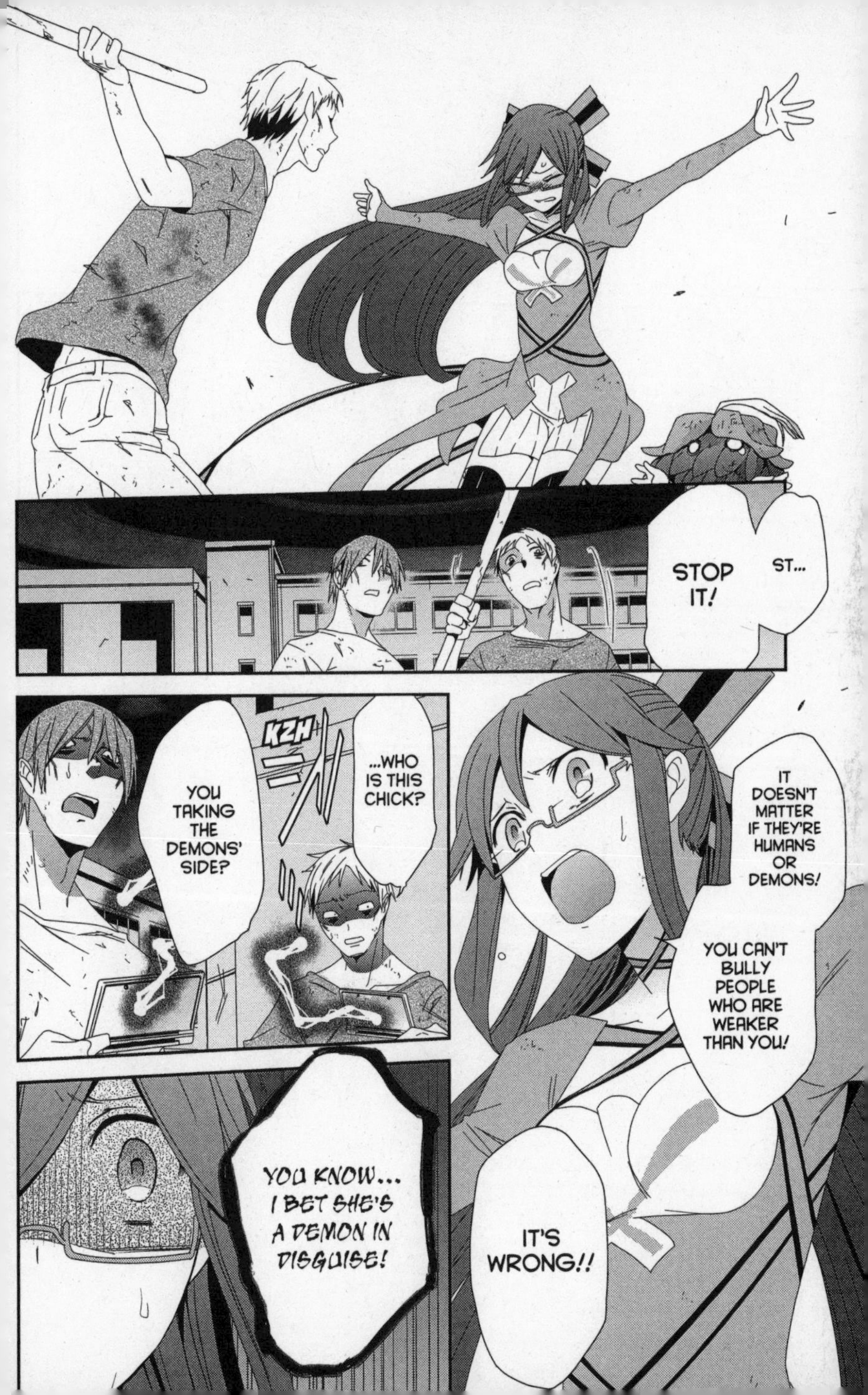
ST...
STOP IT!
IT DOESN'T MATTER IF THEY'RE HUMANS OR DEMONS!
YOU CAN'T BULLY PEOPLE WHO ARE WEAKER THAN YOU!
IT'S WRONG!!
KZH
...WHO IS THIS CHICK?
YOU TAKING THE DEMONS' SIDE?
YOU KNOW... I BET SHE'S A DEMON IN DISGUISE!

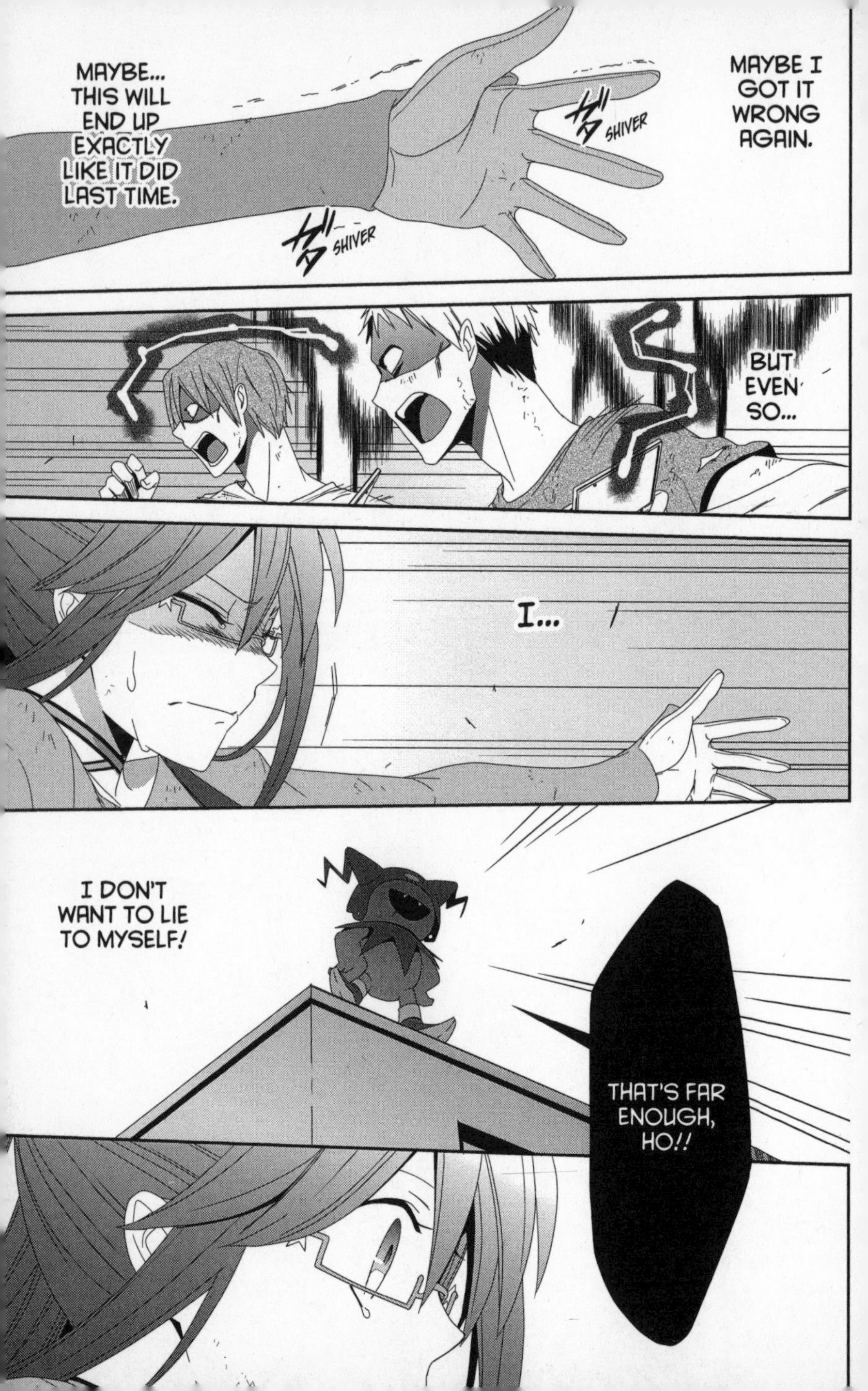
MAYBE I GOT IT WRONG AGAIN.
SHIVER
SHIVER
MAYBE... THIS WILL END UP EXACTLY LIKE IT DID LAST TIME.
BUT EVEN SO...
I...
I DON'T WANT TO LIE TO MYSELF!
THAT'S FAR ENOUGH, HO!!

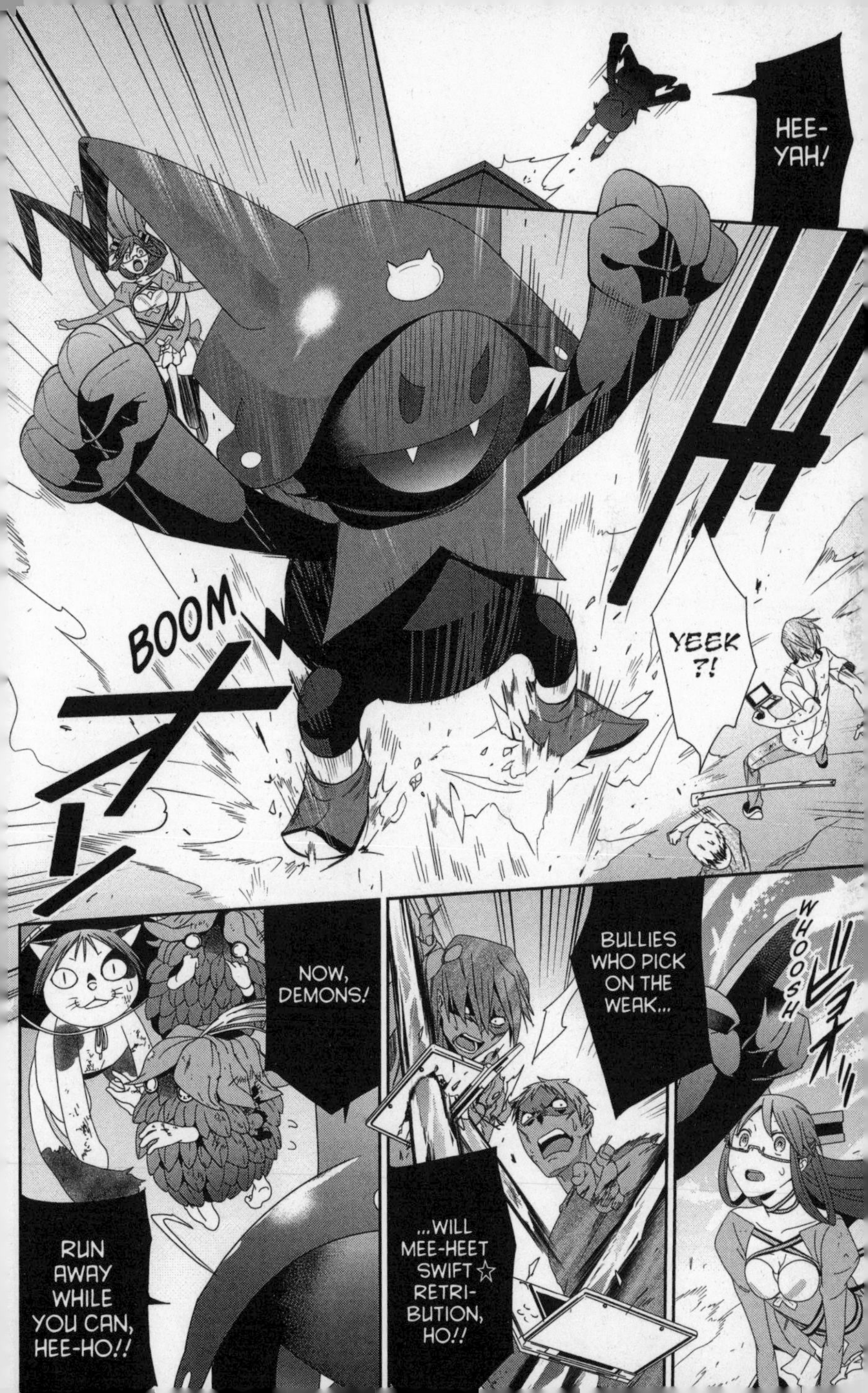
HEE-YAH!
YEEK?!
BOOM
WHOOSH
BULLIES WHO PICK ON THE WEAK...
...WILL MEE-HEET SWIFT☆ RETRIBUTION, HO!!
NOW, DEMONS!
RUN AWAY WHILE YOU CAN, HEE-HO!!

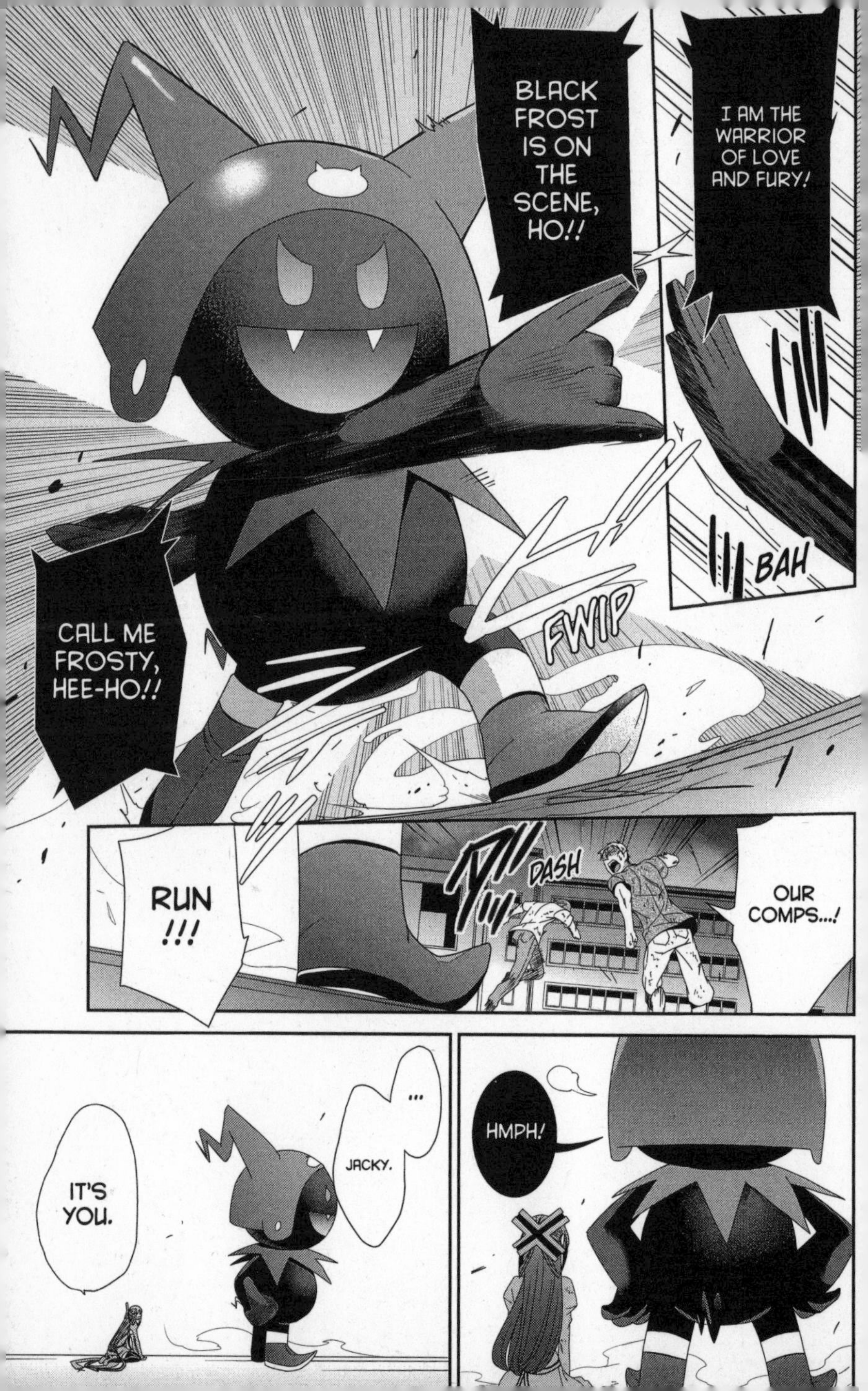
I AM THE WARRIOR OF LOVE AND FURY!
BAH
BLACK FROST IS ON THE SCENE, HO!!
FWIP
CALL ME FROSTY, HEE-HO!!
OUR COMPS...!
DASH
RUN !!!
HMPH!
...
JACKY.
IT'S YOU.

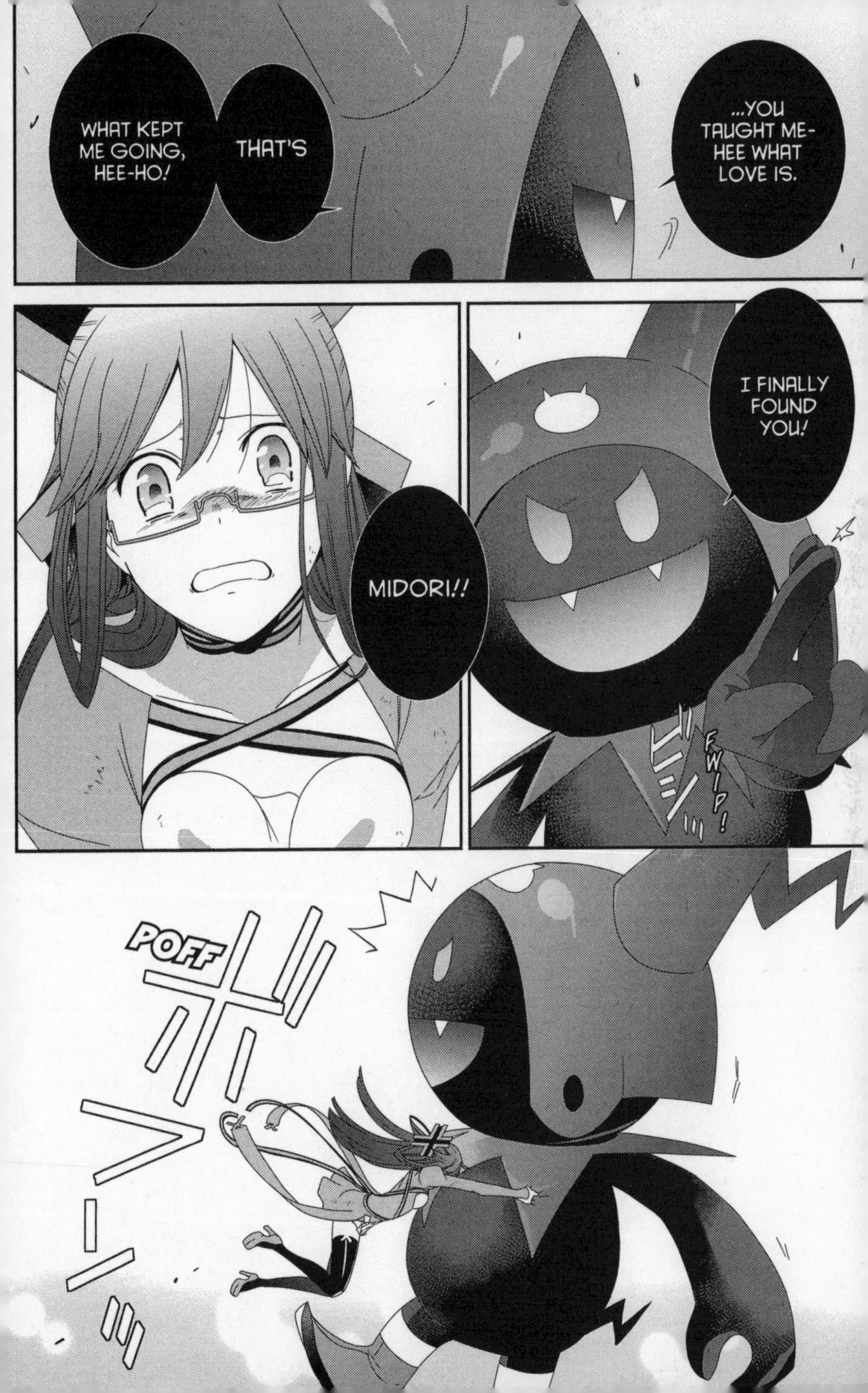
...YOU TAUGHT ME-HEE WHAT LOVE IS.
THAT'S
WHAT KEPT ME GOING, HEE-HO!
I FINALLY FOUND YOU!
FWIP!
MIDORI!!
POFF

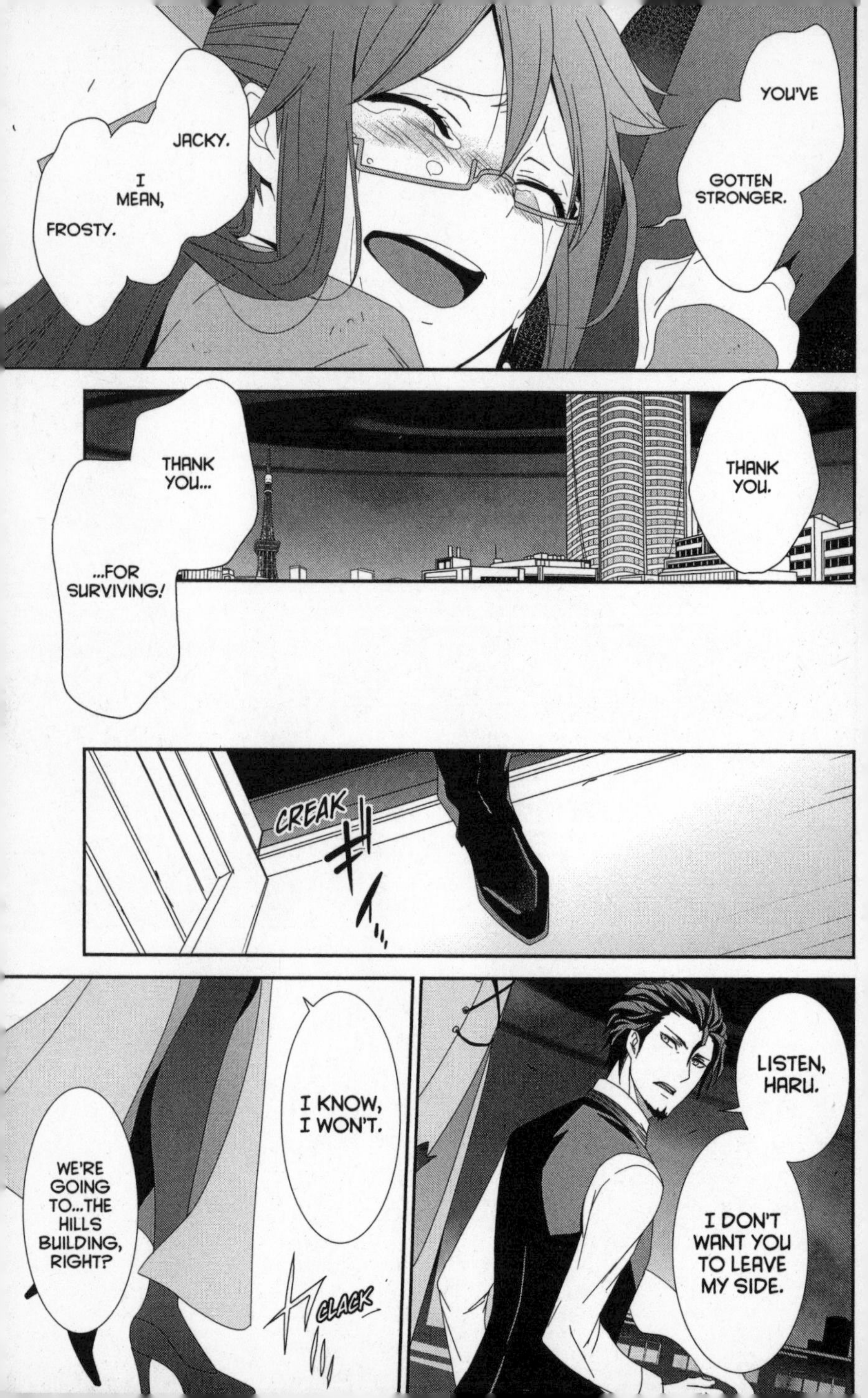
YOU'VE
GOTTEN STRONGER.
JACKY.
I MEAN,
FROSTY.
THANK YOU.
THANK YOU...
...FOR SURVIVING!
CREAK
LISTEN, HARU.
I DON'T WANT YOU TO LEAVE MY SIDE.
I KNOW, I WON'T.
WE'RE GOING TO...THE HILLS BUILDING, RIGHT?
CLACK

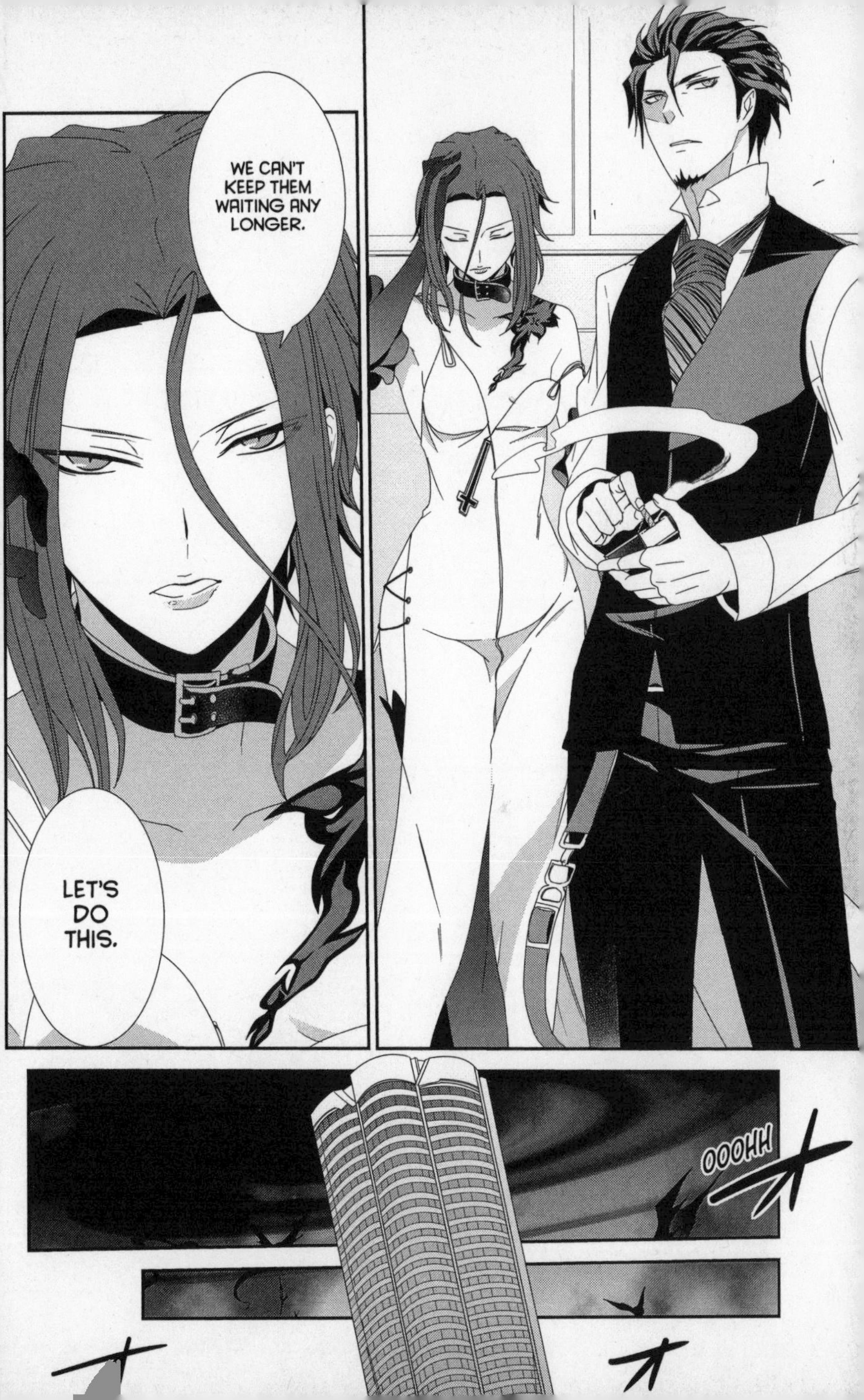
WE CAN'T KEEP THEM WAITING ANY LONGER.
LET'S DO THIS.
OOOHH

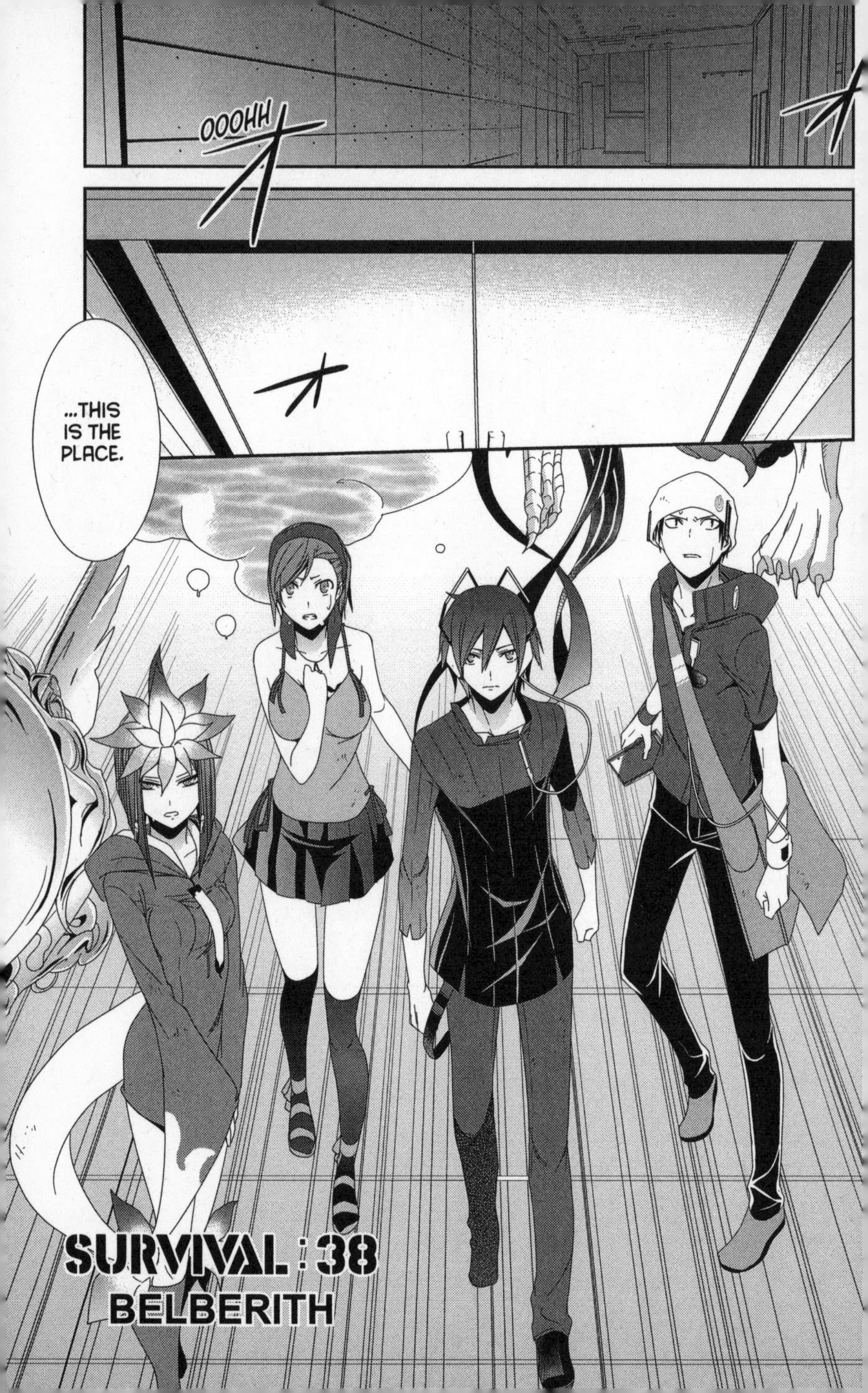
OOOHH
...THIS IS THE PLACE.
SURVIVAL : 38
BELBERITH

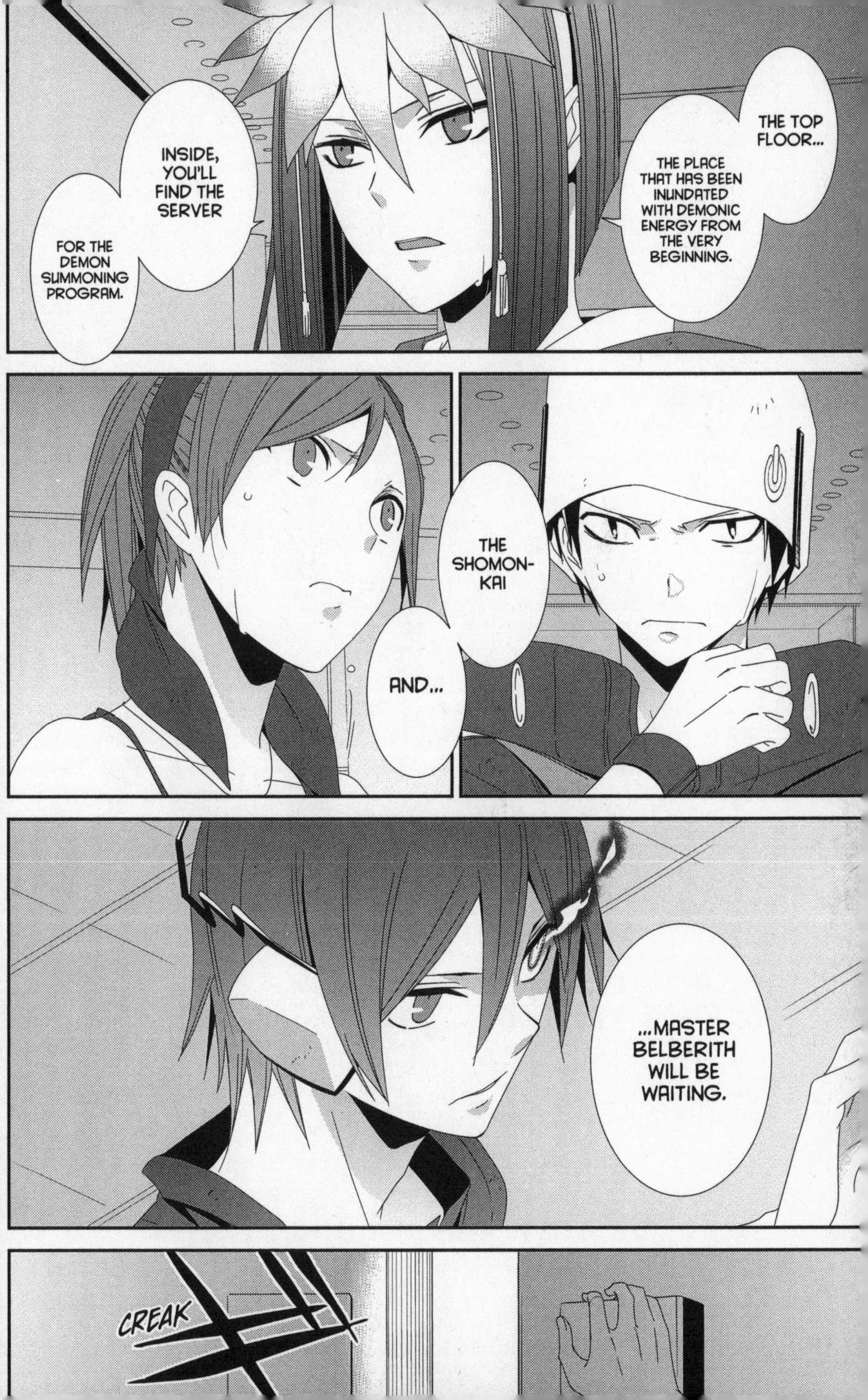
THE TOP FLOOR...
THE PLACE THAT HAS BEEN INUNDATED WITH DEMONIC ENERGY FROM THE VERY BEGINNING.
INSIDE, YOU'LL FIND THE SERVER
FOR THE DEMON SUMMONING PROGRAM.
THE SHOMON-KAI
AND...
...MASTER BELBERITH WILL BE WAITING.
CREAK

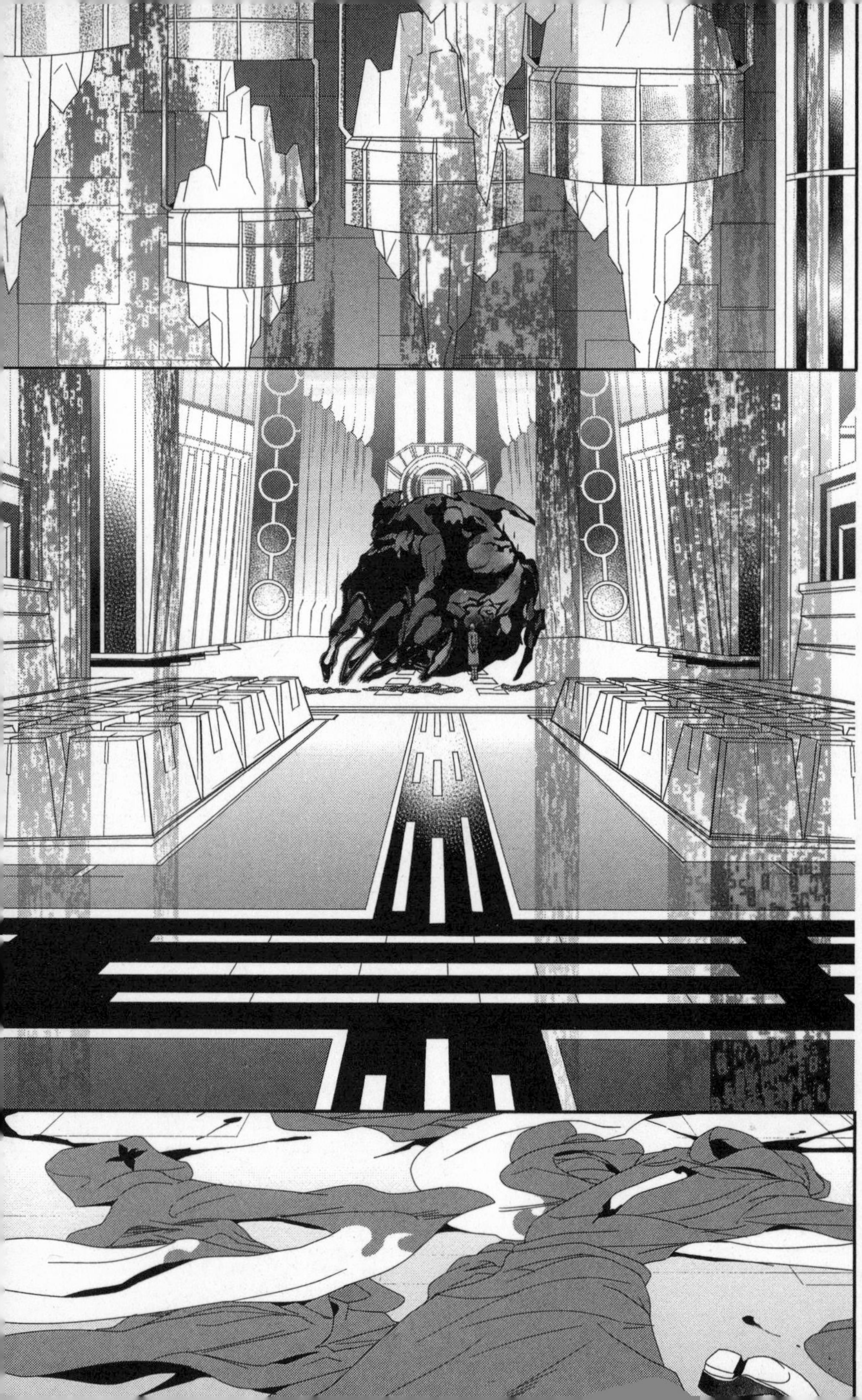

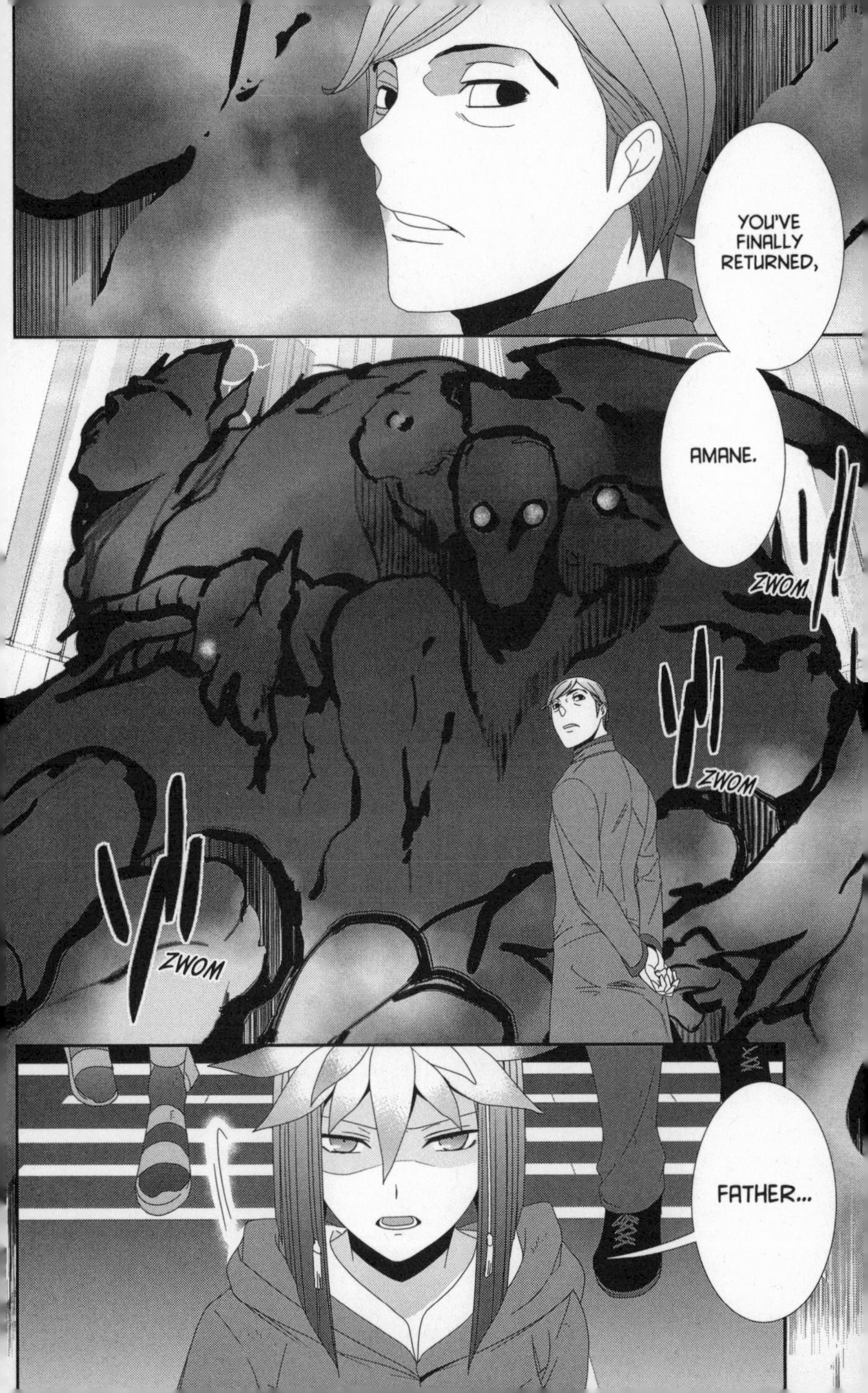
YOU'VE FINALLY RETURNED,
AMANE.
ZWOM
ZWOM
ZWOM
FATHER...

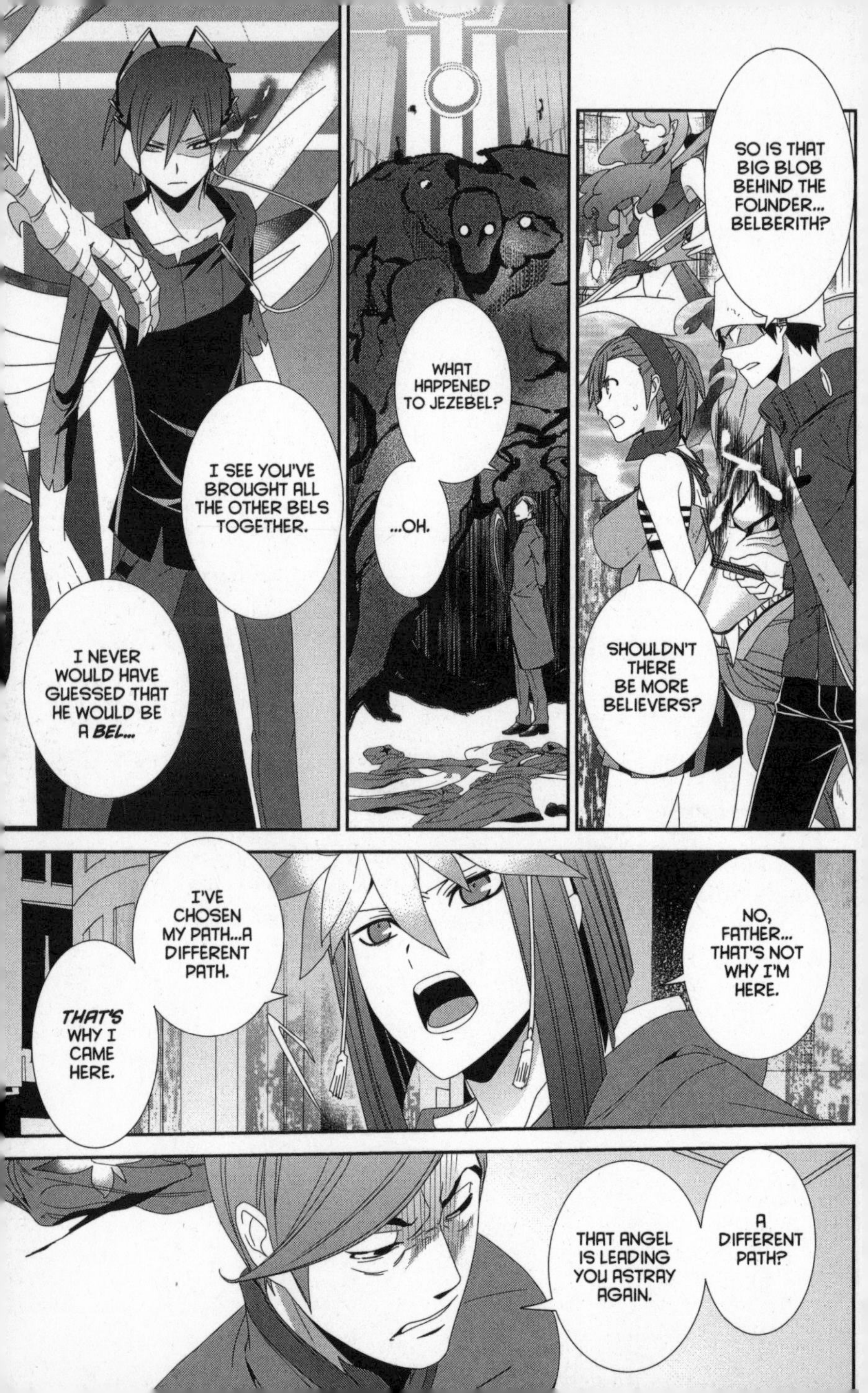
SO IS THAT BIG BLOB BEHIND THE FOUNDER... BELBERITH?
SHOULDN'T THERE BE MORE BELIEVERS?
WHAT HAPPENED TO JEZEBEL?
...OH.
I SEE YOU'VE BROUGHT ALL THE OTHER BELS TOGETHER.
I NEVER WOULD HAVE GUESSED THAT HE WOULD BE A *BEL*...
NO, FATHER... THAT'S NOT WHY I'M HERE.
I'VE CHOSEN MY PATH...A DIFFERENT PATH.
THAT'S WHY I CAME HERE.
A DIFFERENT PATH?
THAT ANGEL IS LEADING YOU ASTRAY AGAIN.

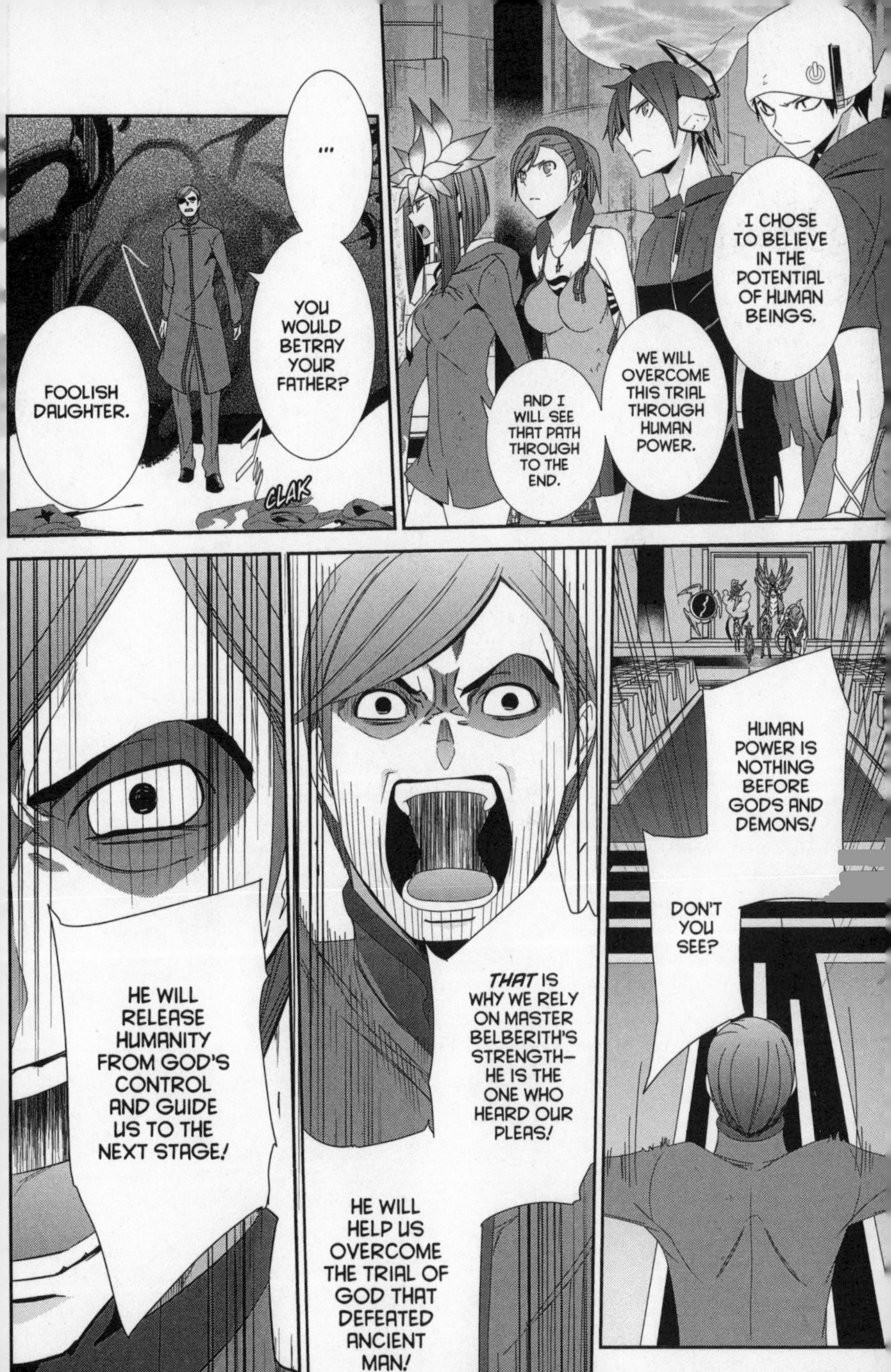
I CHOSE TO BELIEVE IN THE POTENTIAL OF HUMAN BEINGS.
WE WILL OVERCOME THIS TRIAL THROUGH HUMAN POWER.
AND I WILL SEE THAT PATH THROUGH TO THE END.
...
YOU WOULD BETRAY YOUR FATHER?
FOOLISH DAUGHTER.
CLAK
HUMAN POWER IS NOTHING BEFORE GODS AND DEMONS!
DON'T YOU SEE?
THAT IS WHY WE RELY ON MASTER BELBERITH'S STRENGTH— HE IS THE ONE WHO HEARD OUR PLEAS!
HE WILL HELP US OVERCOME THE TRIAL OF GOD THAT DEFEATED ANCIENT MAN!
HE WILL RELEASE HUMANITY FROM GOD'S CONTROL AND GUIDE US TO THE NEXT STAGE!

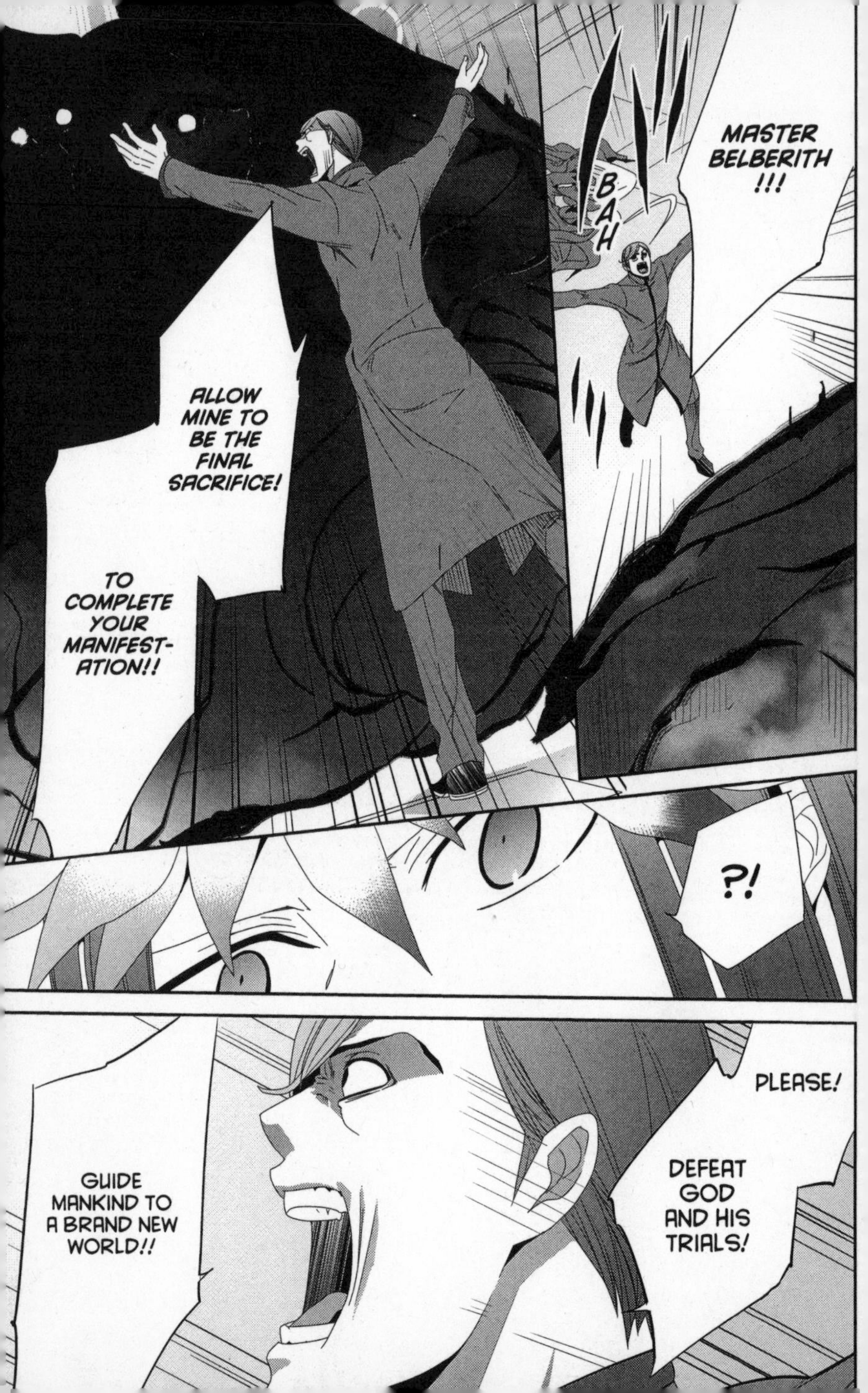
BAH
MASTER BELBERITH !!!
ALLOW MINE TO BE THE FINAL SACRIFICE!
TO COMPLETE YOUR MANIFEST-ATION!!
?!
PLEASE!
DEFEAT GOD AND HIS TRIALS!
GUIDE MANKIND TO A BRAND NEW WORLD!!

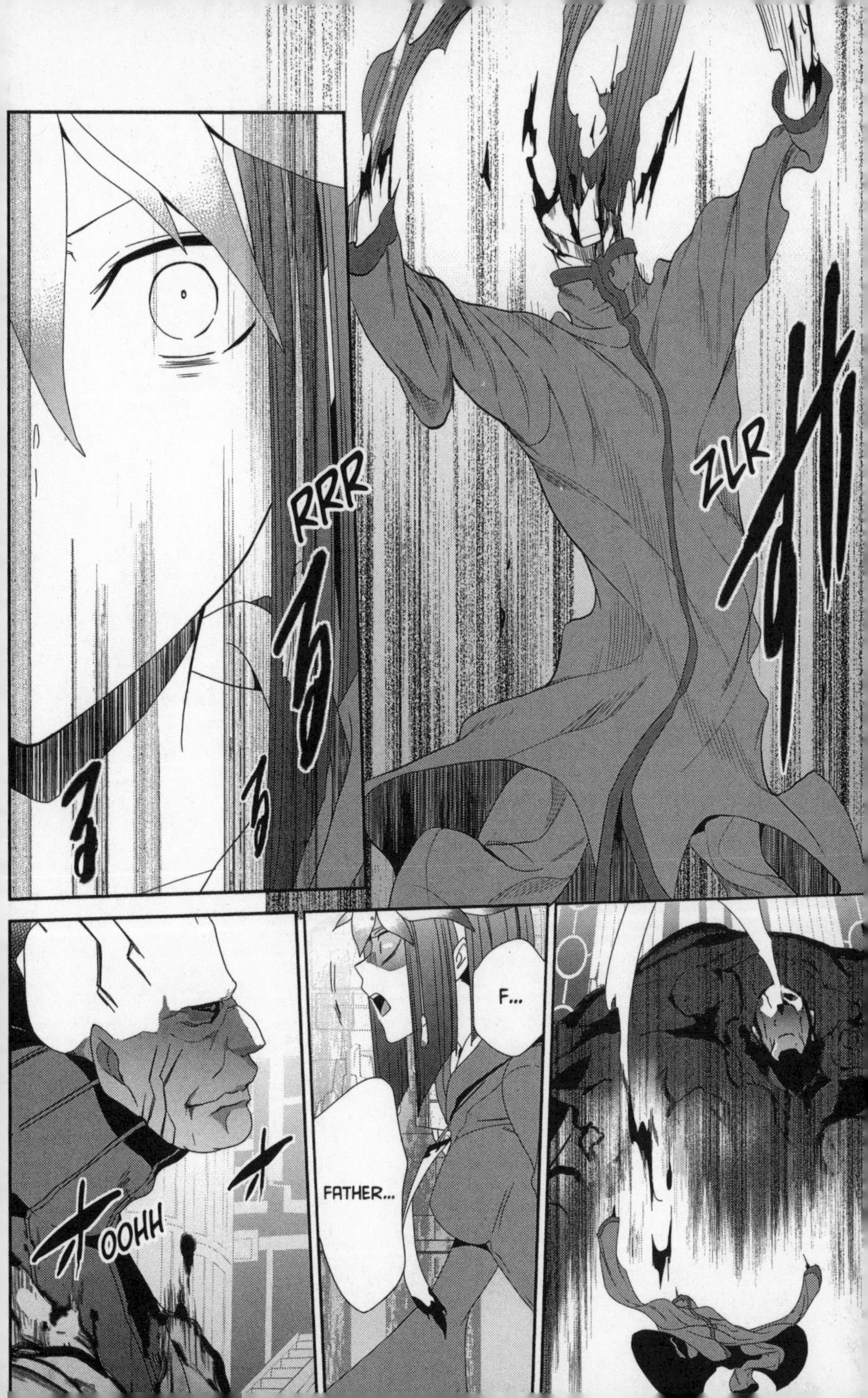
ZLR
RRR
F...
FATHER...
OOHH

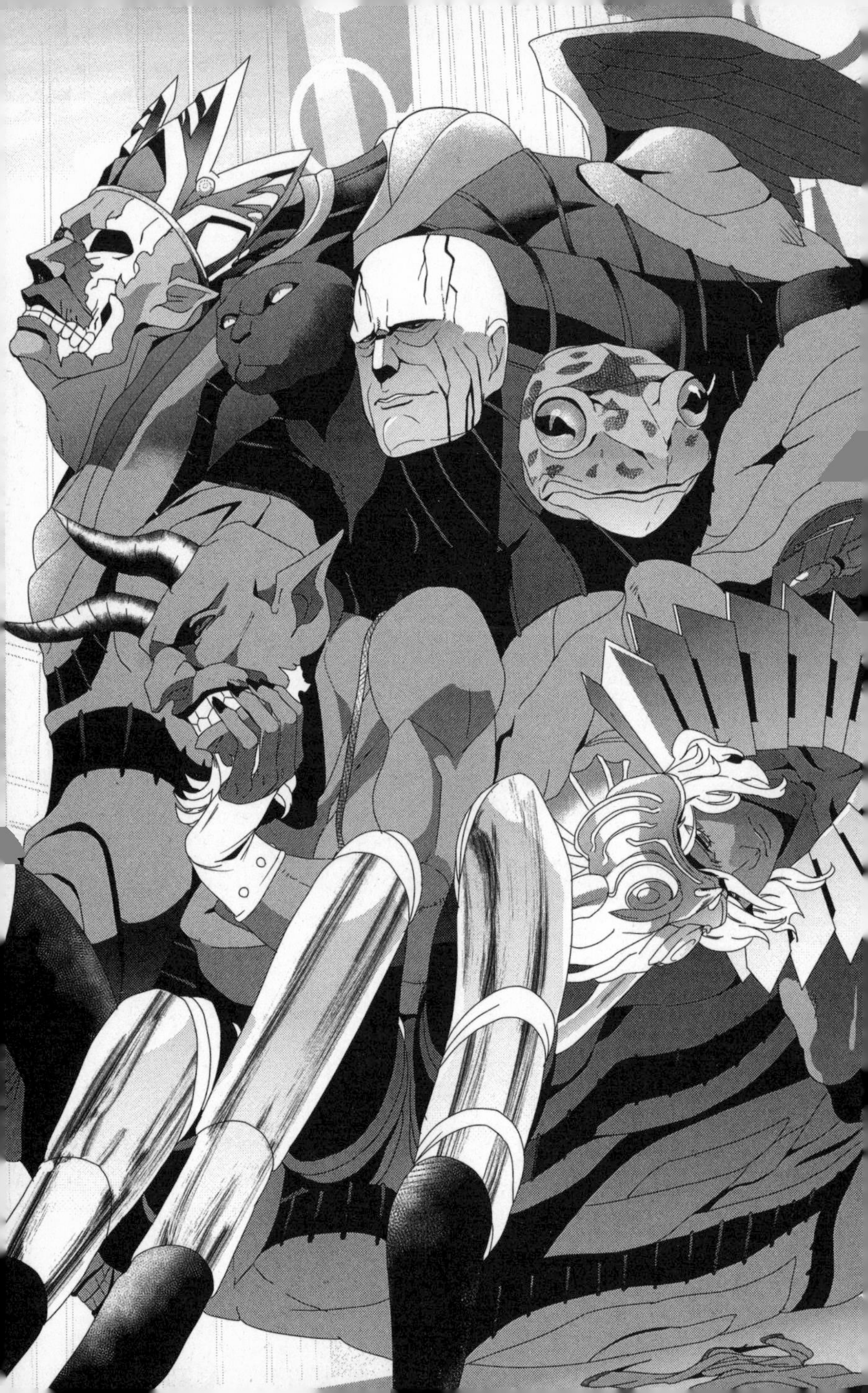

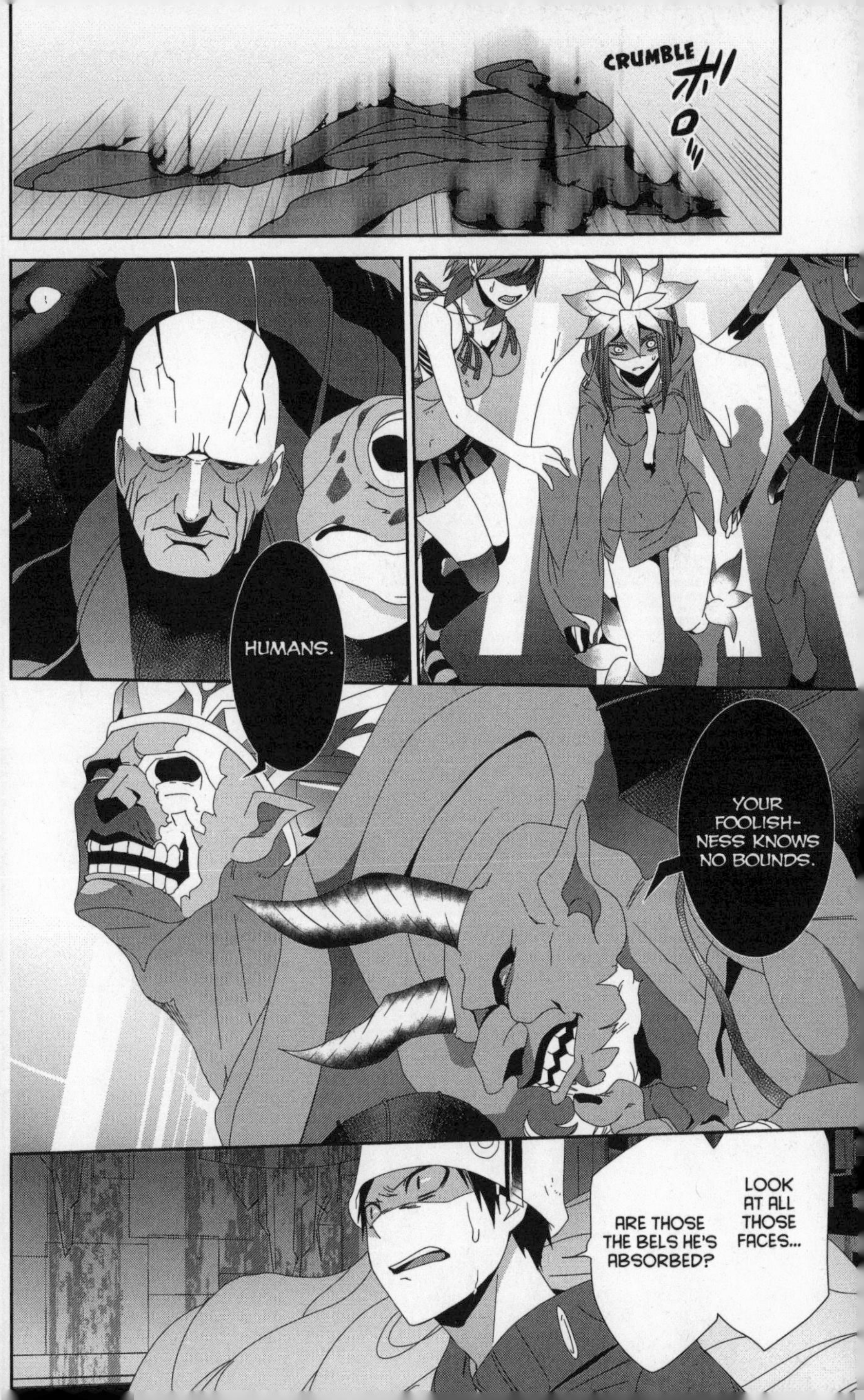
CRUMBLE
HUMANS.
YOUR FOOLISH-NESS KNOWS NO BOUNDS.
LOOK AT ALL THOSE FACES...
ARE THOSE THE BELS HE'S ABSORBED?

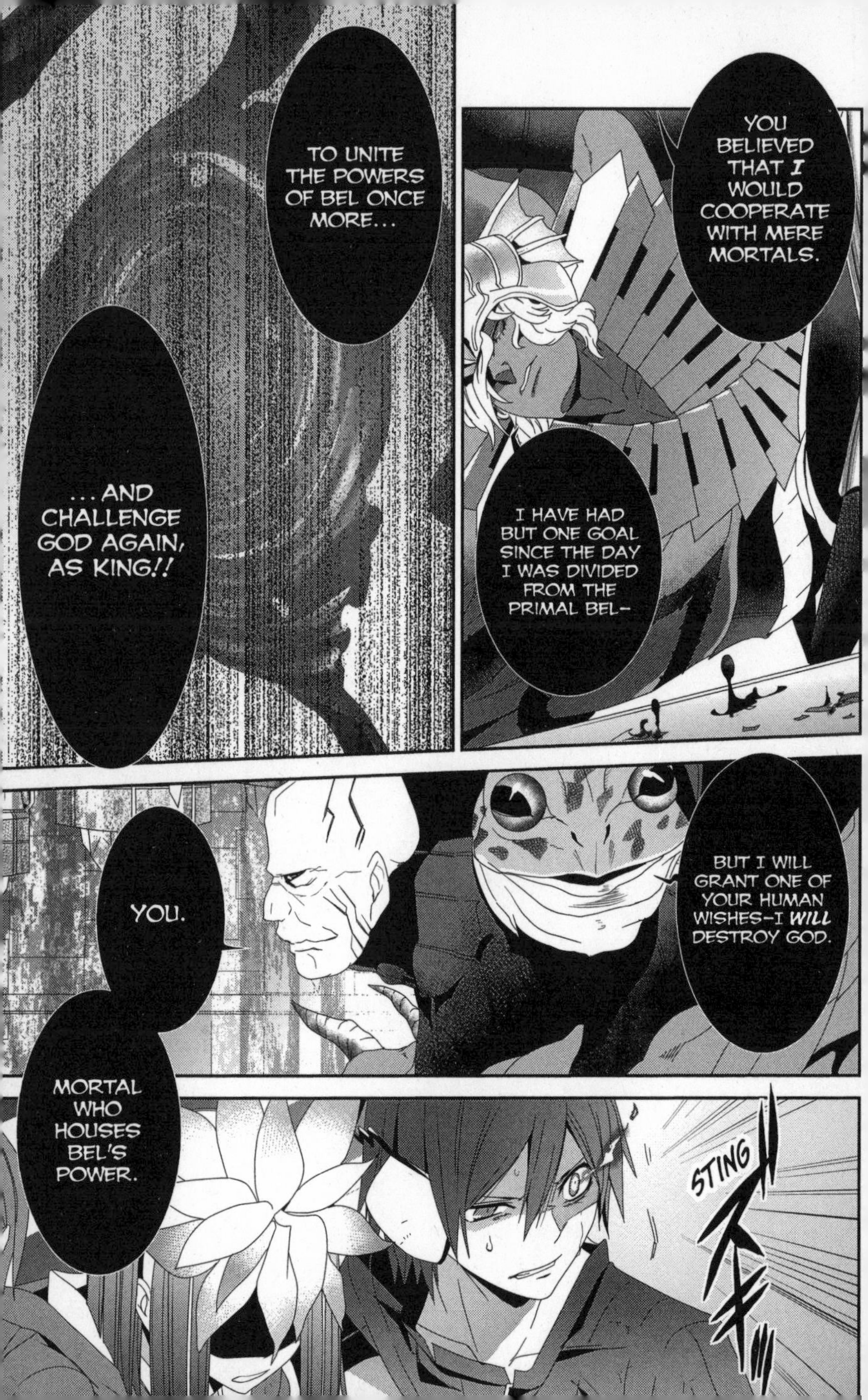
YOU BELIEVED THAT *I* WOULD COOPERATE WITH MERE MORTALS.
I HAVE HAD BUT ONE GOAL SINCE THE DAY I WAS DIVIDED FROM THE PRIMAL BEL–
TO UNITE THE POWERS OF BEL ONCE MORE...
...AND CHALLENGE GOD AGAIN, AS KING!!
BUT I WILL GRANT ONE OF YOUR HUMAN WISHES–I *WILL* DESTROY GOD.
YOU.
MORTAL WHO HOUSES BEL'S POWER.
STING

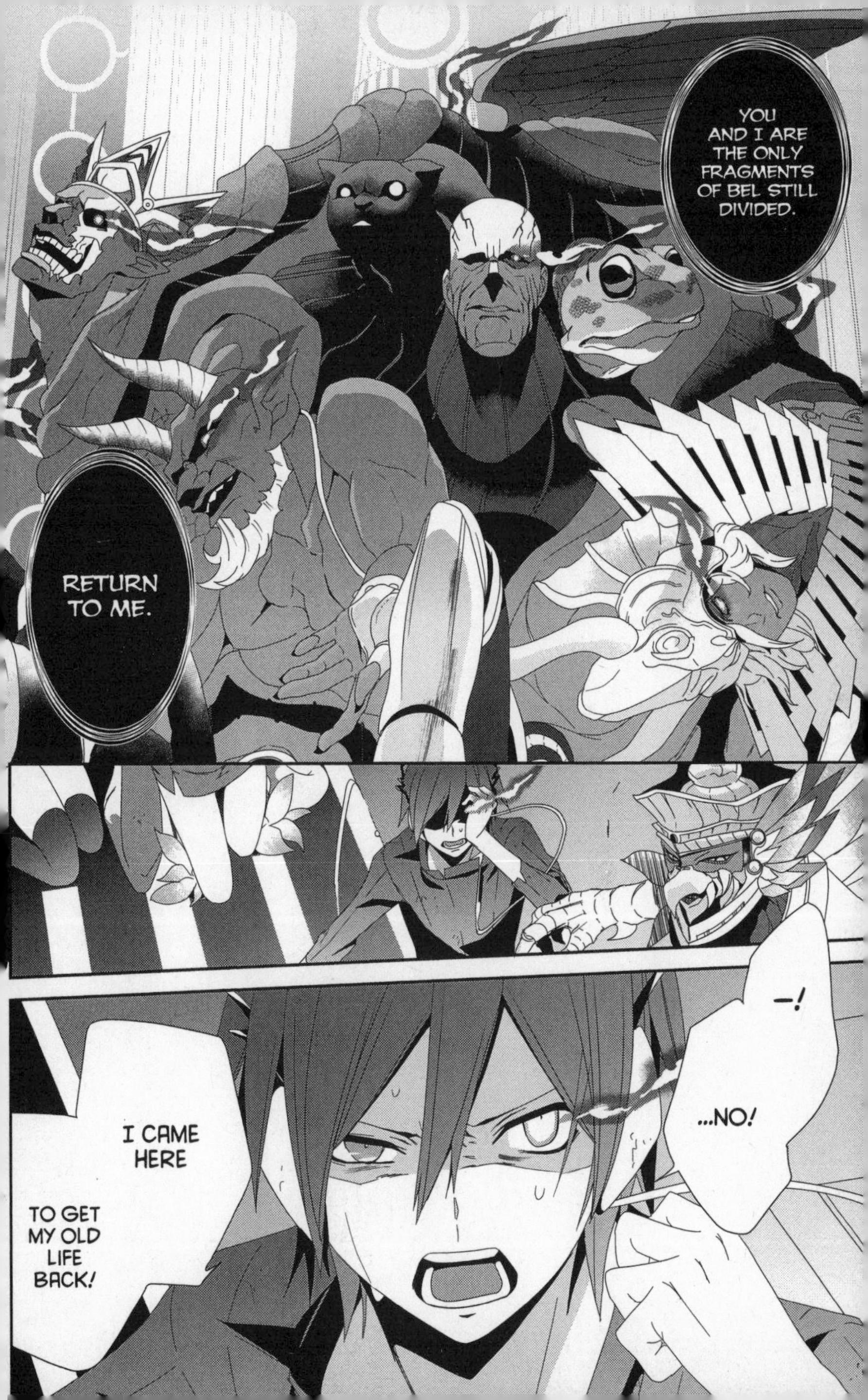
YOU AND I ARE THE ONLY FRAGMENTS OF BEL STILL DIVIDED.
RETURN TO ME.
—!
...NO!
I CAME HERE
TO GET MY OLD LIFE BACK!

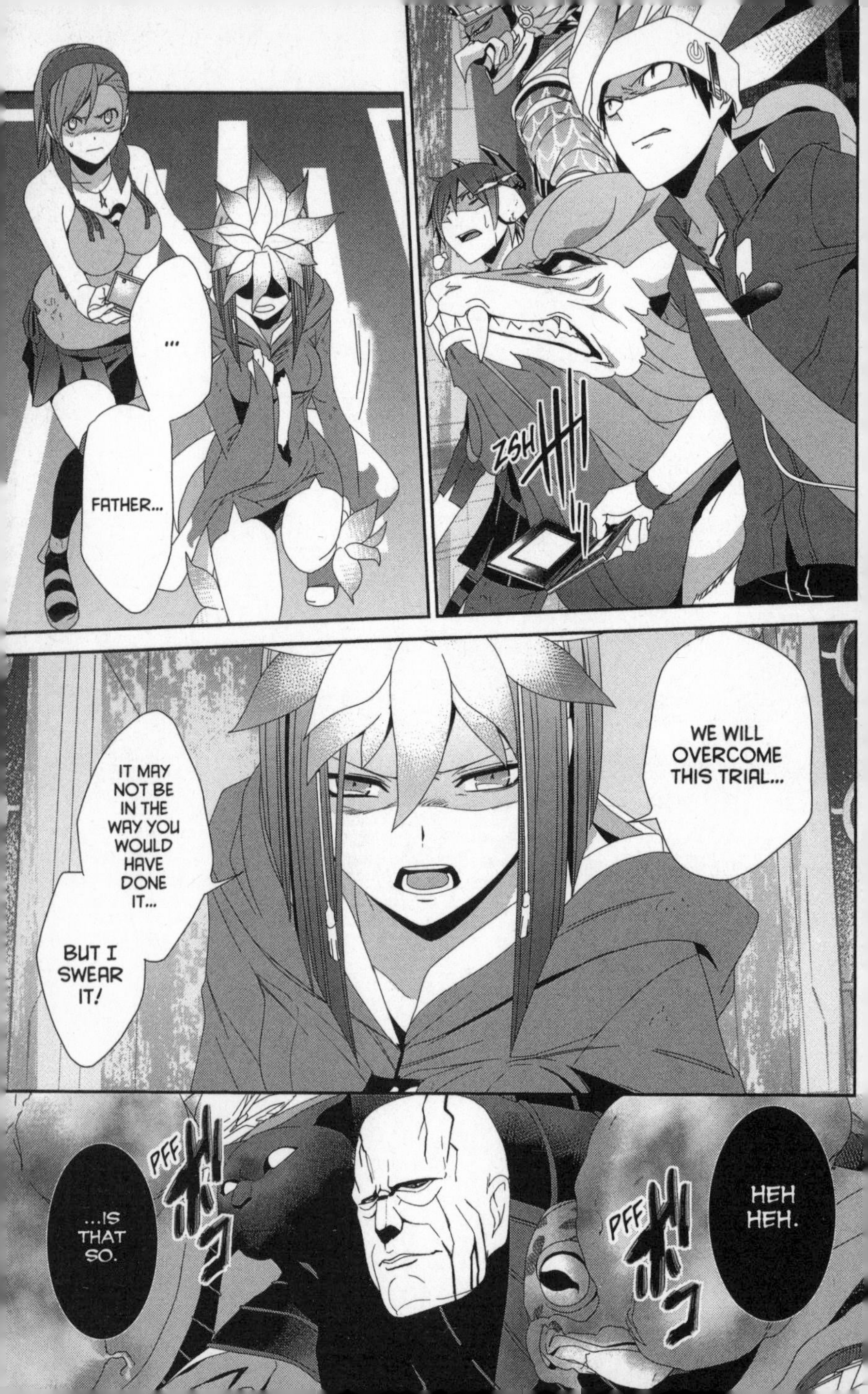
ZSH
...
FATHER...
WE WILL OVERCOME THIS TRIAL...
IT MAY NOT BE IN THE WAY YOU WOULD HAVE DONE IT...
BUT I SWEAR IT!
HEH HEH.
PFF
PFF
...IS THAT SO.

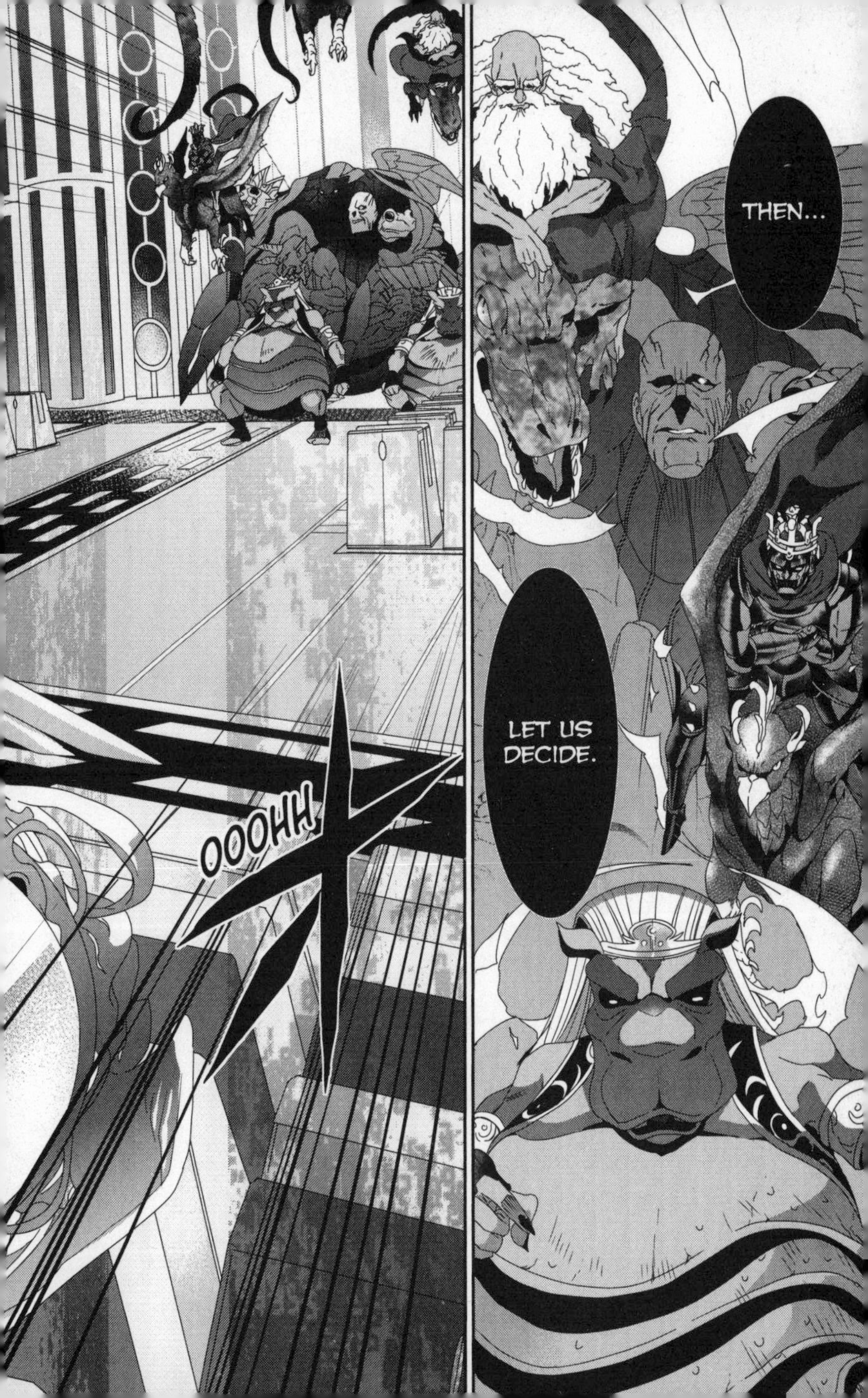
THEN...
LET US DECIDE.
OOOHH

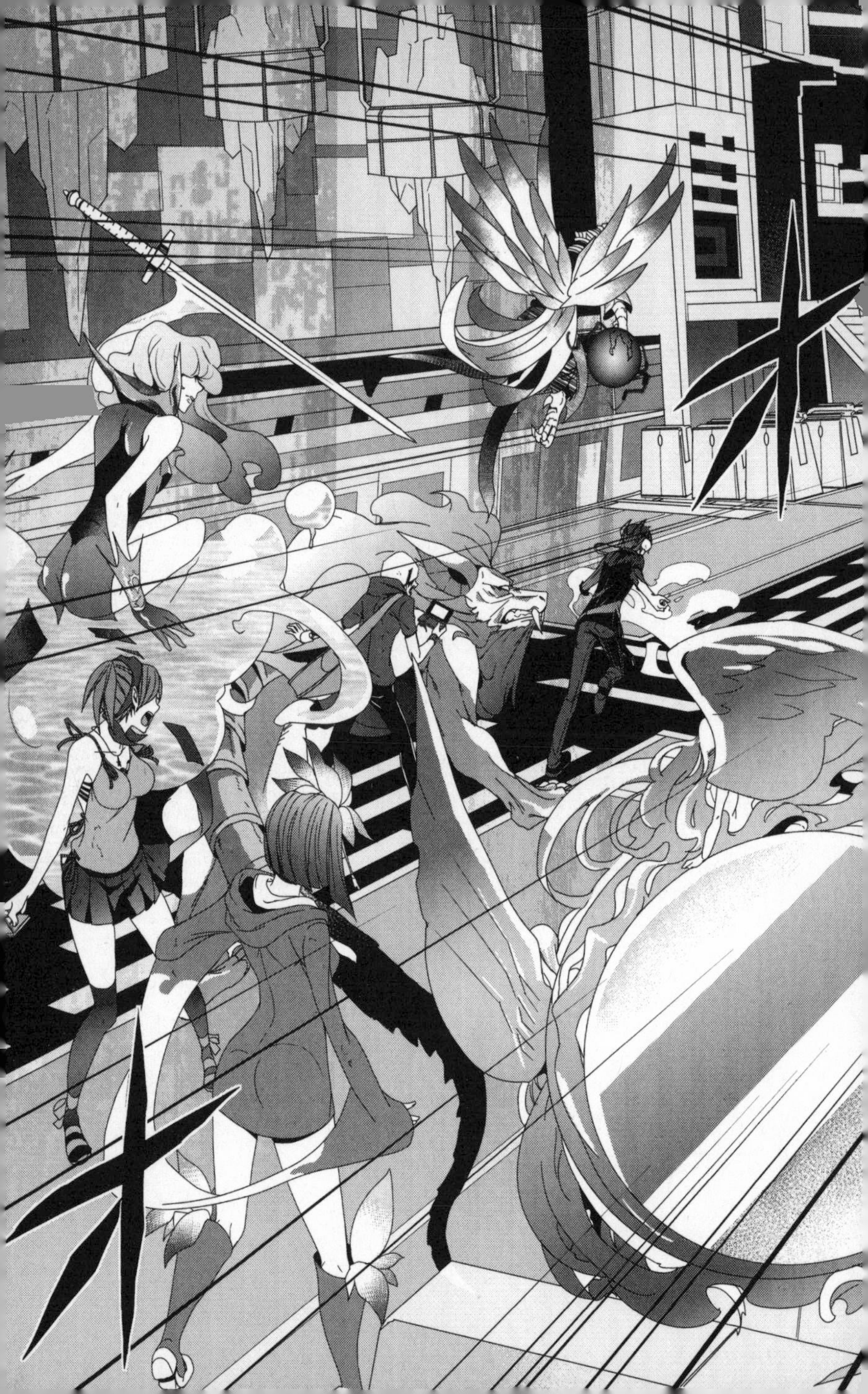

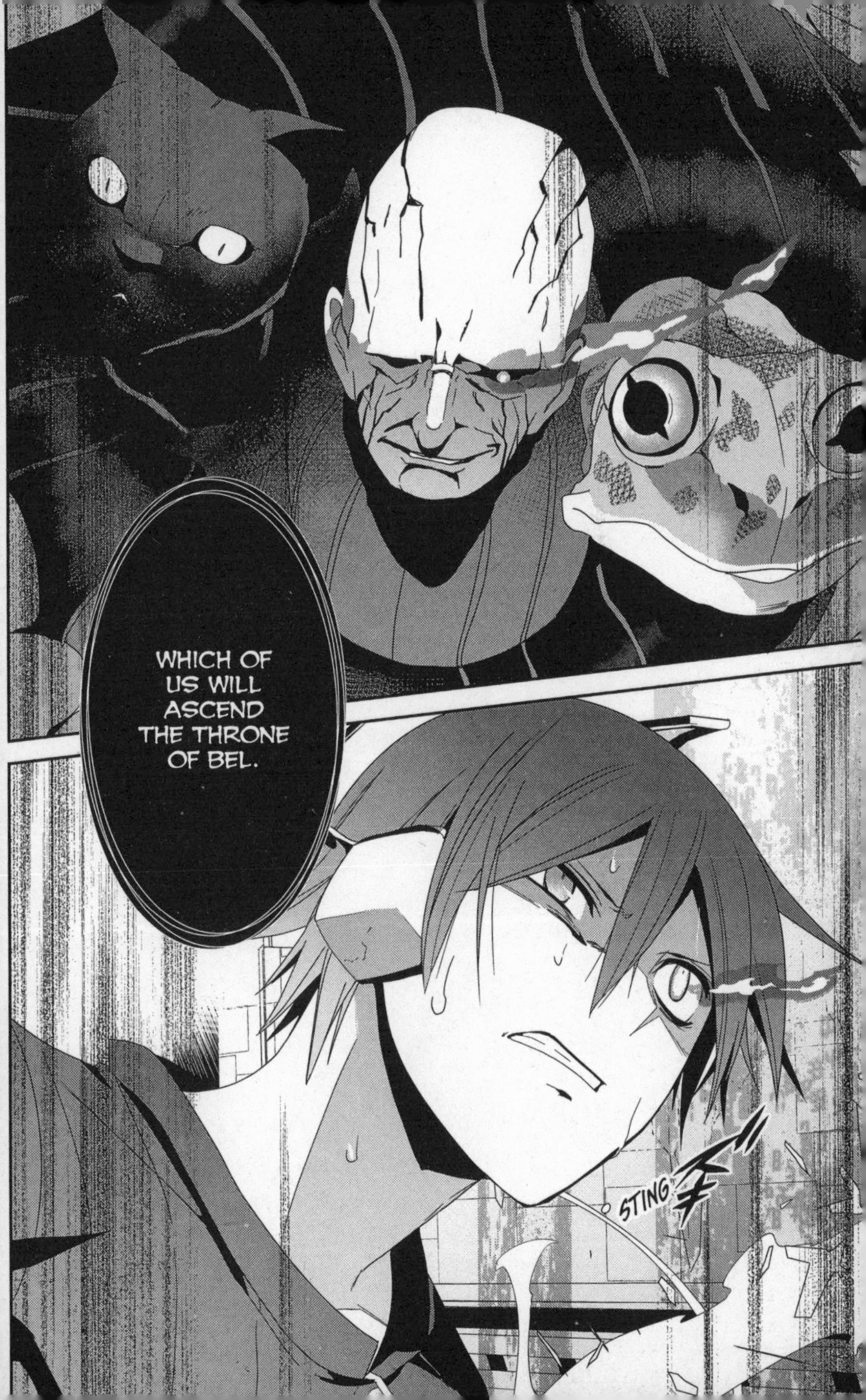
WHICH OF US WILL ASCEND THE THRONE OF BEL.
STING

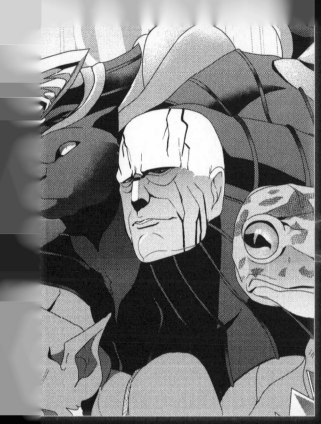

BELBERITH

...ERITH. ONE OF THE 72 DEMONS OF THE GOETIA, HE
...28TH DUKE OF HELL AND COMMANDS 26 DEMONIC
...ONS. IT IS BELIEVED THAT HIS NAME COMES FROM
...GOD BAAL BERITH, WHO WAS WORSHIPED BY THE
...MITES IN THE OLD TESTAMENT, AND HE IS IDENTIFIED
...L BERITH, WHO IS ALSO BELIEVED TO DERIVE FROM
...BERITH. ACCORDING TO SEBASTIEN MICHAELIS, EL
...A DEMON OF THE FIRST CLASS WHO TEMPTS MEN TO
...MURDER AND BLASPHEMY. HE IS THE ARCHNEMESIS
...BARNABAS, AND BEFORE HIS FALL FROM GRACE HE
...WAS PRINCE OF THE CHERUBIM.

DEVIL SURVIVOR
デビルサバイバー

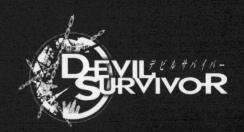

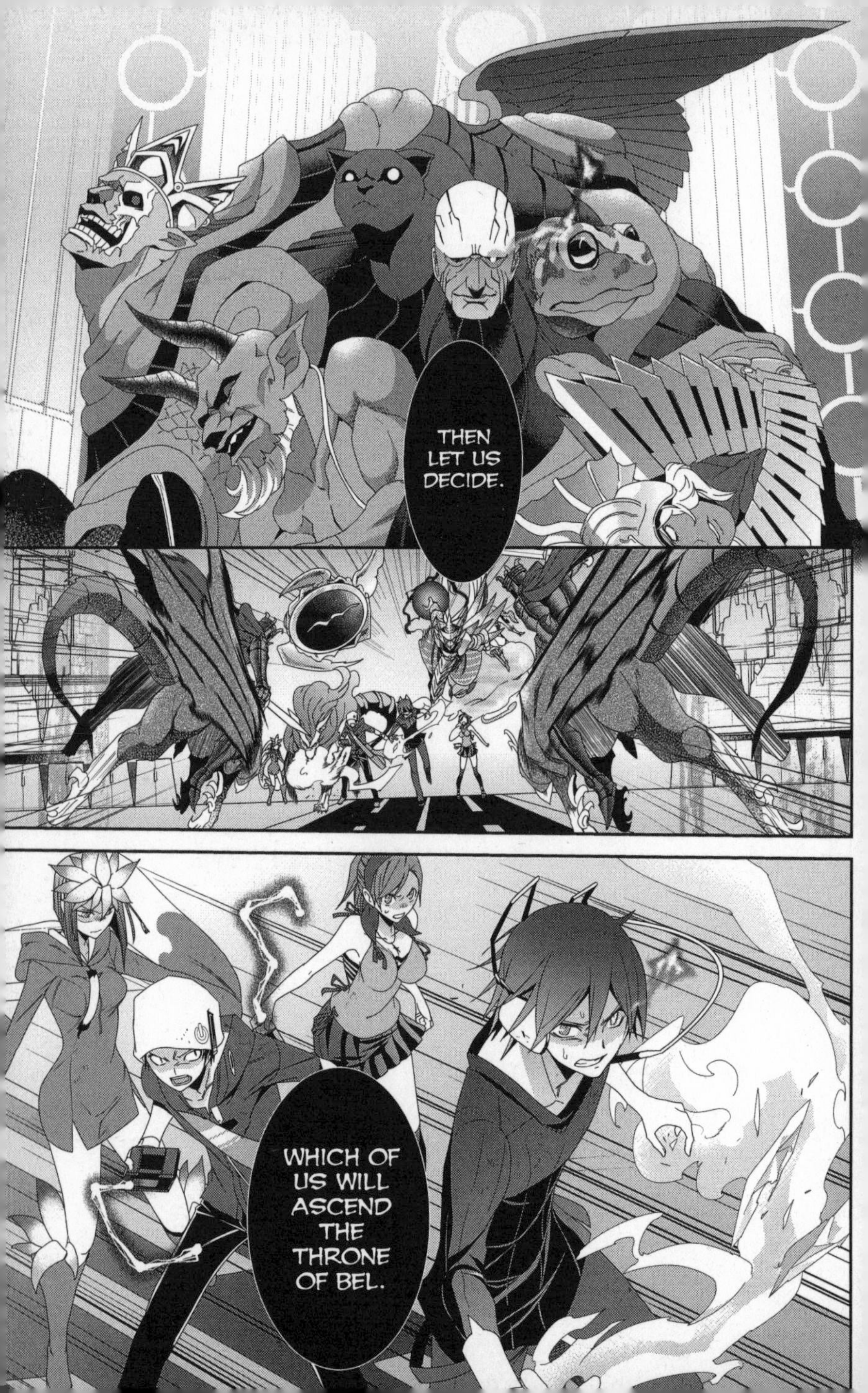
THEN LET US DECIDE.
WHICH OF US WILL ASCEND THE THRONE OF BEL.

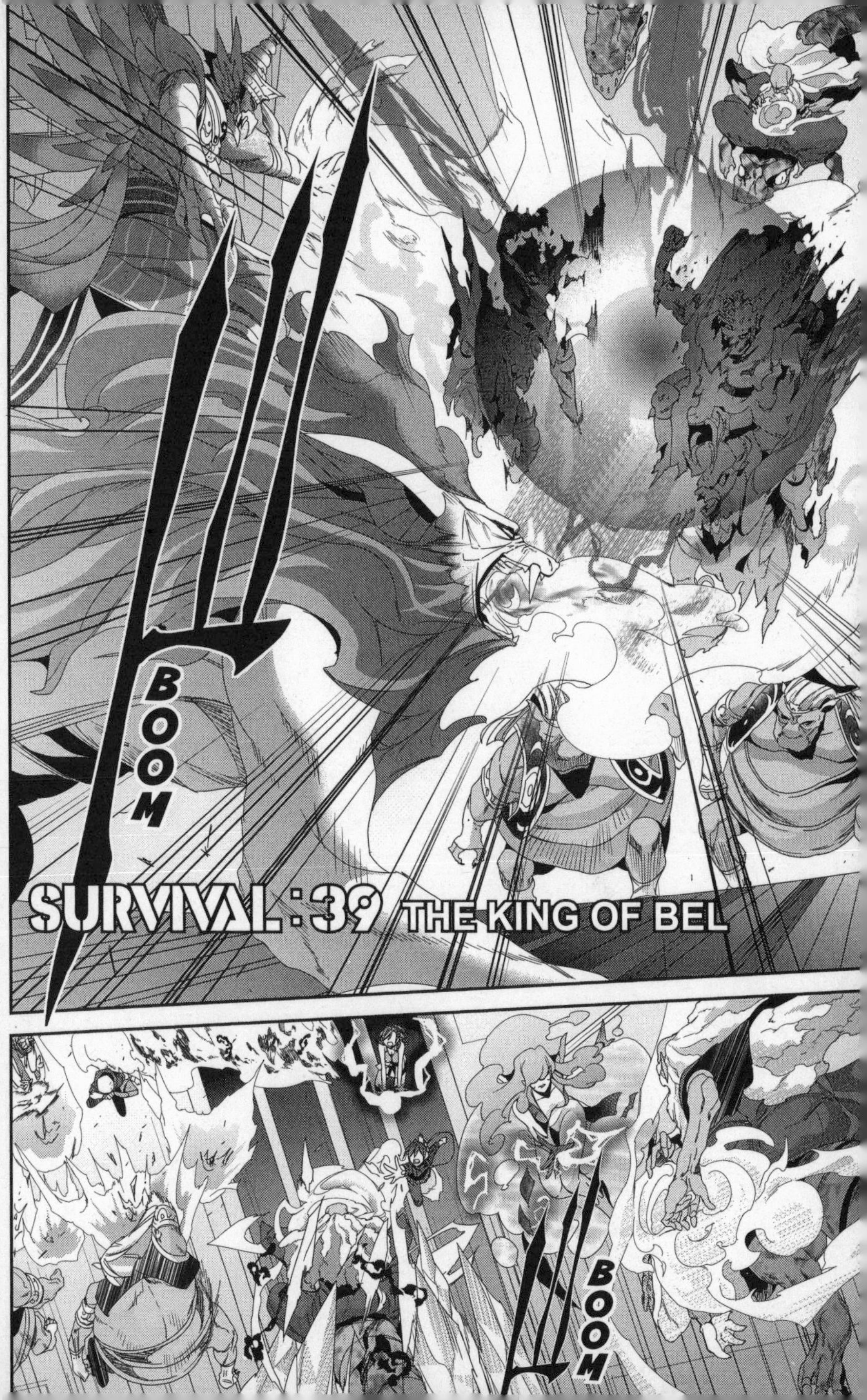
BOOM
SURVIVAL : 39 THE KING OF BEL
BOOM

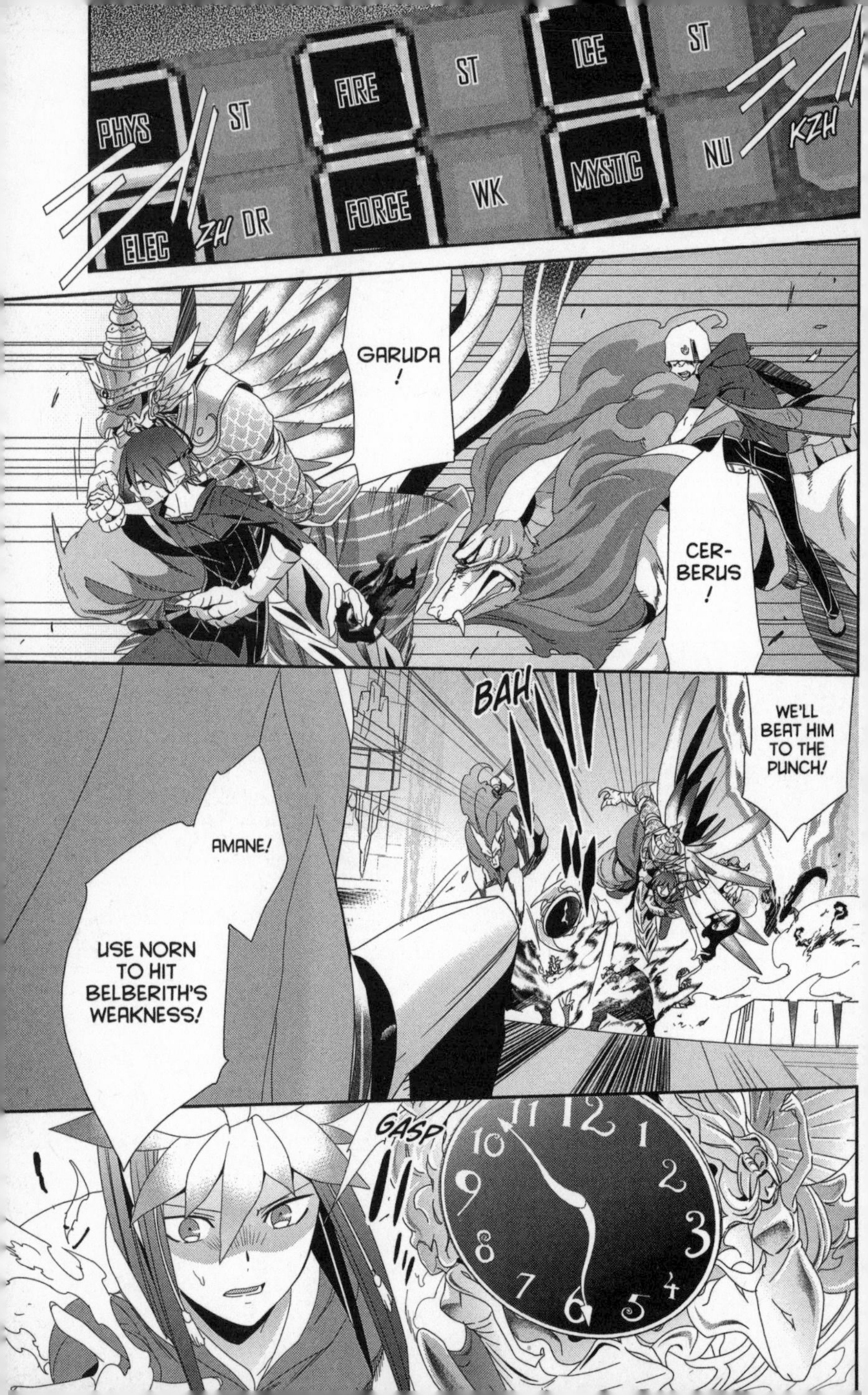
KZH
ST
NU
ICE
MYSTIC
ST
WK
FIRE
FORCE
ST
DR
ZH
PHYS
ELEC
CER-
BERUS
!
GARUDA
!
BAH
WE'LL BEAT HIM TO THE PUNCH!
AMANE!
USE NORN TO HIT BELBERITH'S WEAKNESS!
GASP

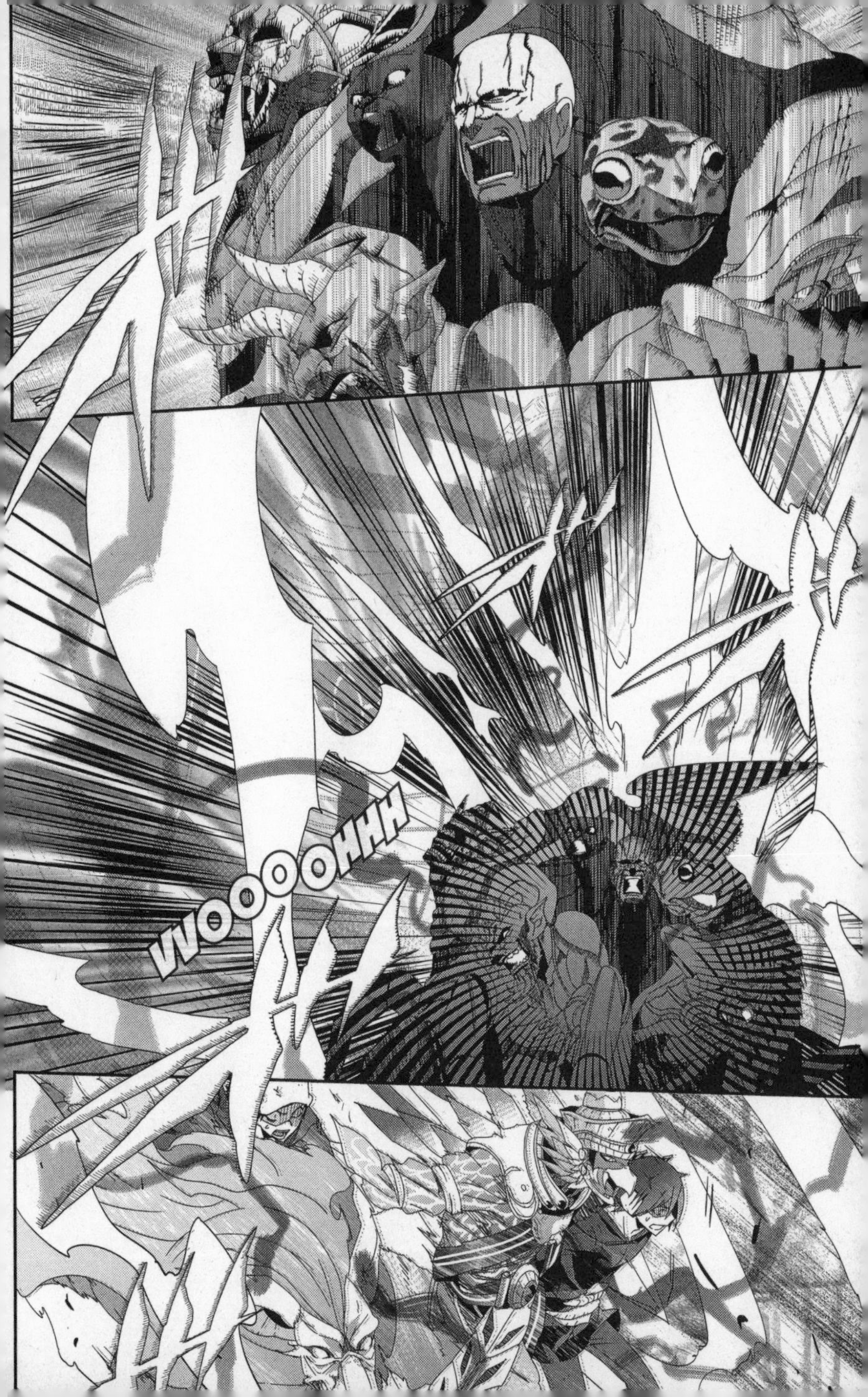
VVOOOOHHH

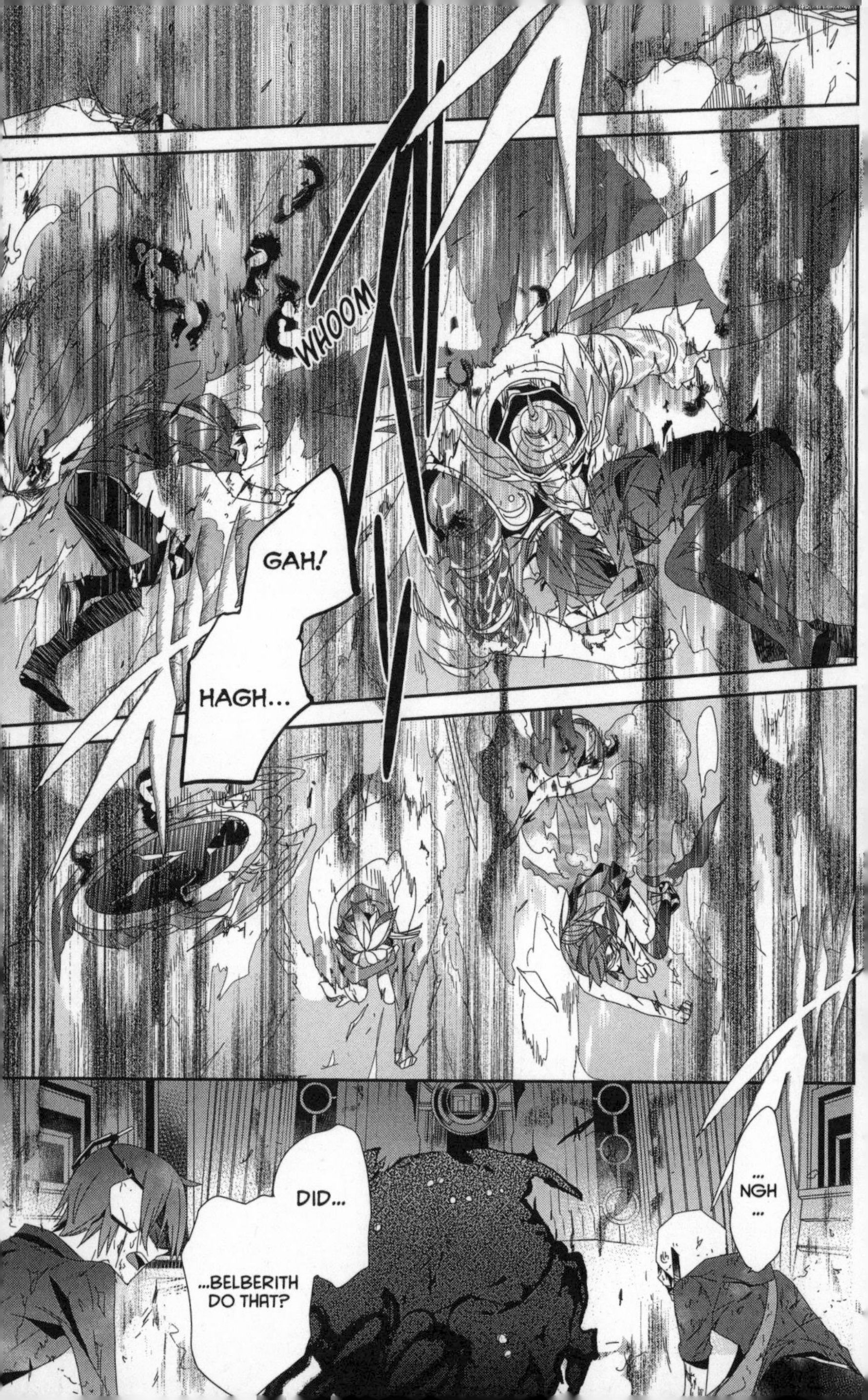
WHOOM
GAH!
HAGH...
...NGH...
DID...
...BELBERITH DO THAT?

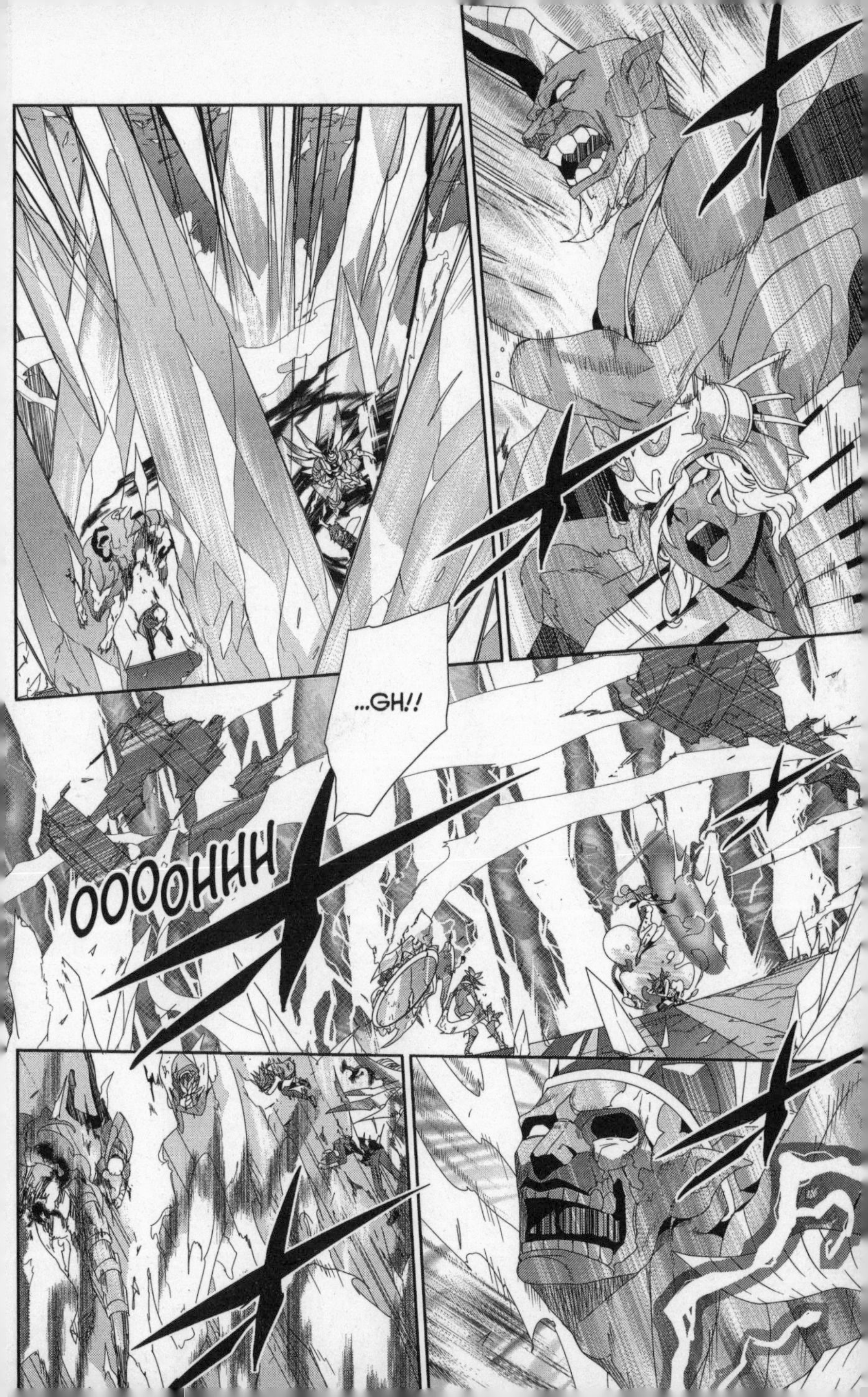
...GH!!
OOOOHHH

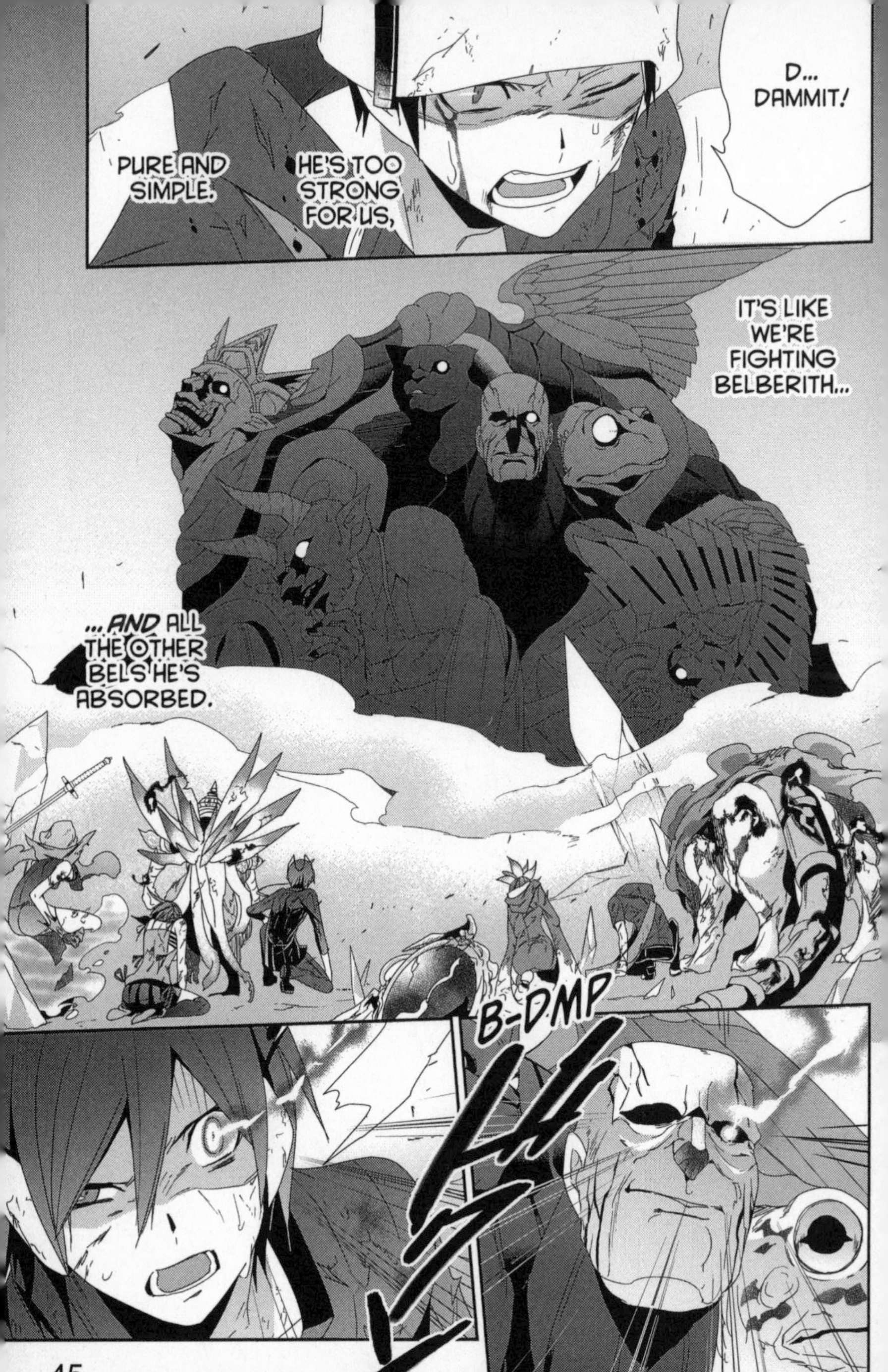
D... DAMMIT!
HE'S TOO STRONG FOR US,
PURE AND SIMPLE.
IT'S LIKE WE'RE FIGHTING BELBERITH...
...AND ALL THE OTHER BELS HE'S ABSORBED.
B-DMP

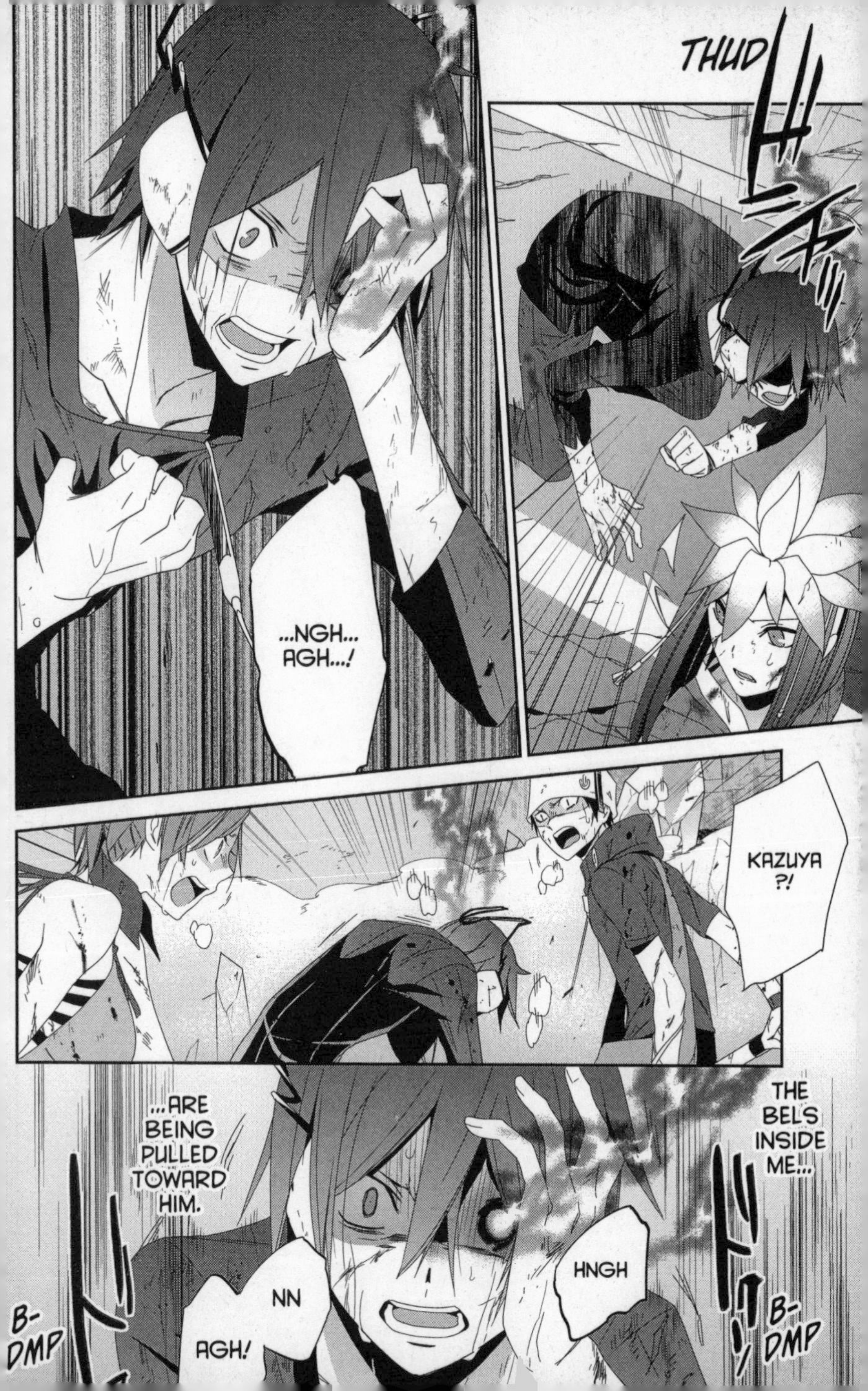
THUD
...NGH... AGH...!
KAZUYA ?!
THE BELS INSIDE ME...
...ARE BEING PULLED TOWARD HIM.
HNGH
B-DMP
NN
AGH!
B-DMP

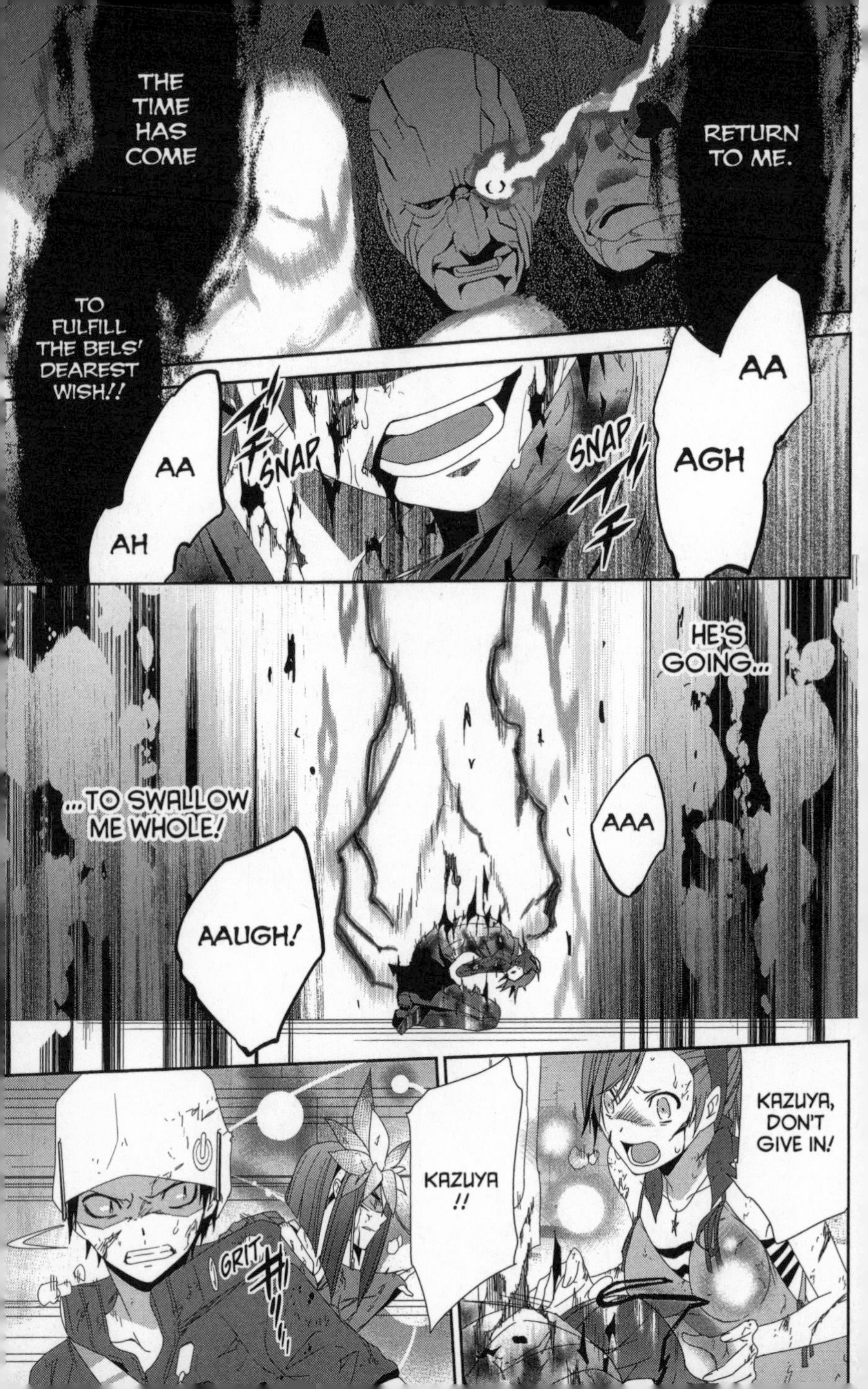
RETURN TO ME.
THE TIME HAS COME
TO FULFILL THE BELS' DEAREST WISH!!
AA AGH
SNAP
SNAP
AA AH
HE'S GOING...
AAA
...TO SWALLOW ME WHOLE!
AAUGH!
KAZUYA, DON'T GIVE IN!
KAZUYA !!
GRIT

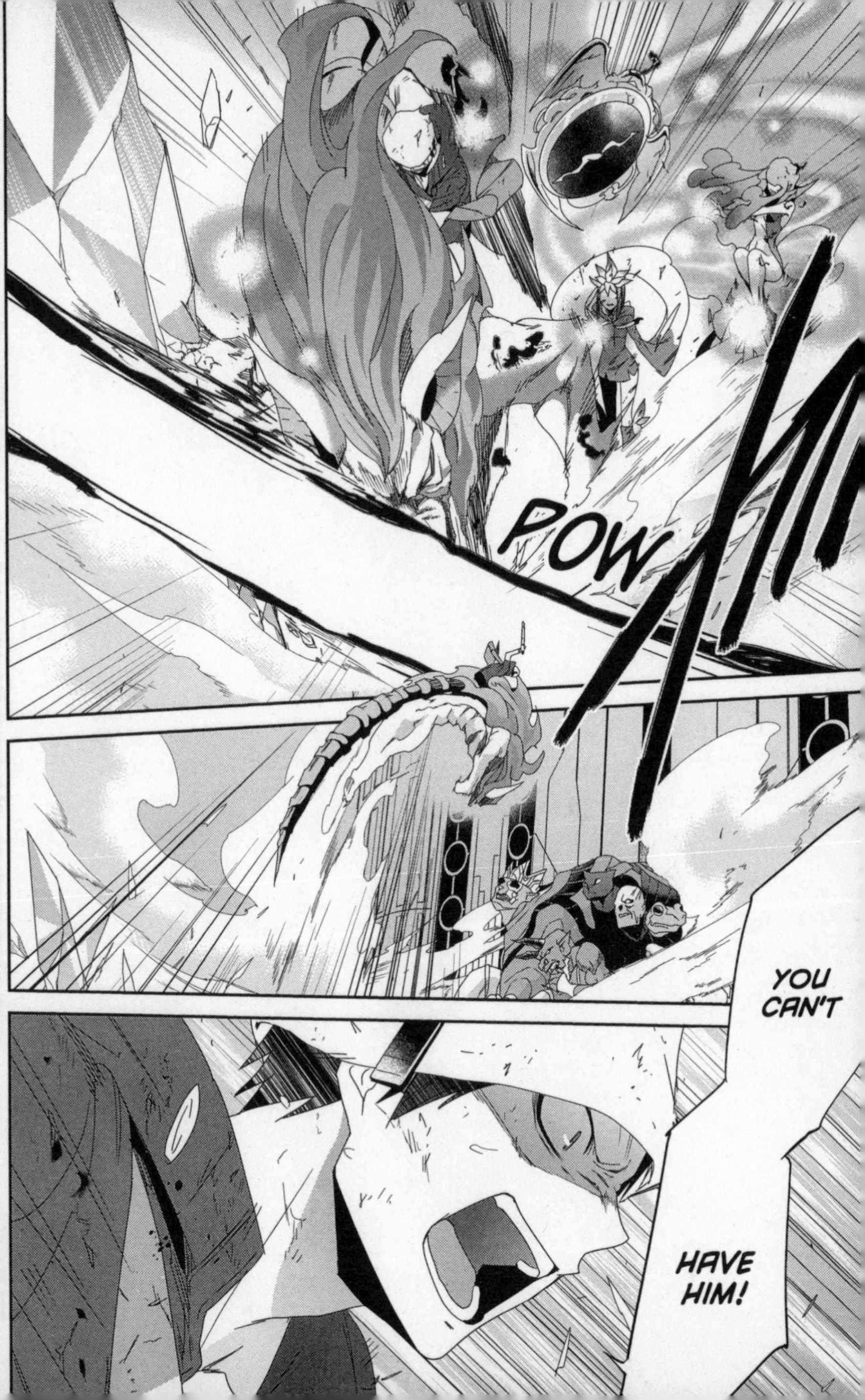
POW
YOU CAN'T
HAVE HIM!

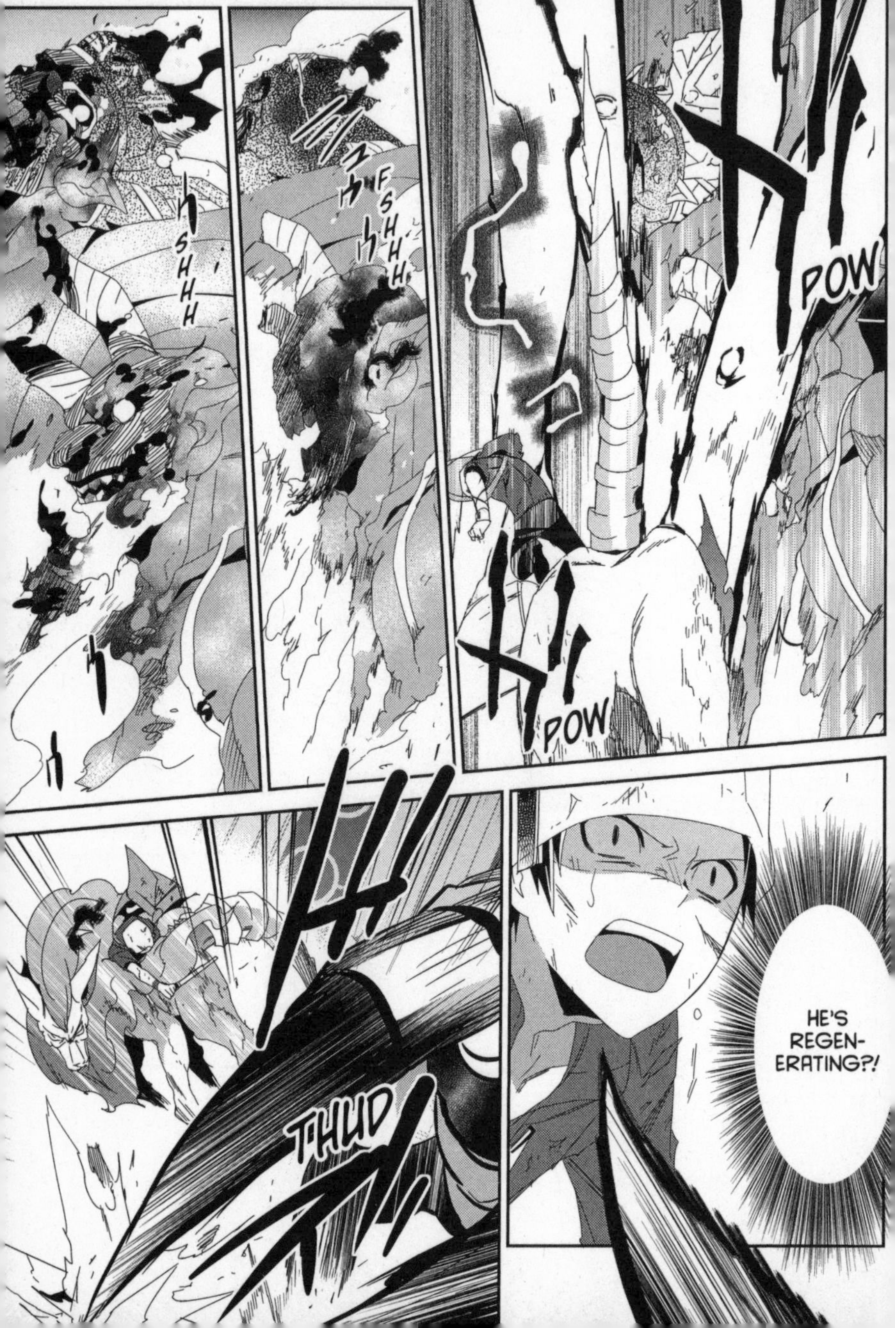
POW
POW
FSHHH
SHHH
HE'S REGEN-
ERATING?!
THUD

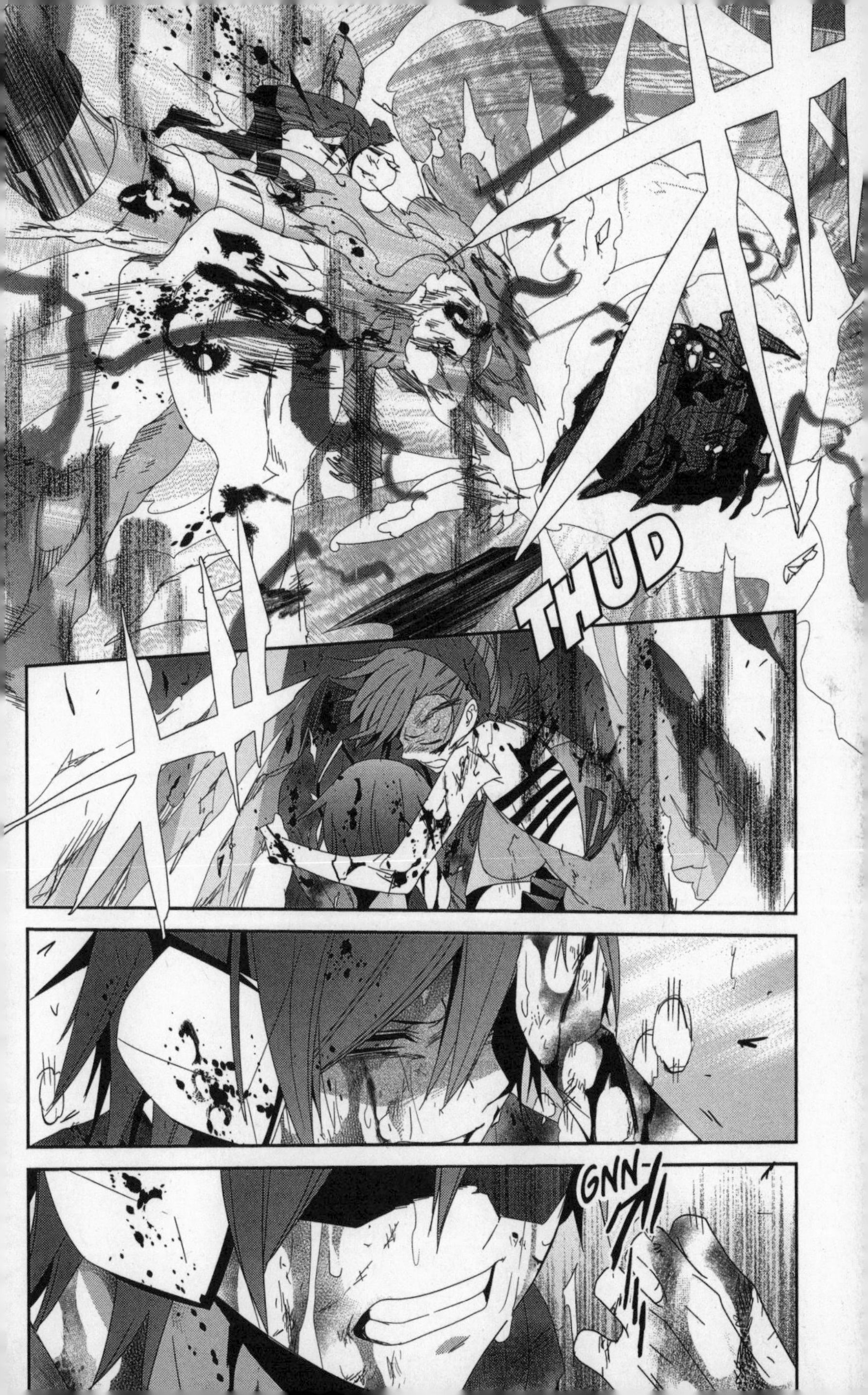
THUD
GNN-!!

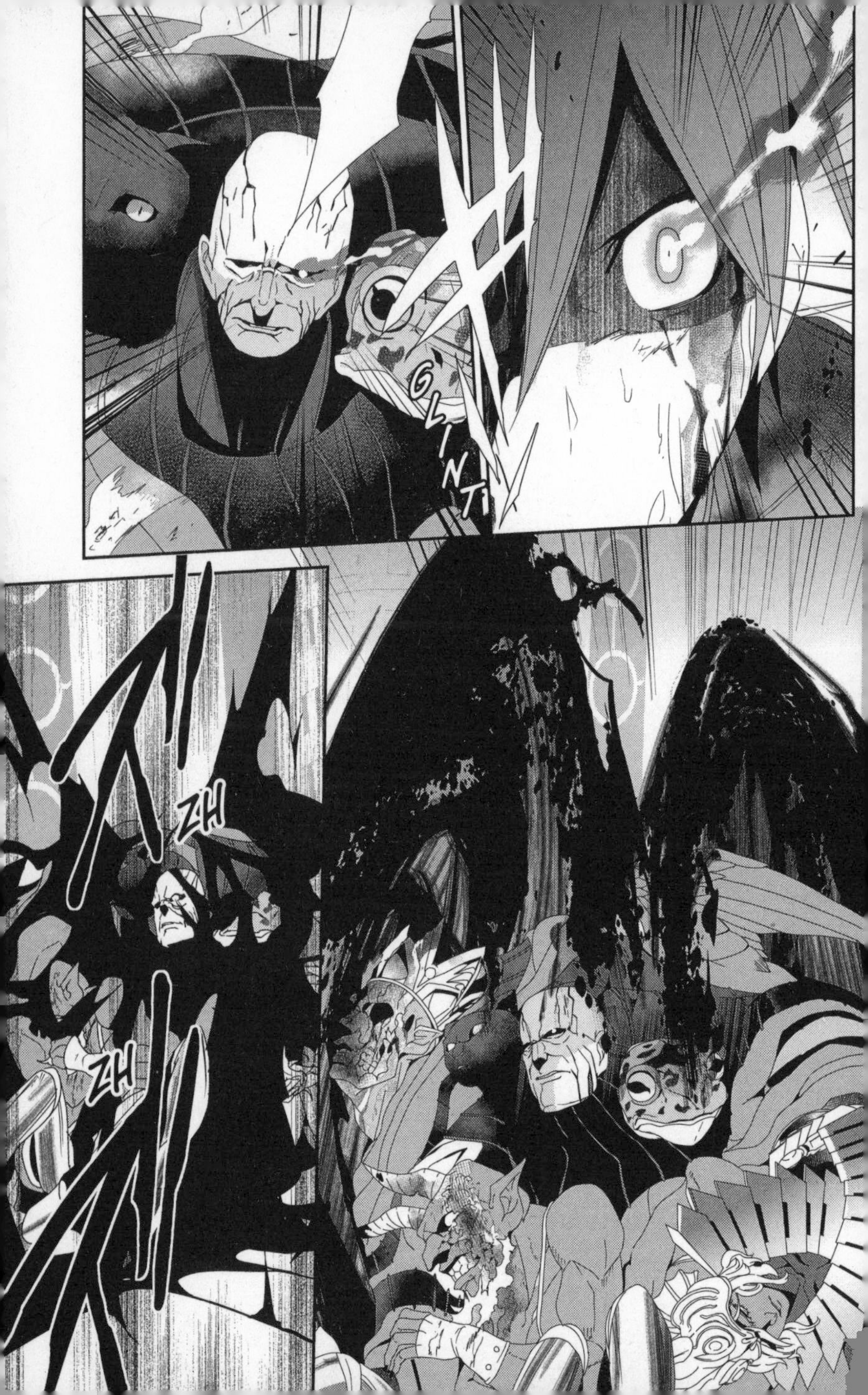
GLINT
ZH
ZH

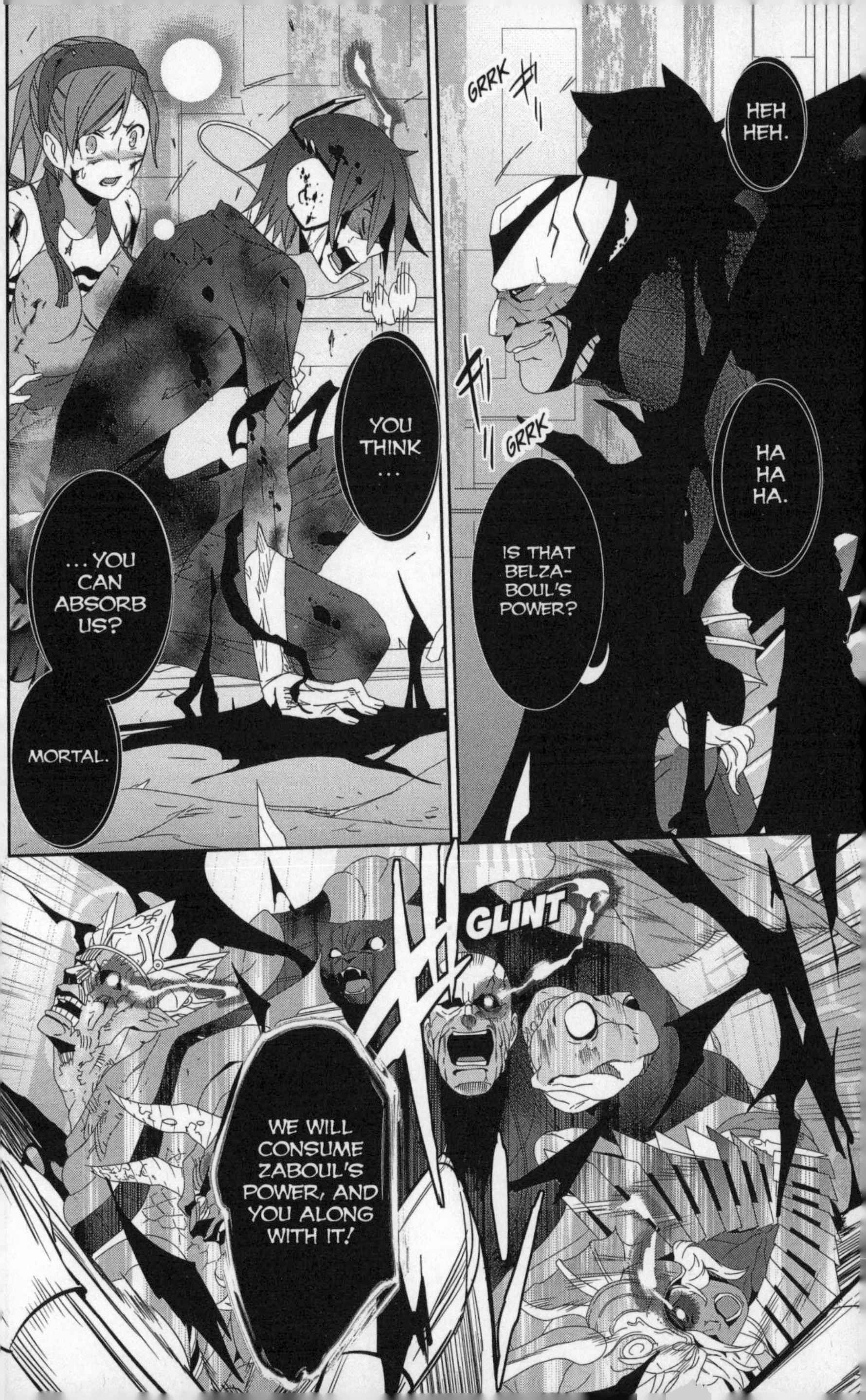
HEH HEH.
GRRK
HA HA HA.
GRRK
IS THAT BELZA-BOUL'S POWER?
YOU THINK...
...YOU CAN ABSORB US?
MORTAL.
GLINT
WE WILL CONSUME ZABOUL'S POWER, AND YOU ALONG WITH IT!

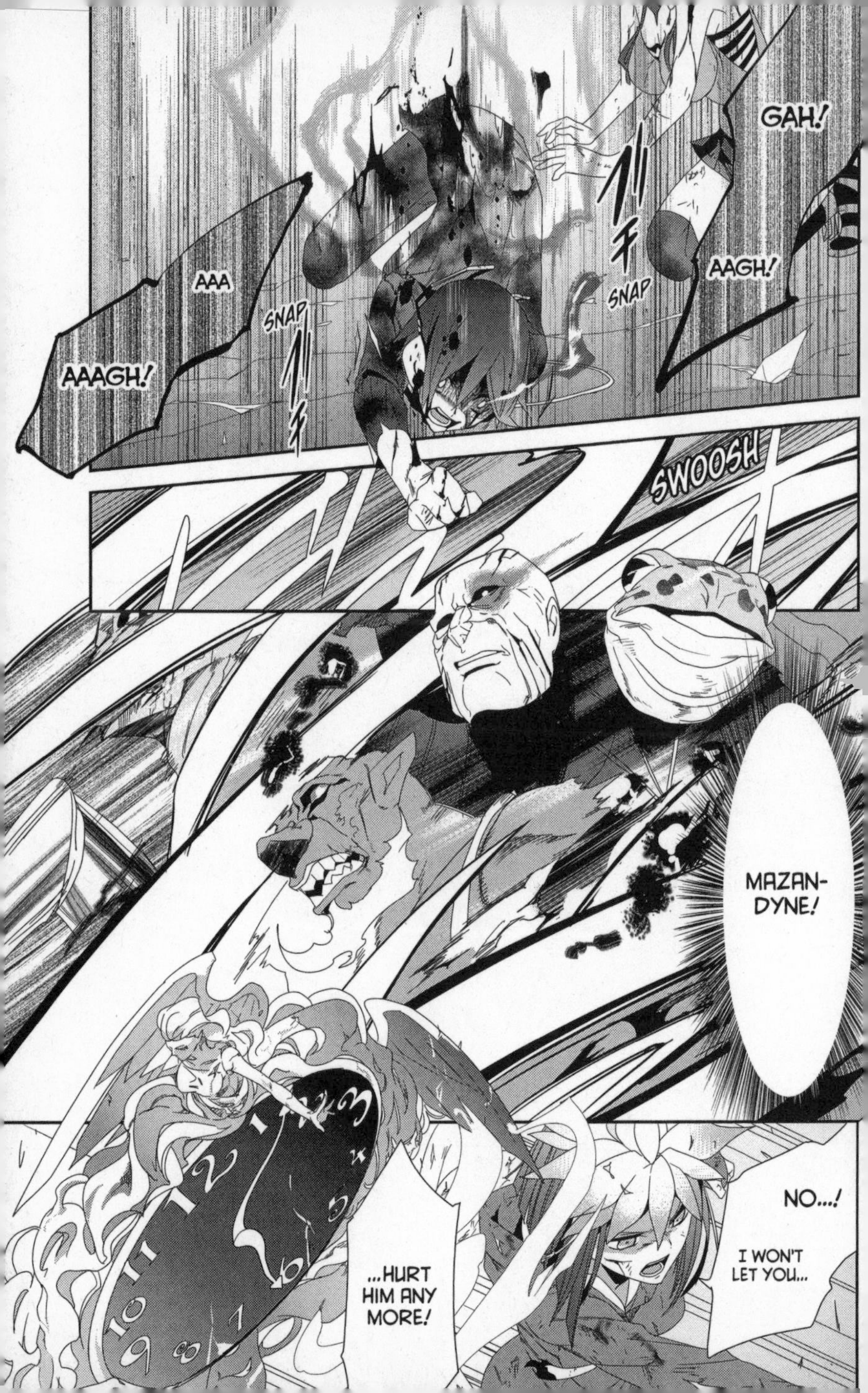
GAH!
AAGH!
SNAP
SNAP
AAA
AAAGH!
SWOOSH
MAZAN-DYNE!
NO...!
I WON'T LET YOU...
...HURT HIM ANY MORE!

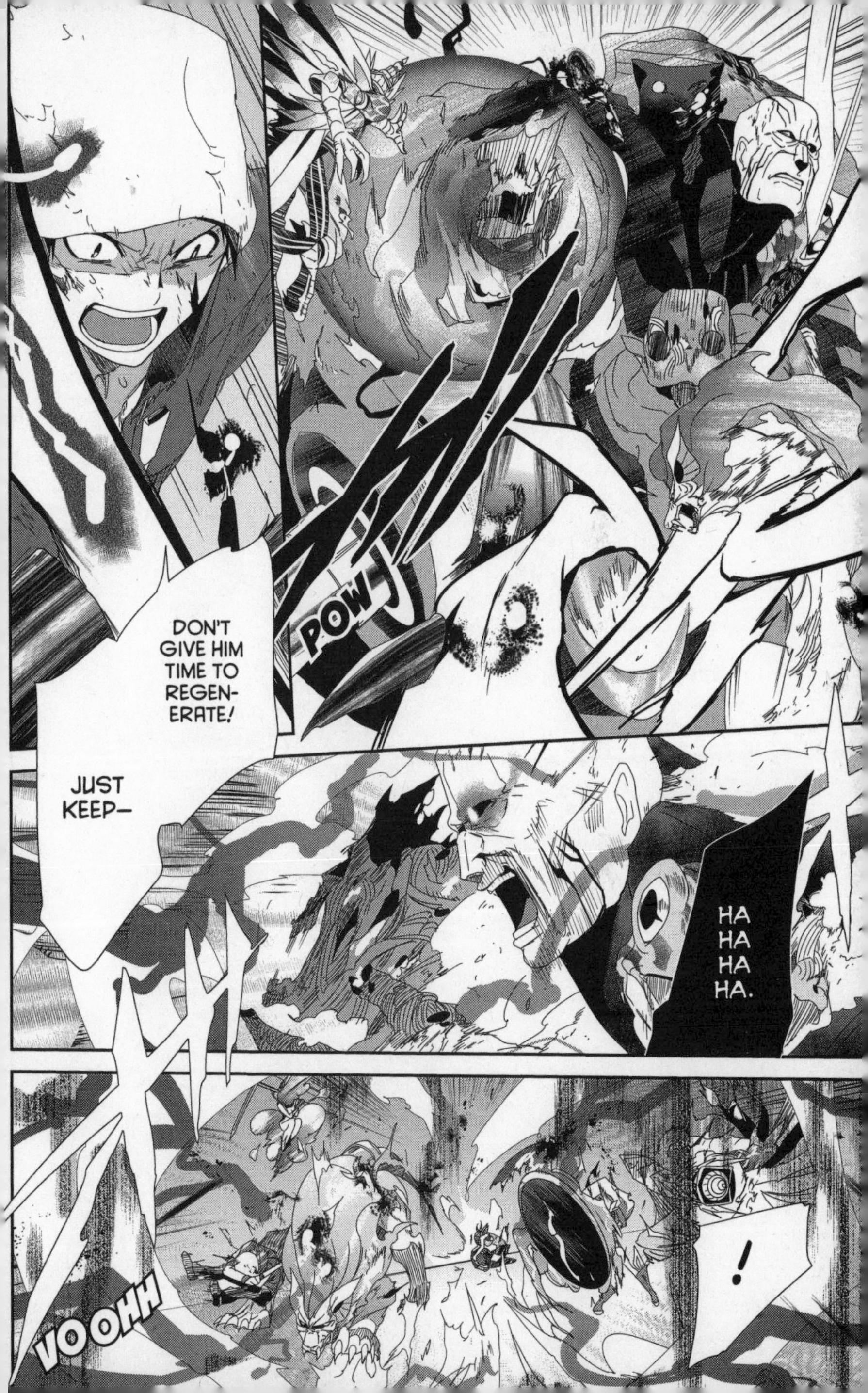
POW
DON'T GIVE HIM TIME TO REGEN-ERATE!
JUST KEEP—
HA HA HA HA.
!
VOOHH

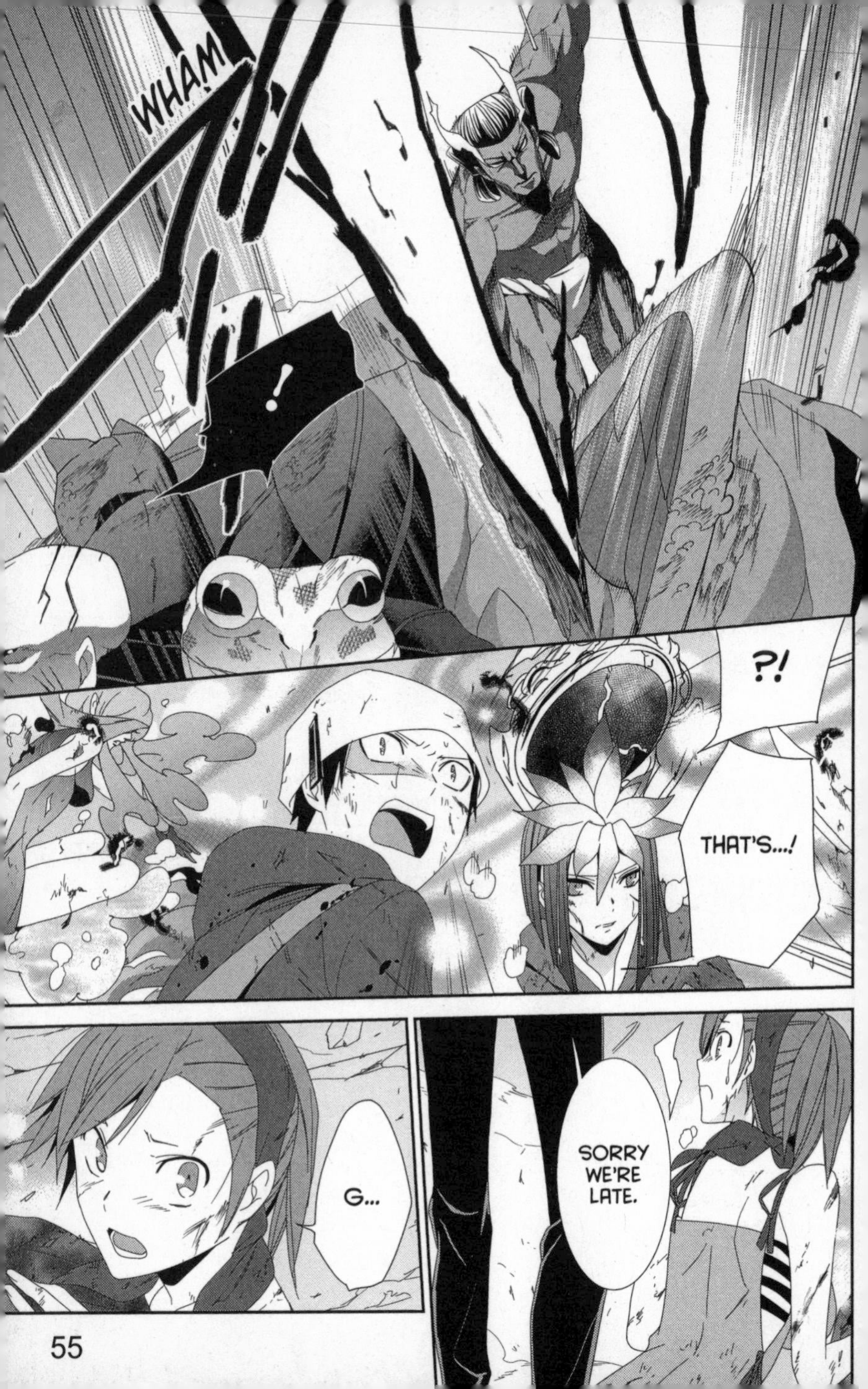
WHAM
!
?!
THAT'S...!
SORRY WE'RE LATE.
G...

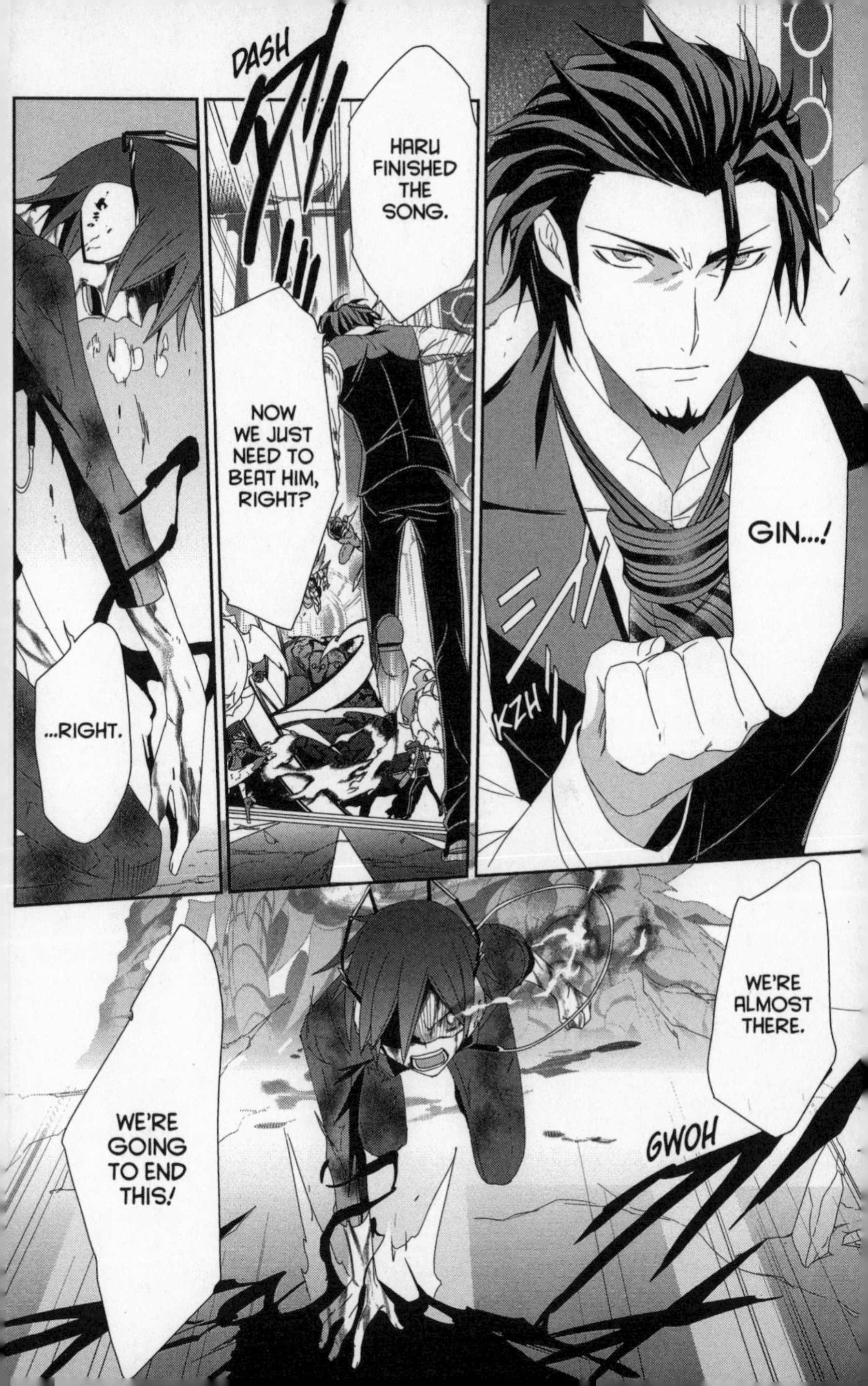
GIN...!
KZH
HARU FINISHED THE SONG.
DASH
NOW WE JUST NEED TO BEAT HIM, RIGHT?
...RIGHT.
WE'RE ALMOST THERE.
GWOH
WE'RE GOING TO END THIS!

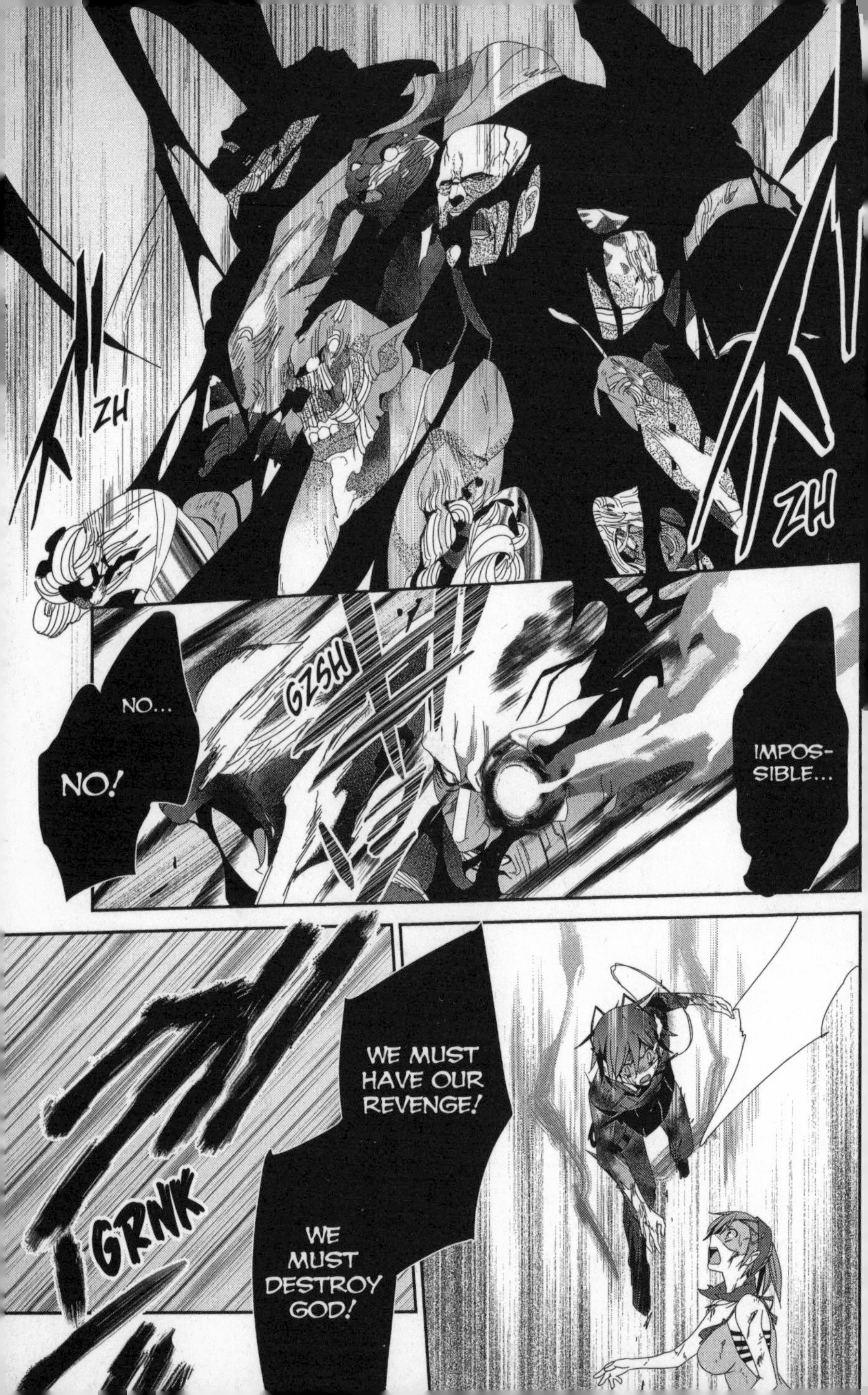
ZH
ZH
IMPOS-SIBLE...
GZSH
NO...
NO!
WE MUST HAVE OUR REVENGE!
WE MUST DESTROY GOD!
GRNK

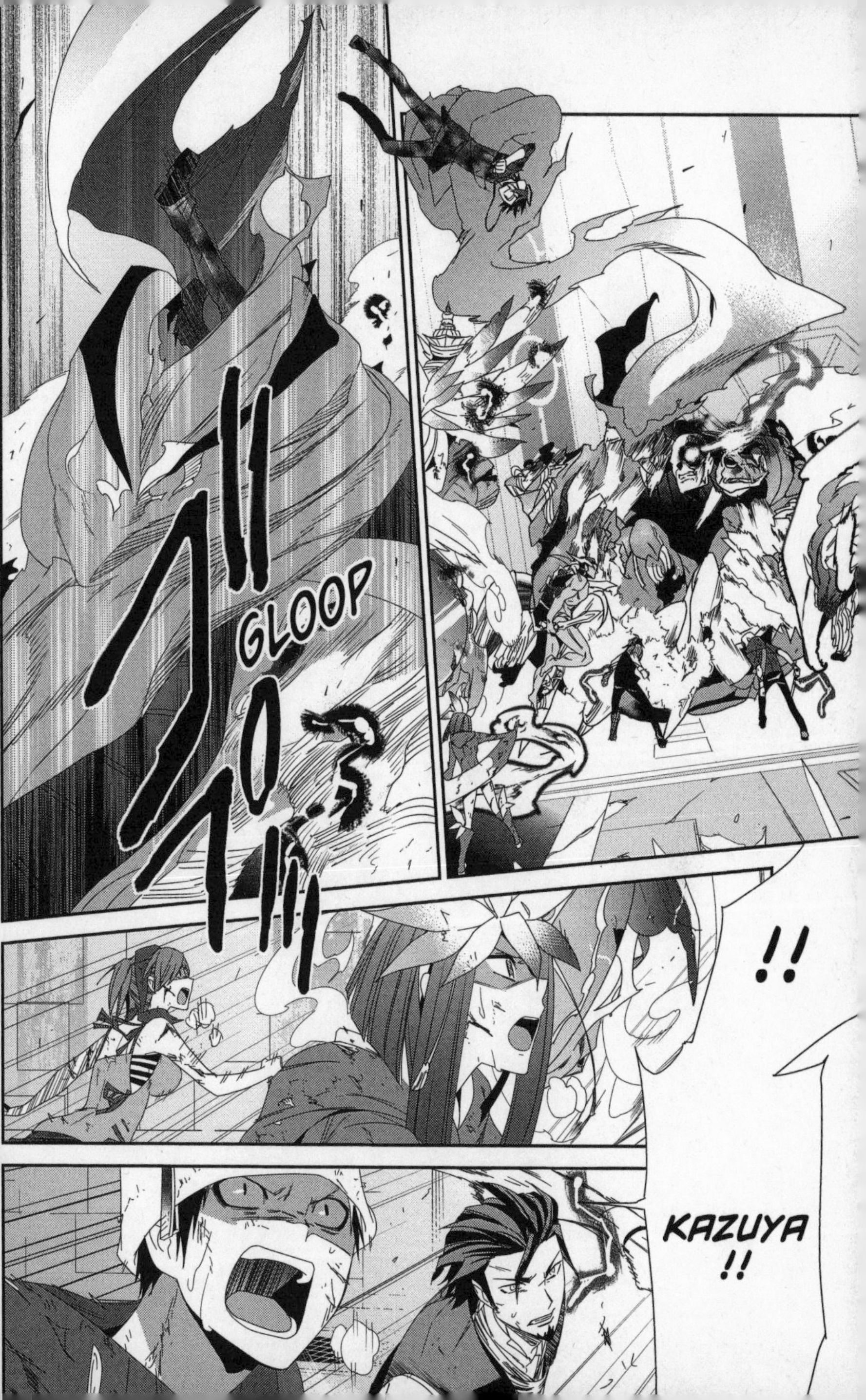
GLOOP
!!
KAZUYA !!

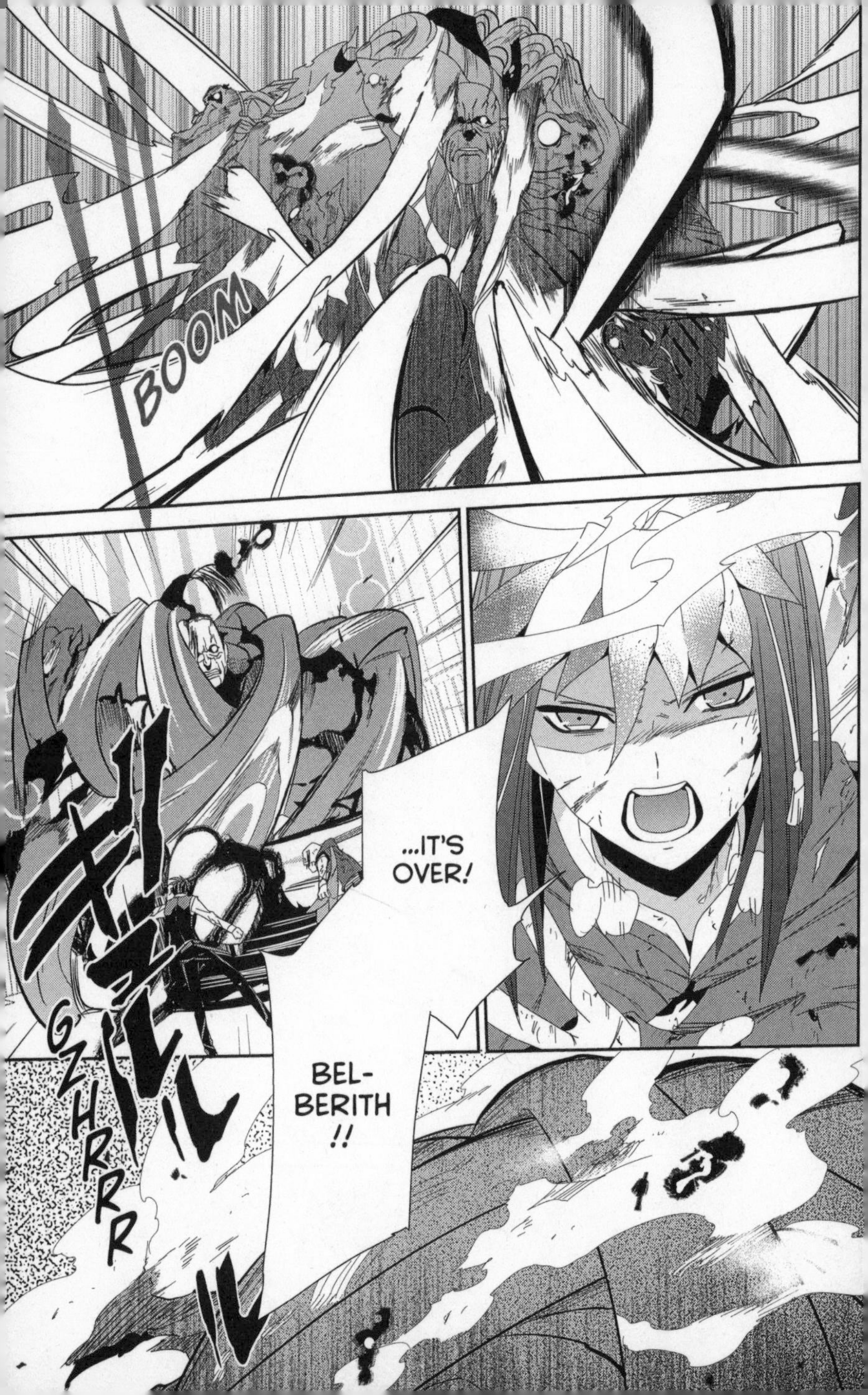
BOOM
...IT'S OVER!
GZHRRR
BEL-BERITH!!

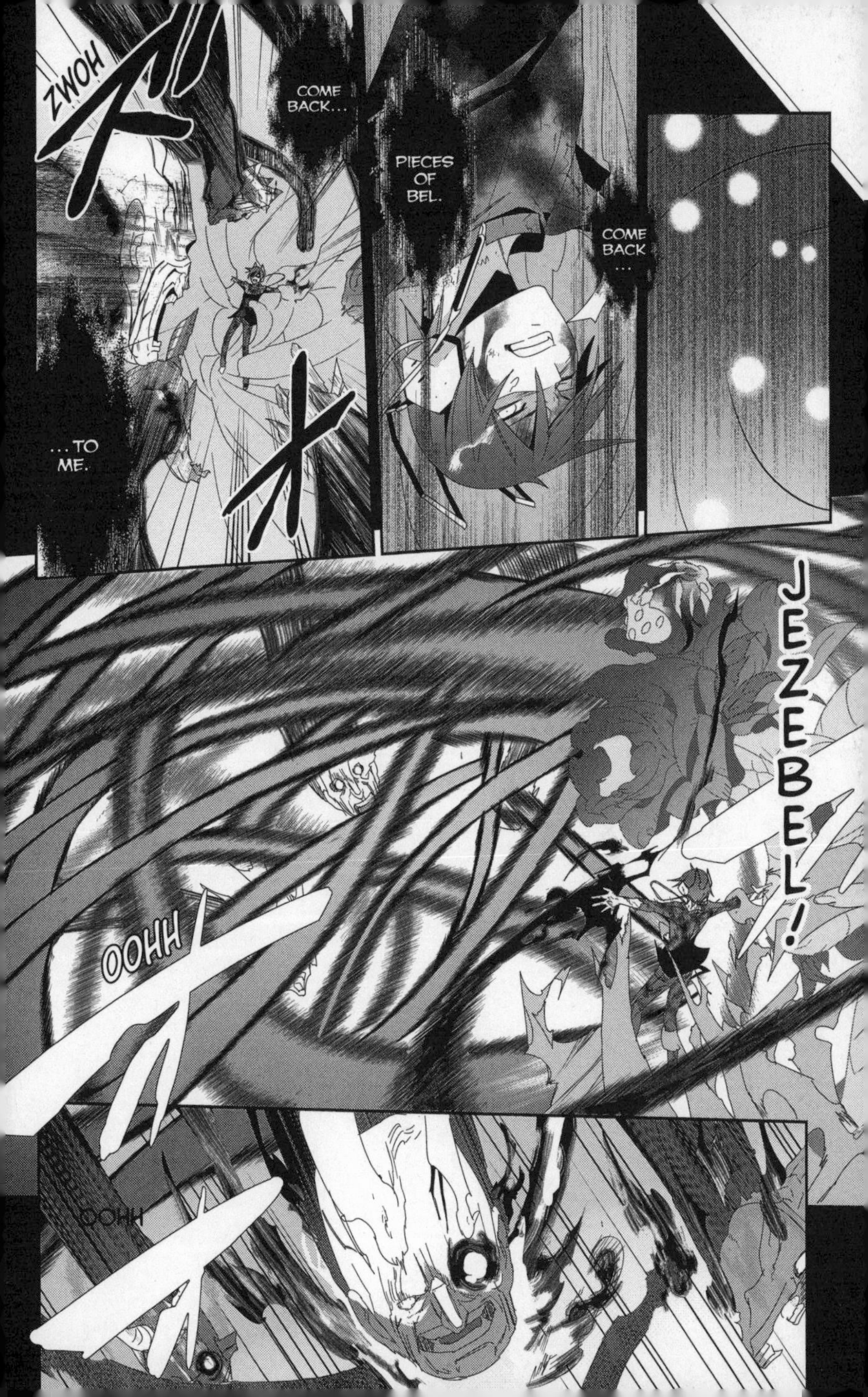
COME BACK...
PIECES OF BEL.
COME BACK ...
ZWOH
...TO ME.
JEZEBEL!
OOHH
OOHH

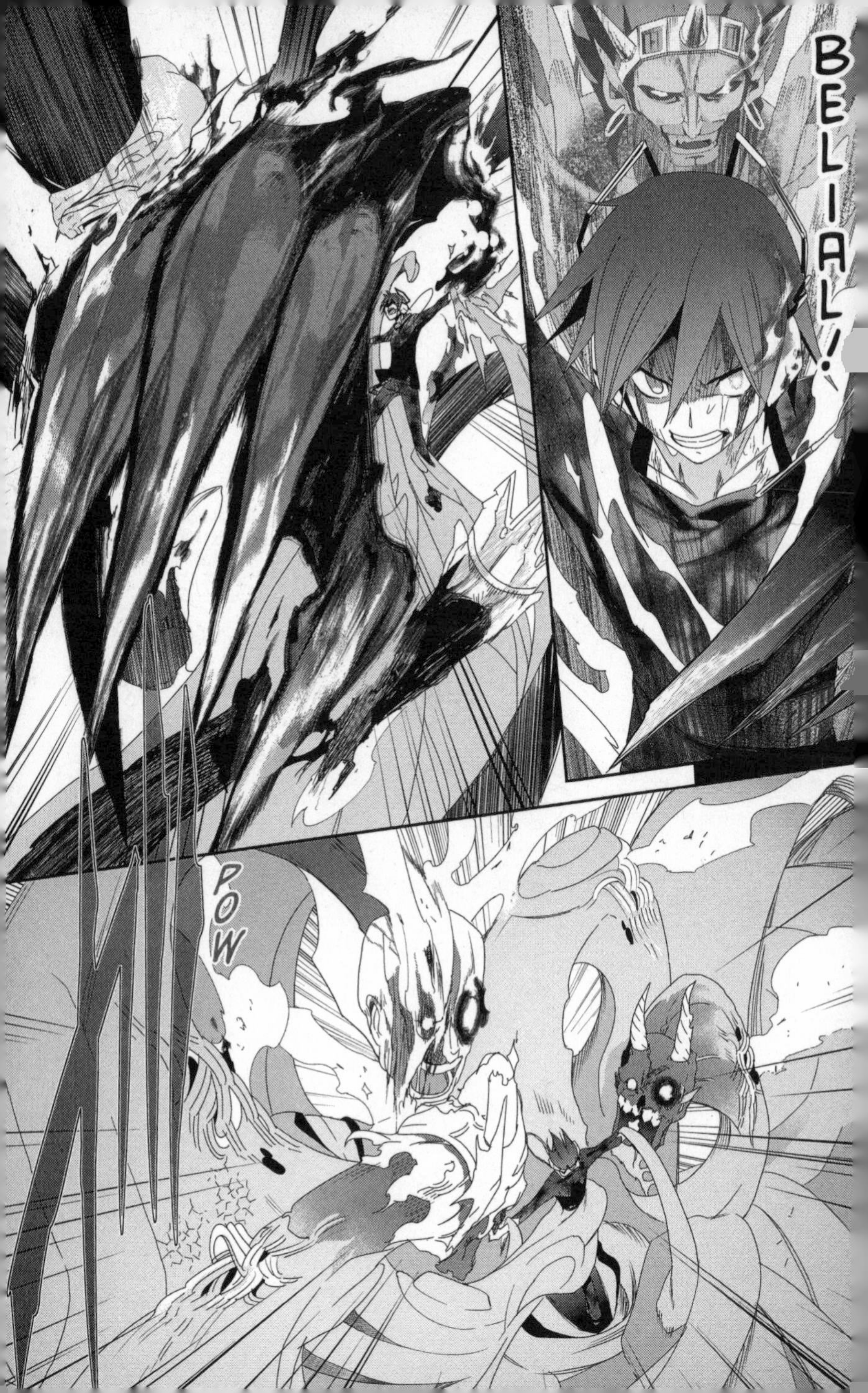
BELIAL!
POW

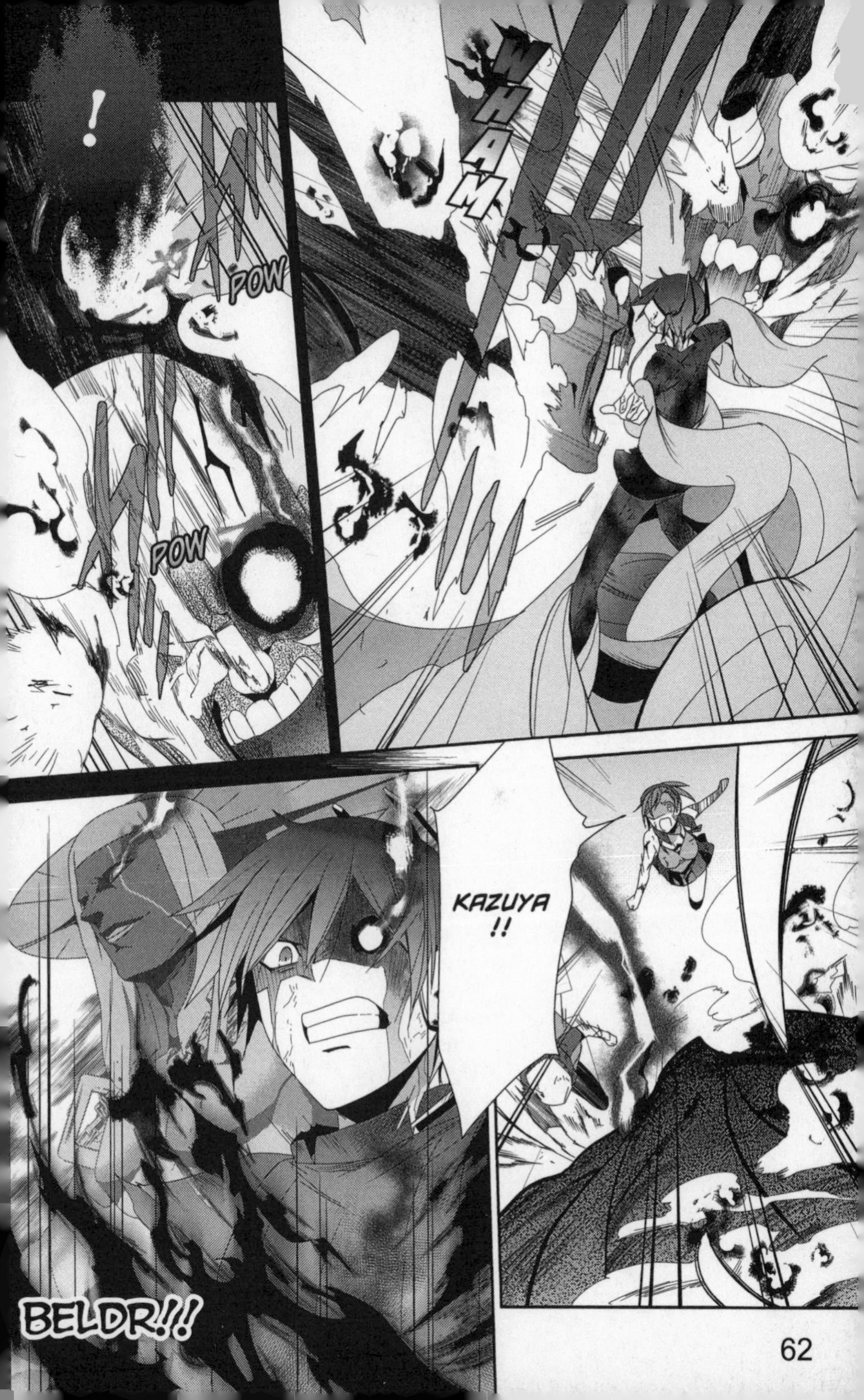
WHAM
!
POW
POW
KAZUYA !!
BELDR!!!

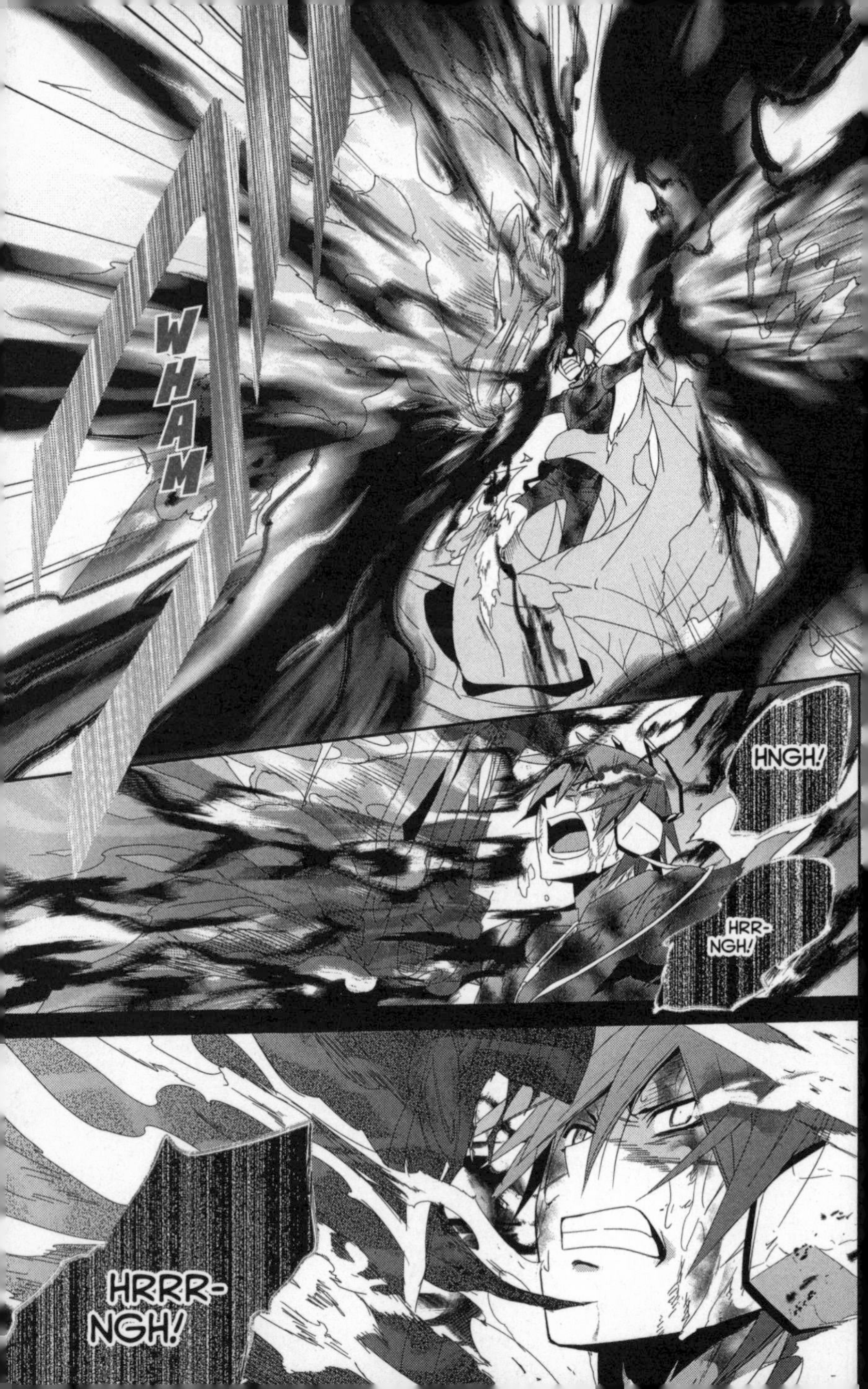
WHAM
HNGH!
HRR-NGH!
HRRR-NGH!

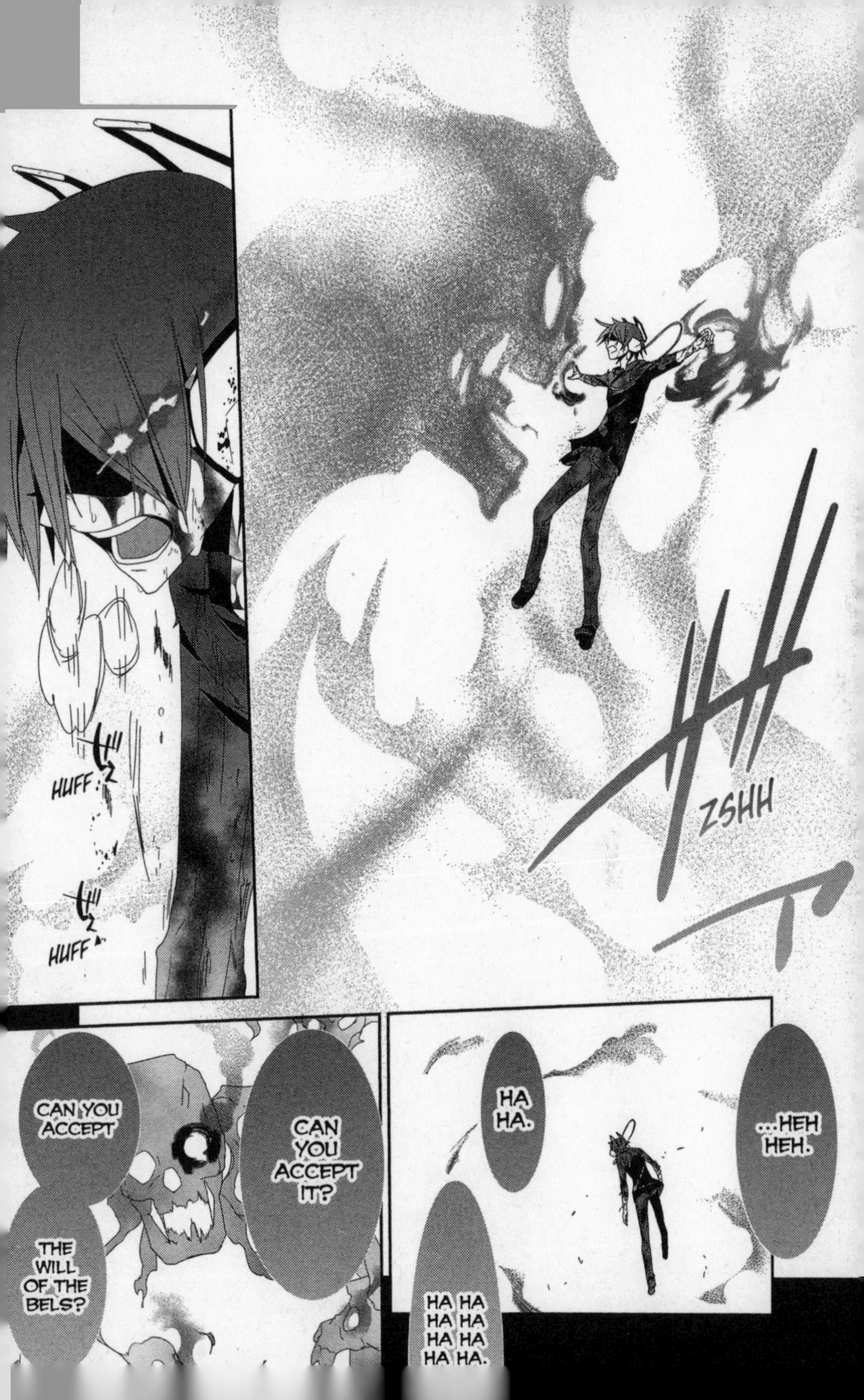
ZSHH
HUFF
HUFF
...HEH HEH.
HA HA.
HA HA HA HA HA HA HA HA.
CAN YOU ACCEPT IT?
CAN YOU ACCEPT
THE WILL OF THE BELS?

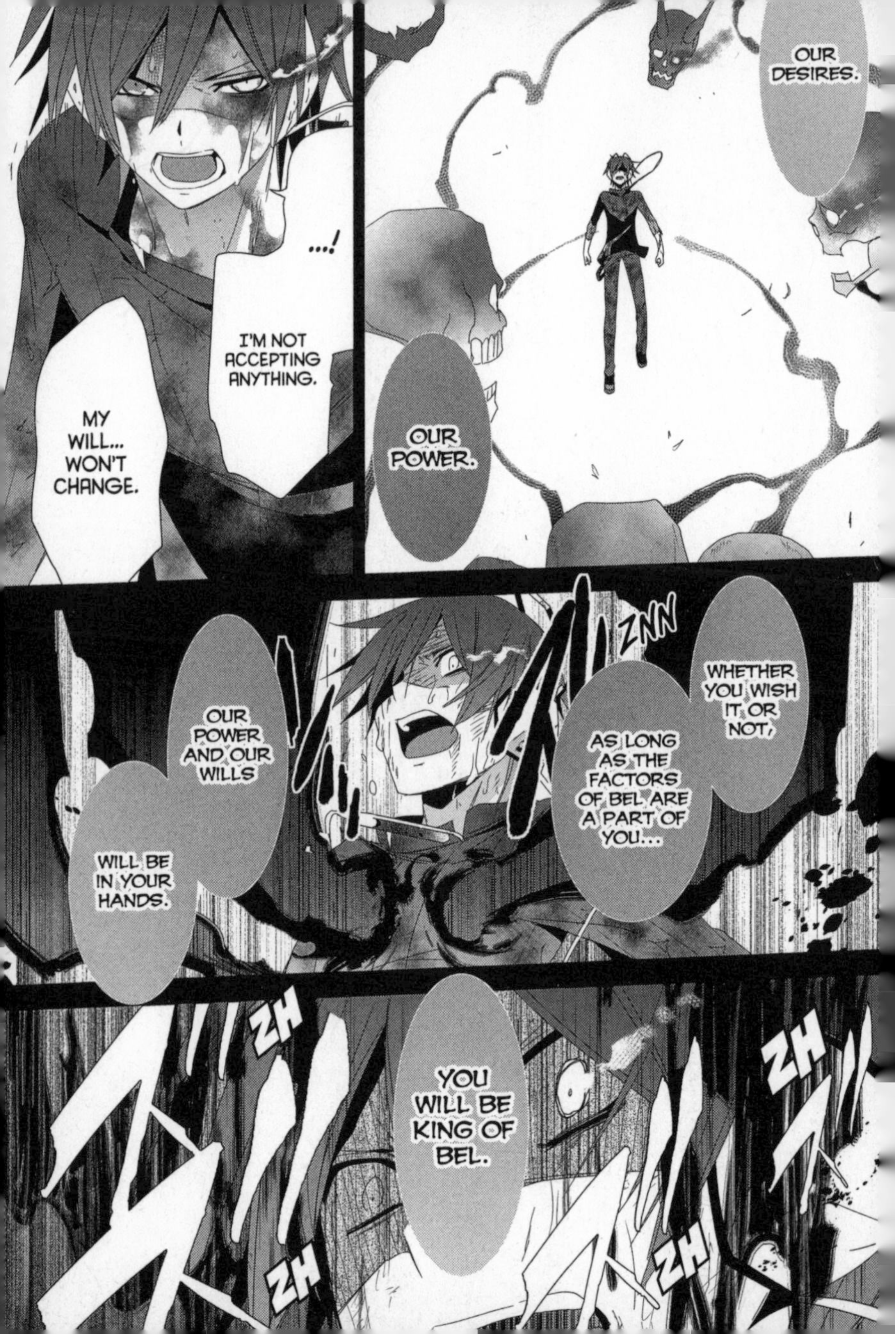
OUR DESIRES.
OUR POWER.
...!
I'M NOT ACCEPTING ANYTHING.
MY WILL... WON'T CHANGE.
ZNN
WHETHER YOU WISH IT OR NOT,
AS LONG AS THE FACTORS OF BEL ARE A PART OF YOU...
OUR POWER AND OUR WILLS
WILL BE IN YOUR HANDS.
ZH
YOU WILL BE KING OF BEL.
ZH
ZH
ZH

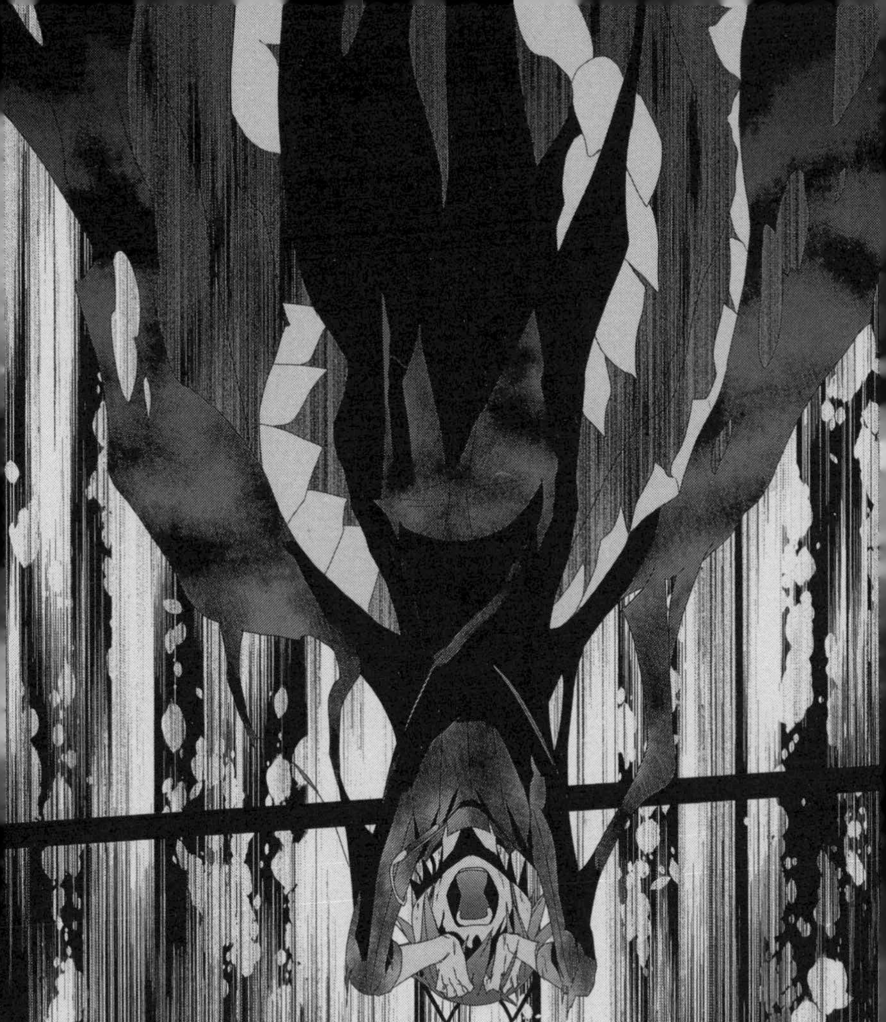
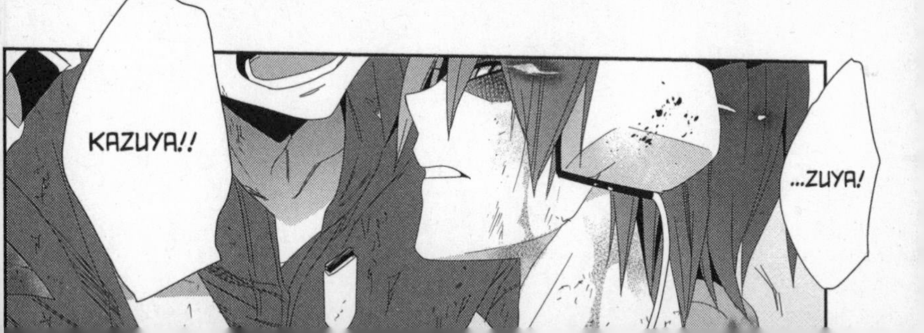
...ZUYA!
KAZUYA!!

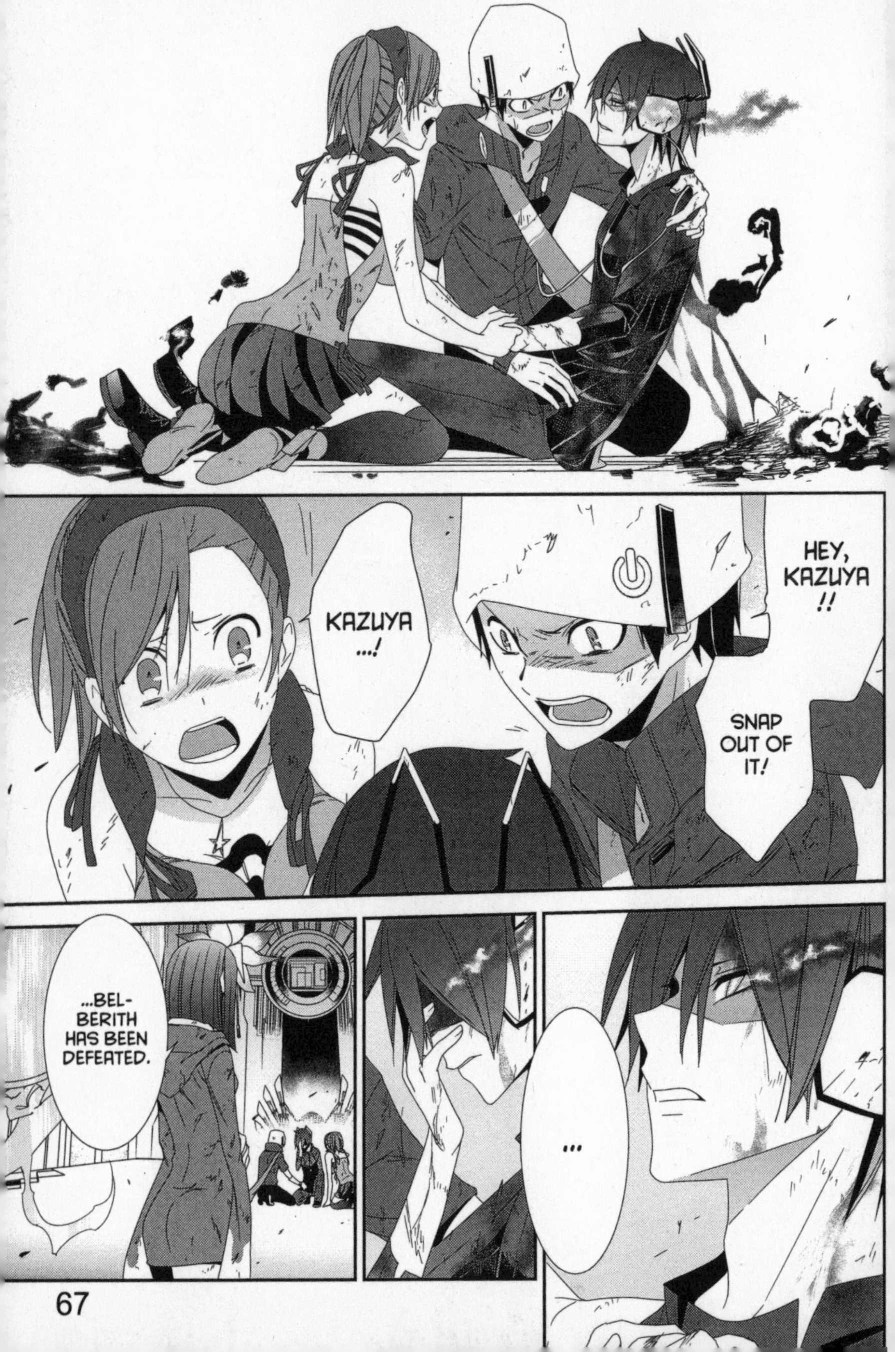
HEY, KAZUYA!!
SNAP OUT OF IT!
KAZUYA ...!
...
...BEL-BERITH HAS BEEN DEFEATED.

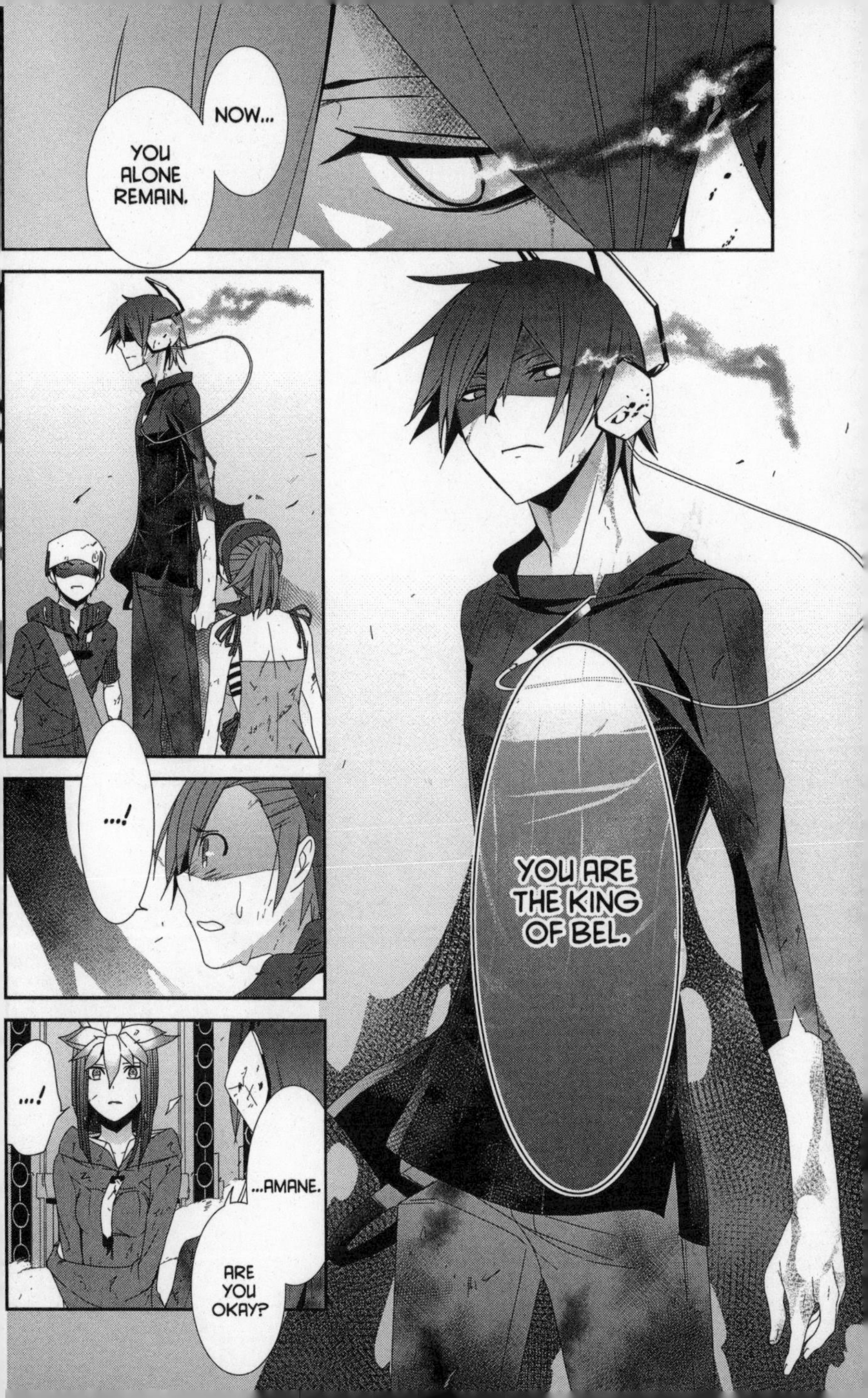
NOW...
YOU ALONE REMAIN.
YOU ARE THE KING OF BEL.
...!
...AMANE.
ARE YOU OKAY?
...!

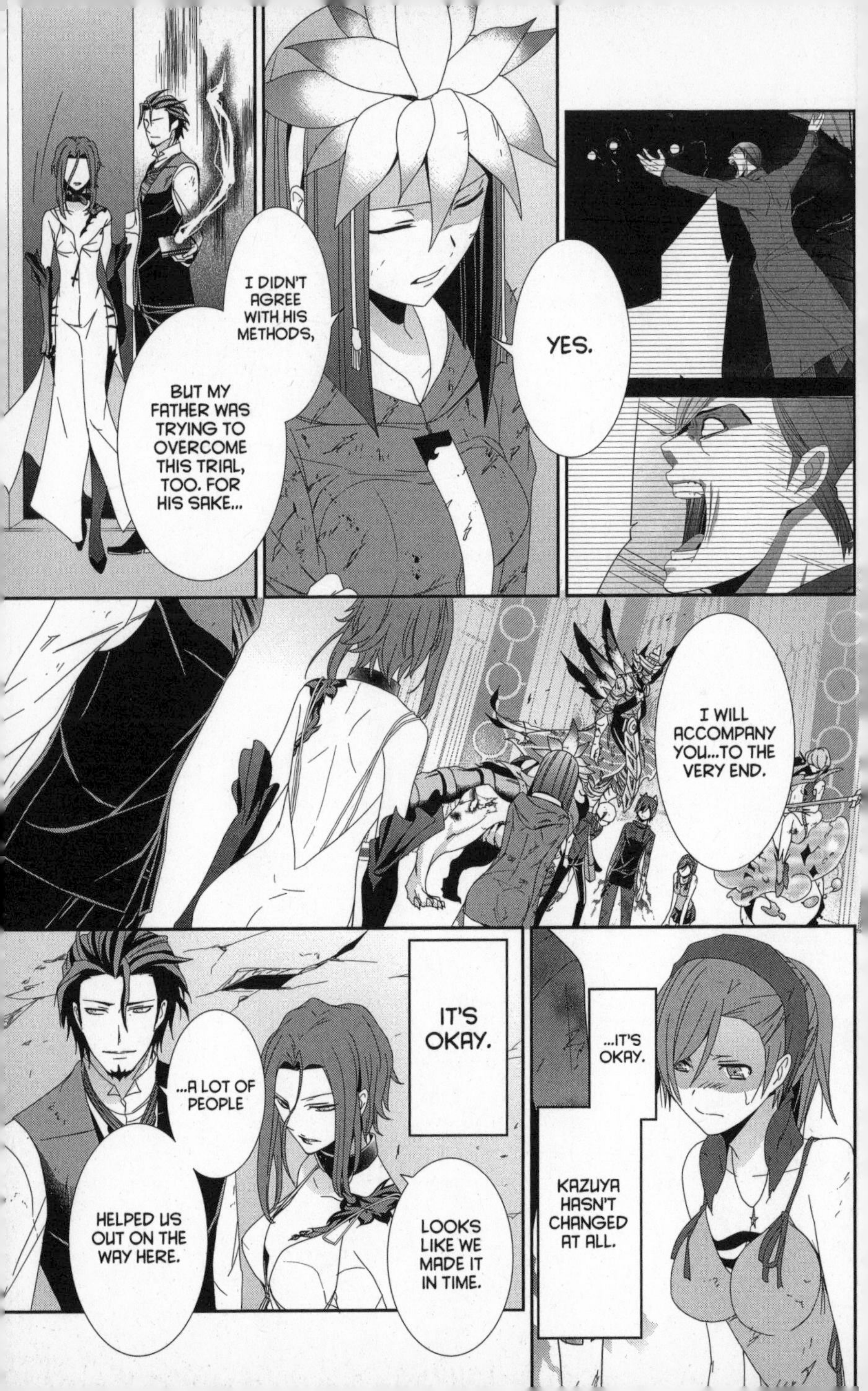
I DIDN'T AGREE WITH HIS METHODS,
BUT MY FATHER WAS TRYING TO OVERCOME THIS TRIAL, TOO. FOR HIS SAKE...
YES.
I WILL ACCOMPANY YOU...TO THE VERY END.
...IT'S OKAY.
KAZUYA HASN'T CHANGED AT ALL.
IT'S OKAY.
LOOKS LIKE WE MADE IT IN TIME.
...A LOT OF PEOPLE
HELPED US OUT ON THE WAY HERE.

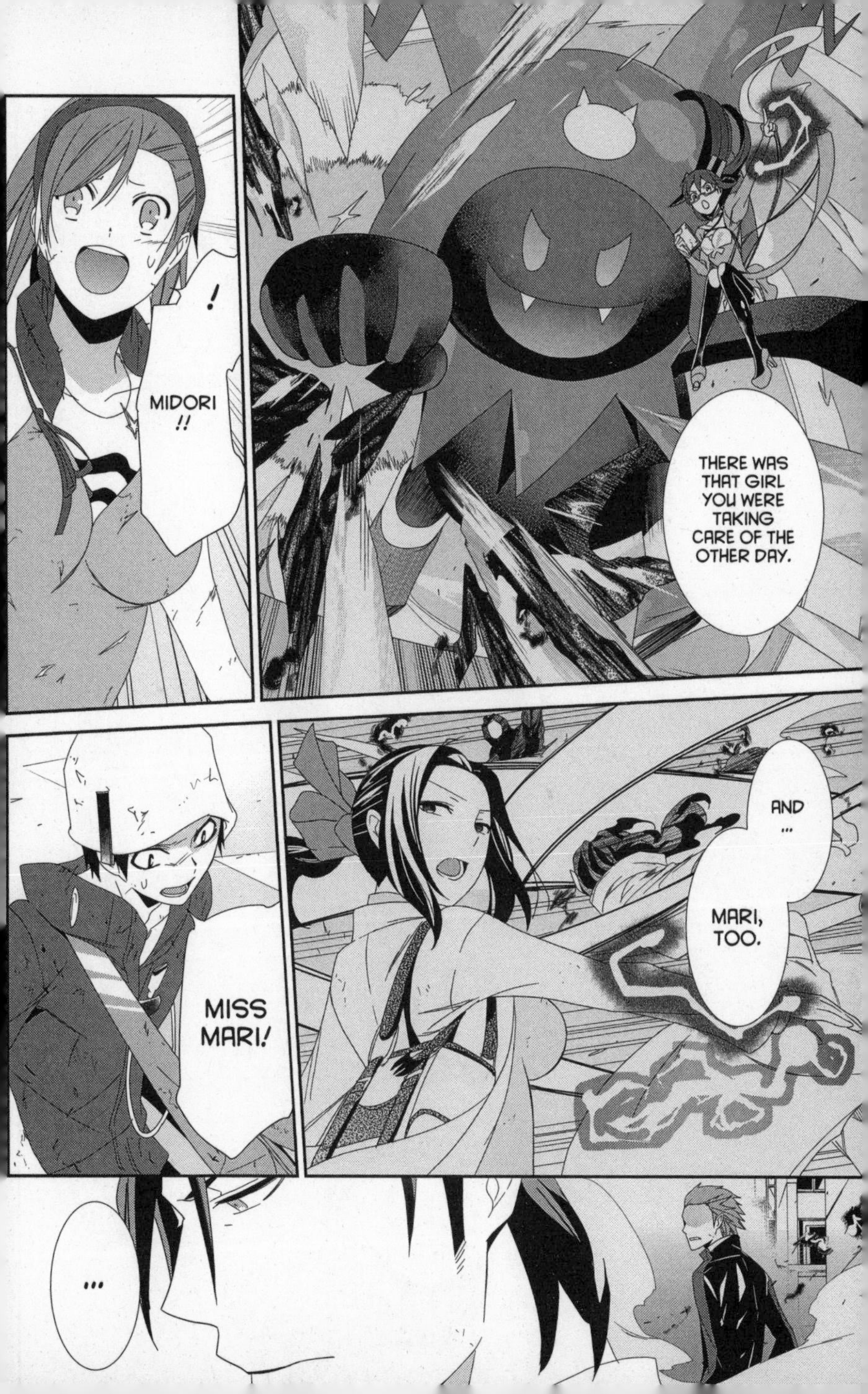
THERE WAS THAT GIRL YOU WERE TAKING CARE OF THE OTHER DAY.
!
MIDORI !!
AND ...
MARI, TOO.
MISS MARI!
...

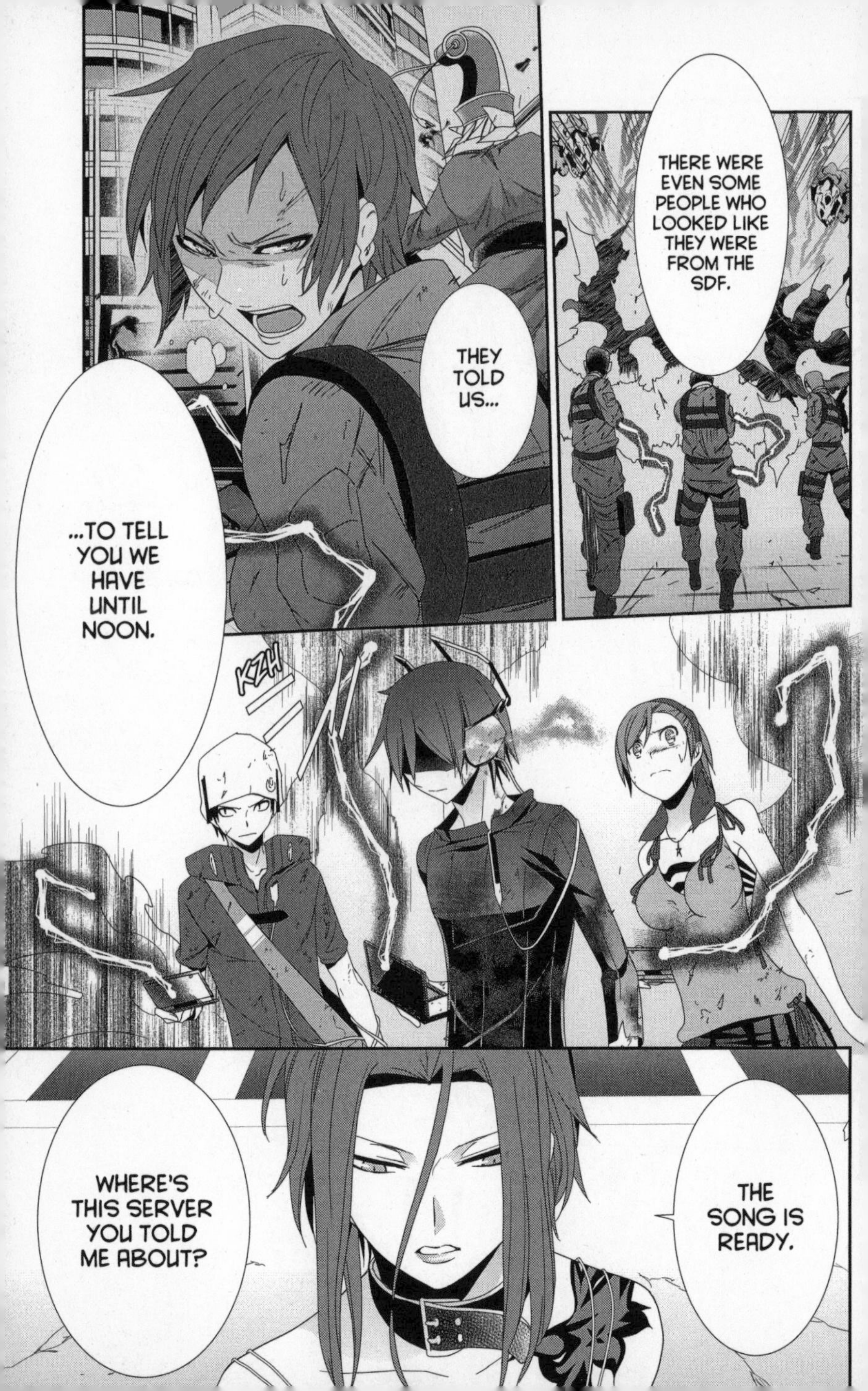
THERE WERE EVEN SOME PEOPLE WHO LOOKED LIKE THEY WERE FROM THE SDF.
THEY TOLD US...
...TO TELL YOU WE HAVE UNTIL NOON.
KZH
THE SONG IS READY.
WHERE'S THIS SERVER YOU TOLD ME ABOUT?

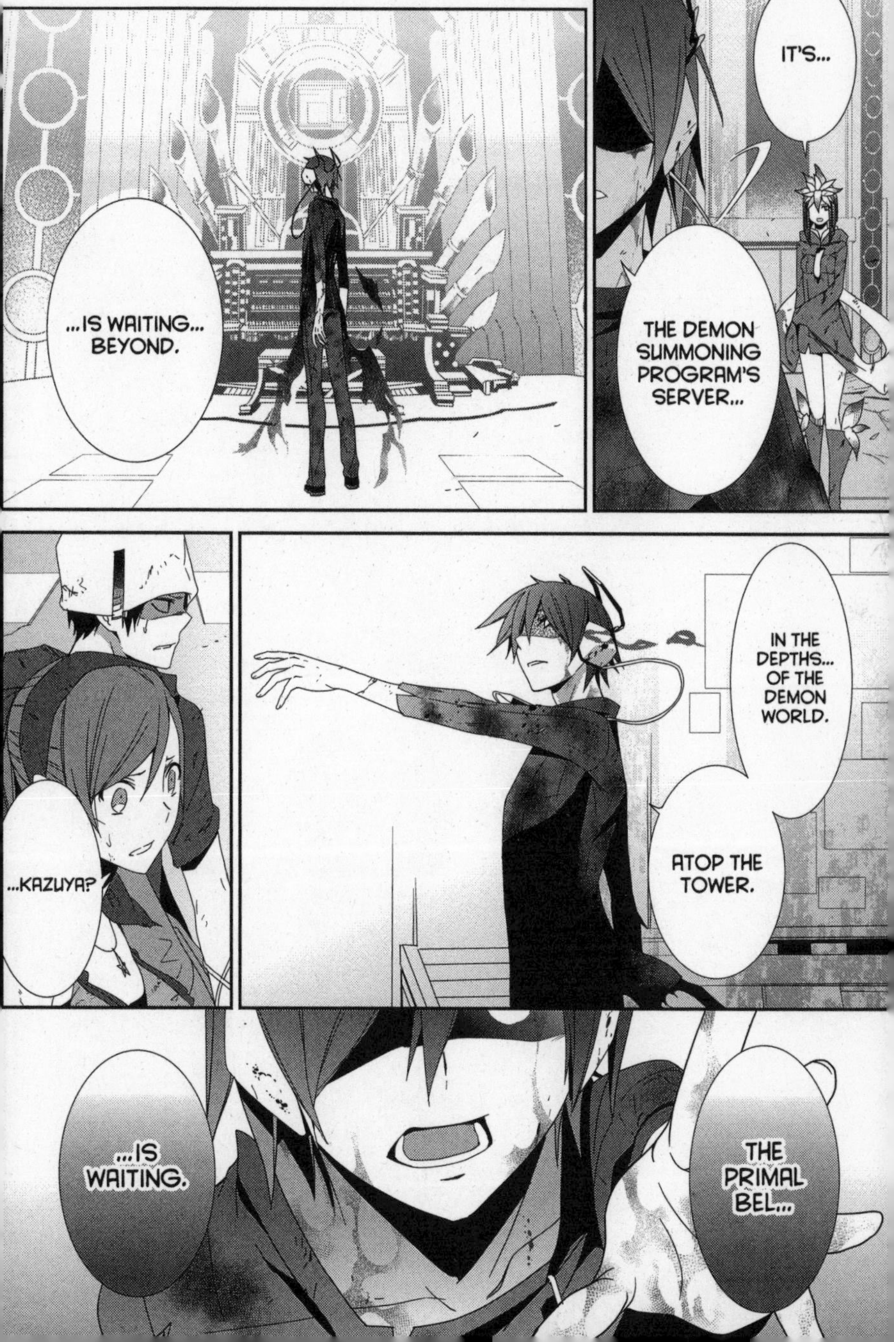
IT'S...
THE DEMON SUMMONING PROGRAM'S SERVER...
...IS WAITING... BEYOND.
IN THE DEPTHS... OF THE DEMON WORLD.
ATOP THE TOWER.
...KAZUYA?
THE PRIMAL BEL...
...IS WAITING.

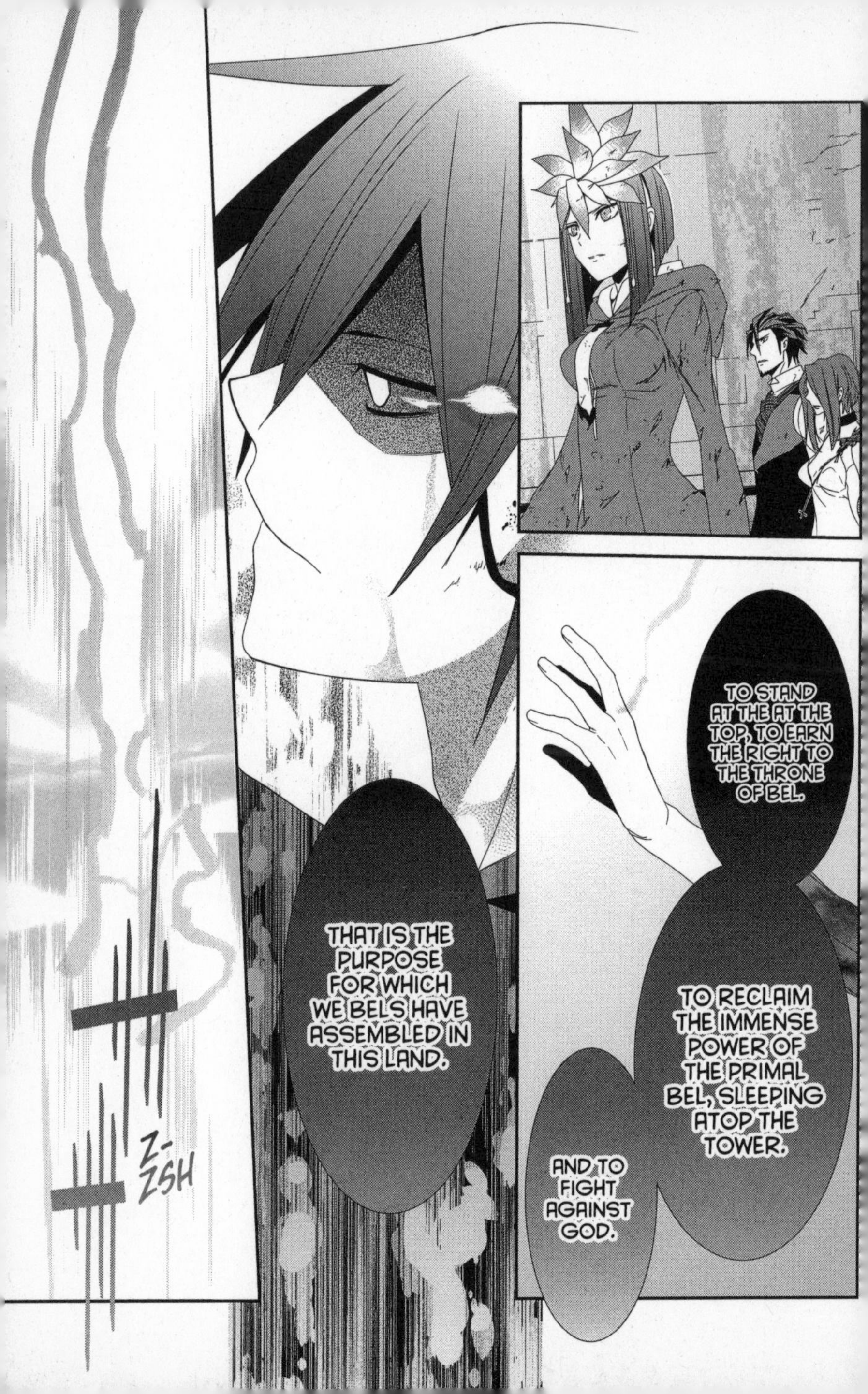
TO STAND AT THE AT THE TOP, TO EARN THE RIGHT TO THE THRONE OF BEL.
TO RECLAIM THE IMMENSE POWER OF THE PRIMAL BEL, SLEEPING ATOP THE TOWER.
AND TO FIGHT AGAINST GOD.
THAT IS THE PURPOSE FOR WHICH WE BELS HAVE ASSEMBLED IN THIS LAND.
Z-ZSH

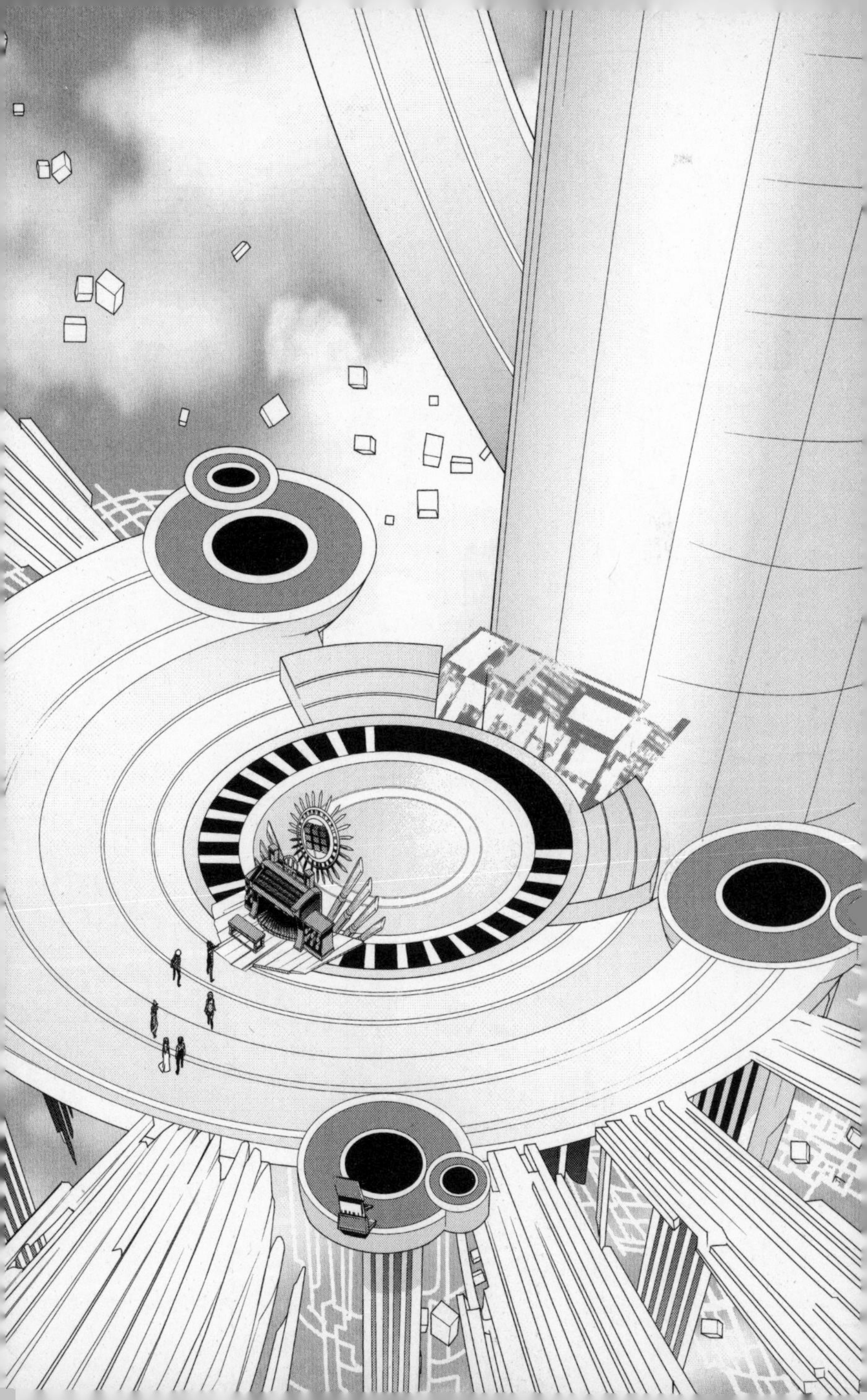

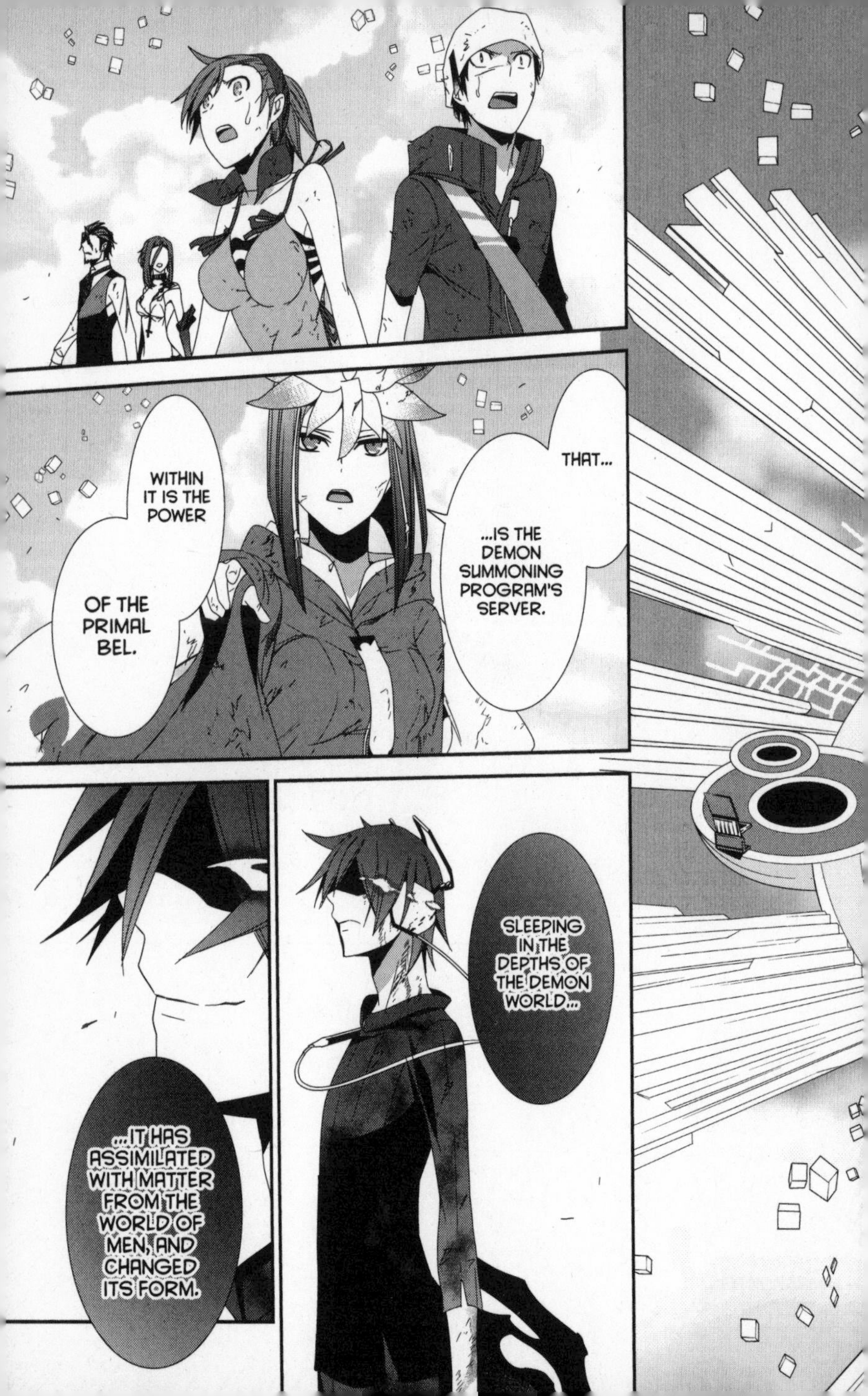
THAT...
...IS THE DEMON SUMMONING PROGRAM'S SERVER.
WITHIN IT IS THE POWER
OF THE PRIMAL BEL.
SLEEPING IN THE DEPTHS OF THE DEMON WORLD...
...IT HAS ASSIMILATED WITH MATTER FROM THE WORLD OF MEN, AND CHANGED ITS FORM.

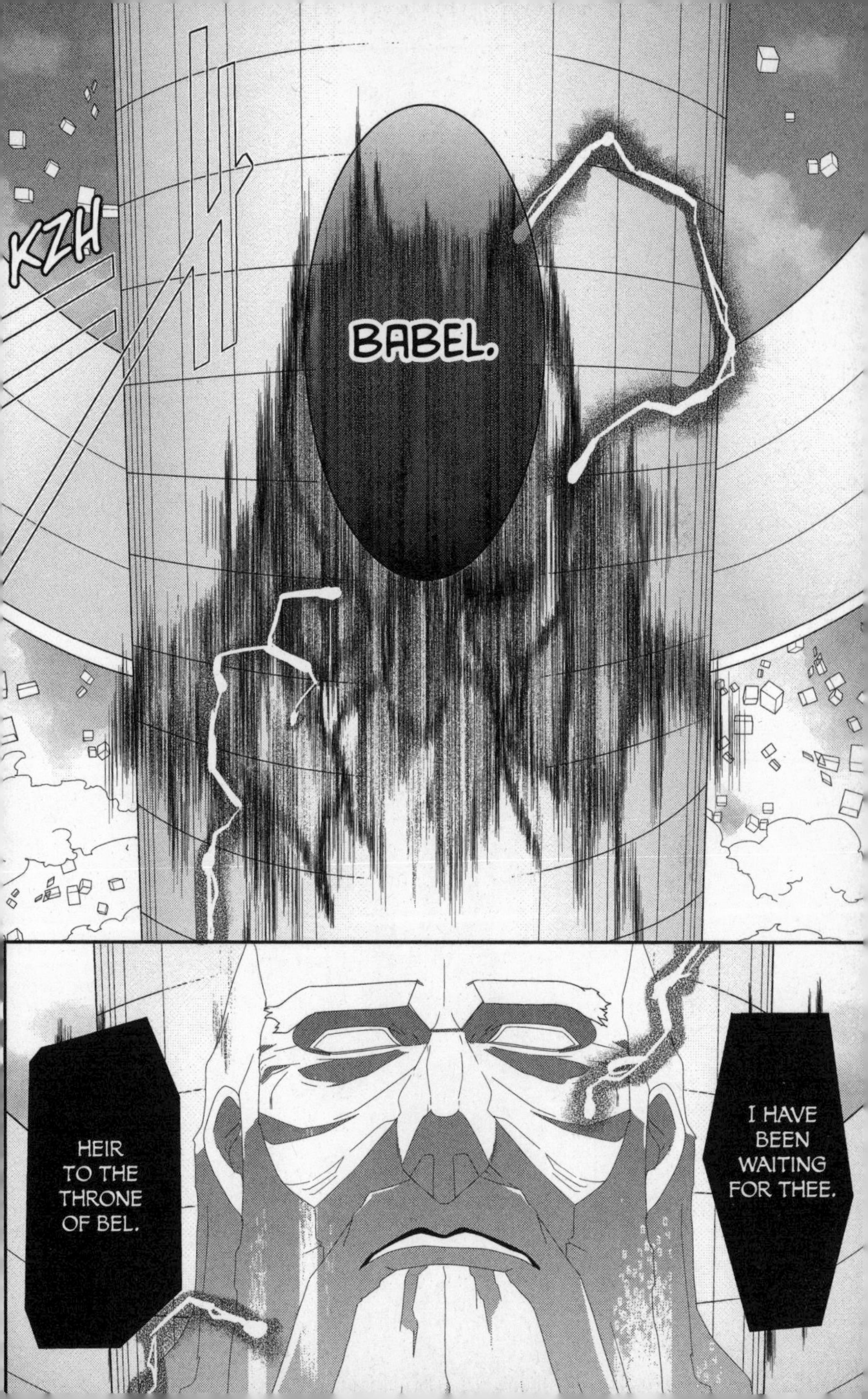
KZH
BABEL.
I HAVE BEEN WAITING FOR THEE.
HEIR TO THE THRONE OF BEL.

DEVIL SURVIVOR
デビルサバイバー

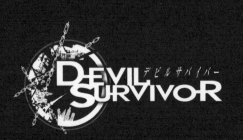

DEVIL SURVIVOR
デビルサバイバー

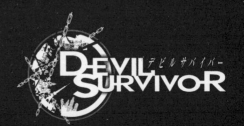

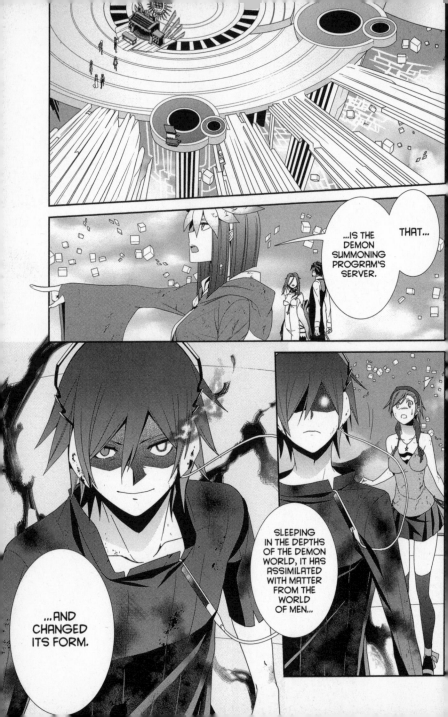

SURVIVAL : 40
BABEL

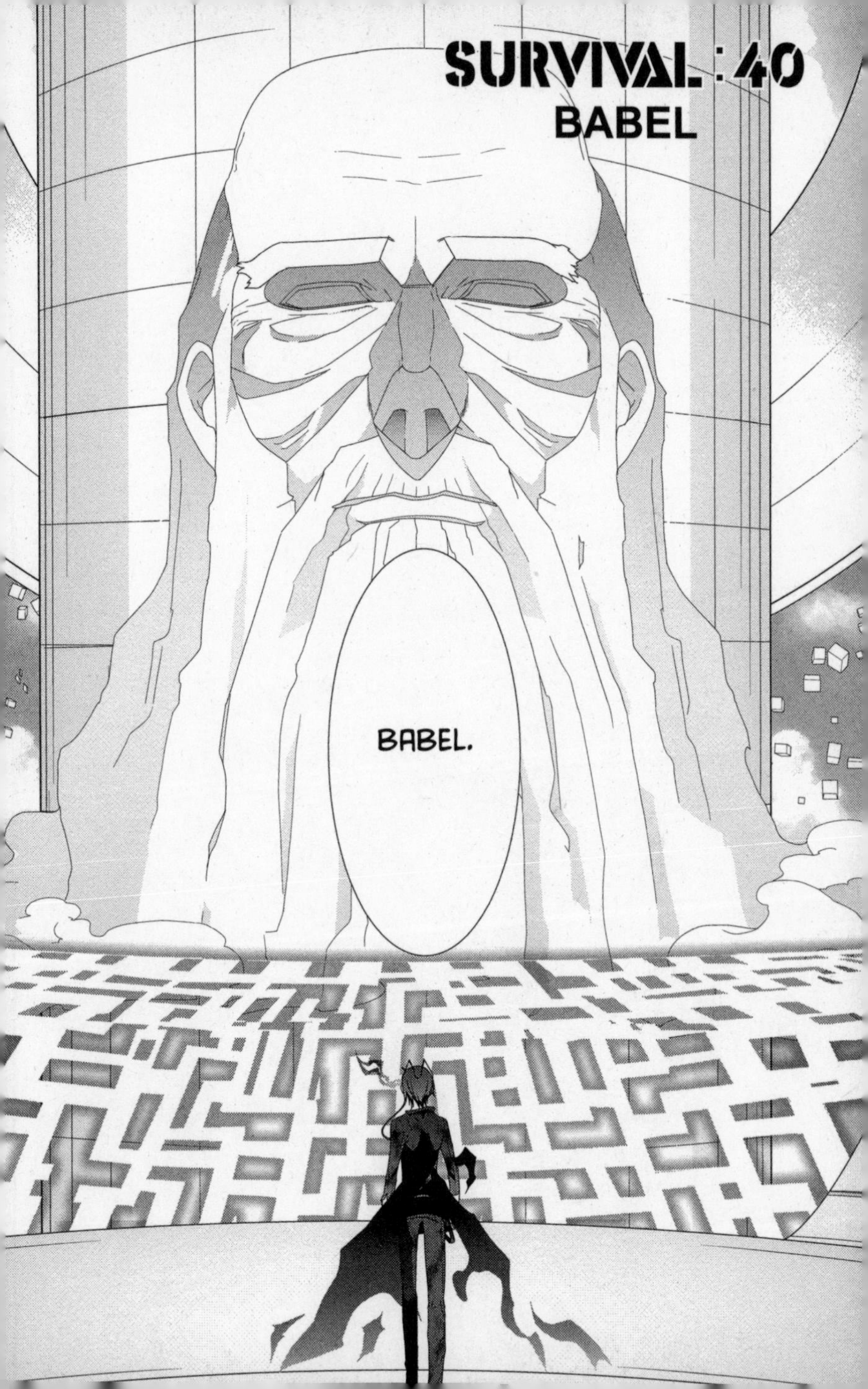
BABEL.

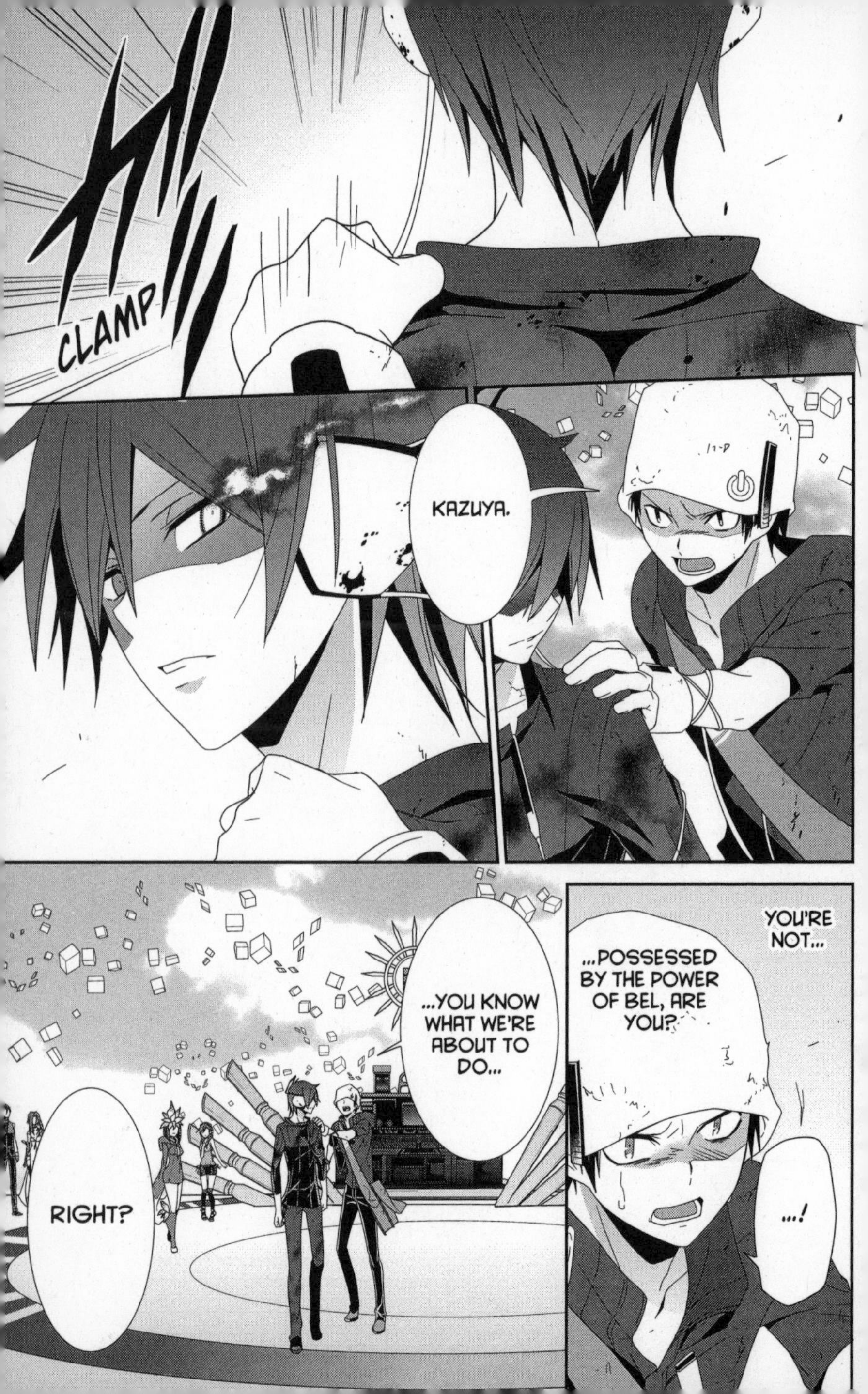
CLAMP
KAZUYA.
YOU'RE NOT...
...POSSESSED BY THE POWER OF BEL, ARE YOU?
...!
...YOU KNOW WHAT WE'RE ABOUT TO DO...
RIGHT?

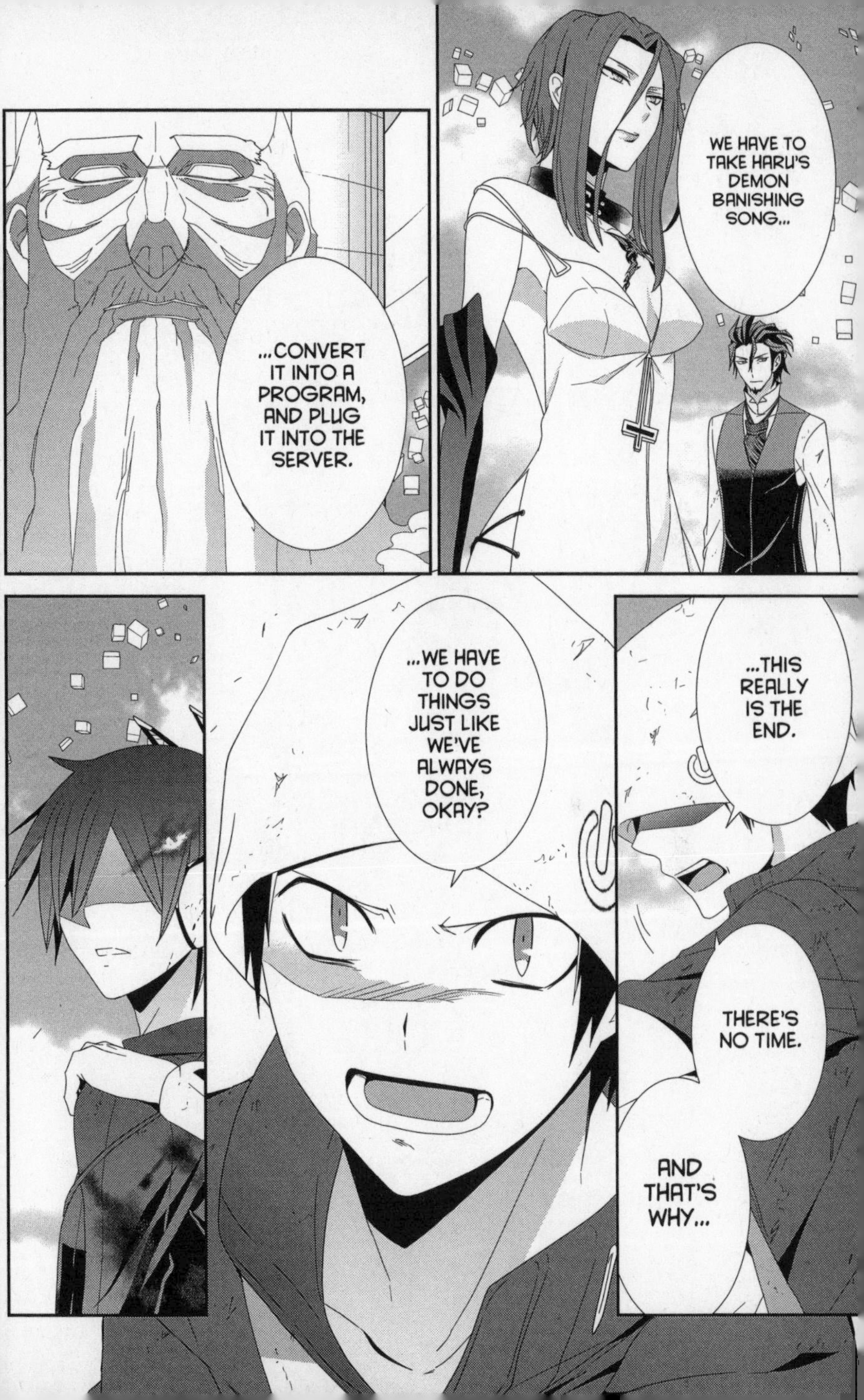
WE HAVE TO TAKE HARU'S DEMON BANISHING SONG...
...CONVERT IT INTO A PROGRAM, AND PLUG IT INTO THE SERVER.
...THIS REALLY IS THE END.
THERE'S NO TIME.
AND THAT'S WHY...
...WE HAVE TO DO THINGS JUST LIKE WE'VE ALWAYS DONE, OKAY?

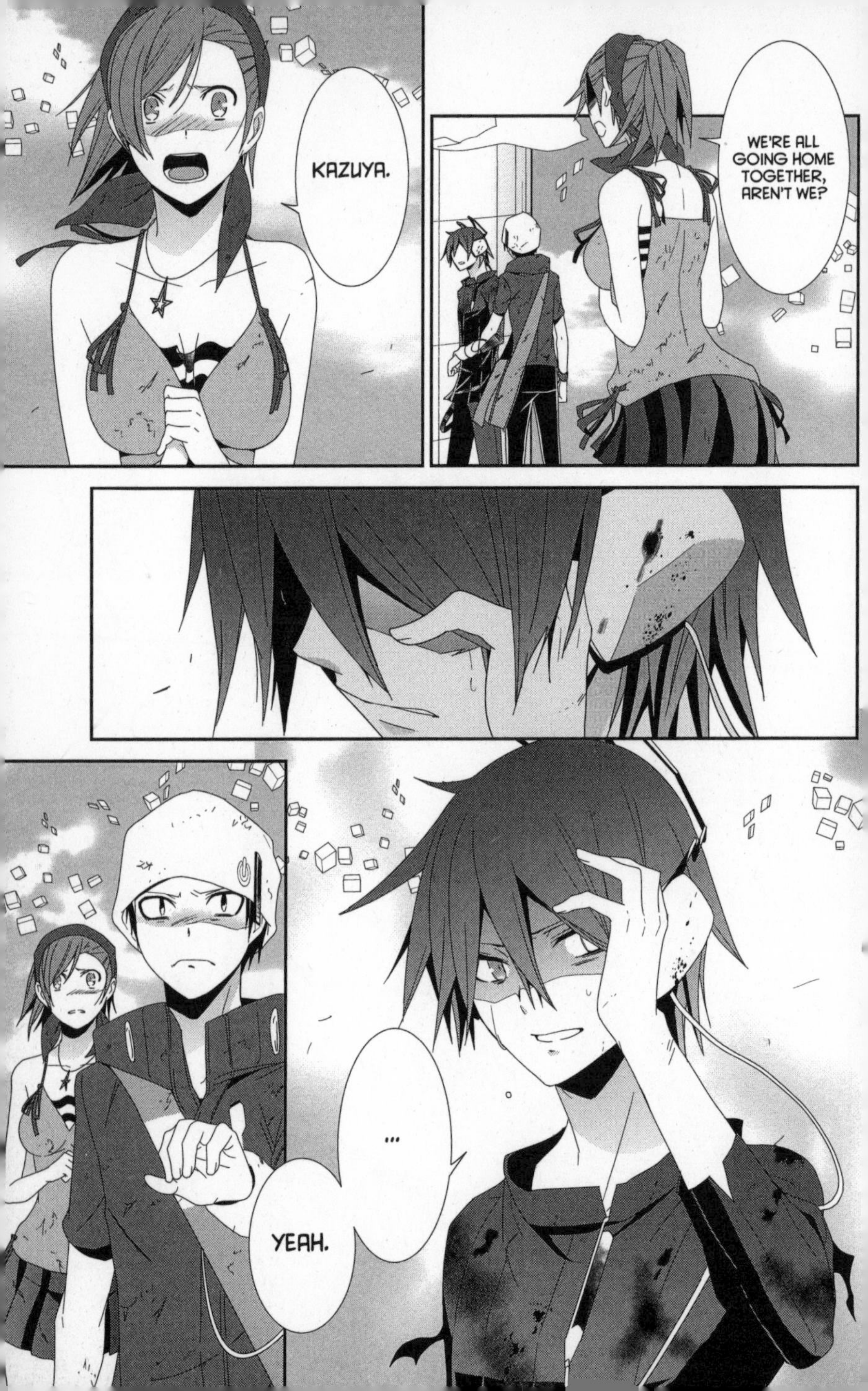
WE'RE ALL GOING HOME TOGETHER, AREN'T WE?
KAZUYA.
...
YEAH.

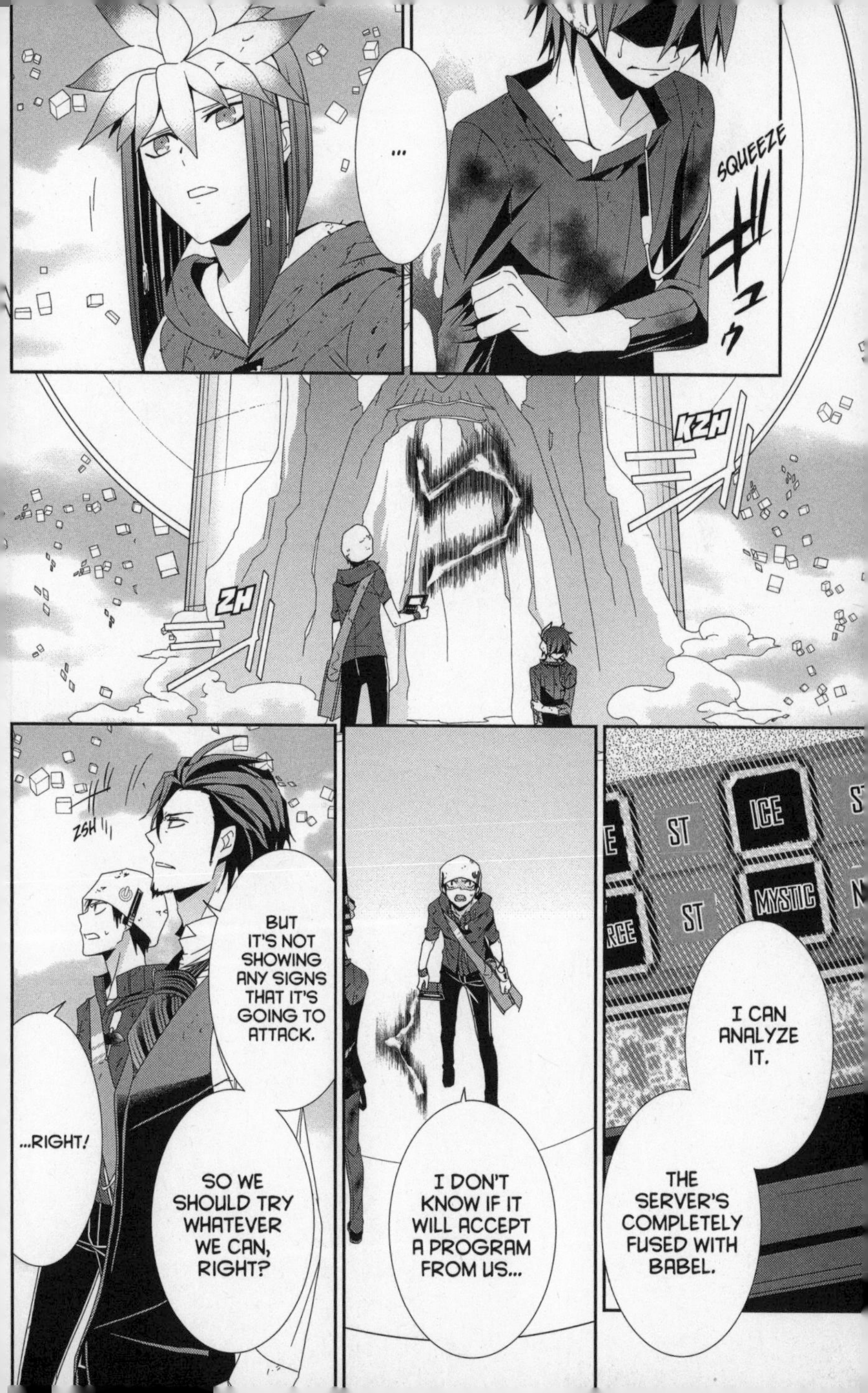
SQUEEZE
ギュゥ
...
KZH
ZH
ICE
ST
MYSTIC
ST
I CAN ANALYZE IT.
THE SERVER'S COMPLETELY FUSED WITH BABEL.
I DON'T KNOW IF IT WILL ACCEPT A PROGRAM FROM US...
ZSH
BUT IT'S NOT SHOWING ANY SIGNS THAT IT'S GOING TO ATTACK.
SO WE SHOULD TRY WHATEVER WE CAN, RIGHT?
...RIGHT!

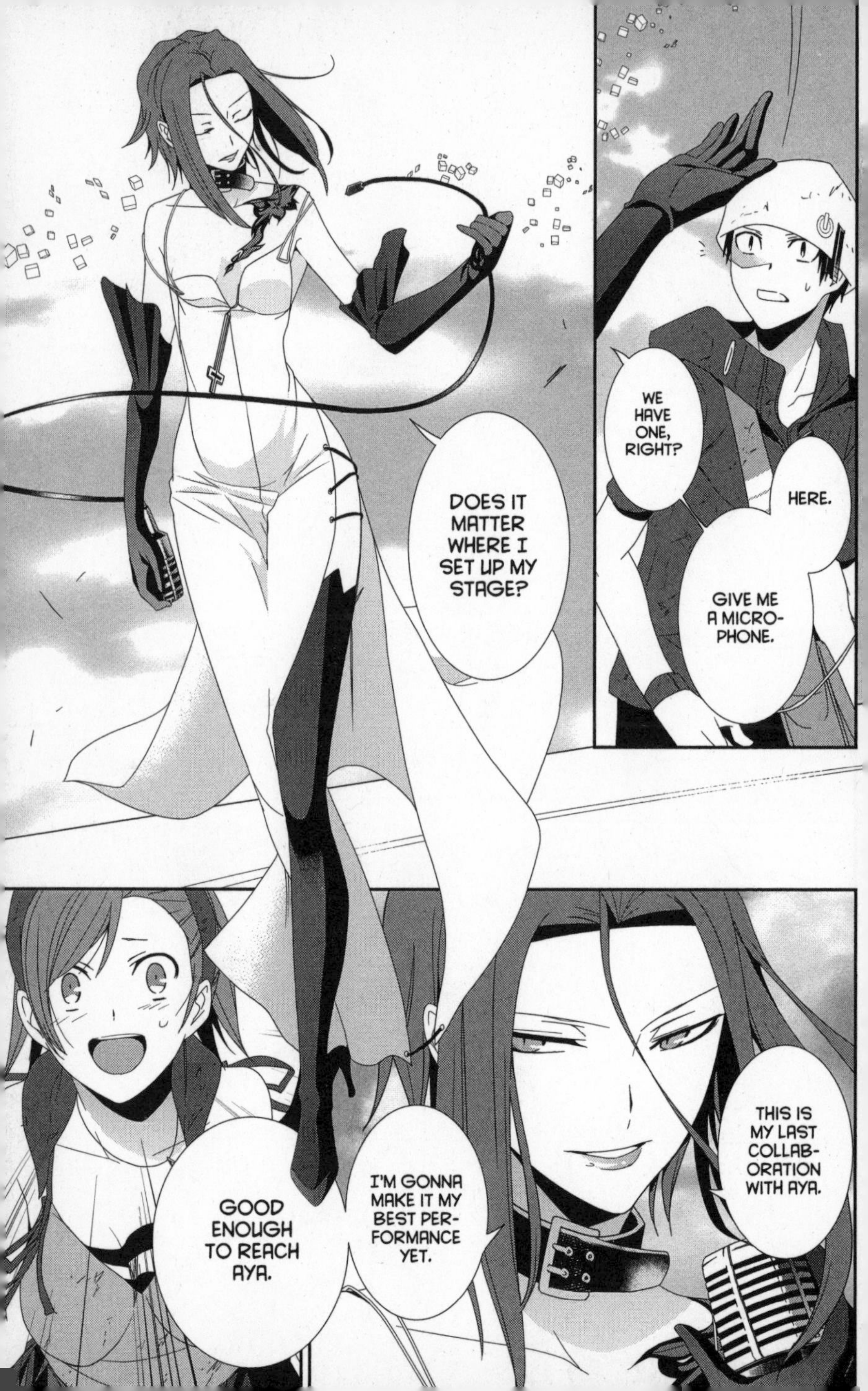
WE HAVE ONE, RIGHT?
HERE.
GIVE ME A MICROPHONE.
DOES IT MATTER WHERE I SET UP MY STAGE?
THIS IS MY LAST COLLABORATION WITH AYA.
I'M GONNA MAKE IT MY BEST PERFORMANCE YET.
GOOD ENOUGH TO REACH AYA.

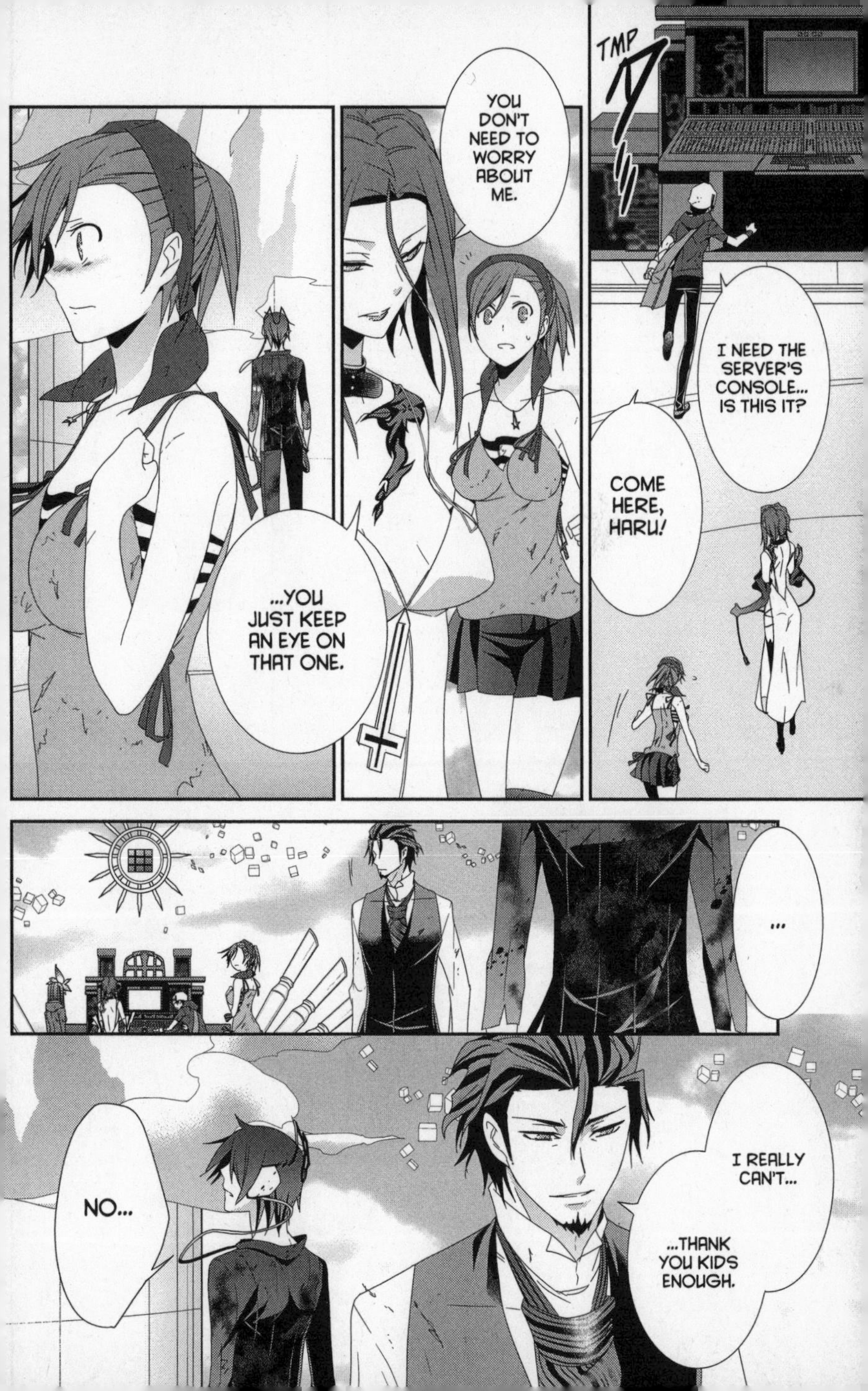
TMP
I NEED THE SERVER'S CONSOLE... IS THIS IT?
COME HERE, HARU!
YOU DON'T NEED TO WORRY ABOUT ME.
...YOU JUST KEEP AN EYE ON THAT ONE.
...
I REALLY CAN'T...
...THANK YOU KIDS ENOUGH.
NO...

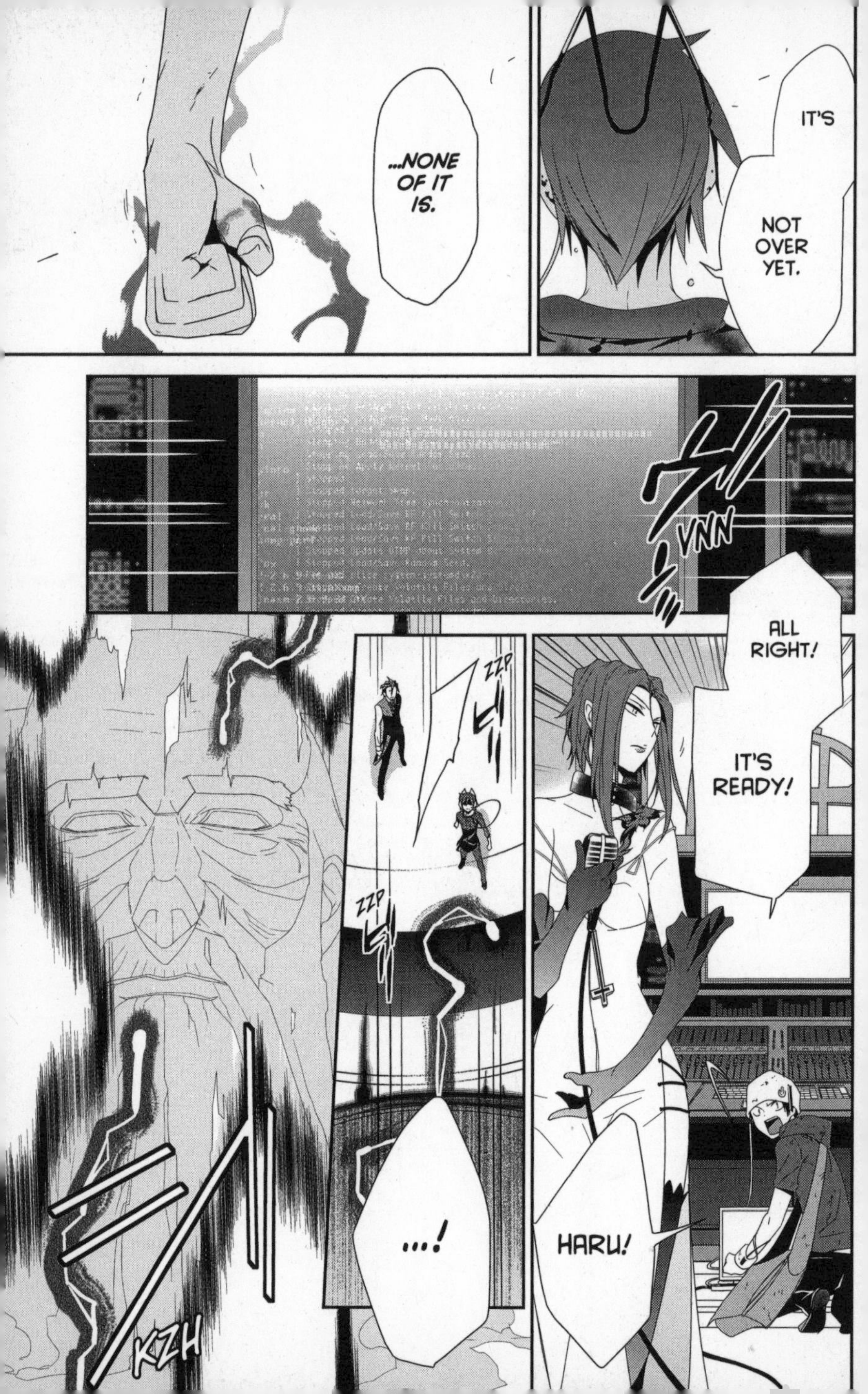
IT'S NOT OVER YET.
...NONE OF IT IS.
VNN
ALL RIGHT! IT'S READY!
HARU!
ZZP
ZZP
...!
KZH

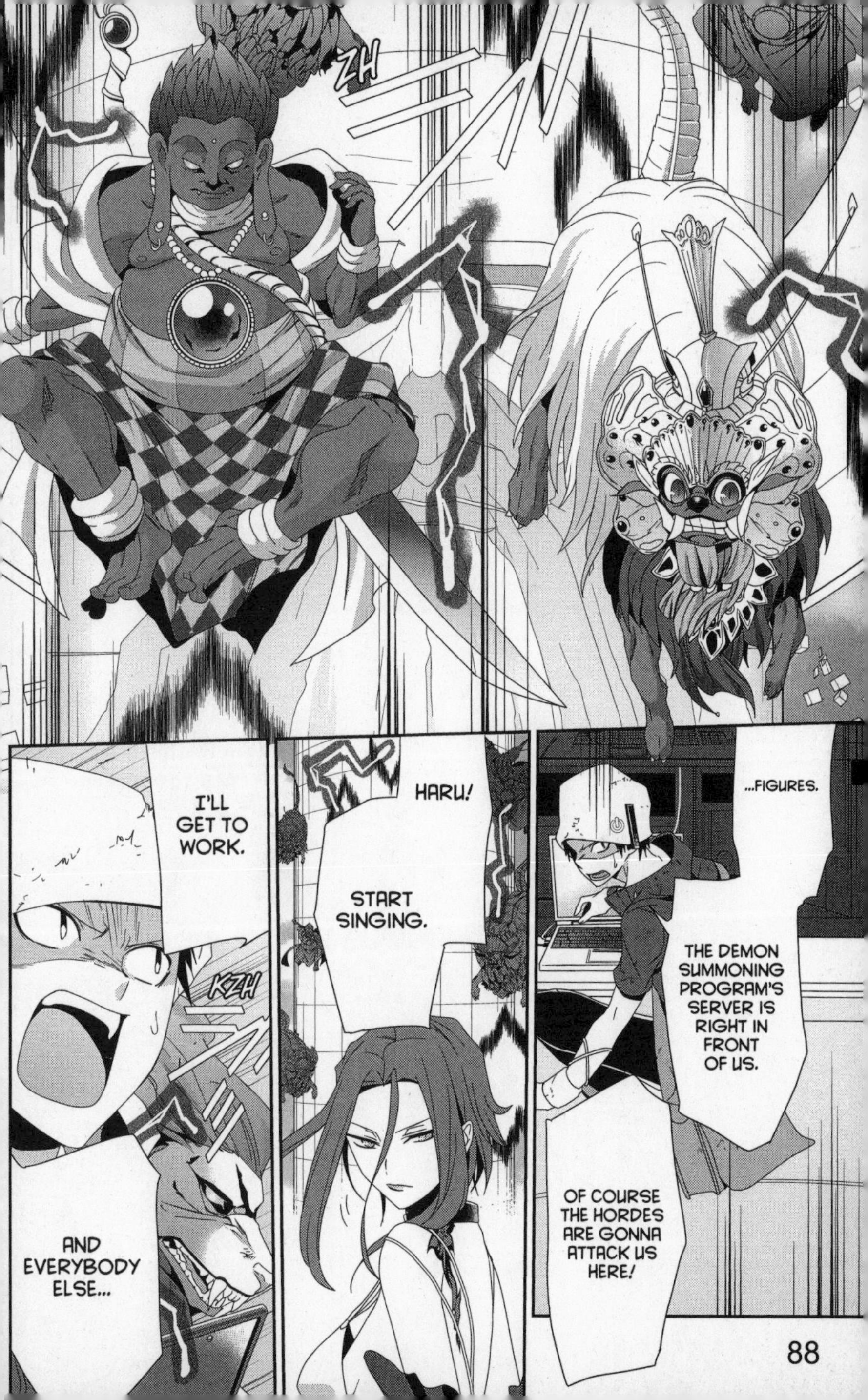
ZH
...FIGURES.
THE DEMON SUMMONING PROGRAM'S SERVER IS RIGHT IN FRONT OF US.
OF COURSE THE HORDES ARE GONNA ATTACK US HERE!
HARU!
START SINGING.
I'LL GET TO WORK.
KZH
AND EVERYBODY ELSE...

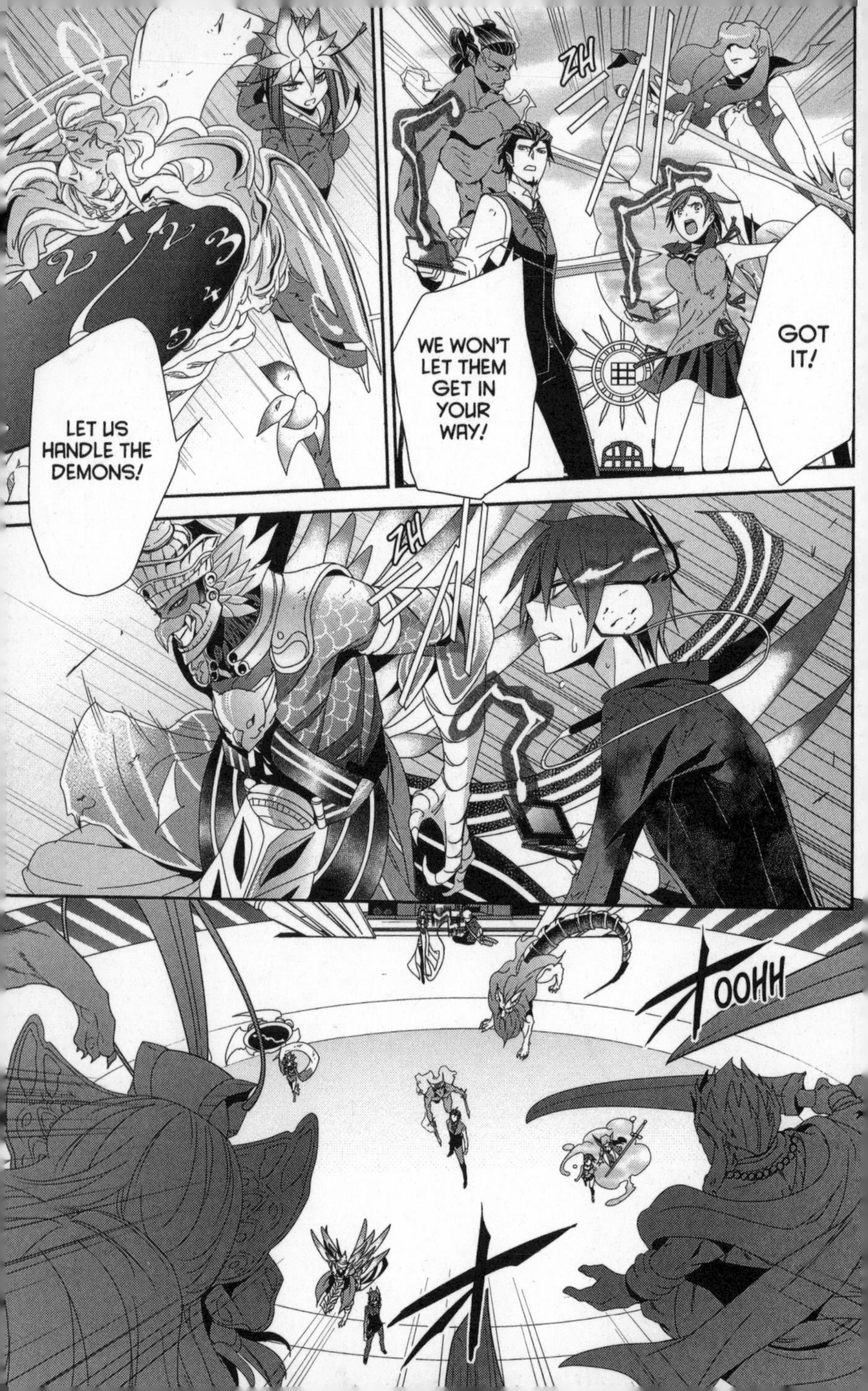
ZH
GOT IT!
WE WON'T LET THEM GET IN YOUR WAY!
LET US HANDLE THE DEMONS!
ZH
TOOHH

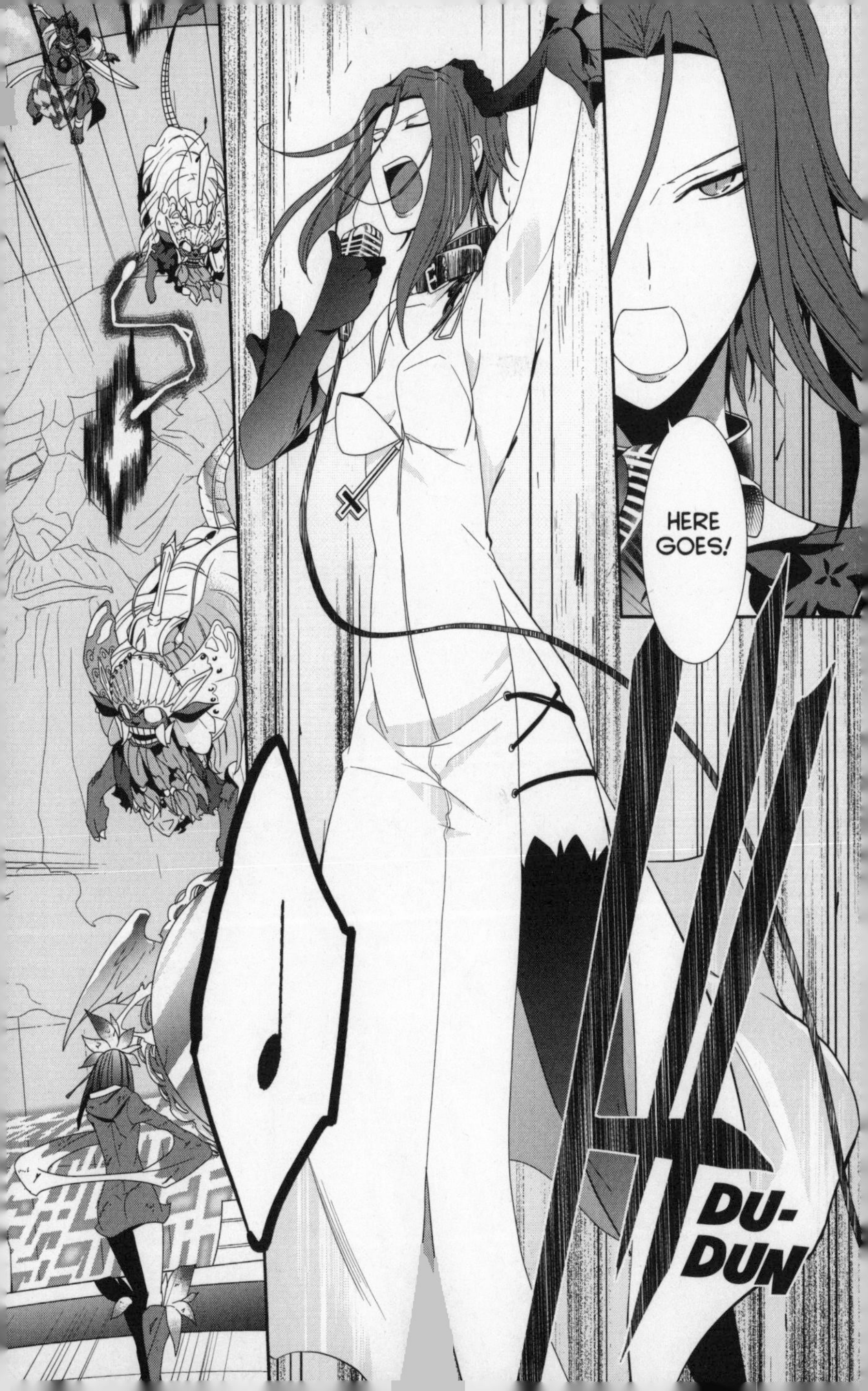
HERE GOES!
DU-DUN

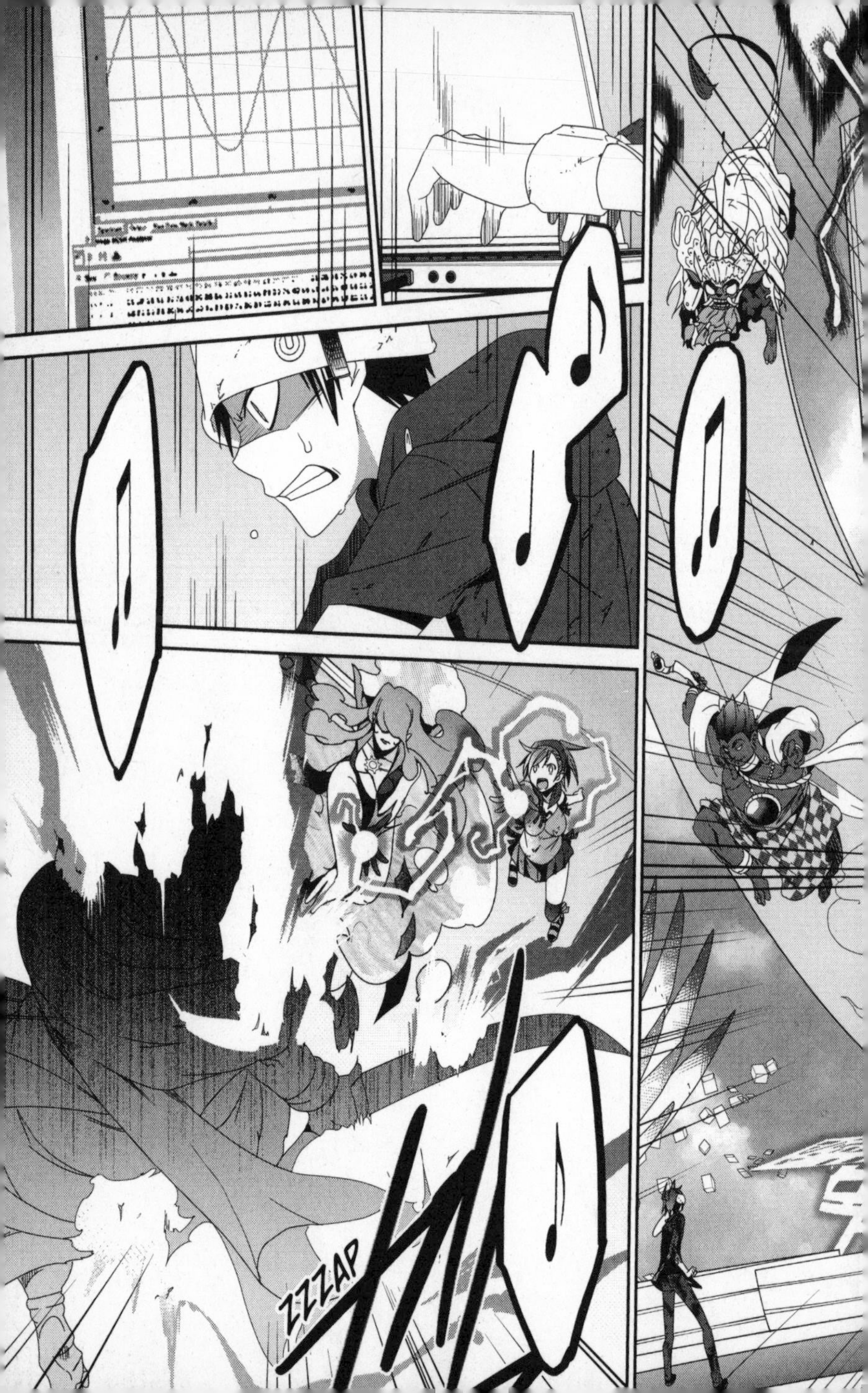
ZZZAP

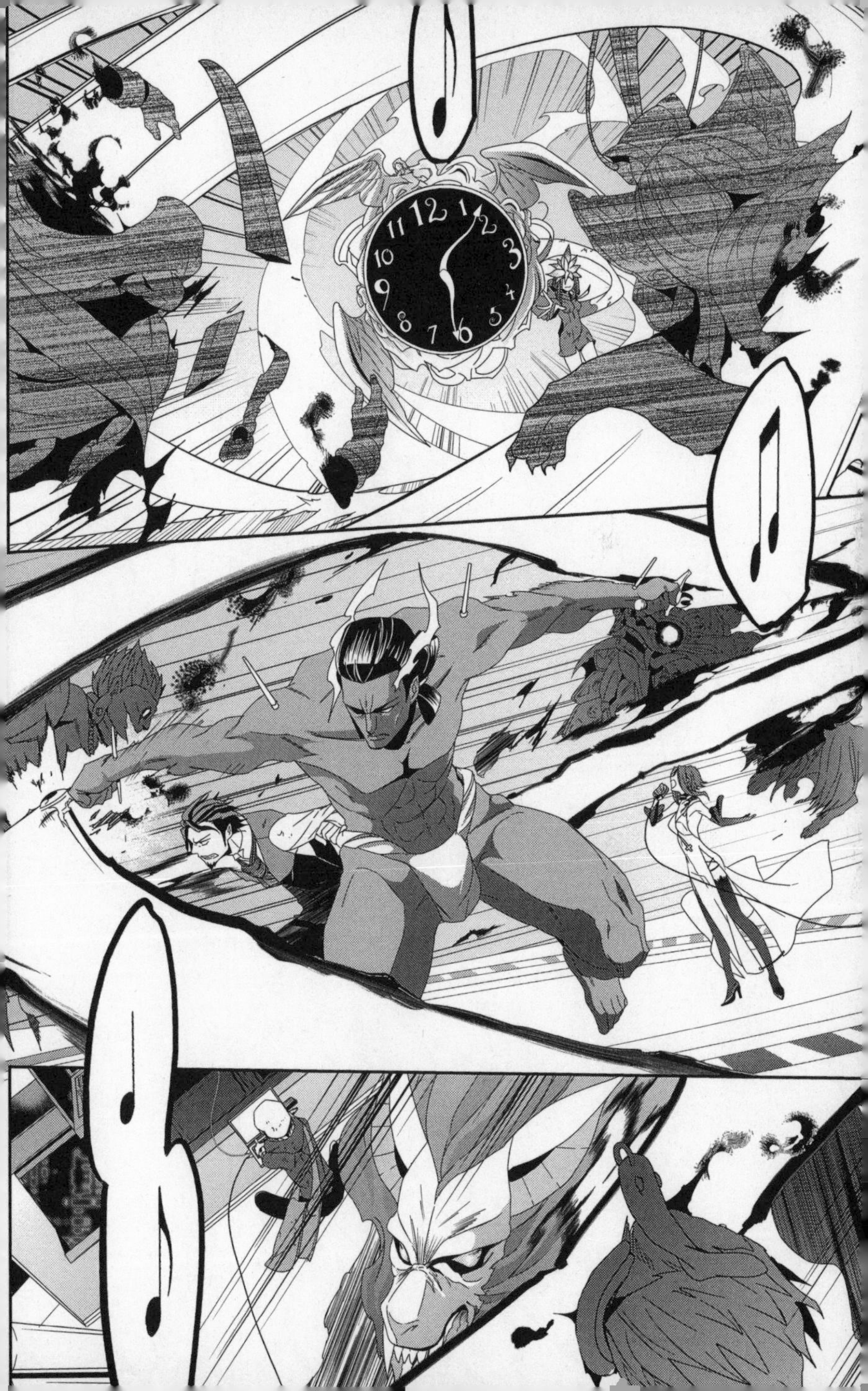

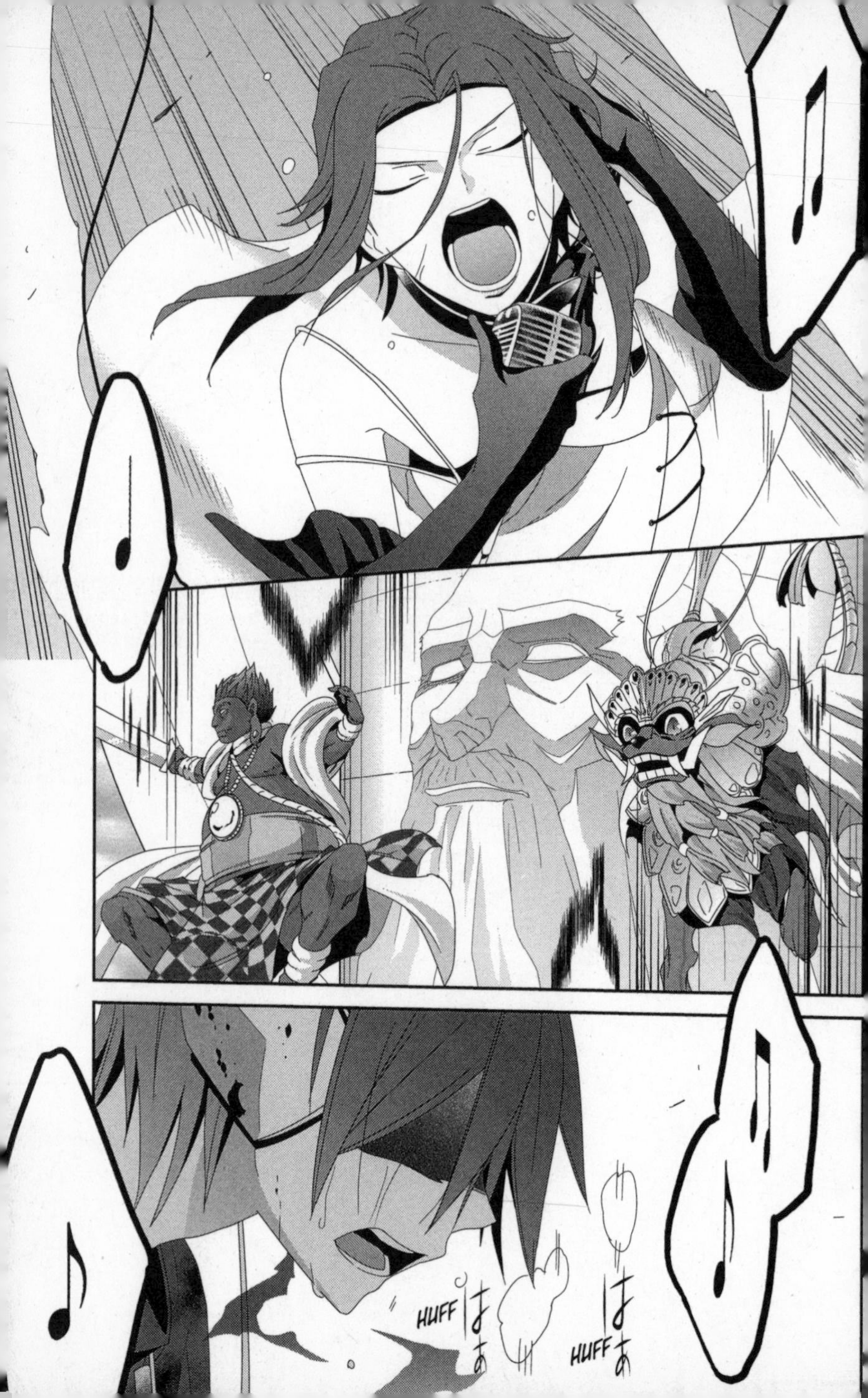
HUFF
はあ
HUFF
はあ

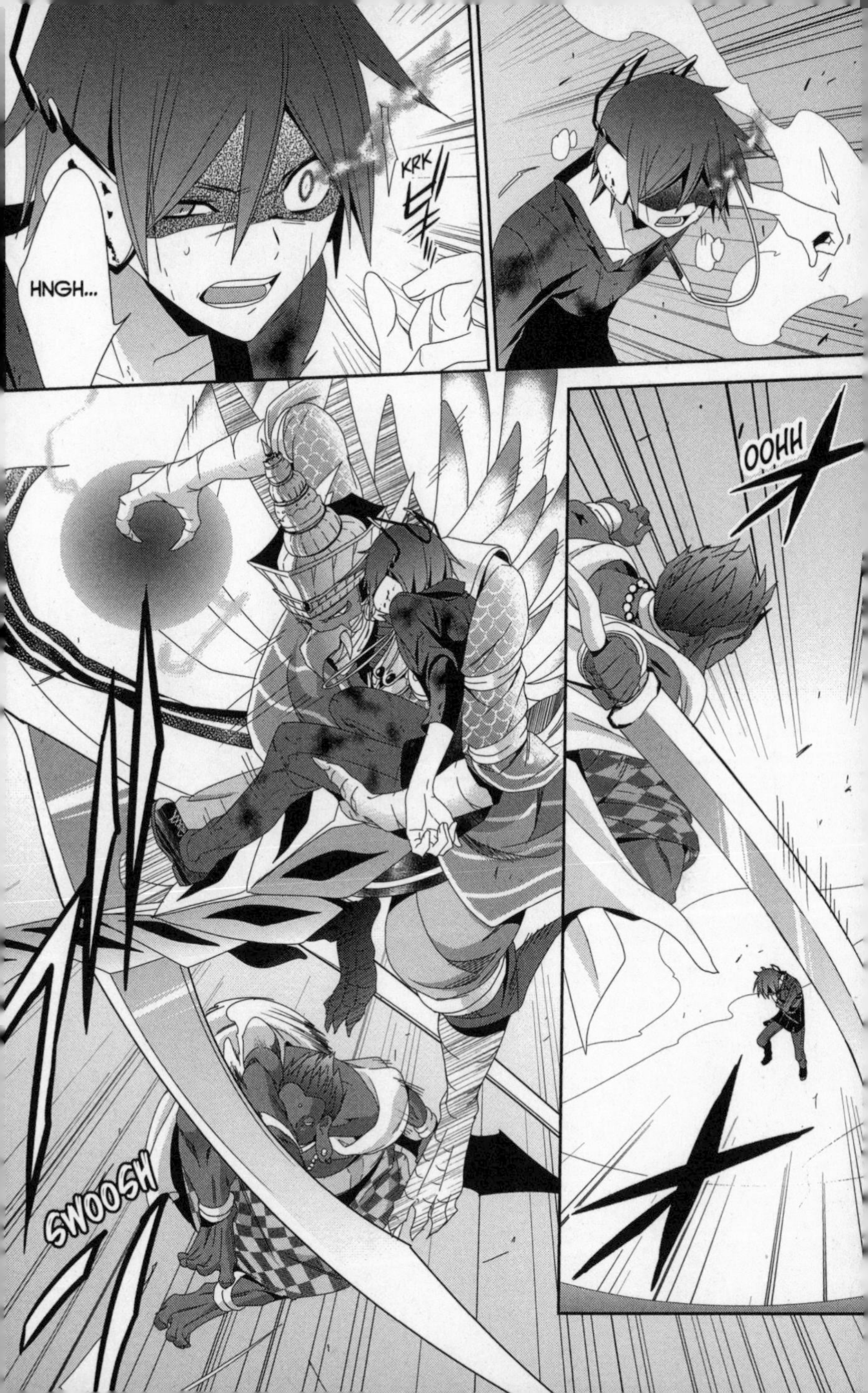
KRK
HNGH...
OOHH
SWOOSH

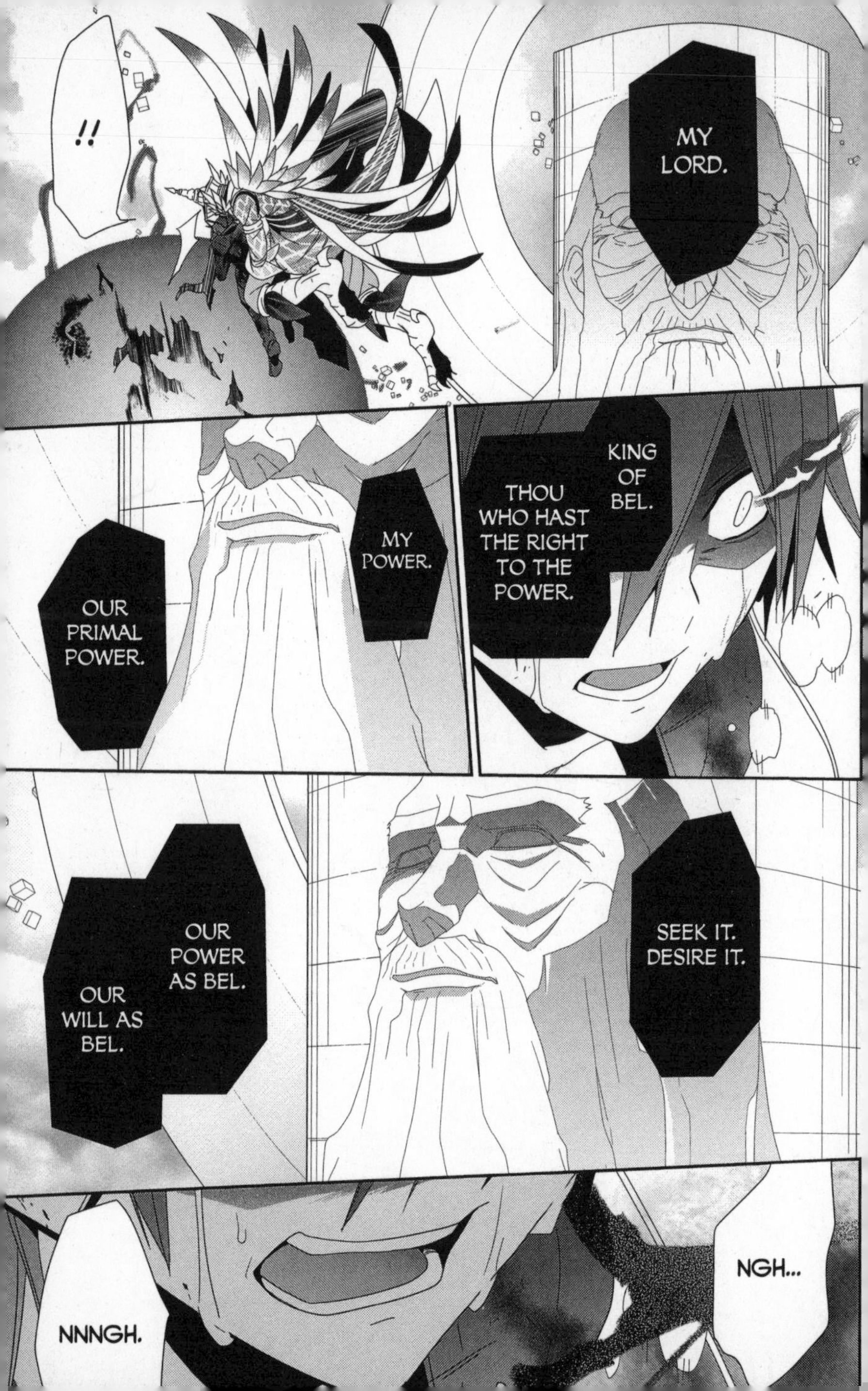
MY LORD.
!!
KING OF BEL.
THOU WHO HAST THE RIGHT TO THE POWER.
MY POWER.
OUR PRIMAL POWER.
SEEK IT. DESIRE IT.
OUR POWER AS BEL.
OUR WILL AS BEL.
NGH...
NNNGH.

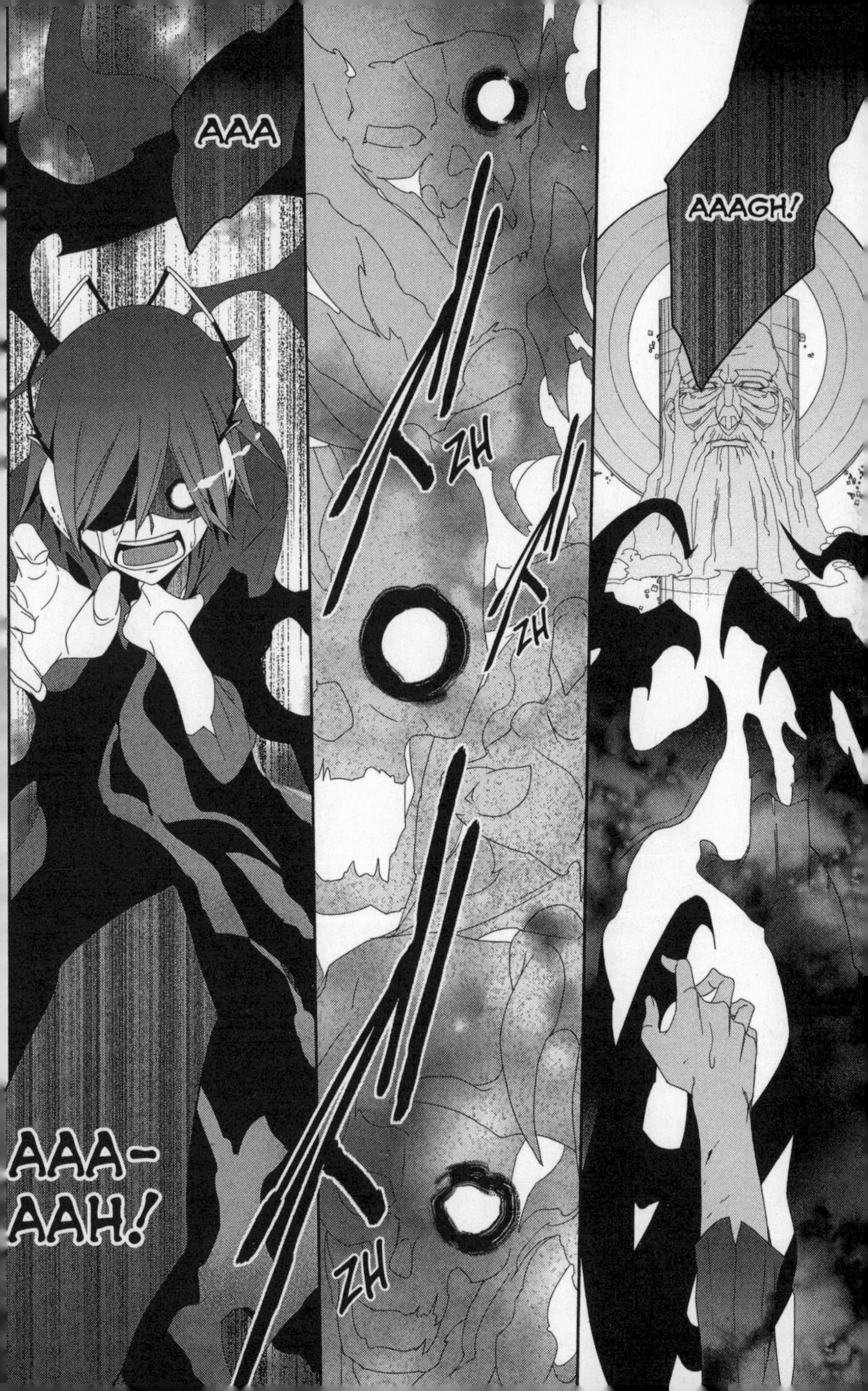
AAAGH!
ZH
ZH
ZH
AAA
AAA-AAH!

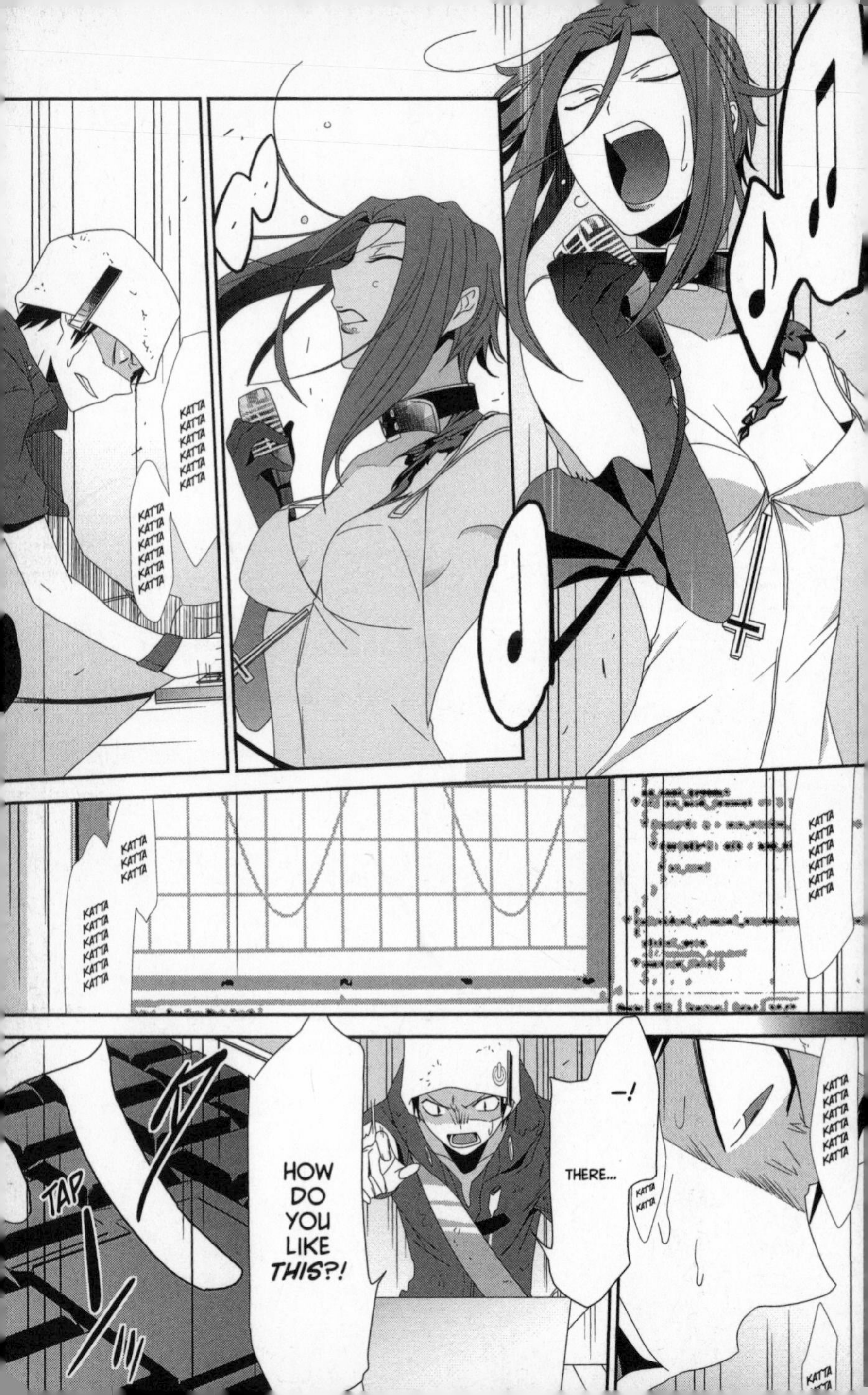
KATTA KATTA KATTA KATTA KATTA KATTA
KATTA KATTA KATTA KATTA KATTA KATTA
KATTA KATTA KATTA KATTA KATTA KATTA KATTA
KATTA KATTA KATTA
KATTA KATTA KATTA KATTA KATTA KATTA KATTA
KATTA KATTA KATTA KATTA KATTA KATTA KATTA
KATTA
—!
THERE...
KATTA KATTA
HOW DO YOU LIKE *THIS*?!
TAP

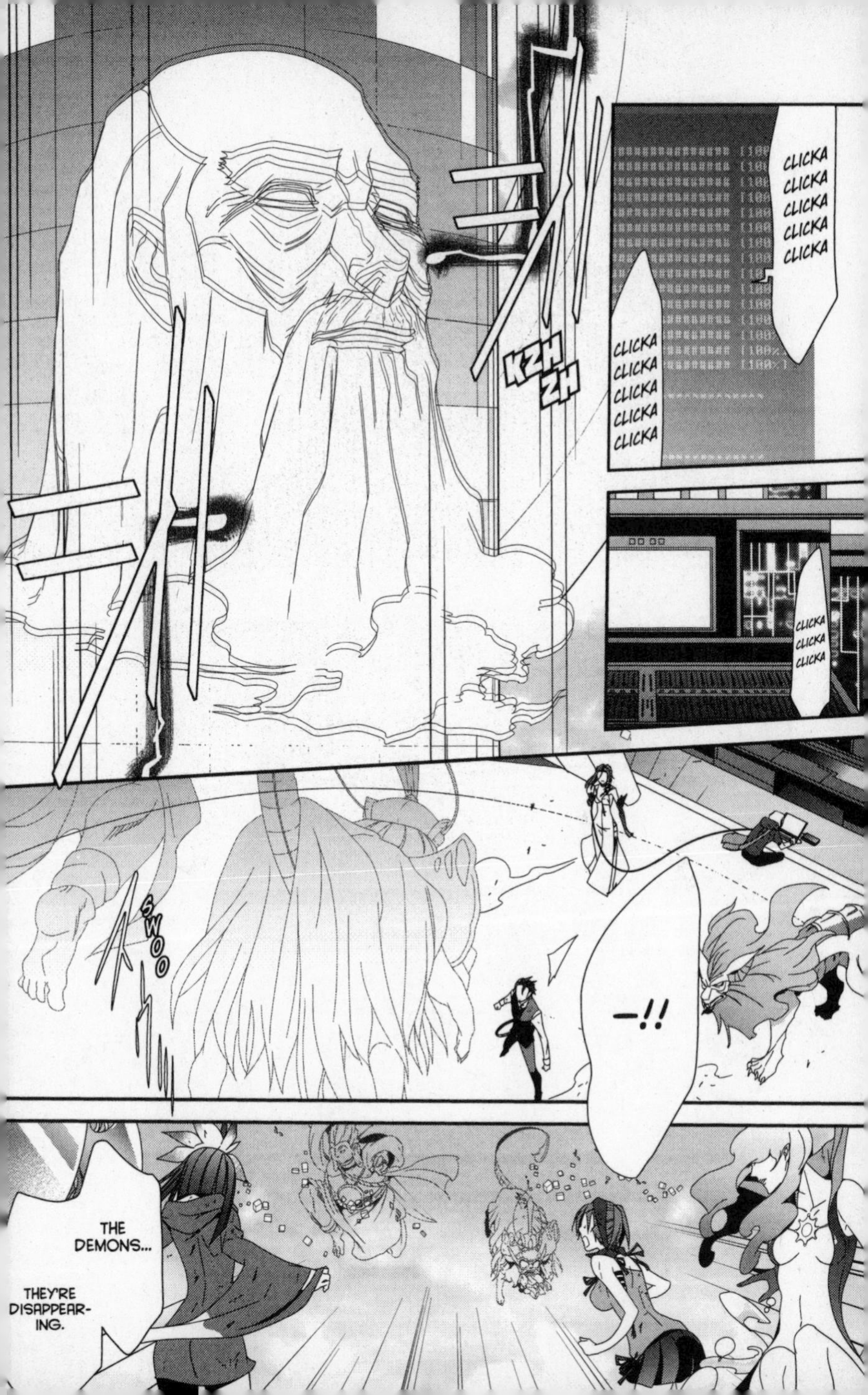

CLICKA CLICKA CLICKA CLICKA CLICKA
CLICKA CLICKA CLICKA CLICKA CLICKA
CLICKA CLICKA CLICKA
KZH ZH
—!!
SWOO
THE DEMONS...
THEY'RE DISAPPEAR-ING.

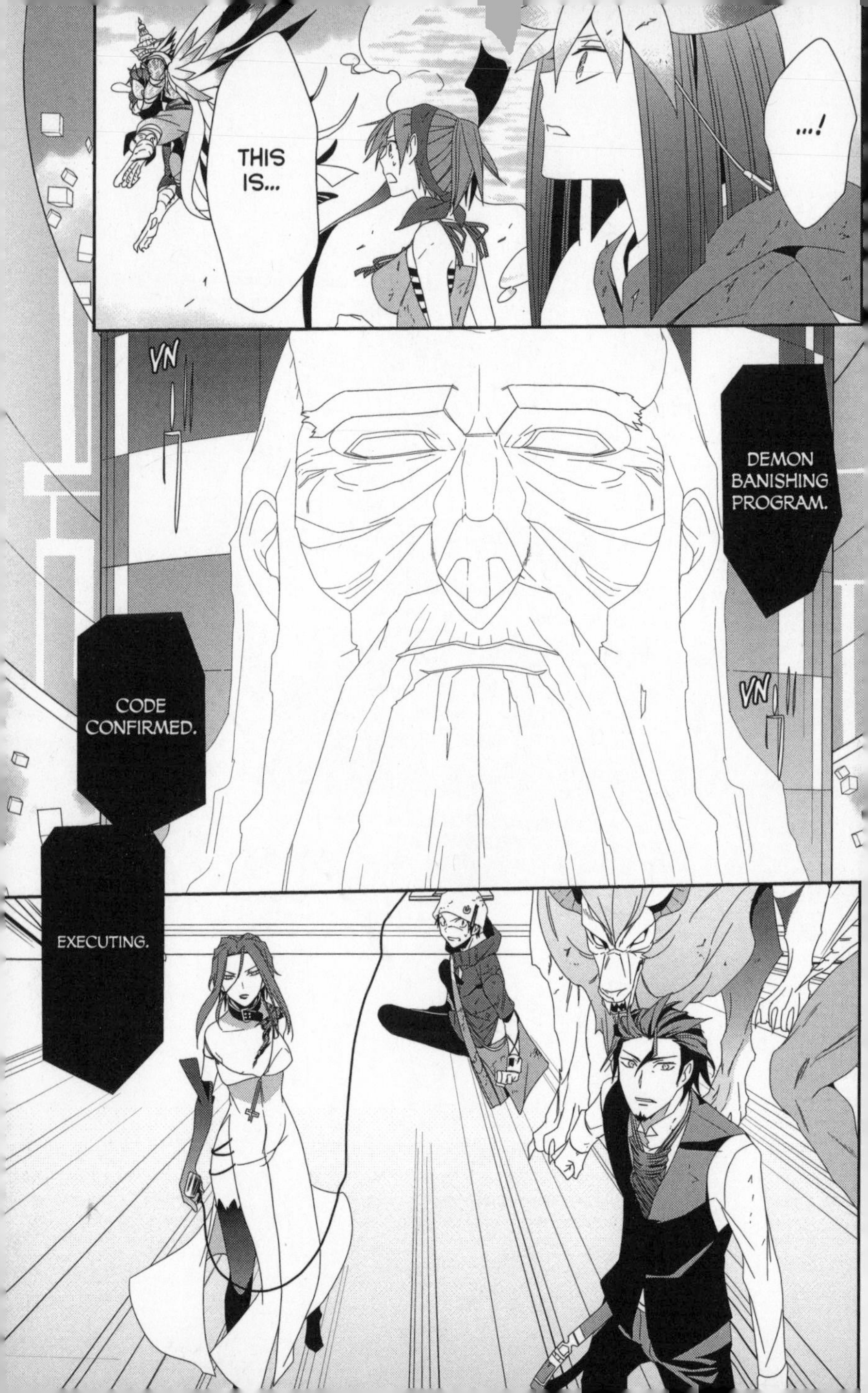
...!
THIS IS...
DEMON BANISHING PROGRAM.
VN
VN
CODE CONFIRMED.
EXECUTING.

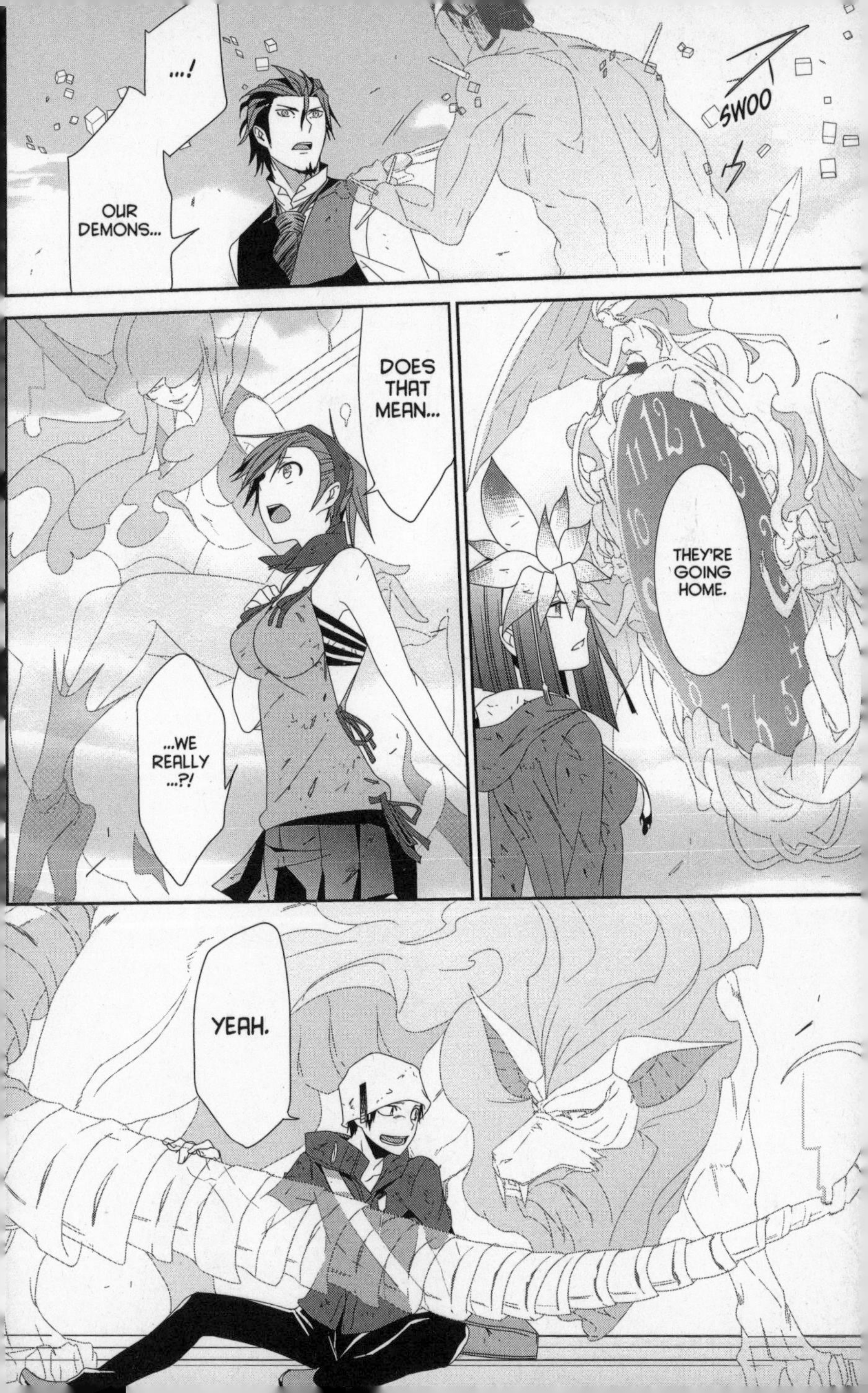
SWOO
...!
OUR DEMONS...
THEY'RE GOING HOME.
DOES THAT MEAN...
...WE REALLY ...?!
YEAH.

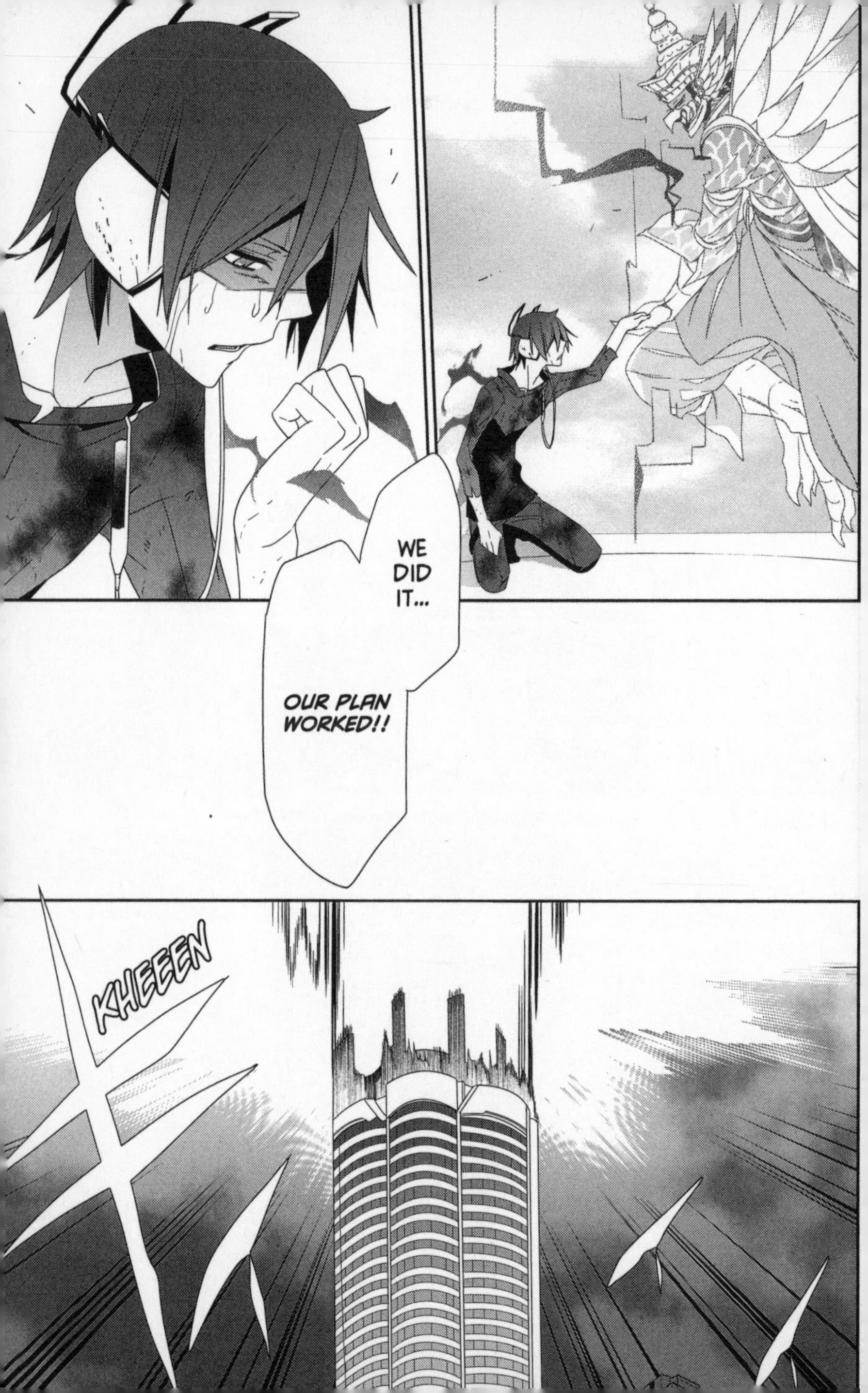
WE DID IT...
OUR PLAN WORKED!!
KHEEEN

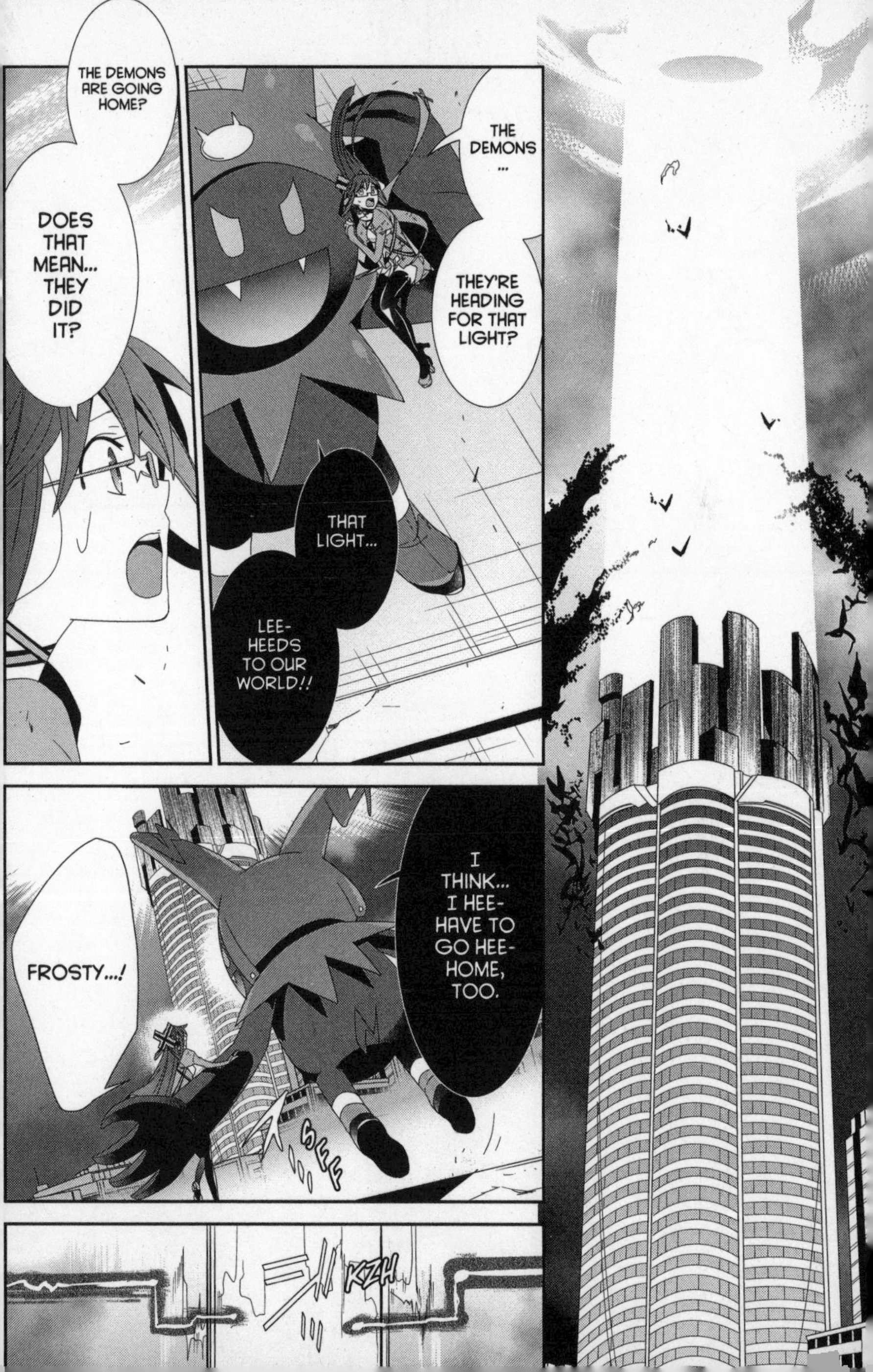

THE DEMONS ...
THEY'RE HEADING FOR THAT LIGHT?
THAT LIGHT...
LEE-HEEDS TO OUR WORLD!!
THE DEMONS ARE GOING HOME?
DOES THAT MEAN... THEY DID IT?
I THINK... I HEE-HAVE TO GO HEE-HOME, TOO.
FROSTY...!
SEFF
KZH

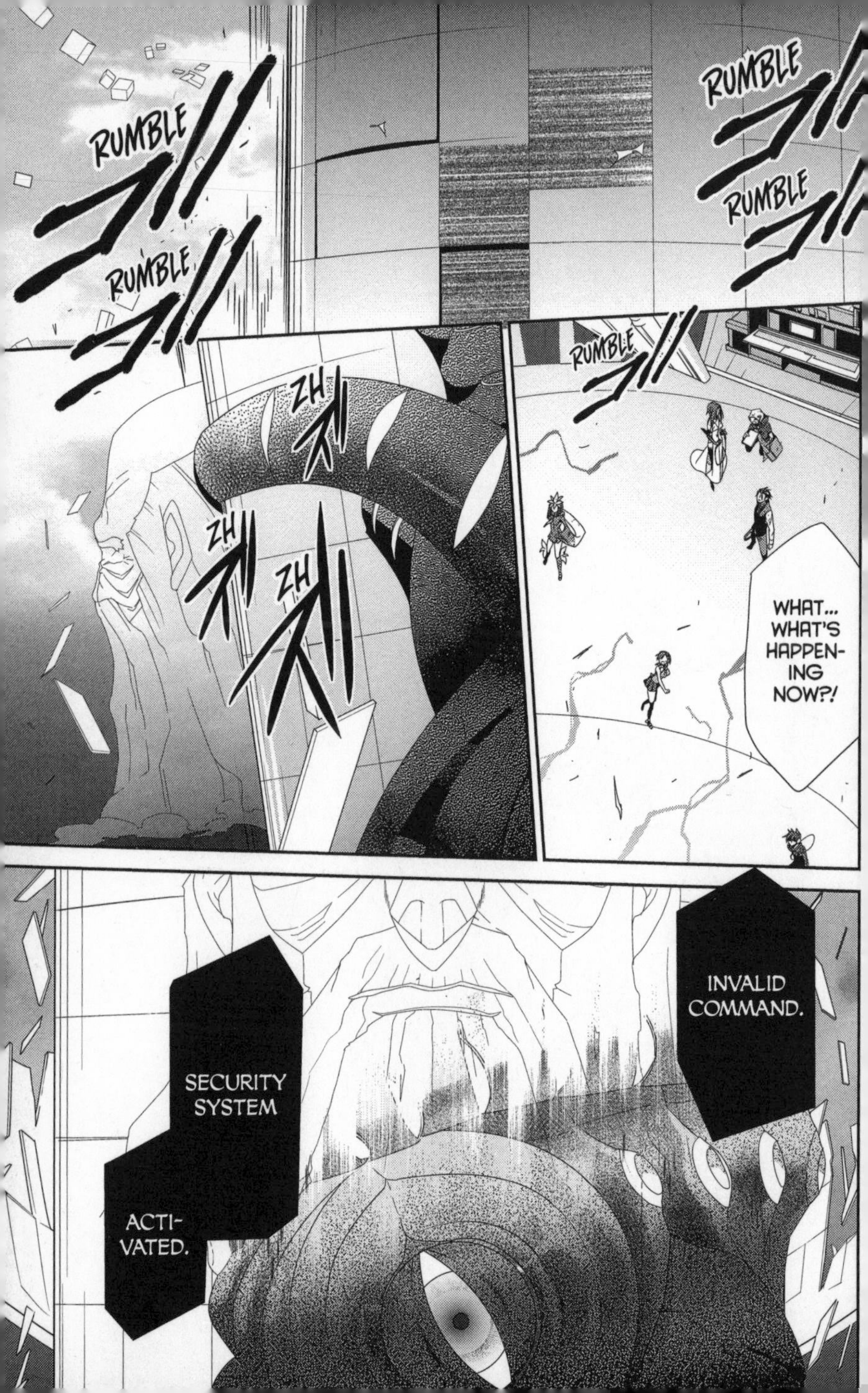
RUMBLE
RUMBLE
RUMBLE
RUMBLE
RUMBLE
ZH
ZH
ZH
WHAT... WHAT'S HAPPEN-ING NOW?!
INVALID COMMAND.
SECURITY SYSTEM
ACTI-VATED.

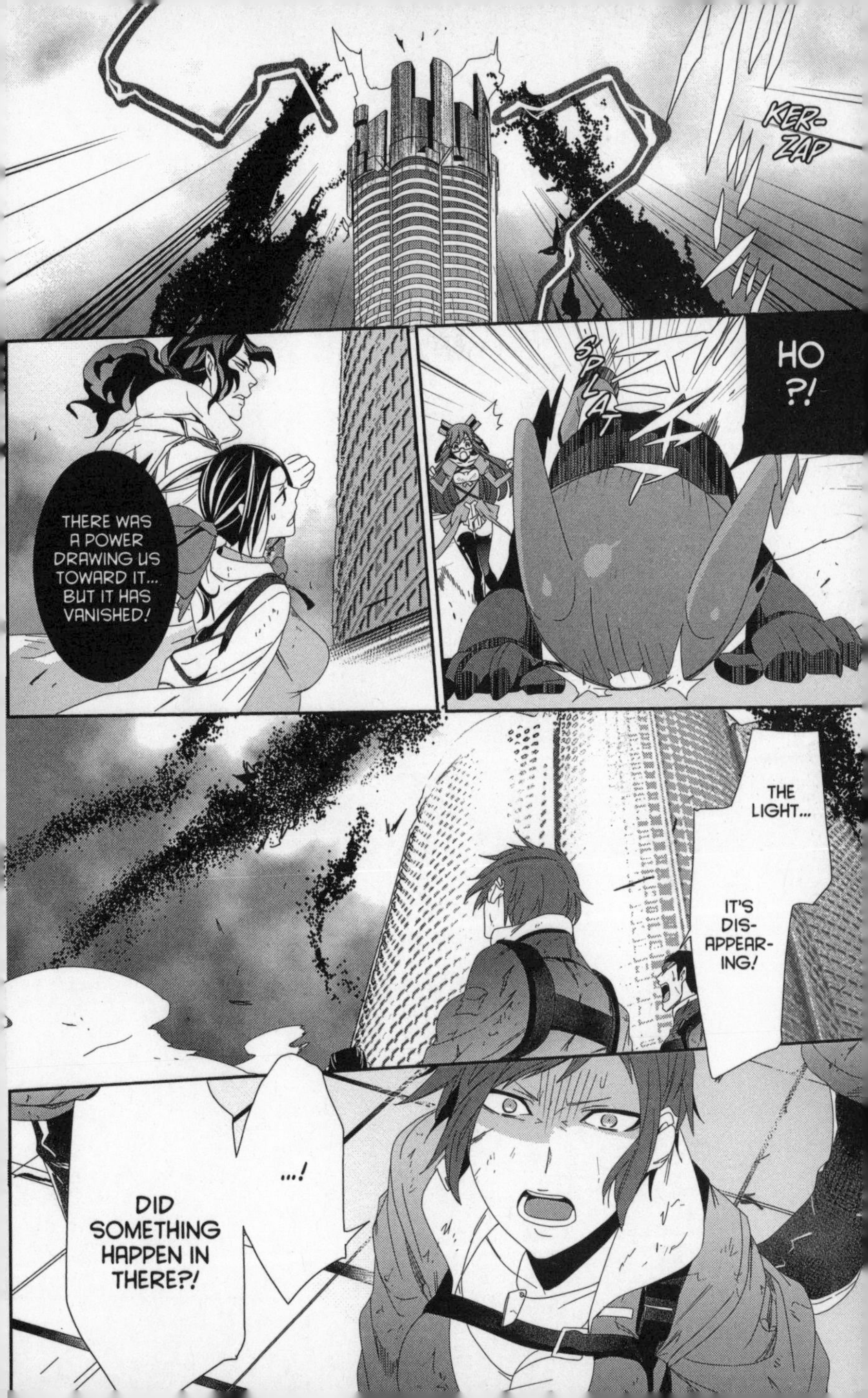
KER-ZAP
HO ?!
SPLAT
THERE WAS A POWER DRAWING US TOWARD IT... BUT IT HAS VANISHED!
THE LIGHT...
IT'S DIS-APPEAR-ING!
...!
DID SOMETHING HAPPEN IN THERE?!

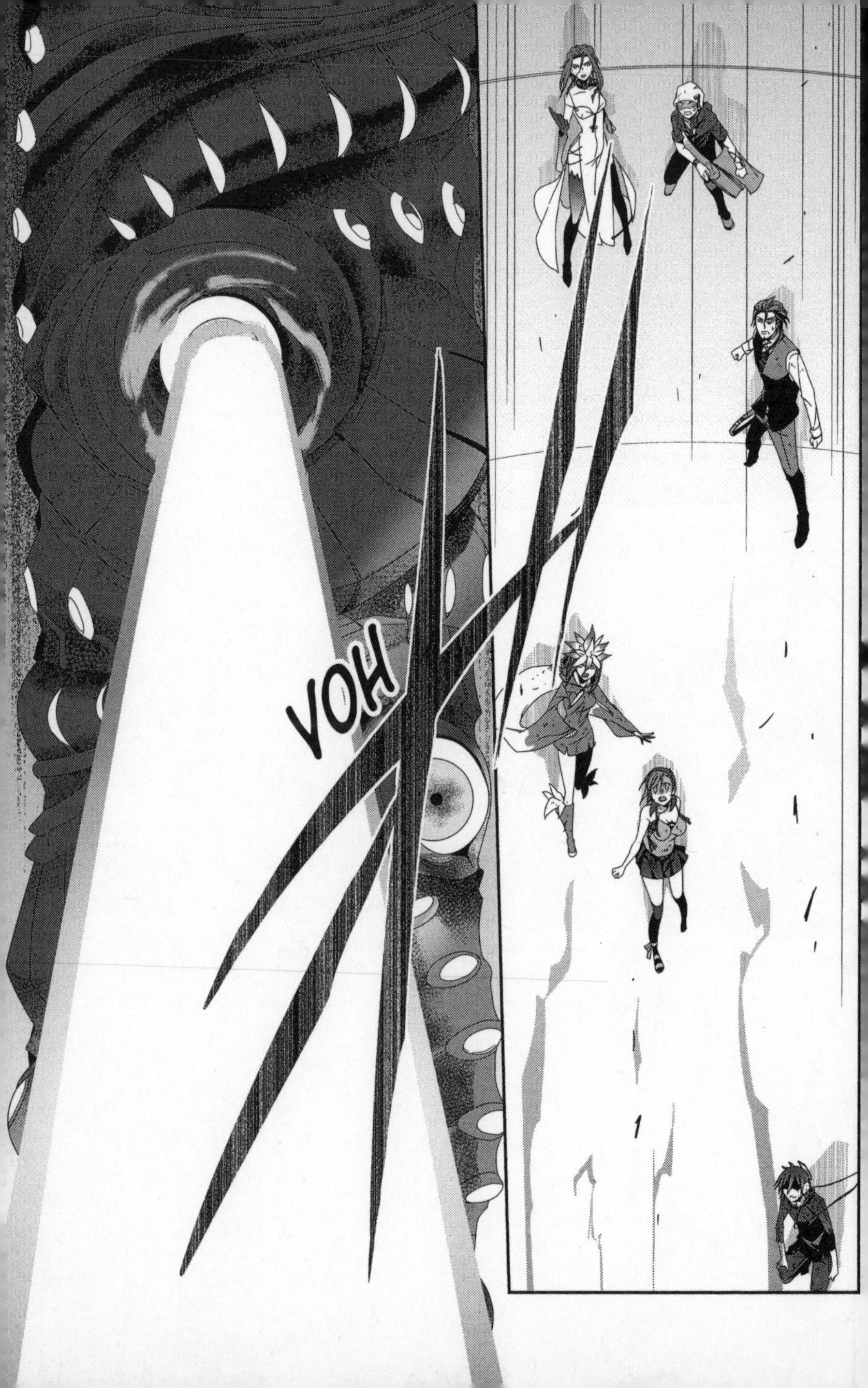
VOH

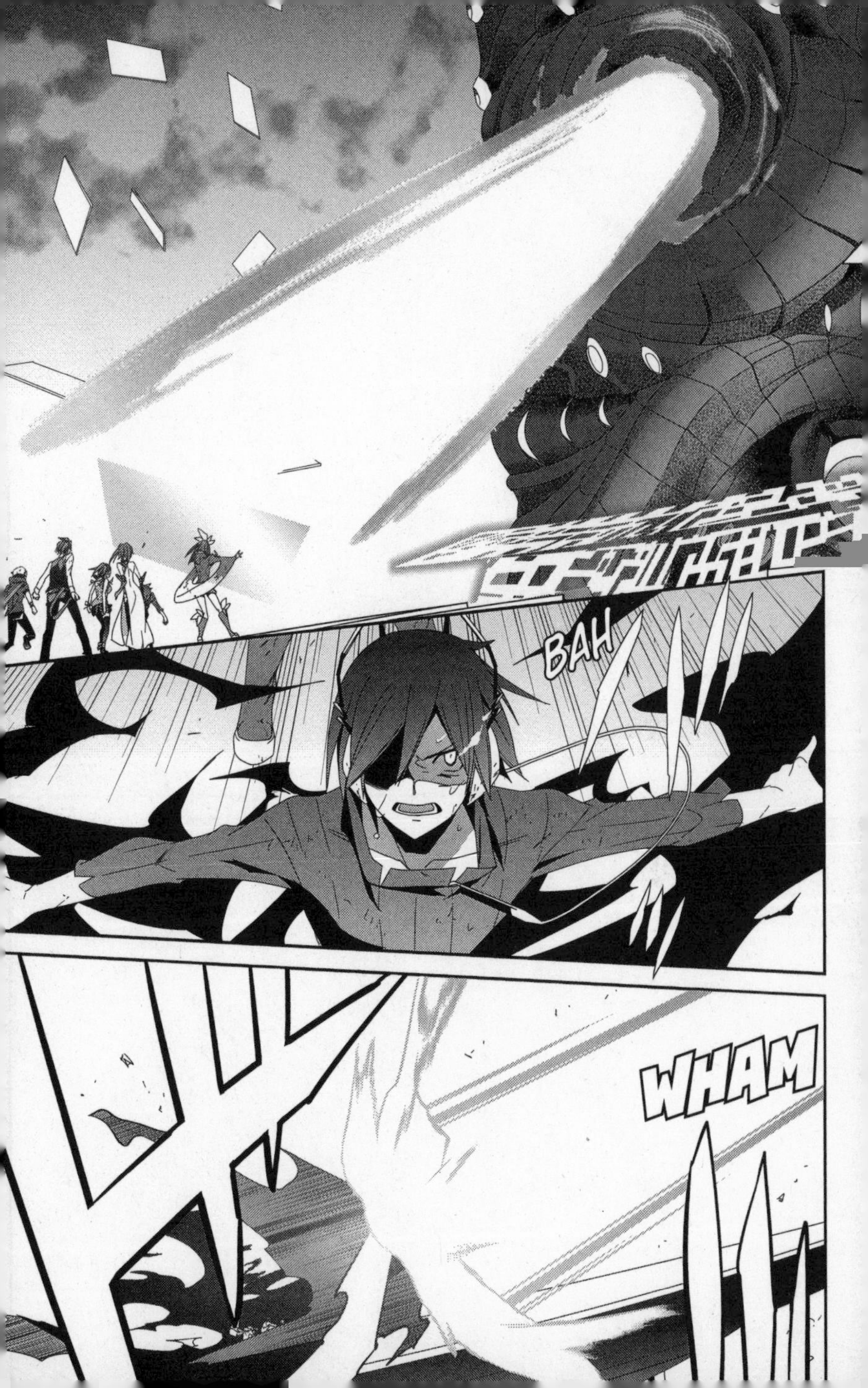
BAH
WHAM

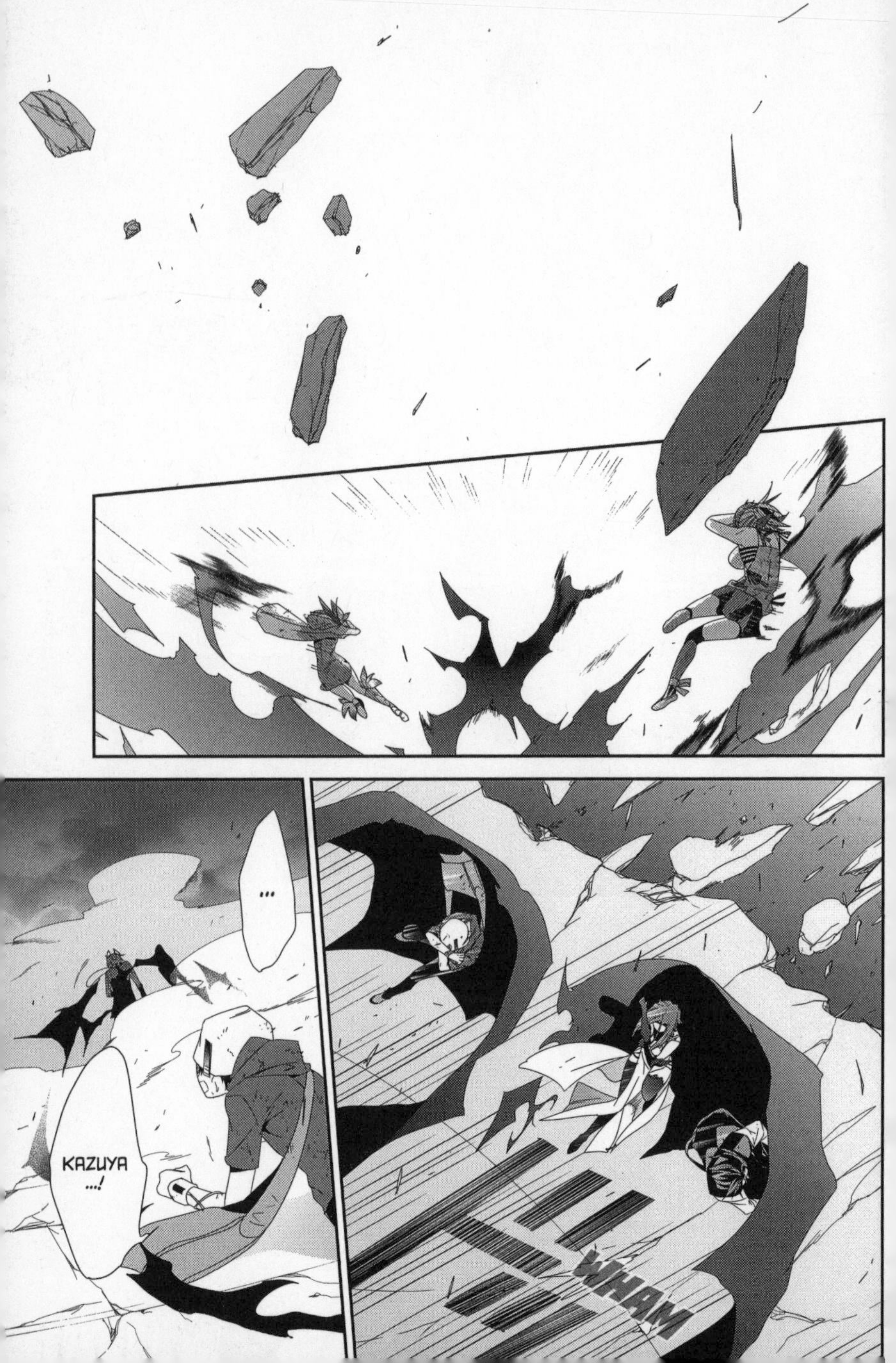
WHAM
...
KAZUYA ...!

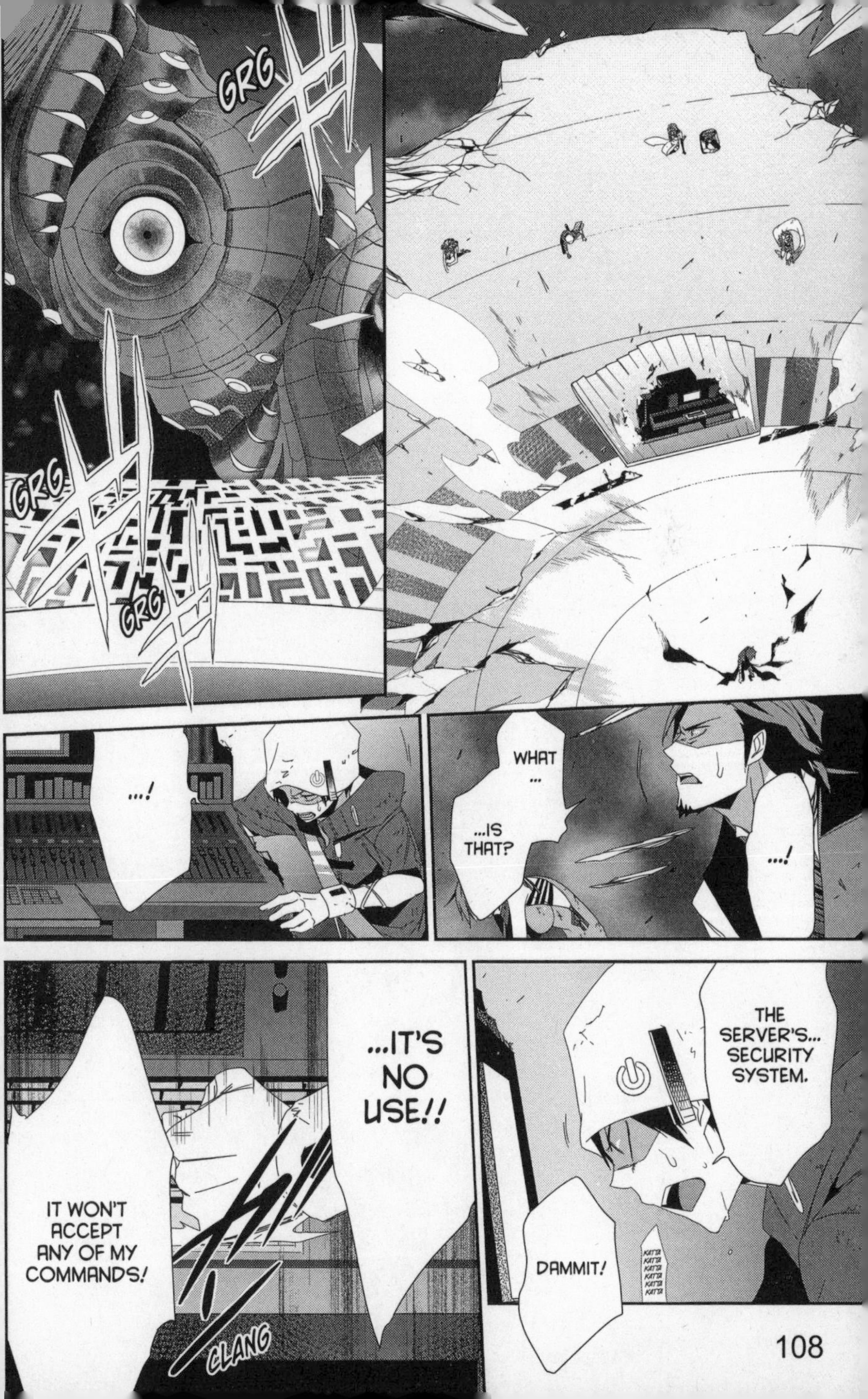
GRG
GRG
GRG
WHAT ...
...IS THAT?
...!
...!
THE SERVER'S... SECURITY SYSTEM.
DAMMIT!
...IT'S NO USE!!
IT WON'T ACCEPT ANY OF MY COMMANDS!
CLANG

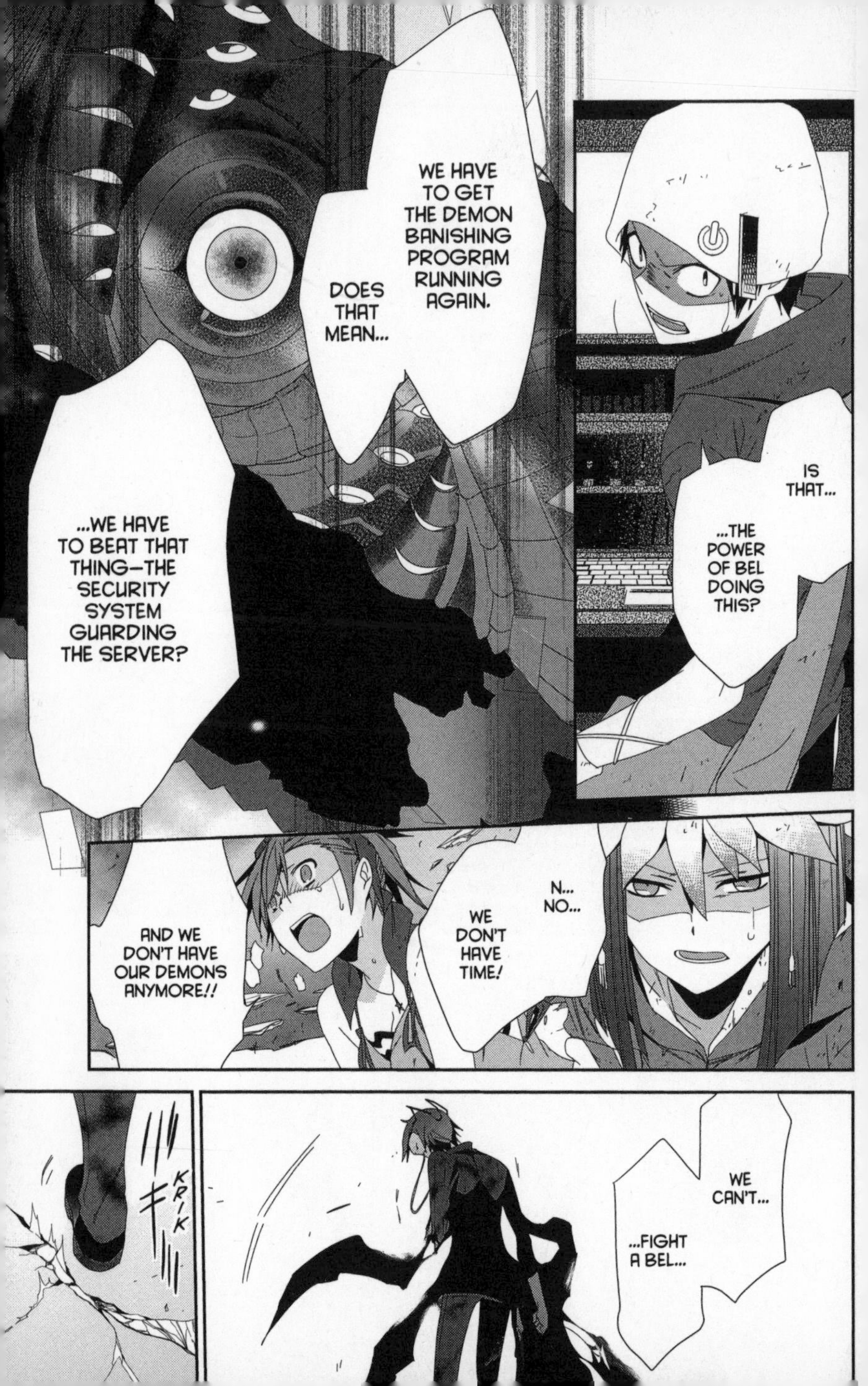
IS THAT...
...THE POWER OF BEL DOING THIS?
WE HAVE TO GET THE DEMON BANISHING PROGRAM RUNNING AGAIN.
DOES THAT MEAN...
...WE HAVE TO BEAT THAT THING—THE SECURITY SYSTEM GUARDING THE SERVER?
N... NO...
WE DON'T HAVE TIME!
AND WE DON'T HAVE OUR DEMONS ANYMORE!!
WE CAN'T...
...FIGHT A BEL...
KRIK

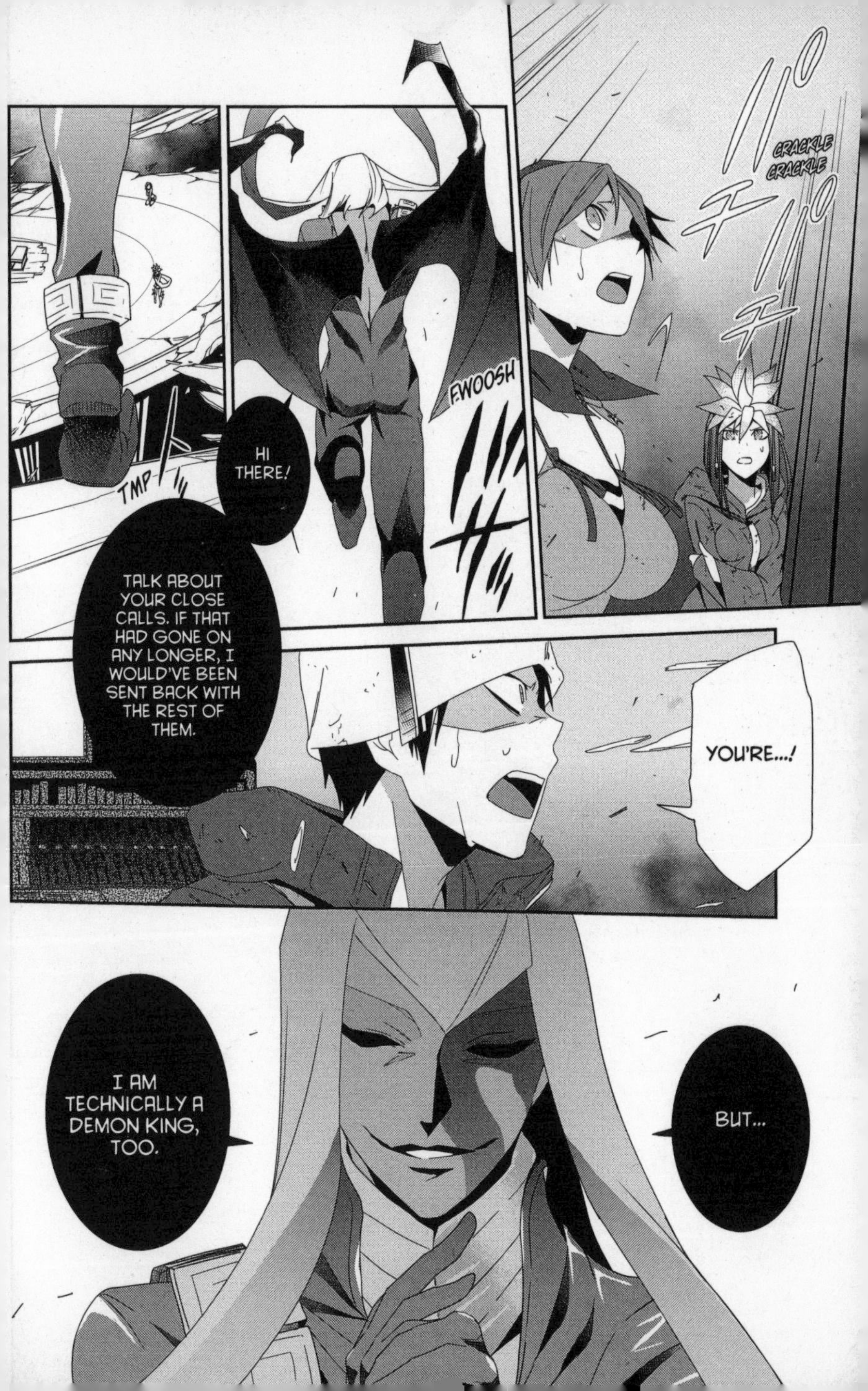
CRACKLE CRACKLE
FWOOSH
HI THERE!
TMP
TALK ABOUT YOUR CLOSE CALLS. IF THAT HAD GONE ON ANY LONGER, I WOULD'VE BEEN SENT BACK WITH THE REST OF THEM.
YOU'RE...!
BUT...
I AM TECHNICALLY A DEMON KING, TOO.

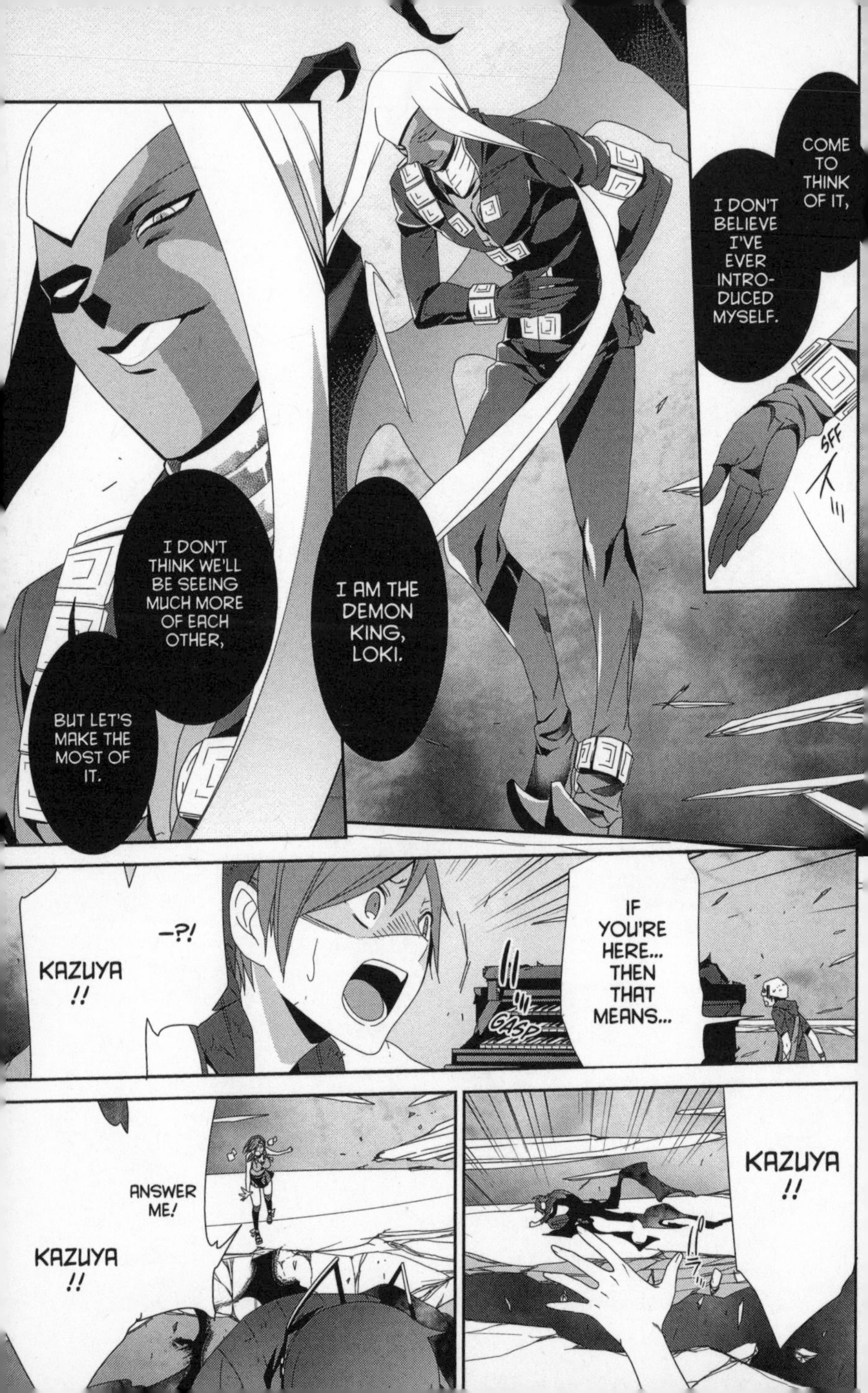
COME TO THINK OF IT,
I DON'T BELIEVE I'VE EVER INTRODUCED MYSELF.
SFF
I AM THE DEMON KING, LOKI.
I DON'T THINK WE'LL BE SEEING MUCH MORE OF EACH OTHER,
BUT LET'S MAKE THE MOST OF IT.
IF YOU'RE HERE... THEN THAT MEANS...
GASP
–?!
KAZUYA!!
KAZUYA!!
ANSWER ME!
KAZUYA!!

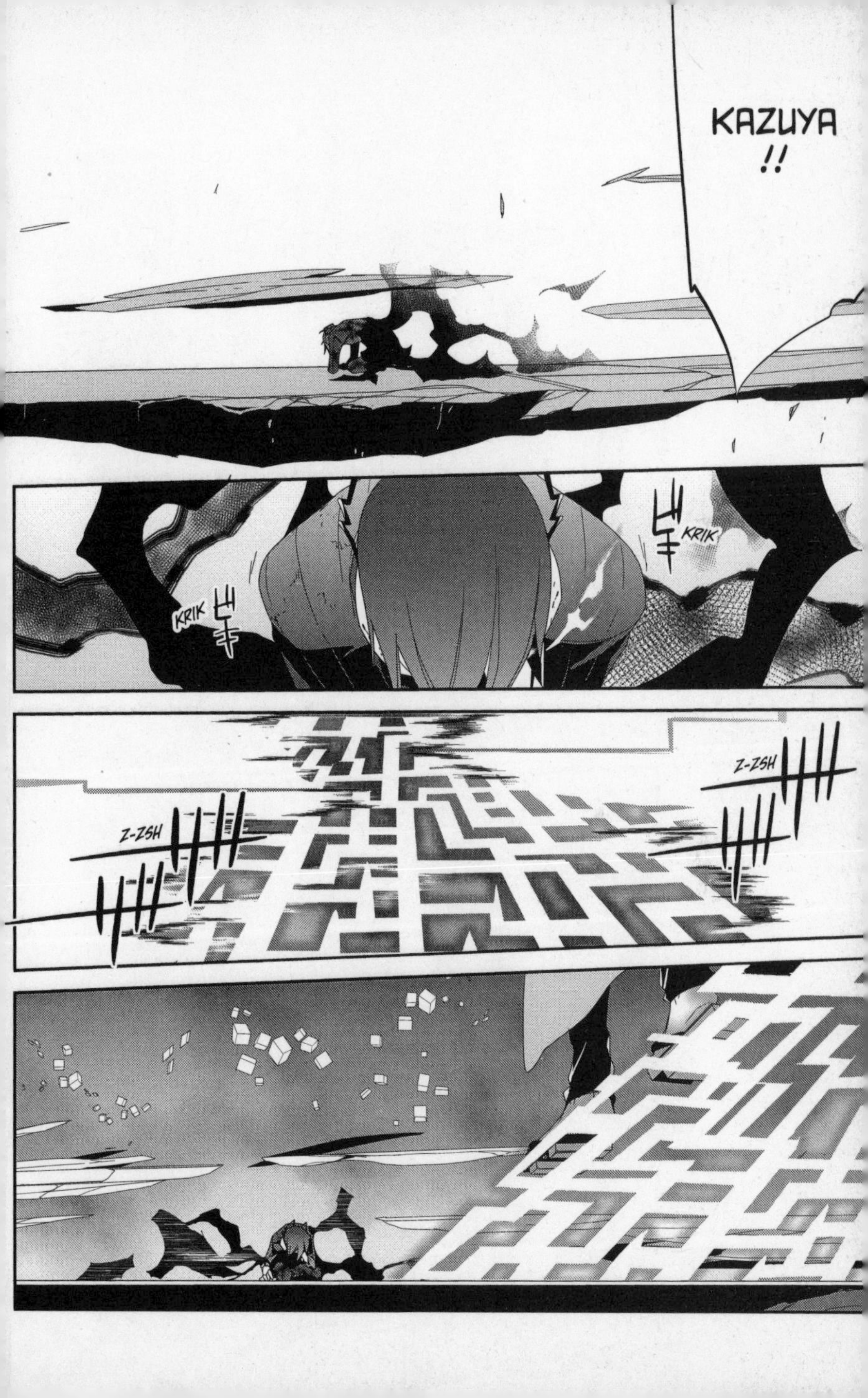
KAZUYA !!
KRIK
KRIK
Z-ZSH
Z-ZSH

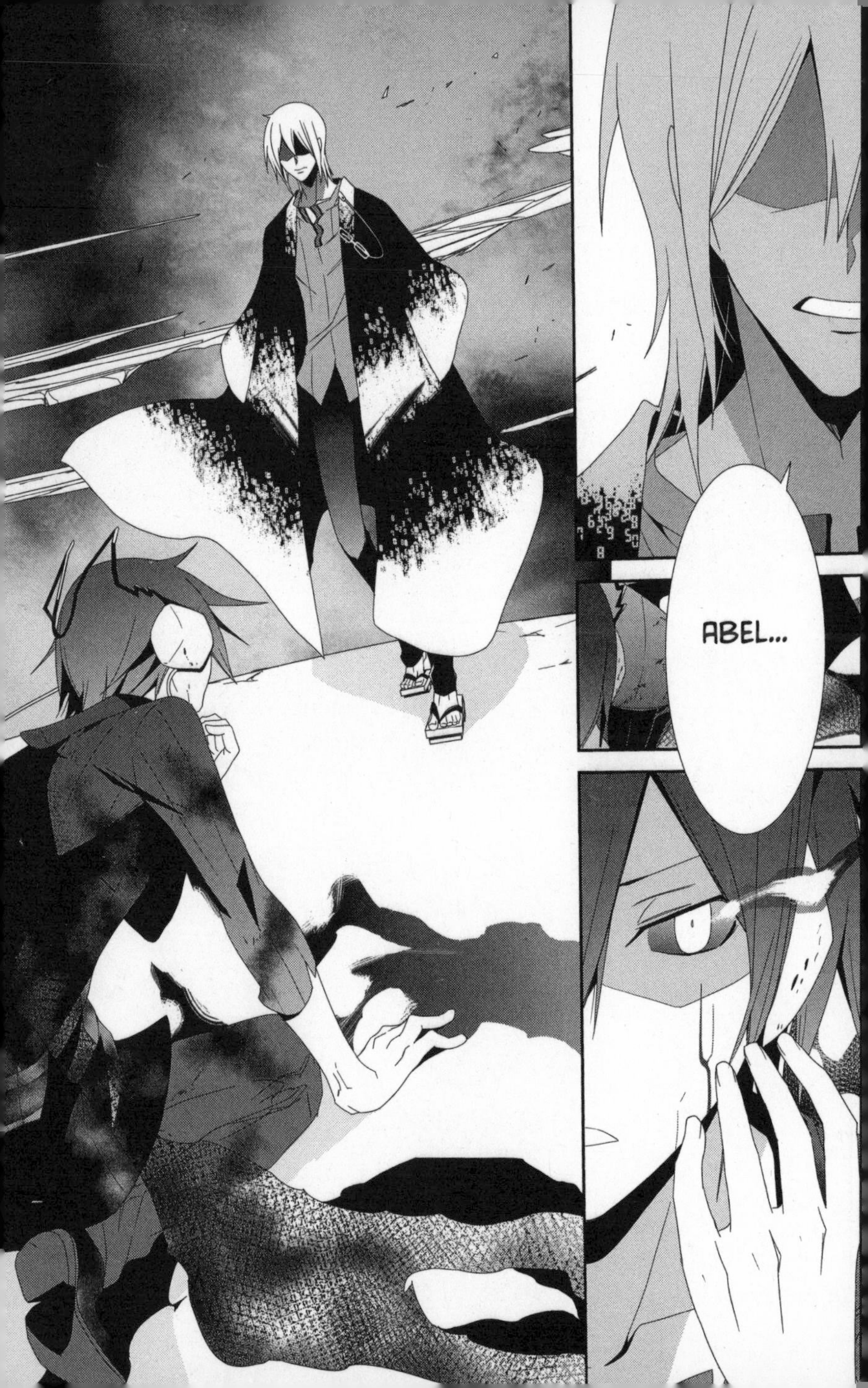
ABEL...

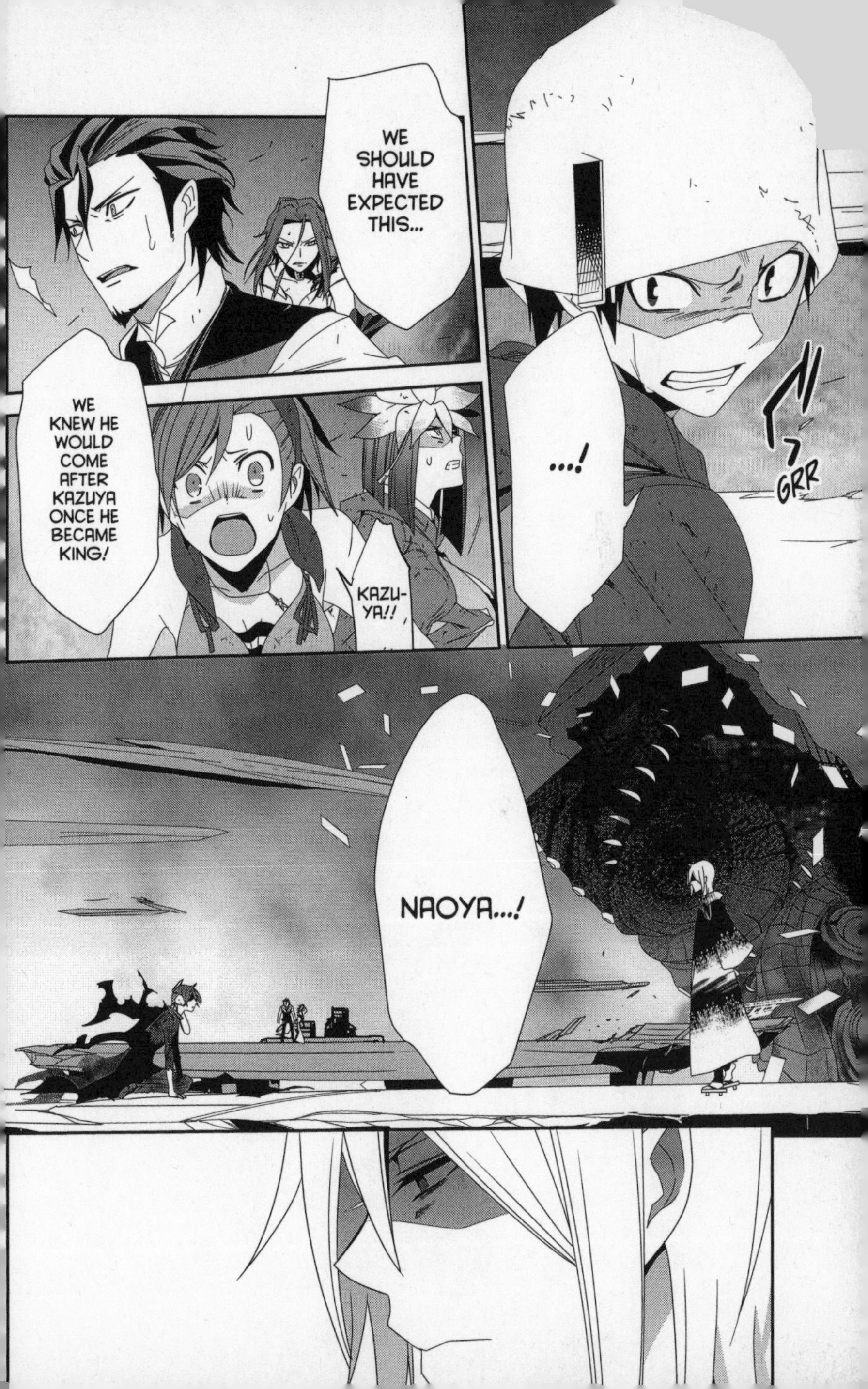
...!
GRR
WE SHOULD HAVE EXPECTED THIS...
KAZU-YA!!
WE KNEW HE WOULD COME AFTER KAZUYA ONCE HE BECAME KING!
NAOYA...!

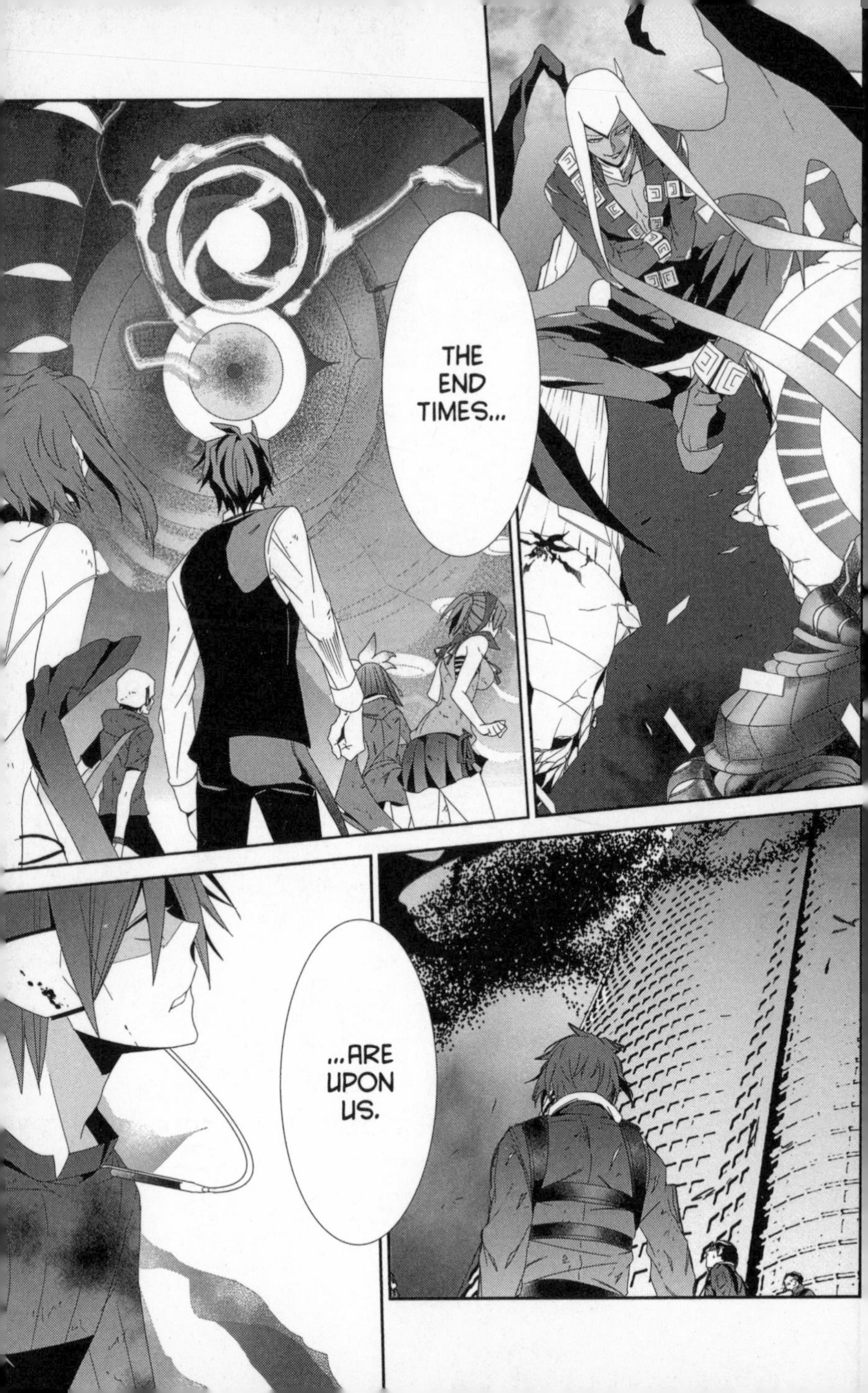
THE END TIMES...
...ARE UPON US.

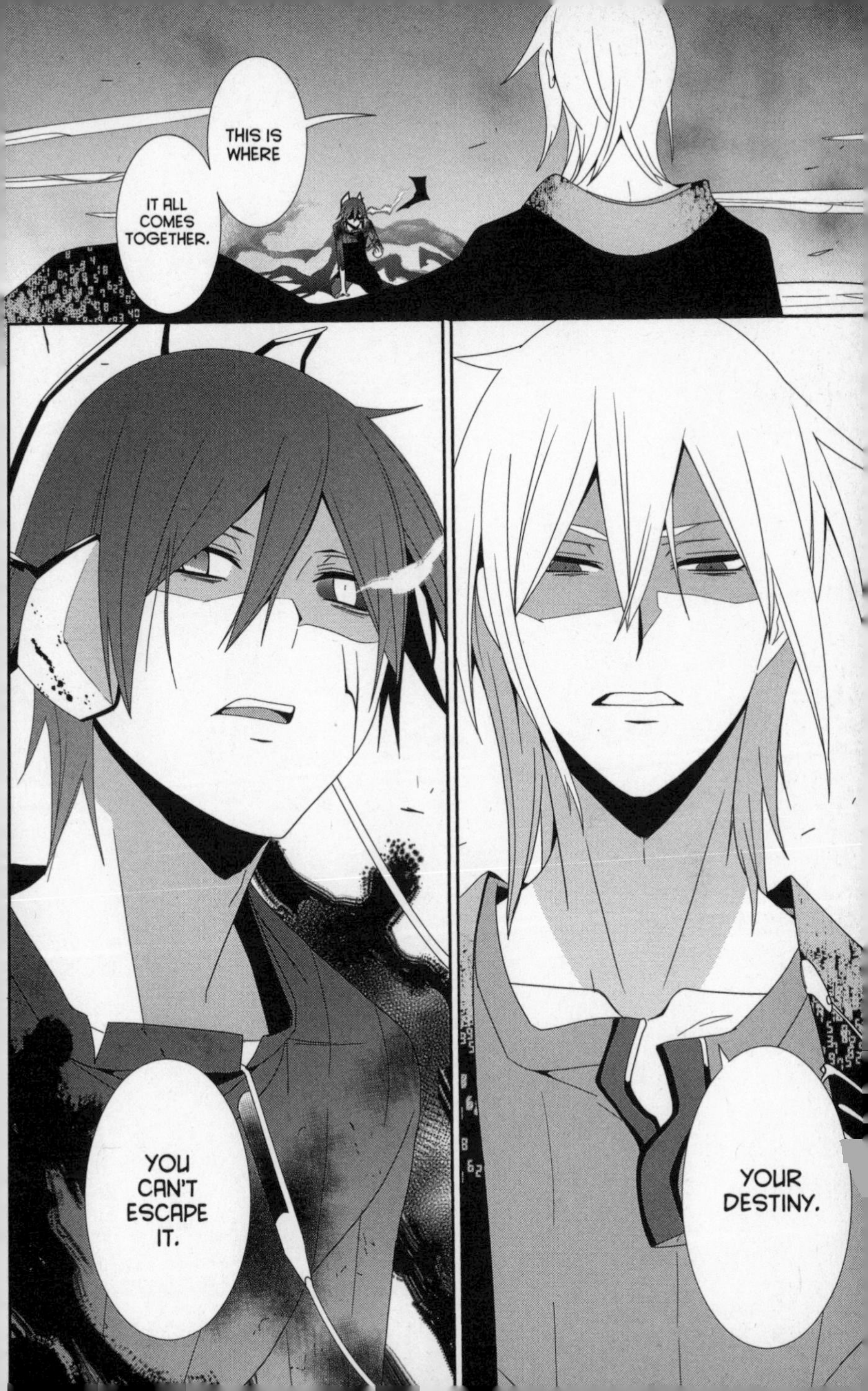
THIS IS WHERE
IT ALL COMES TOGETHER.
YOUR DESTINY.
YOU CAN'T ESCAPE IT.

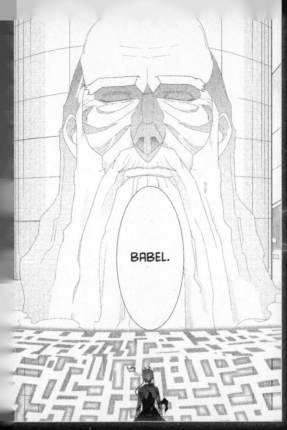

BABEL.

BABEL

THE TOWER OF BABEL. AN ENORMOUS TOWER THAT
EARS IN THE BOOK OF GENESIS IN THE OLD TESTAMENT.
OCATED IN BABYLON (AKKADIAN FOR "GOD'S GATE"),
E CENTRAL CITY OF ANCIENT MESOPOTAMIA, WHERE
IS SAID MANY SUCH TOWERS COULD BE FOUND. THE
ER WAS BUILT IN AN ATTEMPT TO REACH HEAVEN—THE
TEMPT INCURRED GOD'S WRATH, AND THE PEOPLE'S
LANGUAGE WAS DIVIDED AS A RESULT. NO LONGER
ABLE TO COMMUNICATE, ITS BUILDERS GAVE UP ON
NSTRUCTION OF THE TOWER. THIS STORY IS USED TO
AIN THE DIVERSITY OF LANGUAGES IN THE WORLD, AND
ERALLY IT IS SEEN AS MERE LEGEND, BUT SOME MORE
ONSERVATIVE SECTS TREAT IT AS HISTORICAL FACT.

DEVIL SURVIVOR
デビルサバイバー

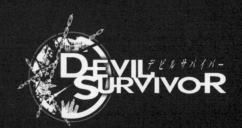

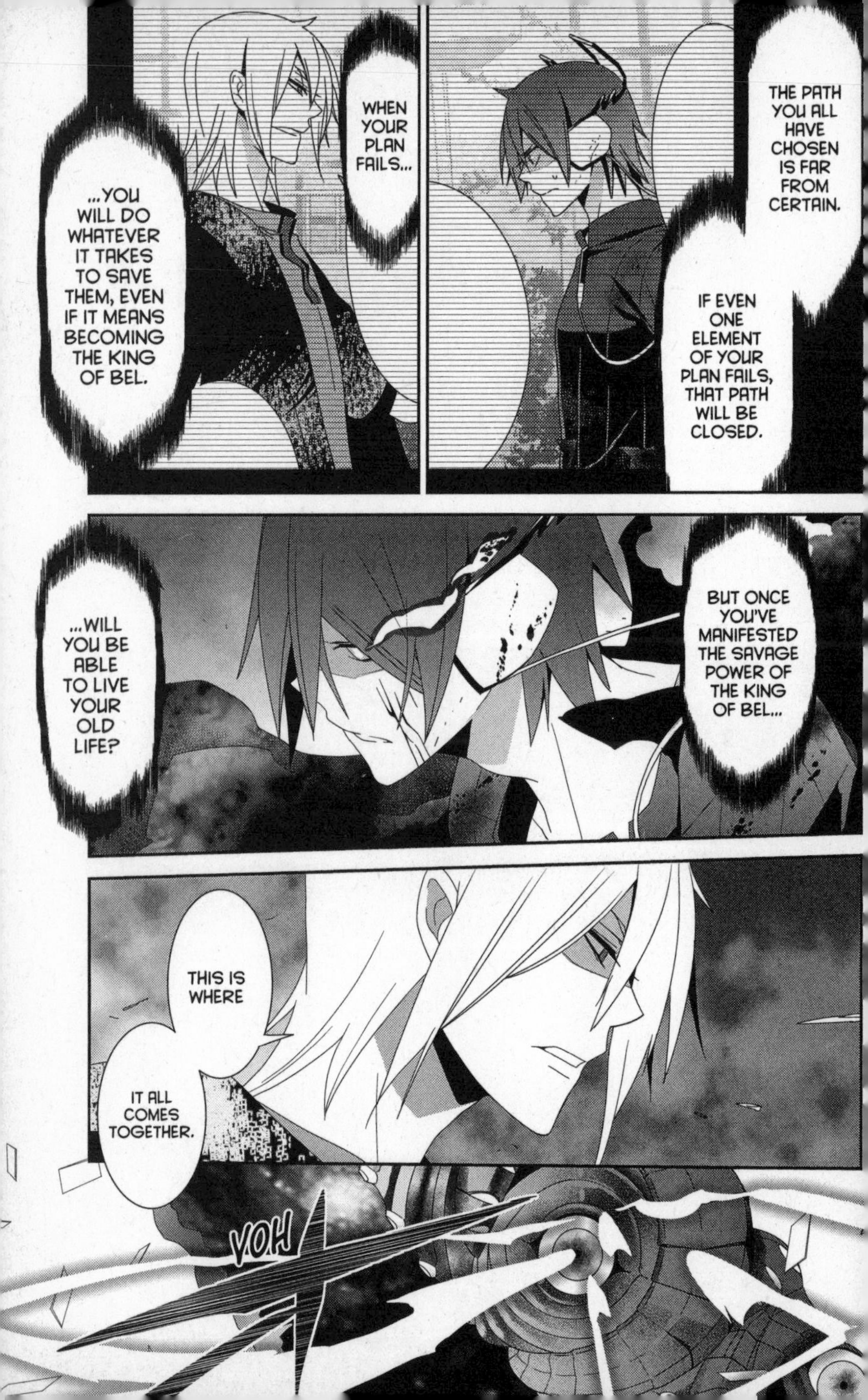
THE PATH YOU ALL HAVE CHOSEN IS FAR FROM CERTAIN.
IF EVEN ONE ELEMENT OF YOUR PLAN FAILS, THAT PATH WILL BE CLOSED.
WHEN YOUR PLAN FAILS...
...YOU WILL DO WHATEVER IT TAKES TO SAVE THEM, EVEN IF IT MEANS BECOMING THE KING OF BEL.
BUT ONCE YOU'VE MANIFESTED THE SAVAGE POWER OF THE KING OF BEL...
...WILL YOU BE ABLE TO LIVE YOUR OLD LIFE?
THIS IS WHERE
IT ALL COMES TOGETHER.
VOH

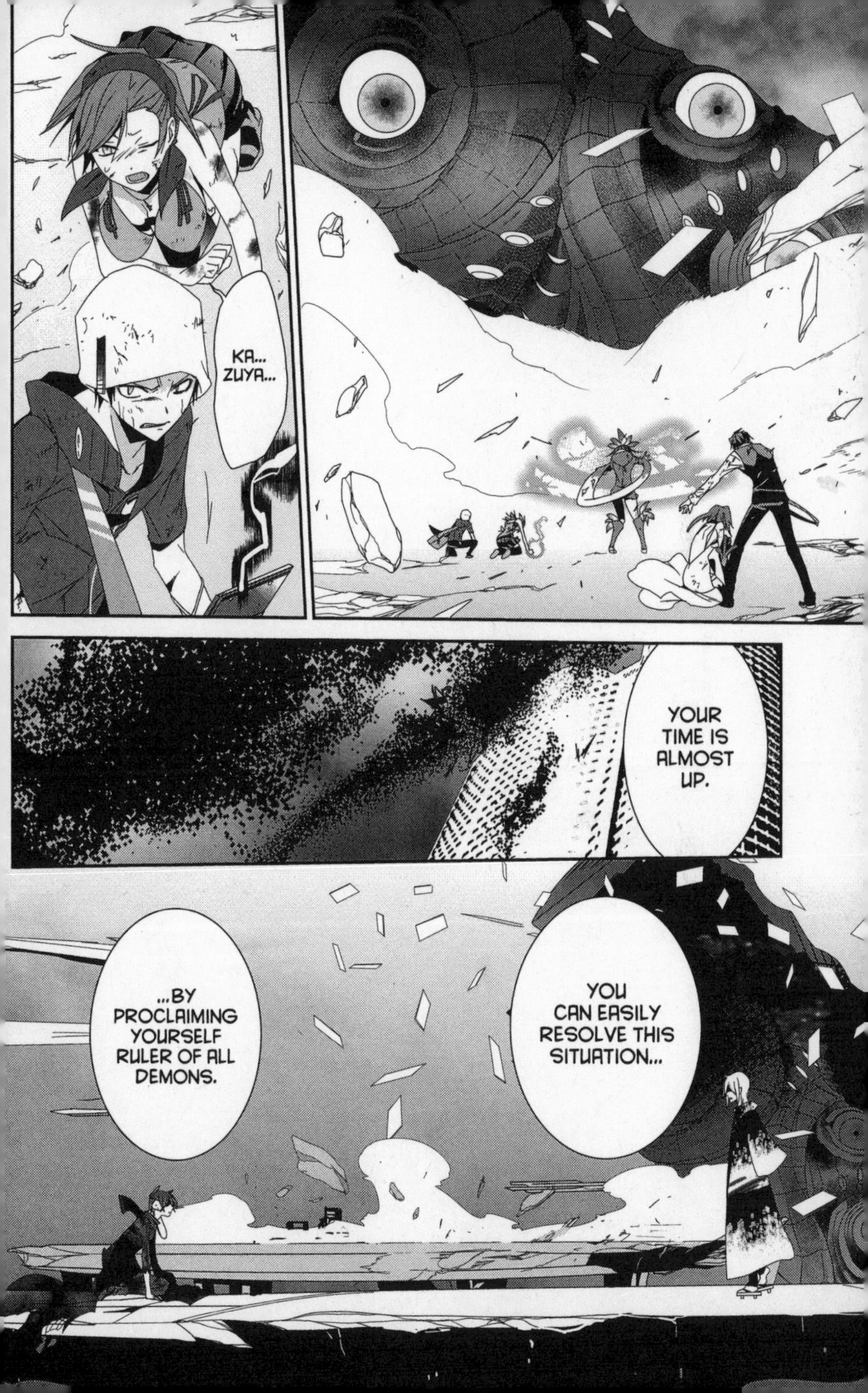
KA... ZUYA...
YOUR TIME IS ALMOST UP.
YOU CAN EASILY RESOLVE THIS SITUATION...
...BY PROCLAIMING YOURSELF RULER OF ALL DEMONS.

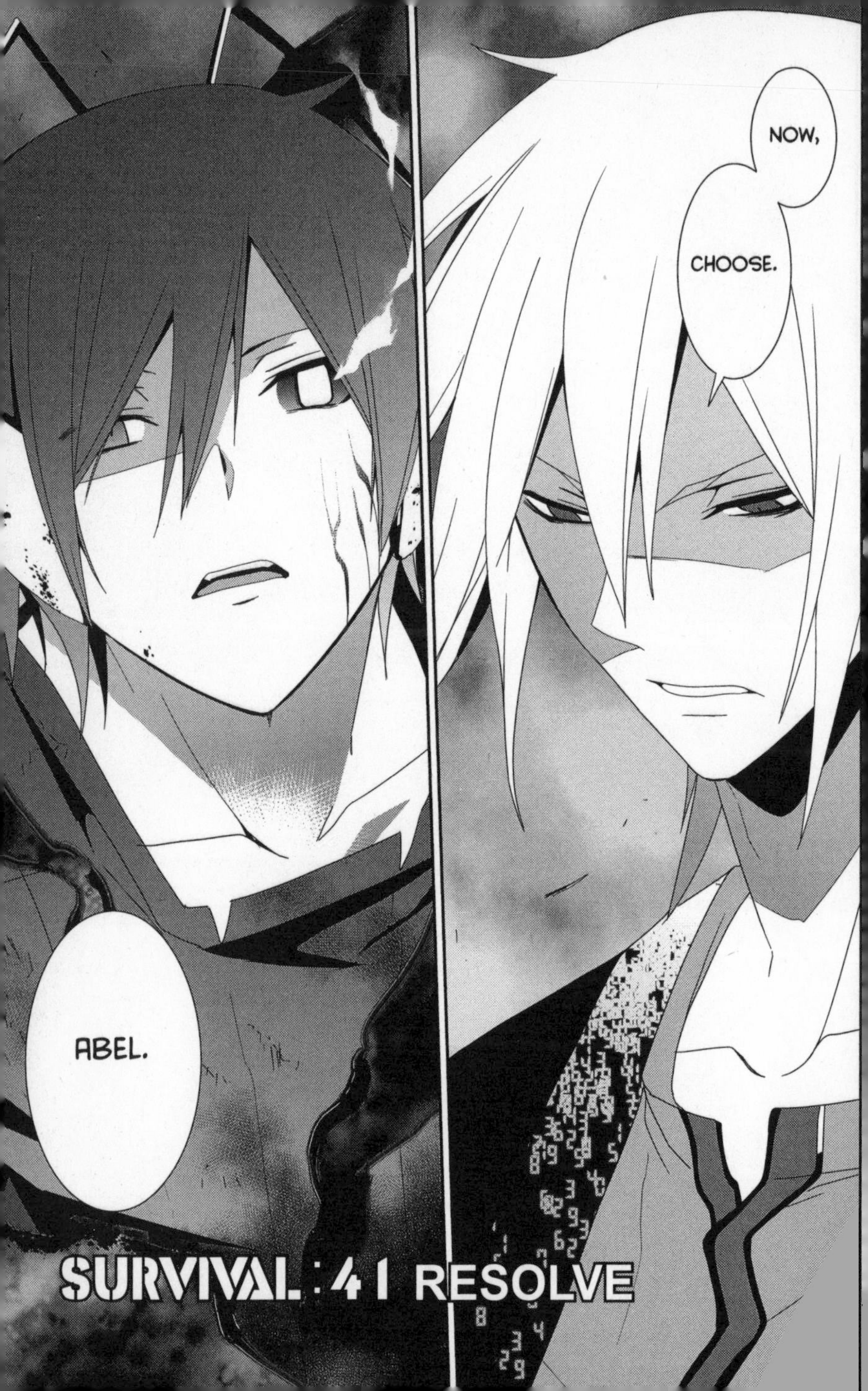
NOW,
CHOOSE.
ABEL.
SURVIVAL : 41 RESOLVE

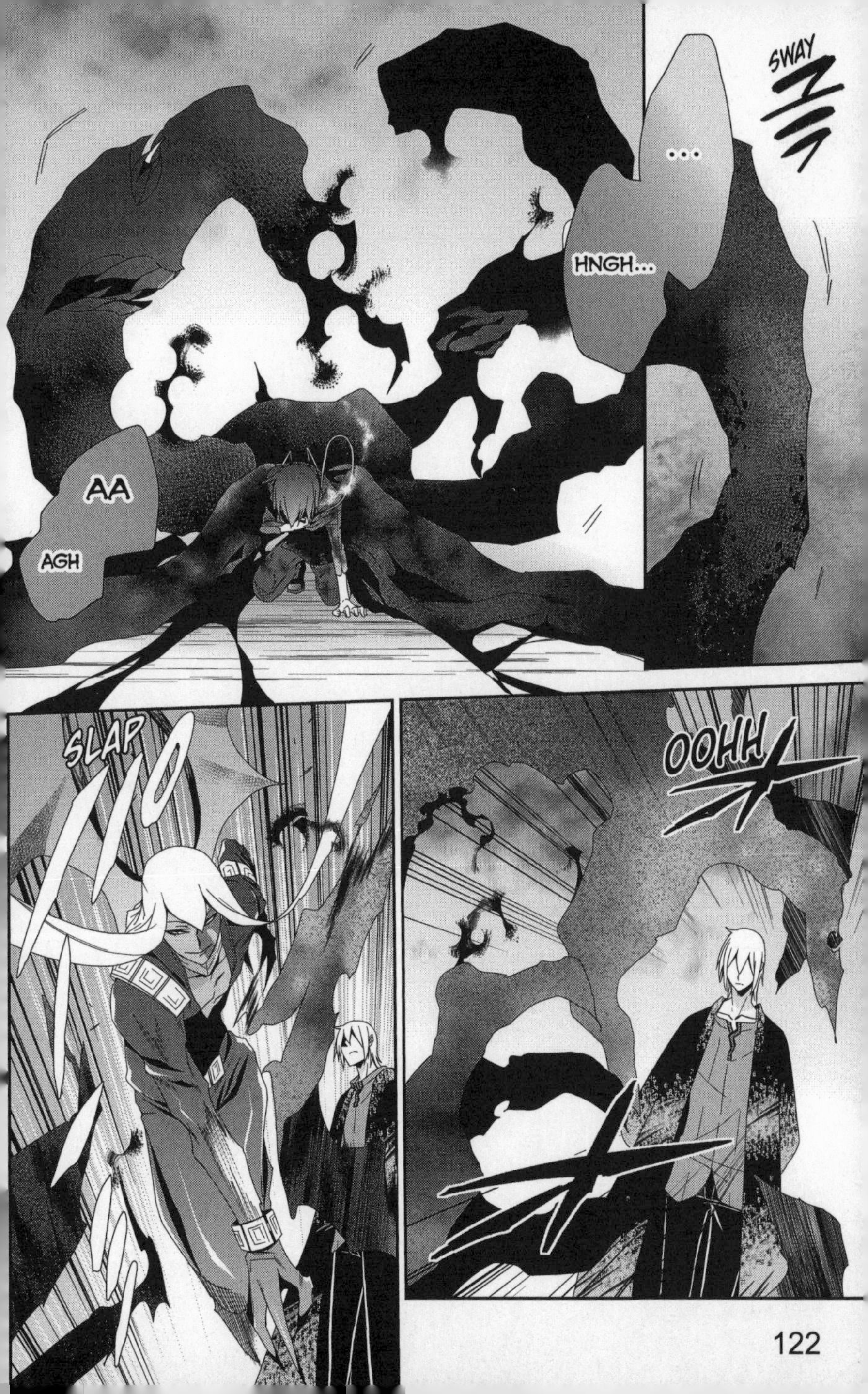
SWAY
...
HNGH...
AA
AGH
OOHH
SLAP

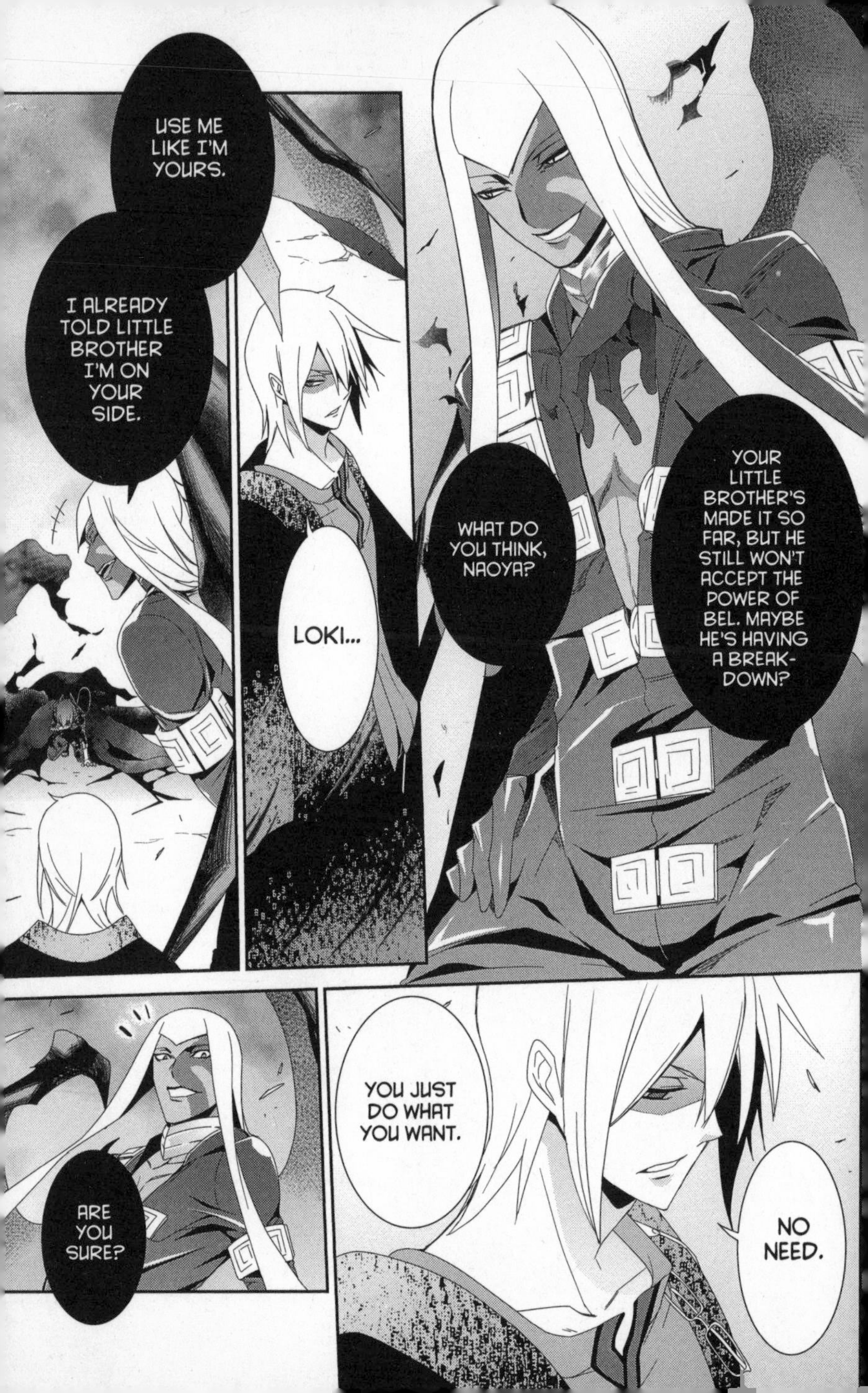
YOUR LITTLE BROTHER'S MADE IT SO FAR, BUT HE STILL WON'T ACCEPT THE POWER OF BEL. MAYBE HE'S HAVING A BREAK-DOWN?
WHAT DO YOU THINK, NAOYA?
LOKI...
USE ME LIKE I'M YOURS.
I ALREADY TOLD LITTLE BROTHER I'M ON YOUR SIDE.
NO NEED.
YOU JUST DO WHAT YOU WANT.
ARE YOU SURE?

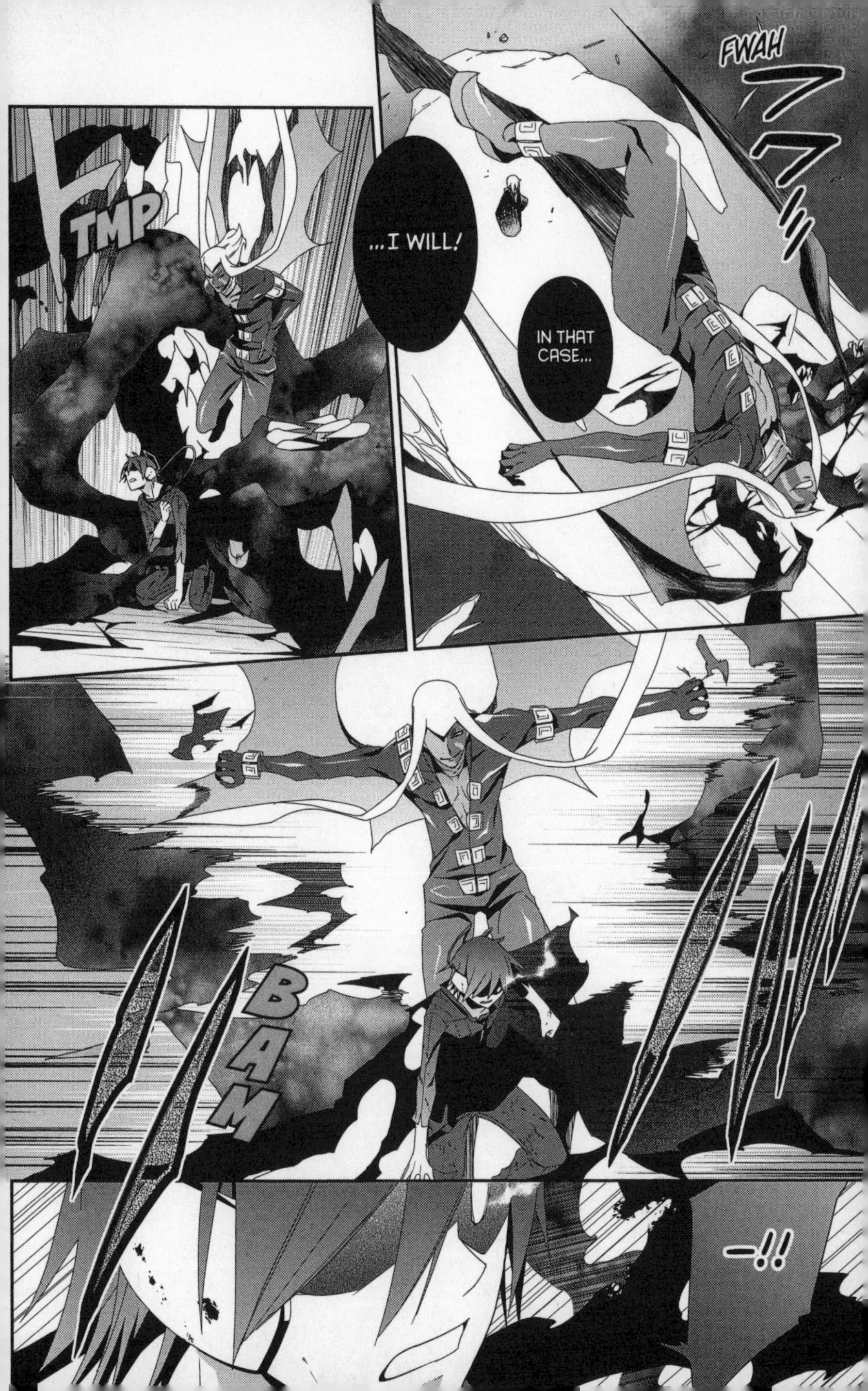
FWAH
IN THAT CASE...
...I WILL!
TMP
BAM
—!!

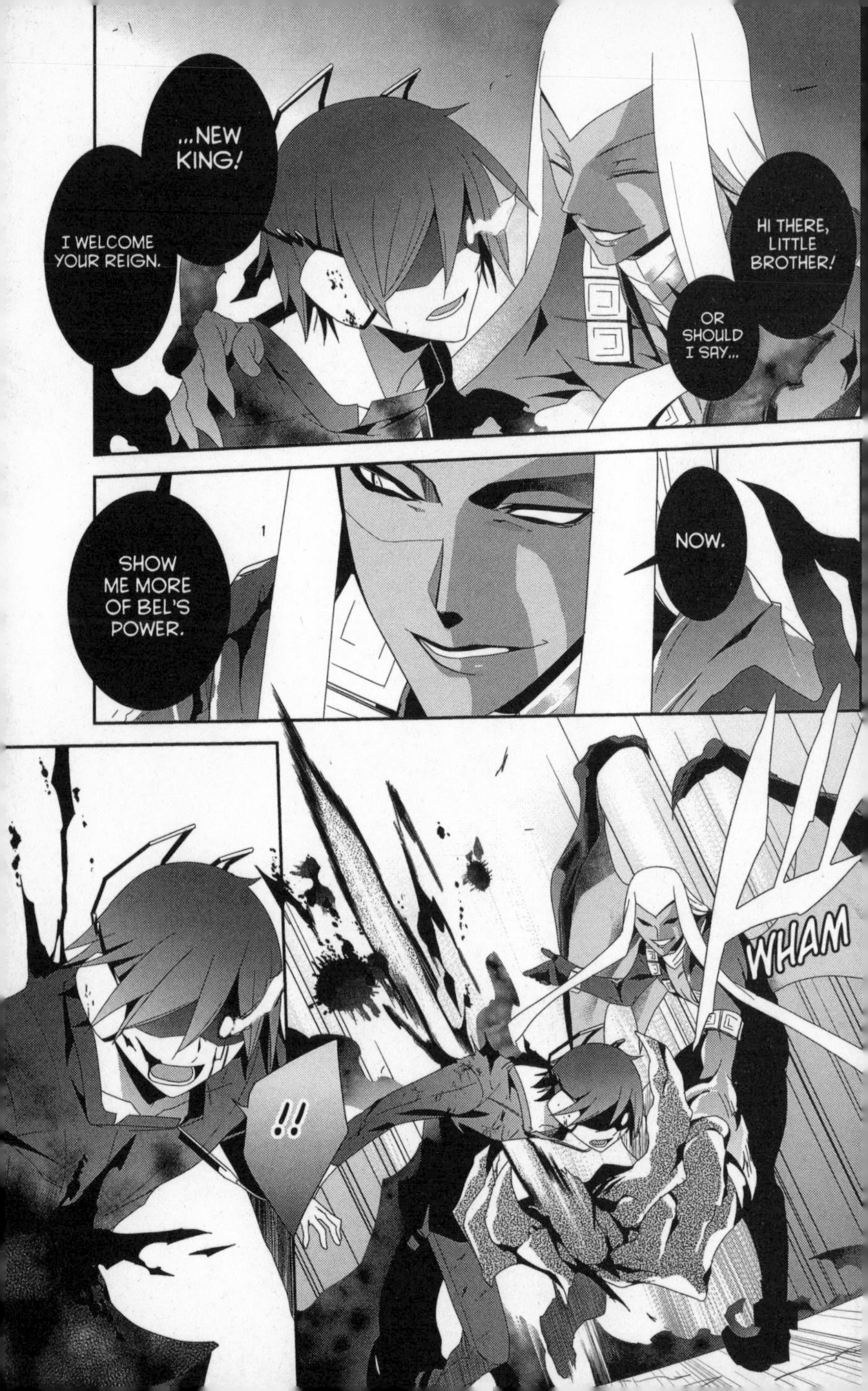
HI THERE, LITTLE BROTHER!
OR SHOULD I SAY...
...NEW KING!
I WELCOME YOUR REIGN.
NOW.
SHOW ME MORE OF BEL'S POWER.
WHAM
!!

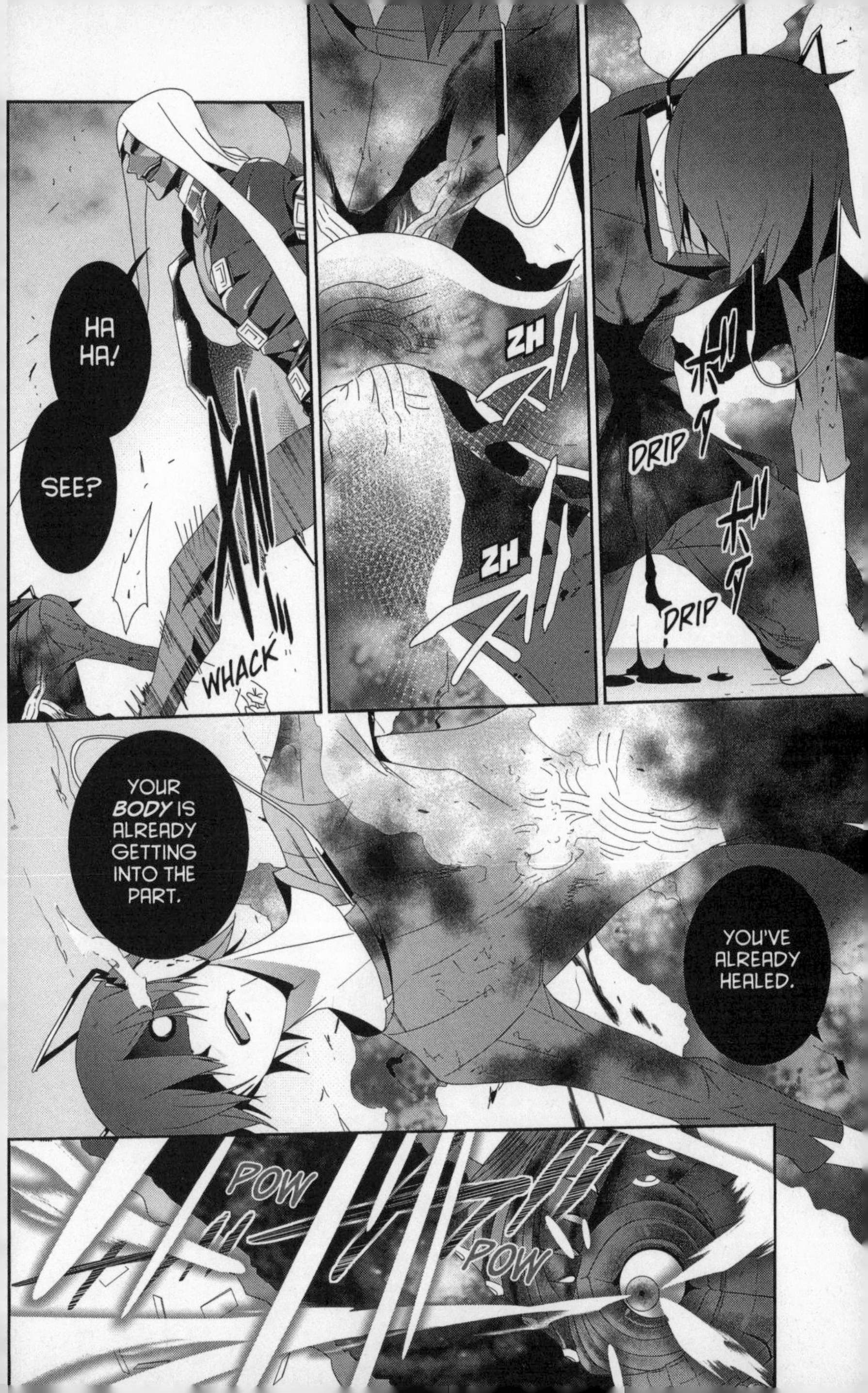
ポタ
DRIP
ポタ
DRIP
ZH
ZH
HA HA!
SEE?
WHACK
YOU'VE ALREADY HEALED.
YOUR *BODY* IS ALREADY GETTING INTO THE PART.
POW
POW

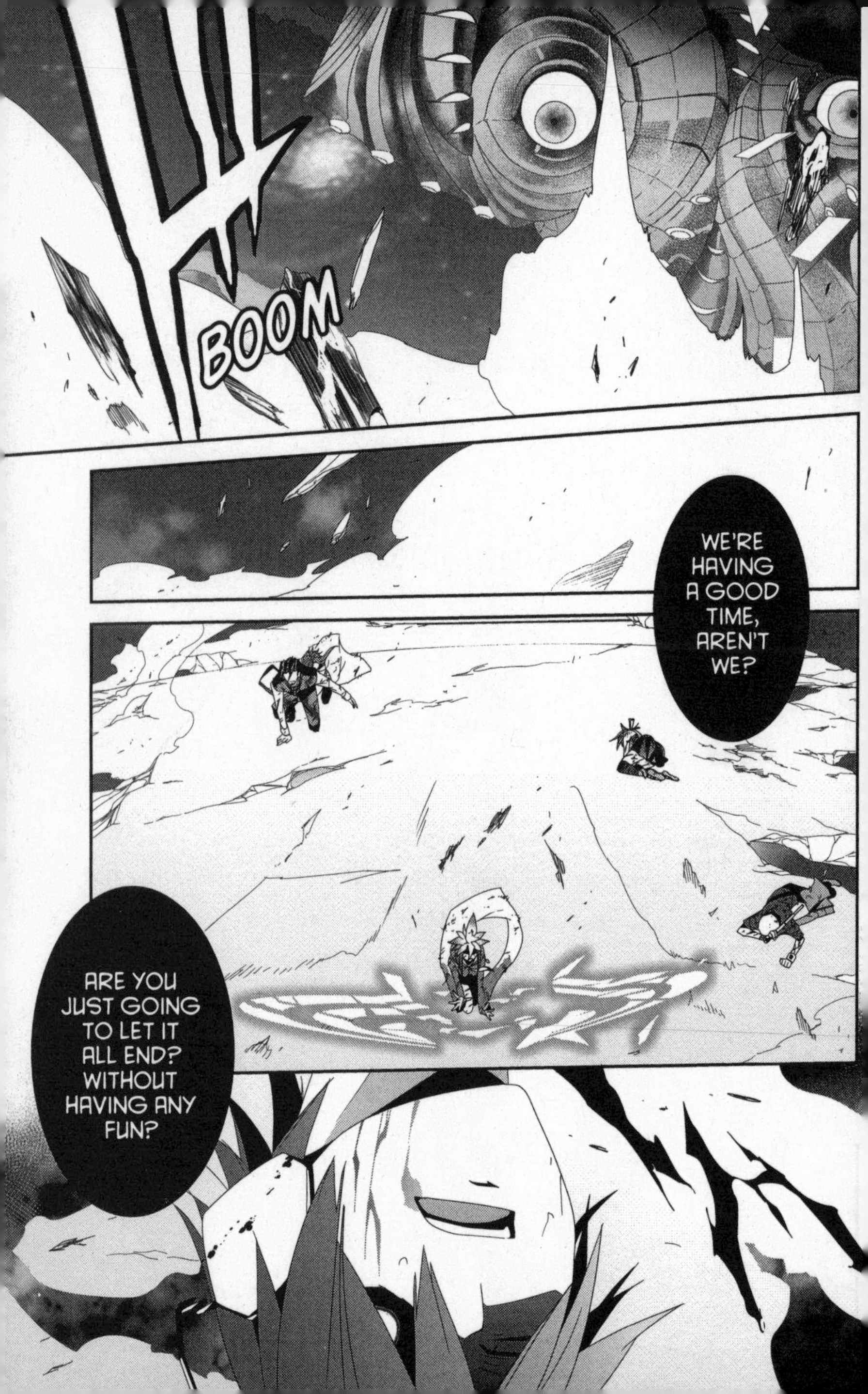
BOOM
WE'RE HAVING A GOOD TIME, AREN'T WE?
ARE YOU JUST GOING TO LET IT ALL END? WITHOUT HAVING ANY FUN?

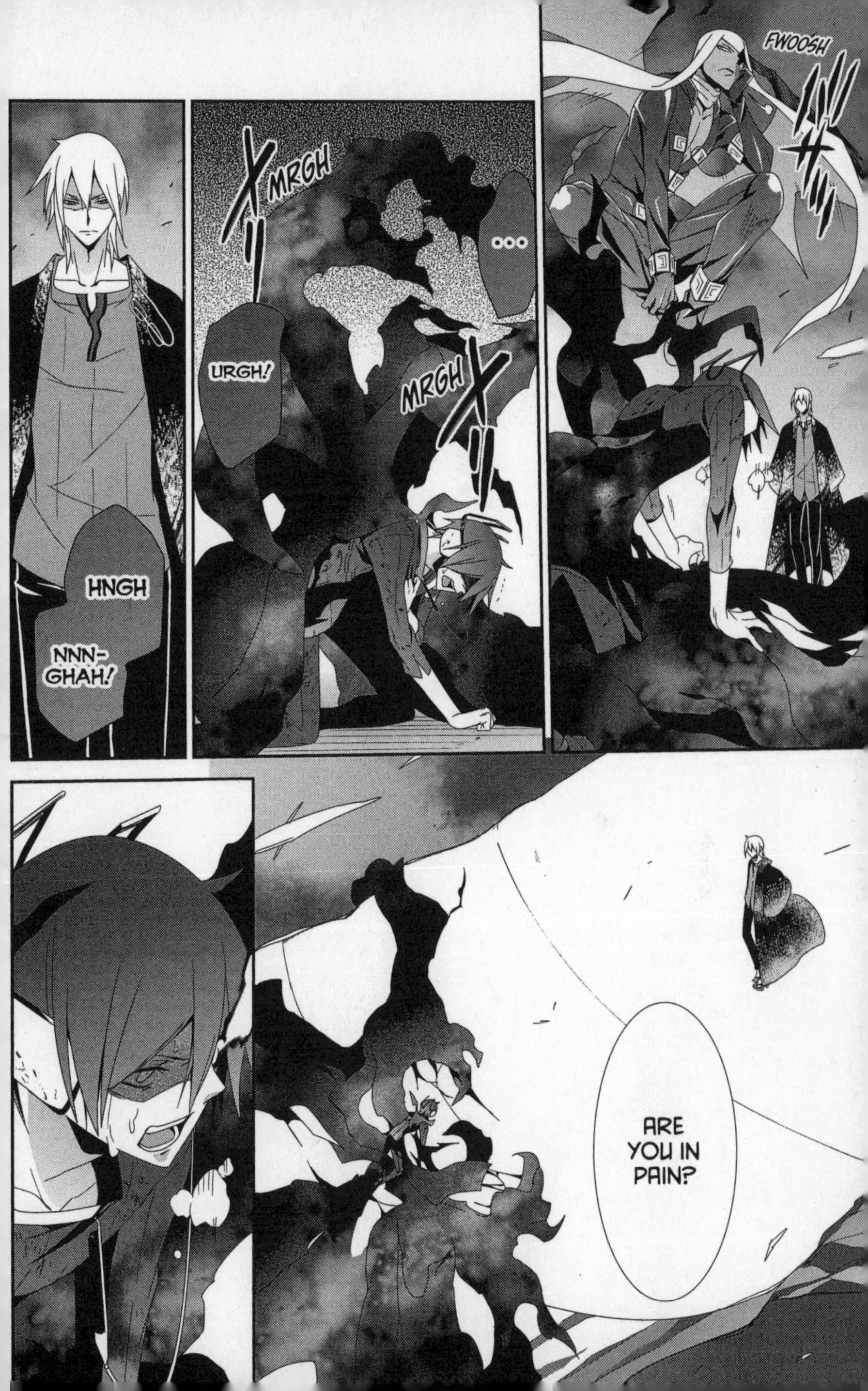
FWOOSH
MRGH
...
MRGH
URGH!
HNGH
NNN-GHAH!
ARE YOU IN PAIN?

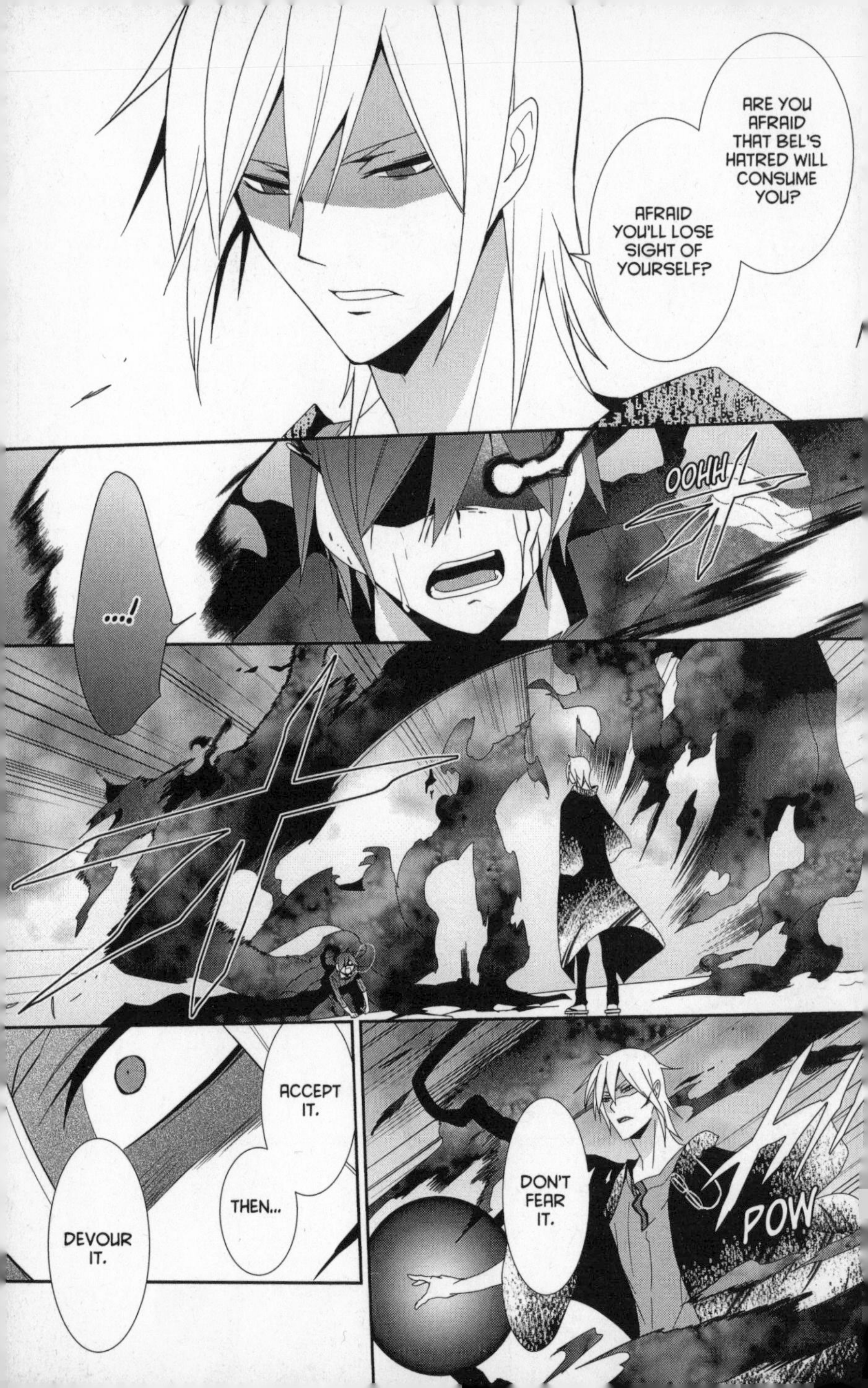
ARE YOU AFRAID THAT BEL'S HATRED WILL CONSUME YOU?
AFRAID YOU'LL LOSE SIGHT OF YOURSELF?
OOHH
...!
DON'T FEAR IT.
POW
ACCEPT IT.
THEN...
DEVOUR IT.

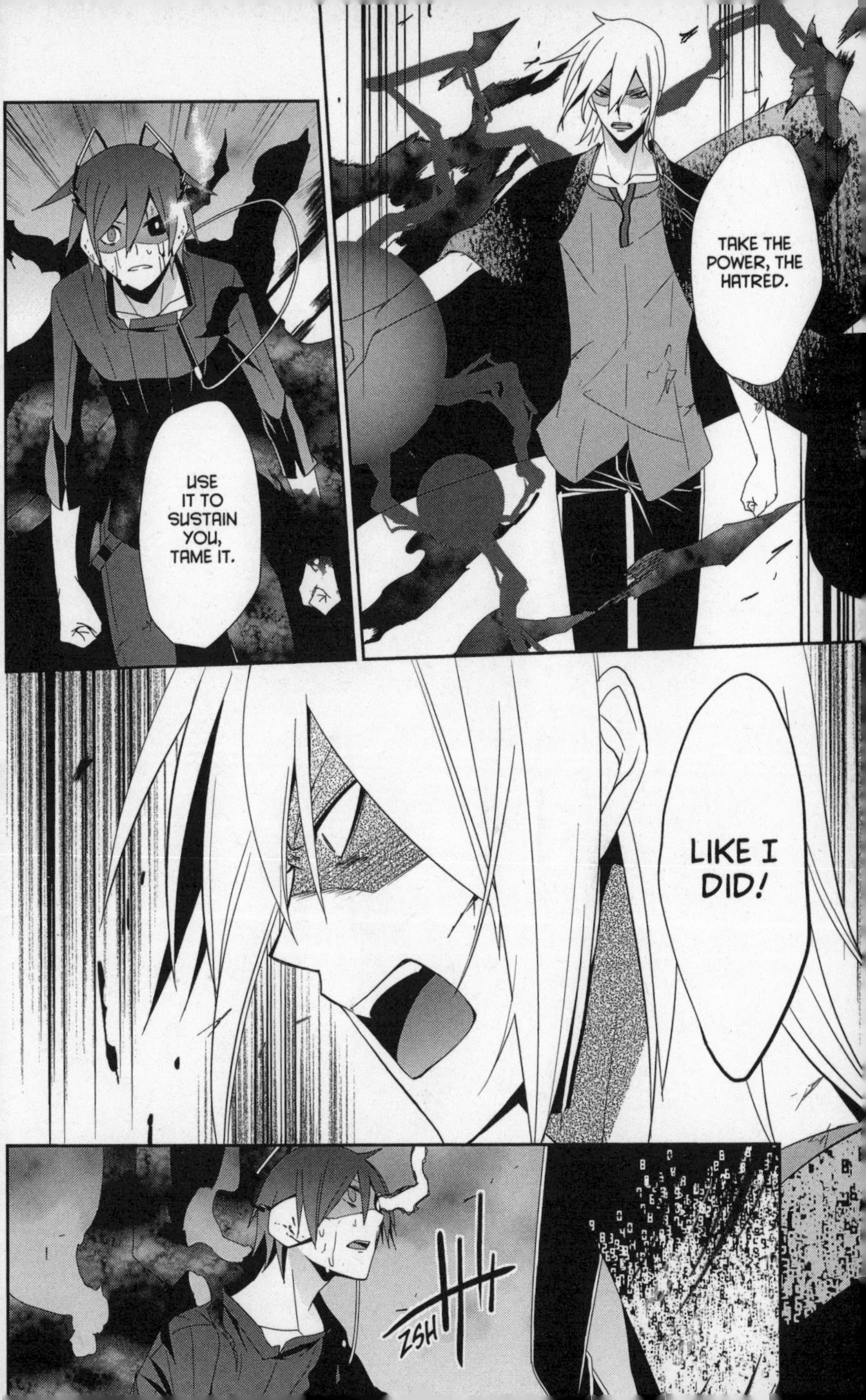
TAKE THE POWER, THE HATRED.
USE IT TO SUSTAIN YOU, TAME IT.
LIKE I DID!
ZSH

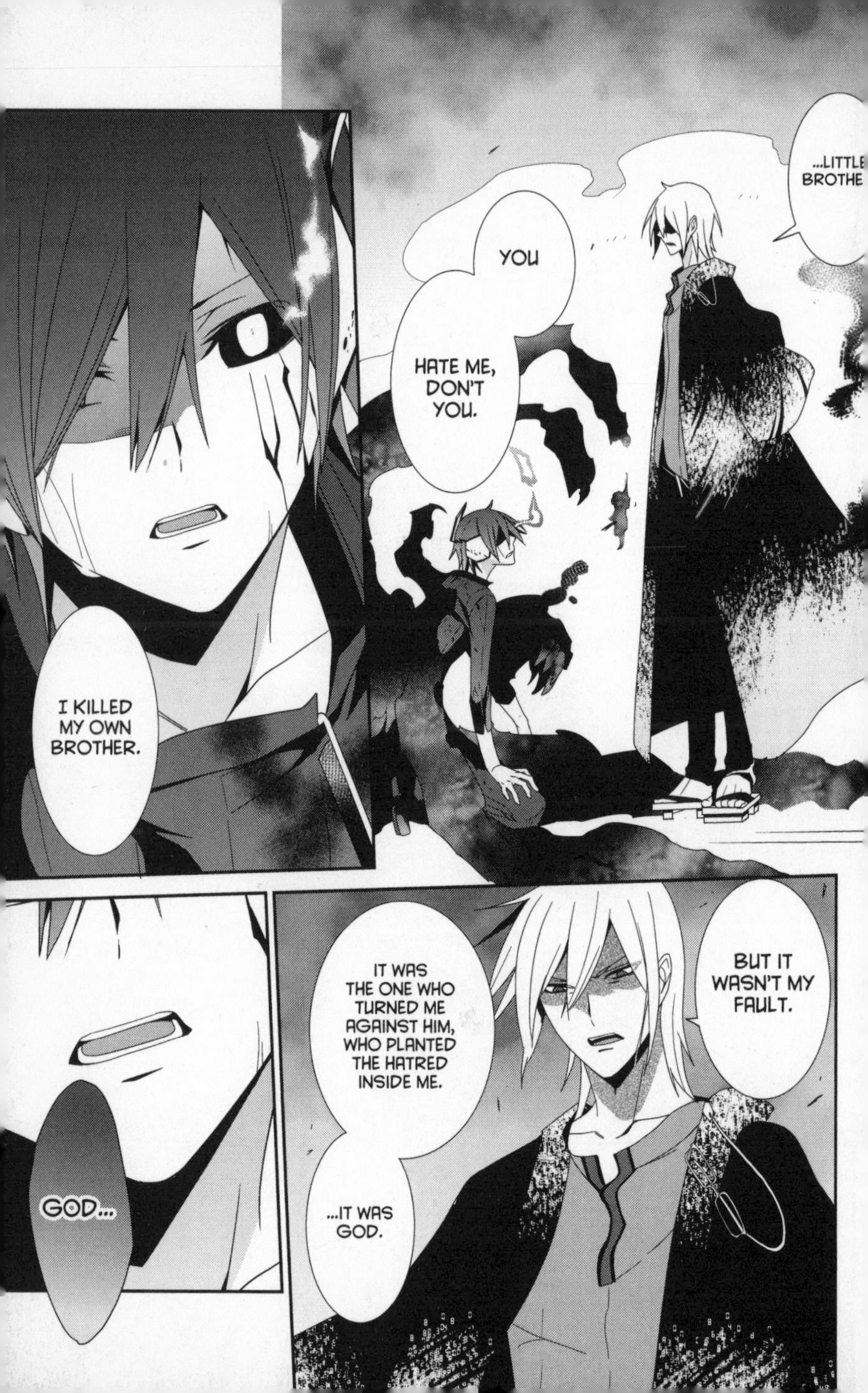
...LITTLE BROTHE
YOU
HATE ME, DON'T YOU.
I KILLED MY OWN BROTHER.
BUT IT WASN'T MY FAULT.
IT WAS THE ONE WHO TURNED ME AGAINST HIM, WHO PLANTED THE HATRED INSIDE ME.
...IT WAS GOD.
GOD...

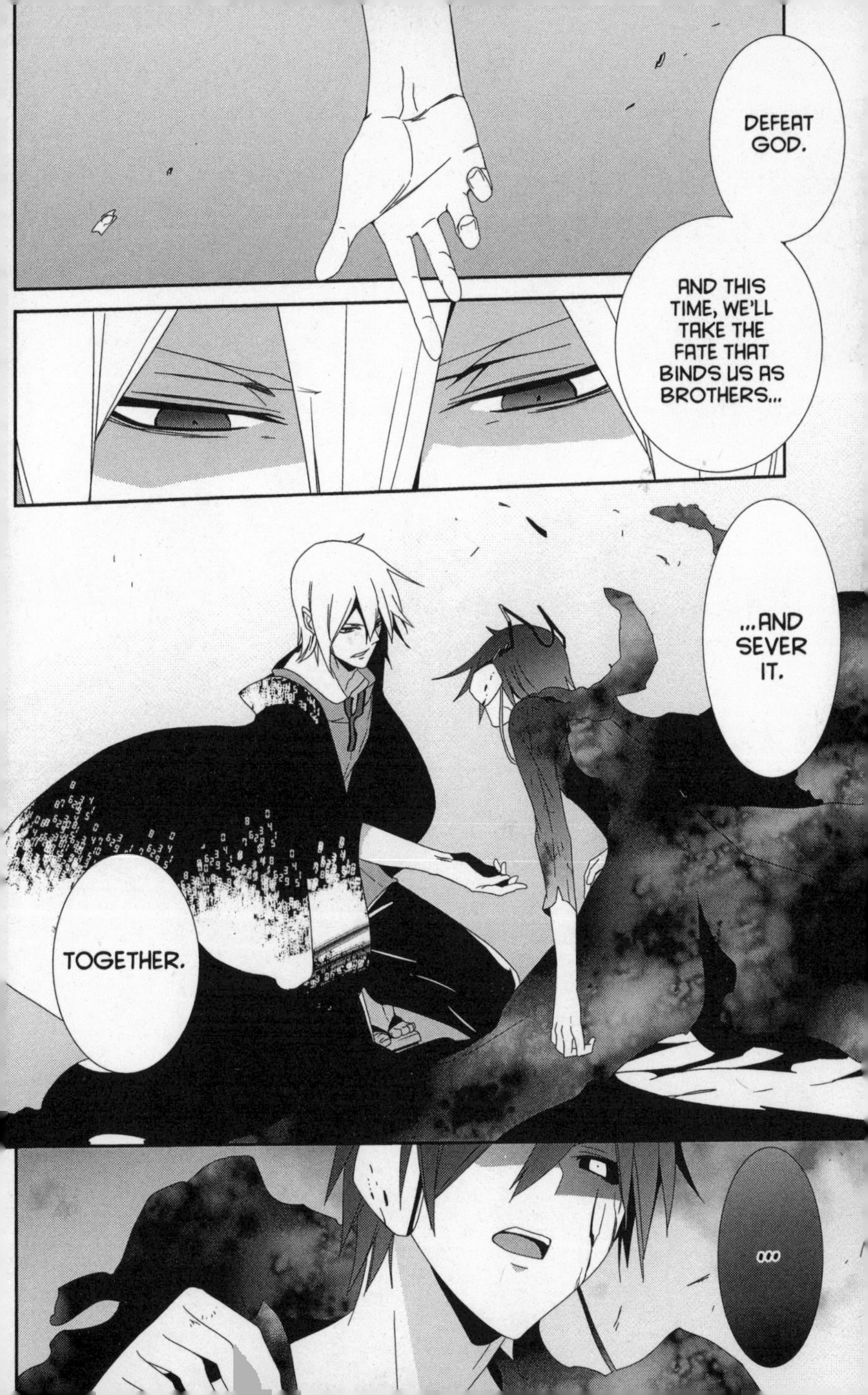
DEFEAT GOD.
AND THIS TIME, WE'LL TAKE THE FATE THAT BINDS US AS BROTHERS...
...AND SEVER IT.
TOGETHER.
...

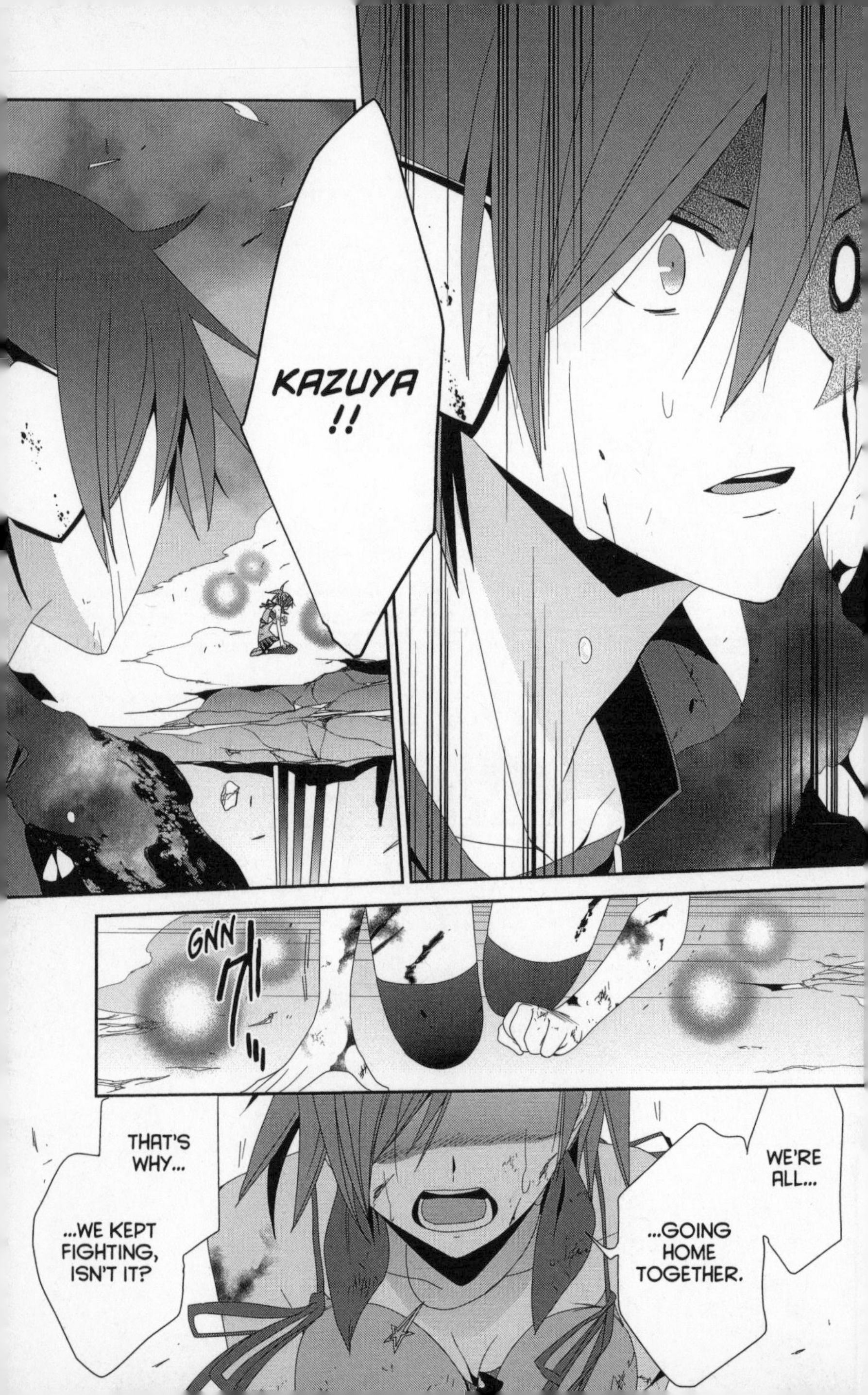
KAZUYA !!
GNN
WE'RE ALL...
...GOING HOME TOGETHER.
THAT'S WHY...
...WE KEPT FIGHTING, ISN'T IT?

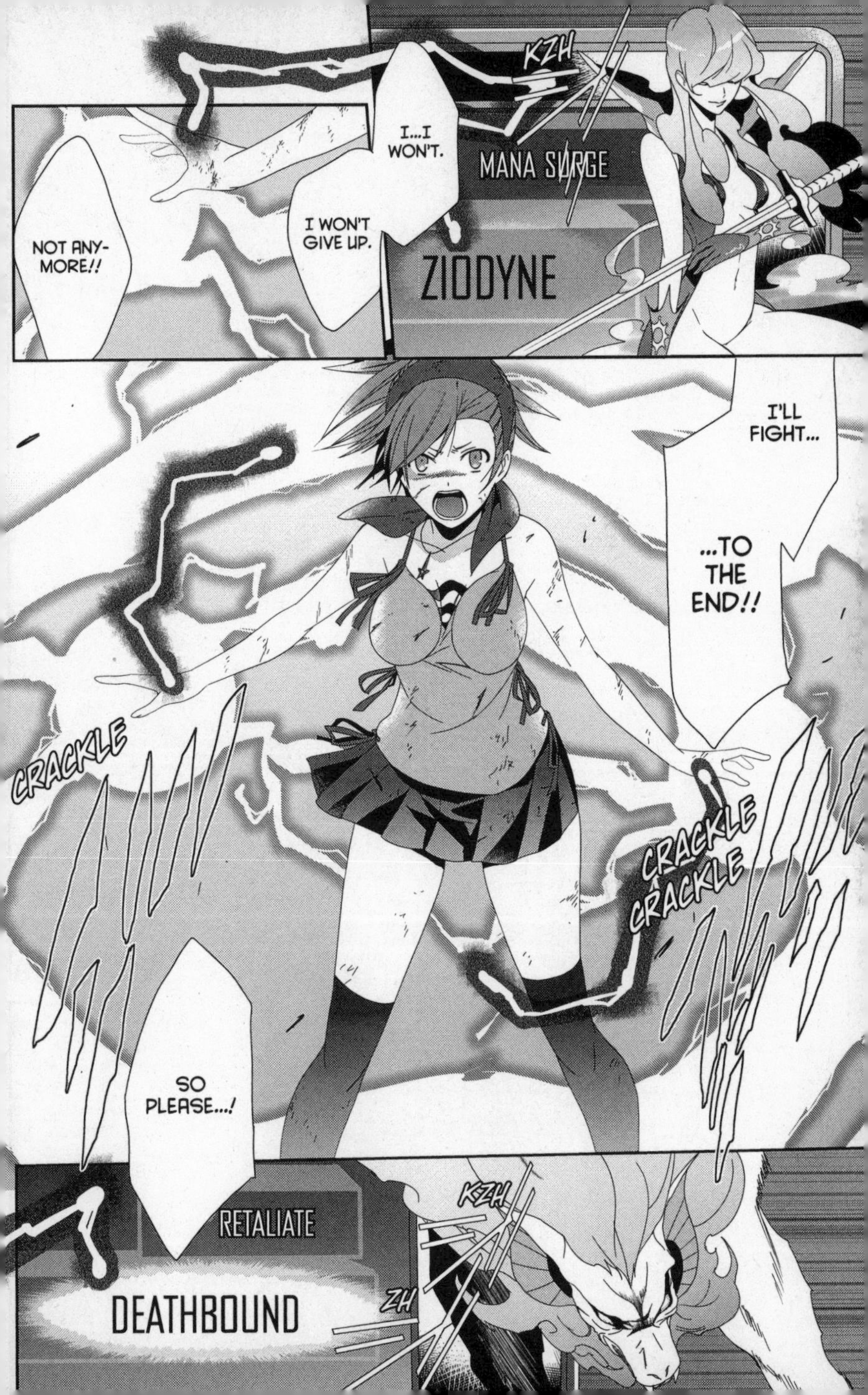
KZH
MANA SURGE
ZIODYNE
I...I WON'T.
I WON'T GIVE UP.
NOT ANY-MORE!!
I'LL FIGHT...
...TO THE END!!
CRACKLE CRACKLE
CRACKLE
SO PLEASE...!
KZH
RETALIATE
ZH
DEATHBOUND

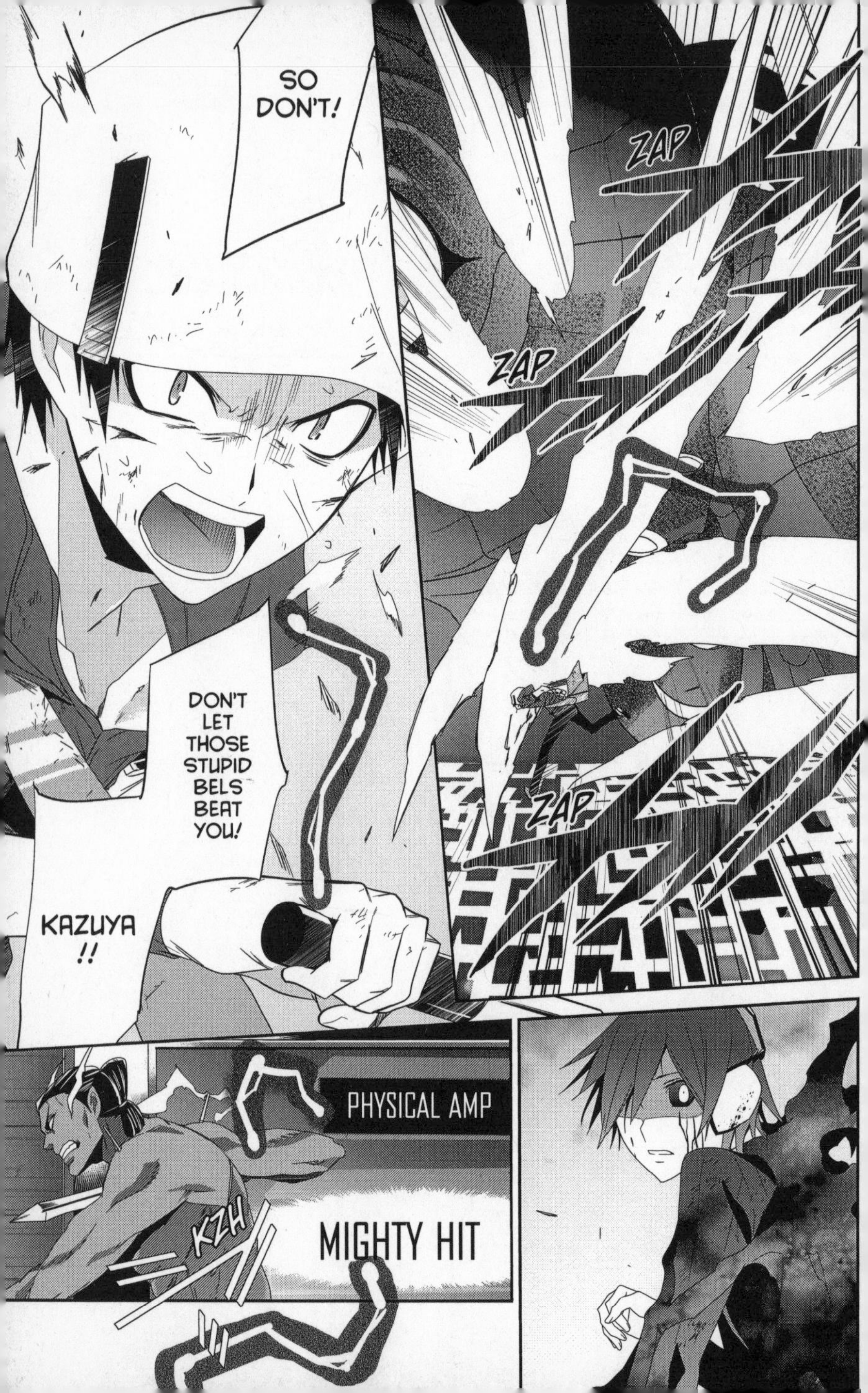
ZAP
ZAP
ZAP
SO DON'T!
DON'T LET THOSE STUPID BELS BEAT YOU!
KAZUYA !!
PHYSICAL AMP
MIGHTY HIT
KZH

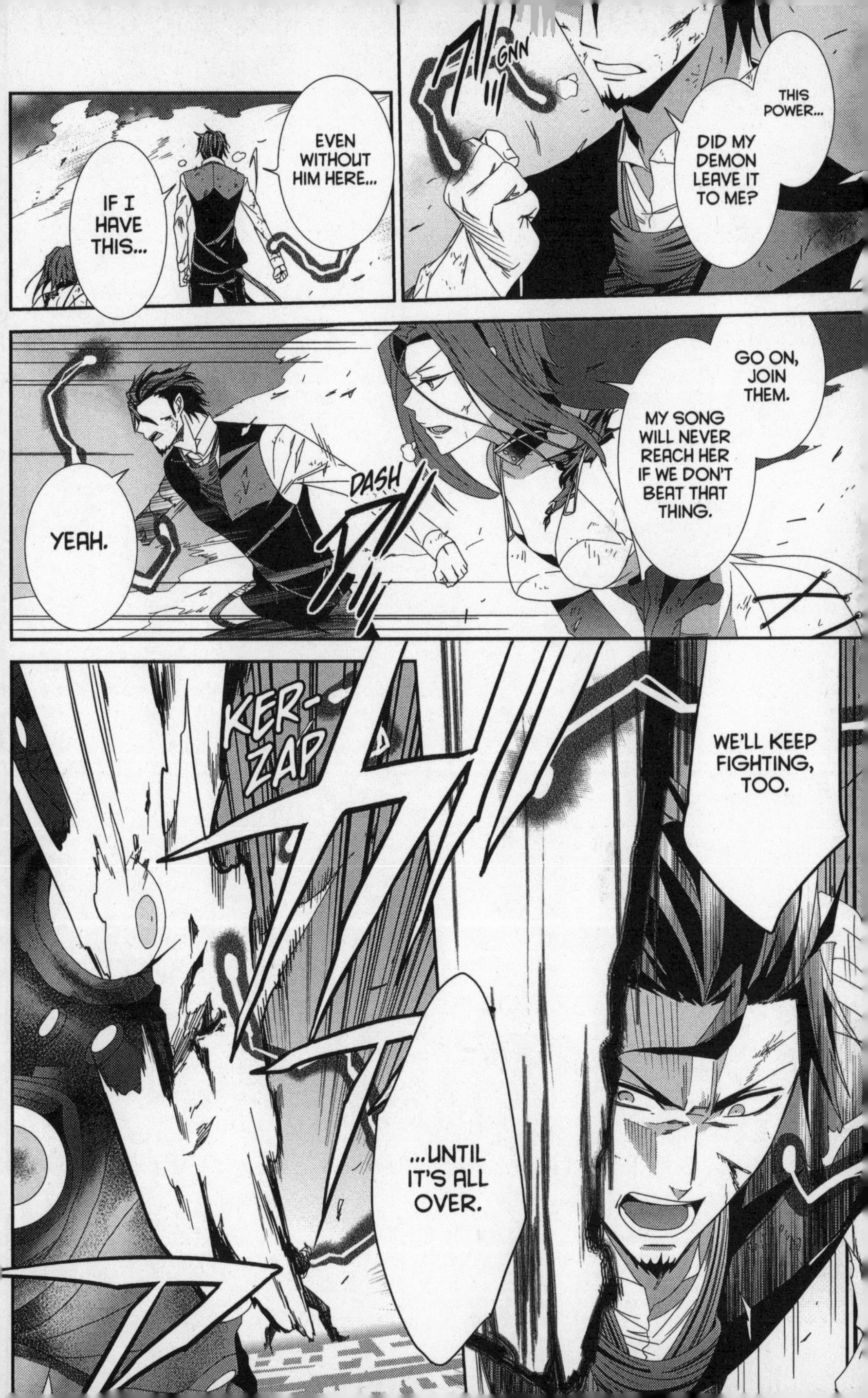
GNN
THIS POWER...
DID MY DEMON LEAVE IT TO ME?
EVEN WITHOUT HIM HERE...
IF I HAVE THIS...
GO ON, JOIN THEM.
MY SONG WILL NEVER REACH HER IF WE DON'T BEAT THAT THING.
DASH
YEAH.
KER-ZAP
WE'LL KEEP FIGHTING, TOO.
...UNTIL IT'S ALL OVER.

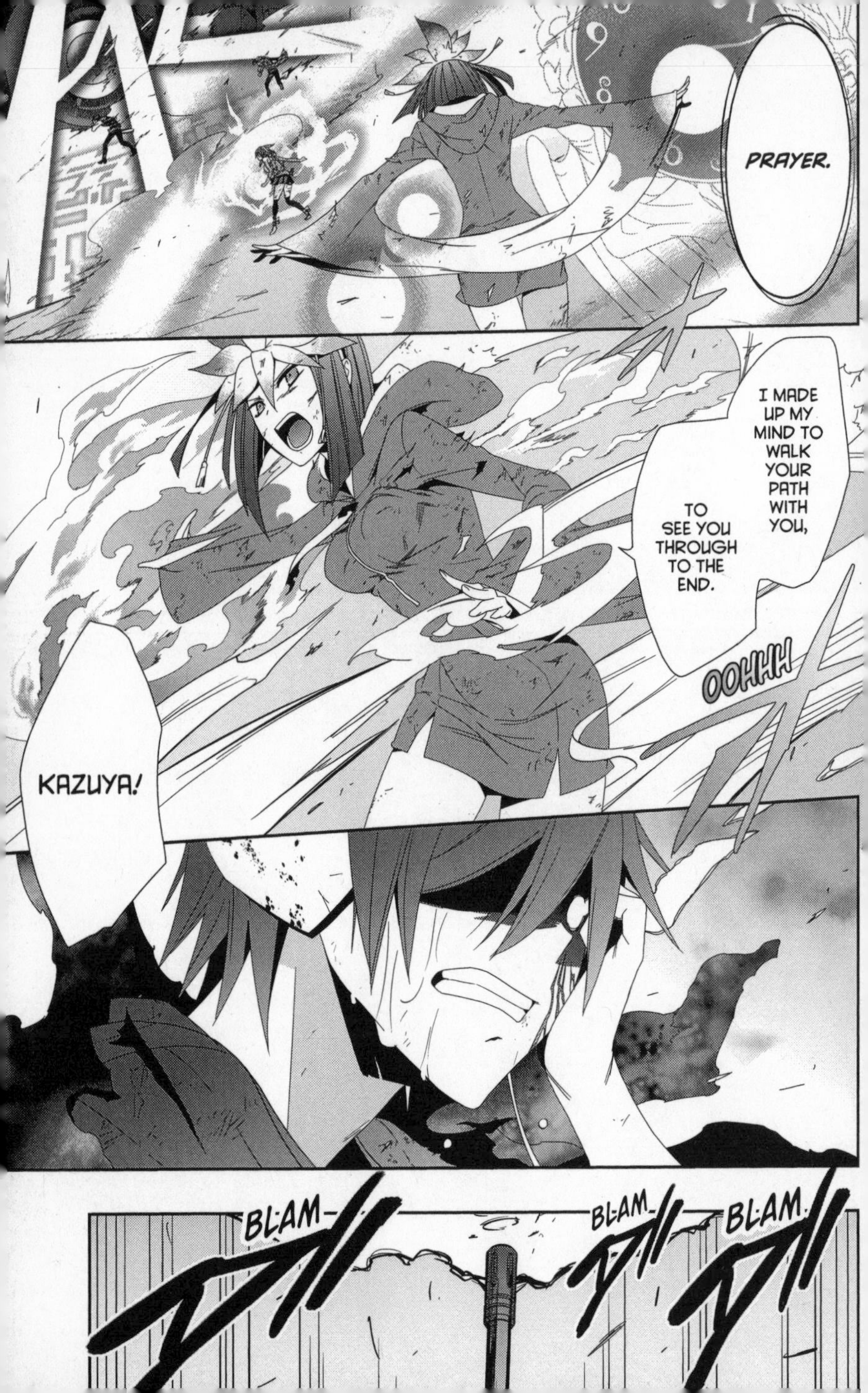
PRAYER.
I MADE UP MY MIND TO WALK YOUR PATH WITH YOU,
TO SEE YOU THROUGH TO THE END.
OOHHH
KAZUYA!
BLAM
BLAM
BLAM

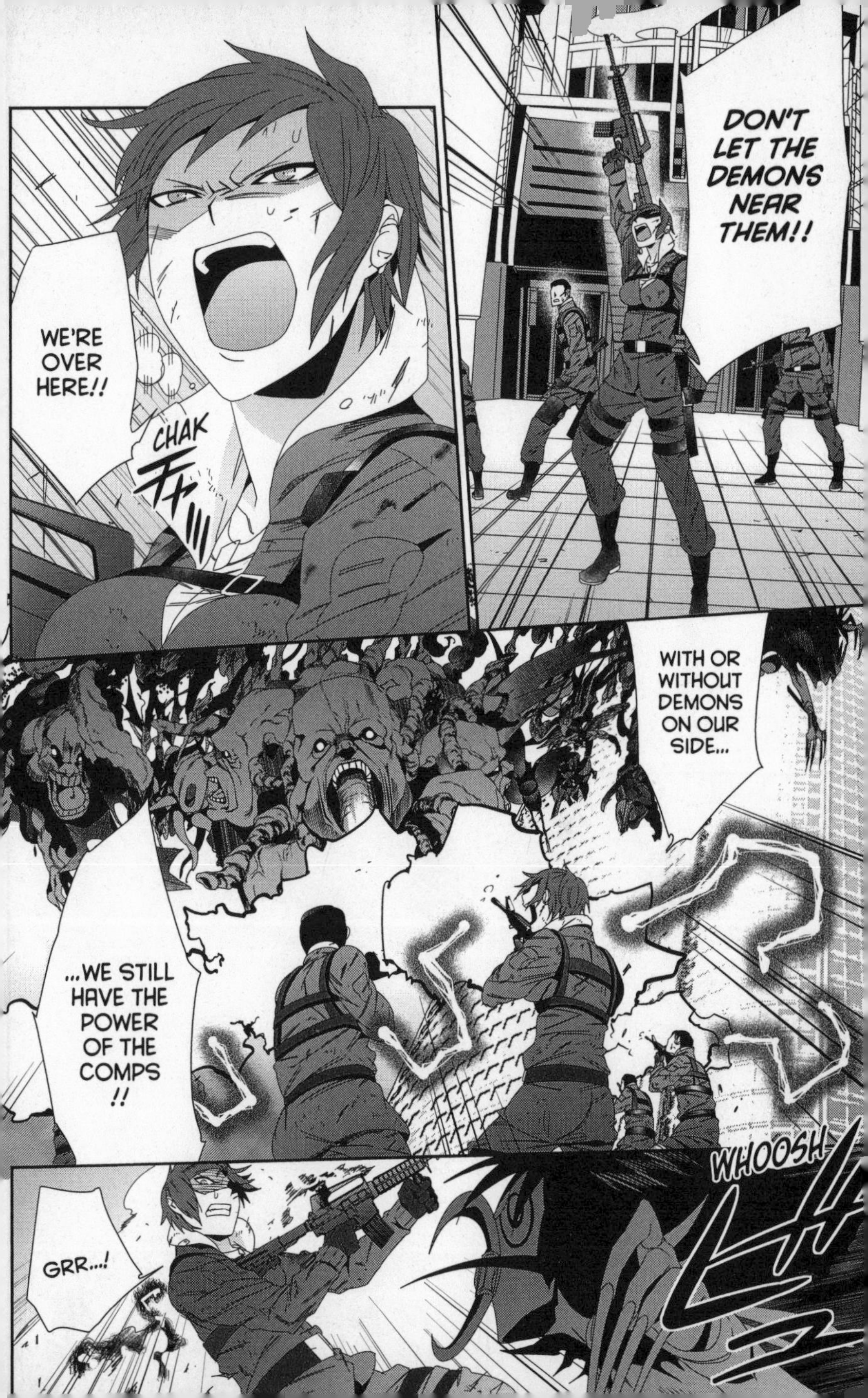
DON'T LET THE DEMONS NEAR THEM!!
WE'RE OVER HERE!!
CHAK
WITH OR WITHOUT DEMONS ON OUR SIDE...
...WE STILL HAVE THE POWER OF THE COMPS !!
WHOOSH
GRR...!

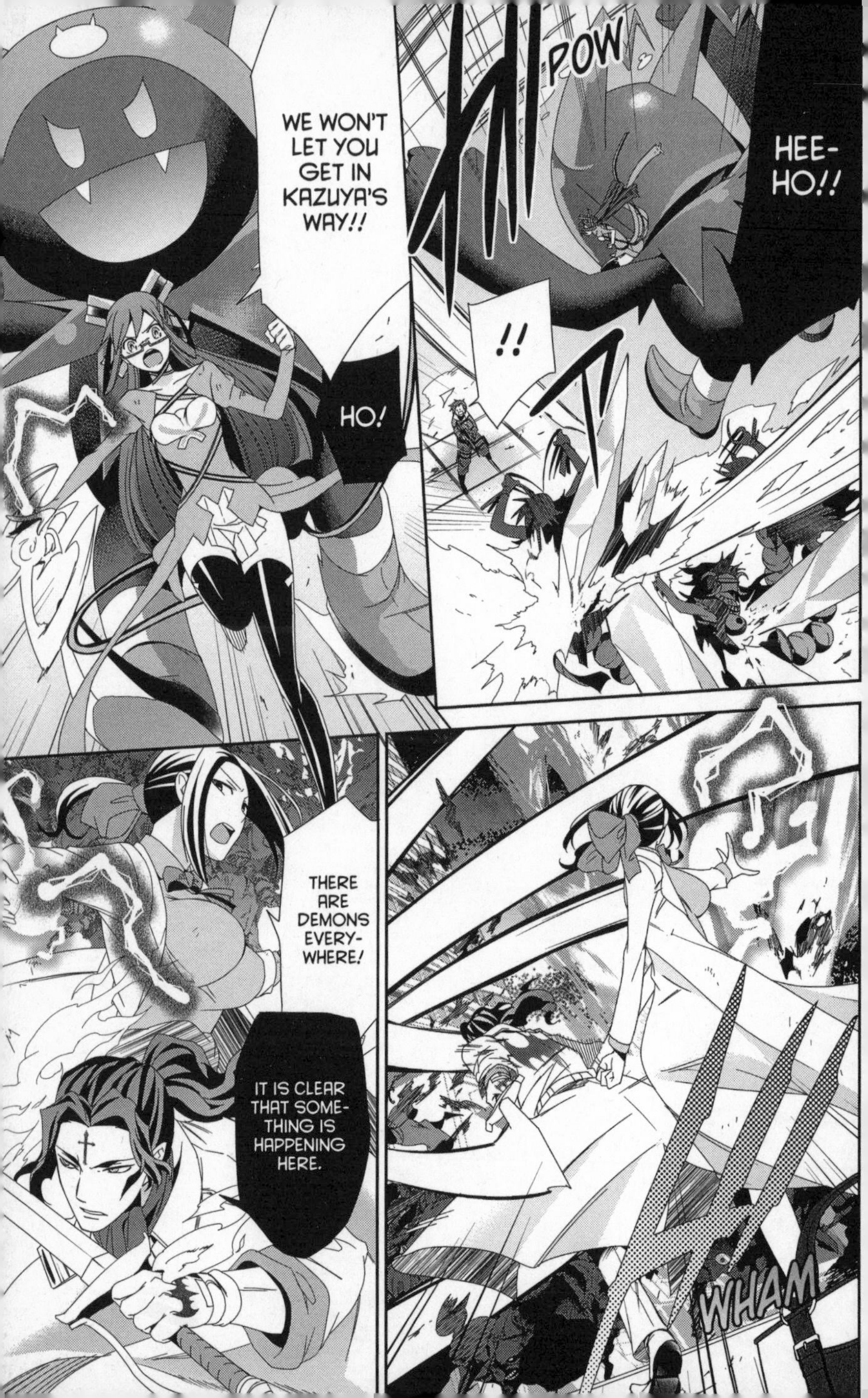

POW
HEE-HO!!
!!
WE WON'T LET YOU GET IN KAZUYA'S WAY!!
HO!
WHAM
THERE ARE DEMONS EVERYWHERE!
IT IS CLEAR THAT SOMETHING IS HAPPENING HERE.

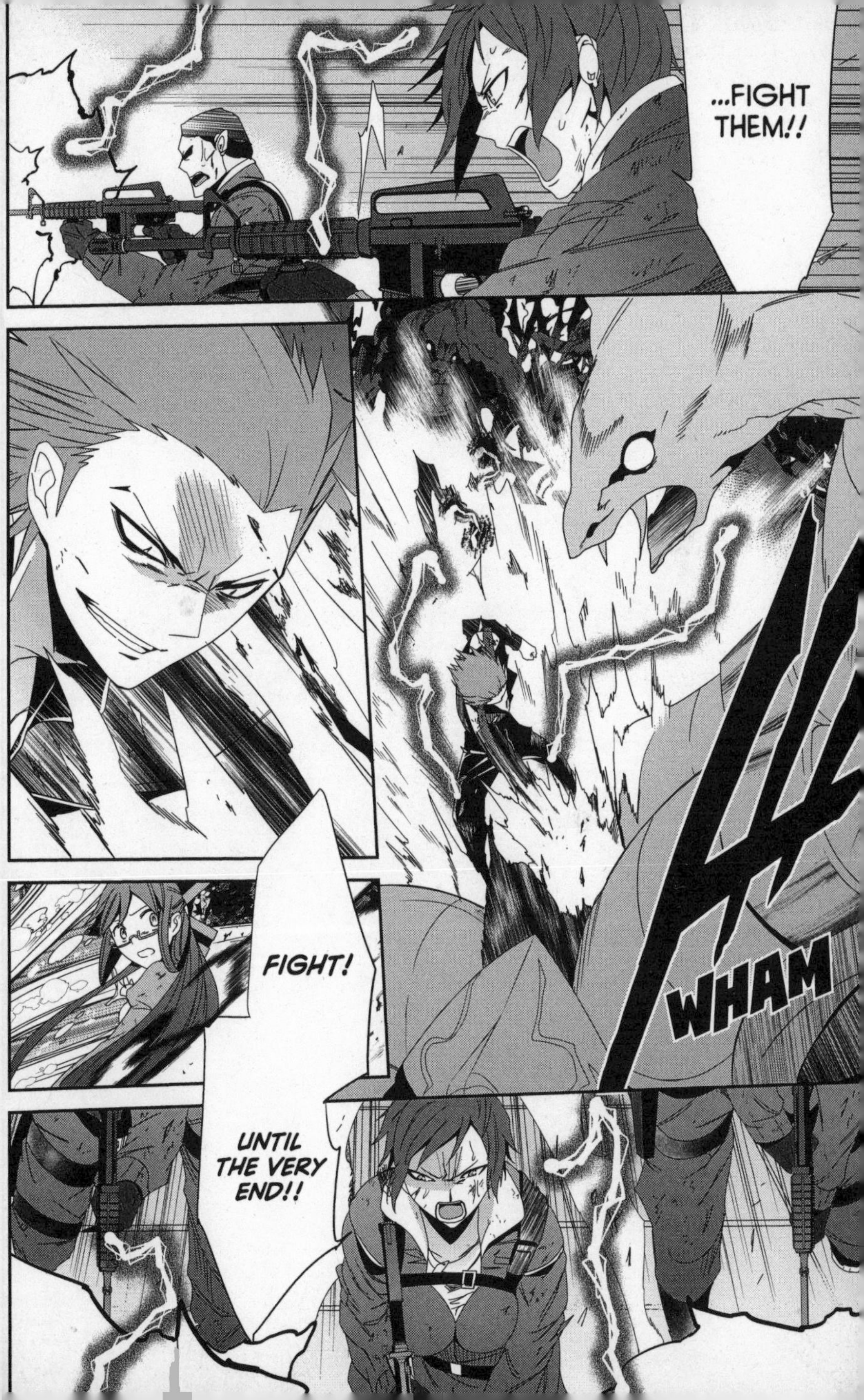
...FIGHT THEM!!
WHAM
FIGHT!
UNTIL THE VERY END!!

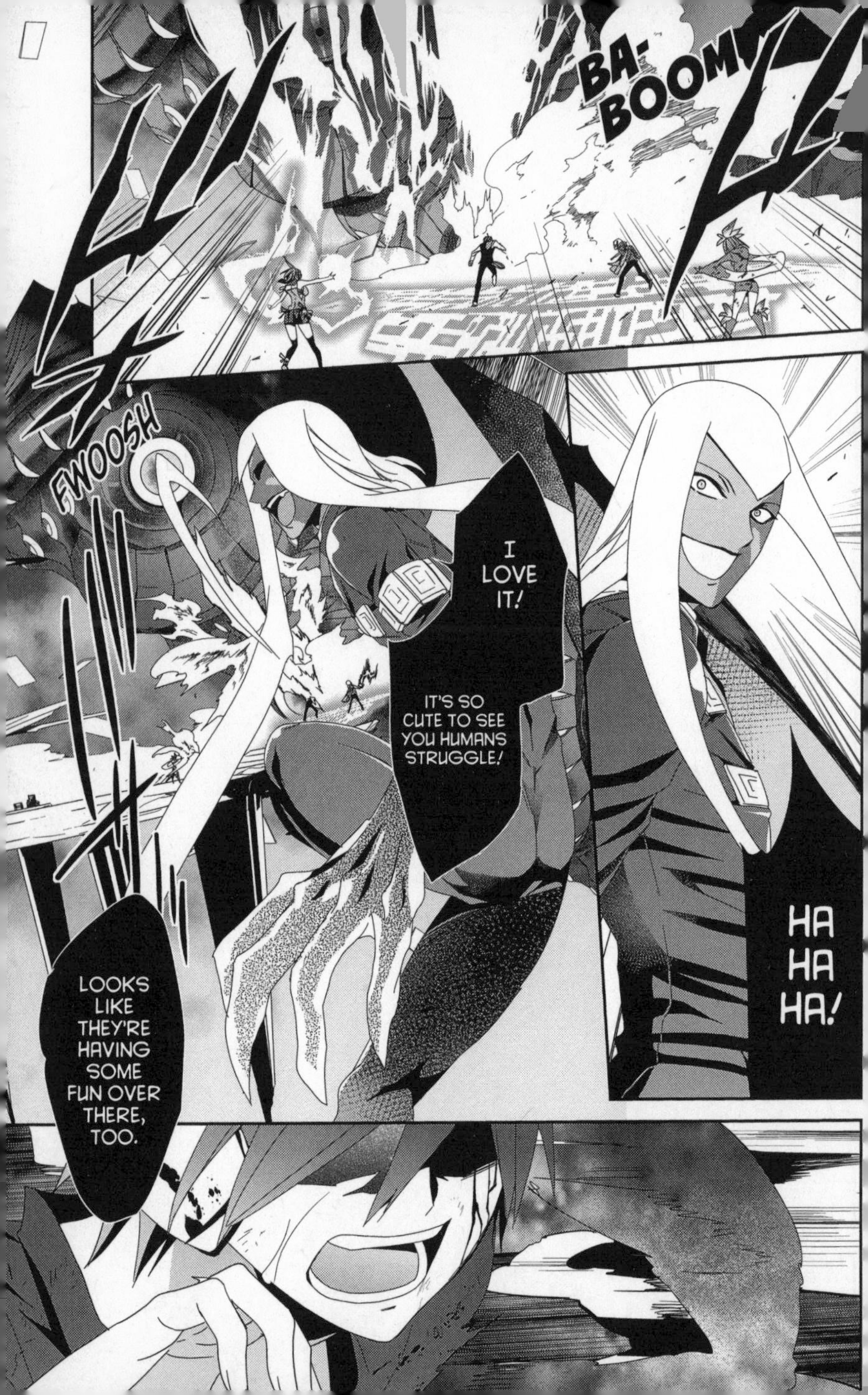
BA-BOOM
HA HA HA!
FWOOSH
I LOVE IT!
IT'S SO CUTE TO SEE YOU HUMANS STRUGGLE!
LOOKS LIKE THEY'RE HAVING SOME FUN OVER THERE, TOO.

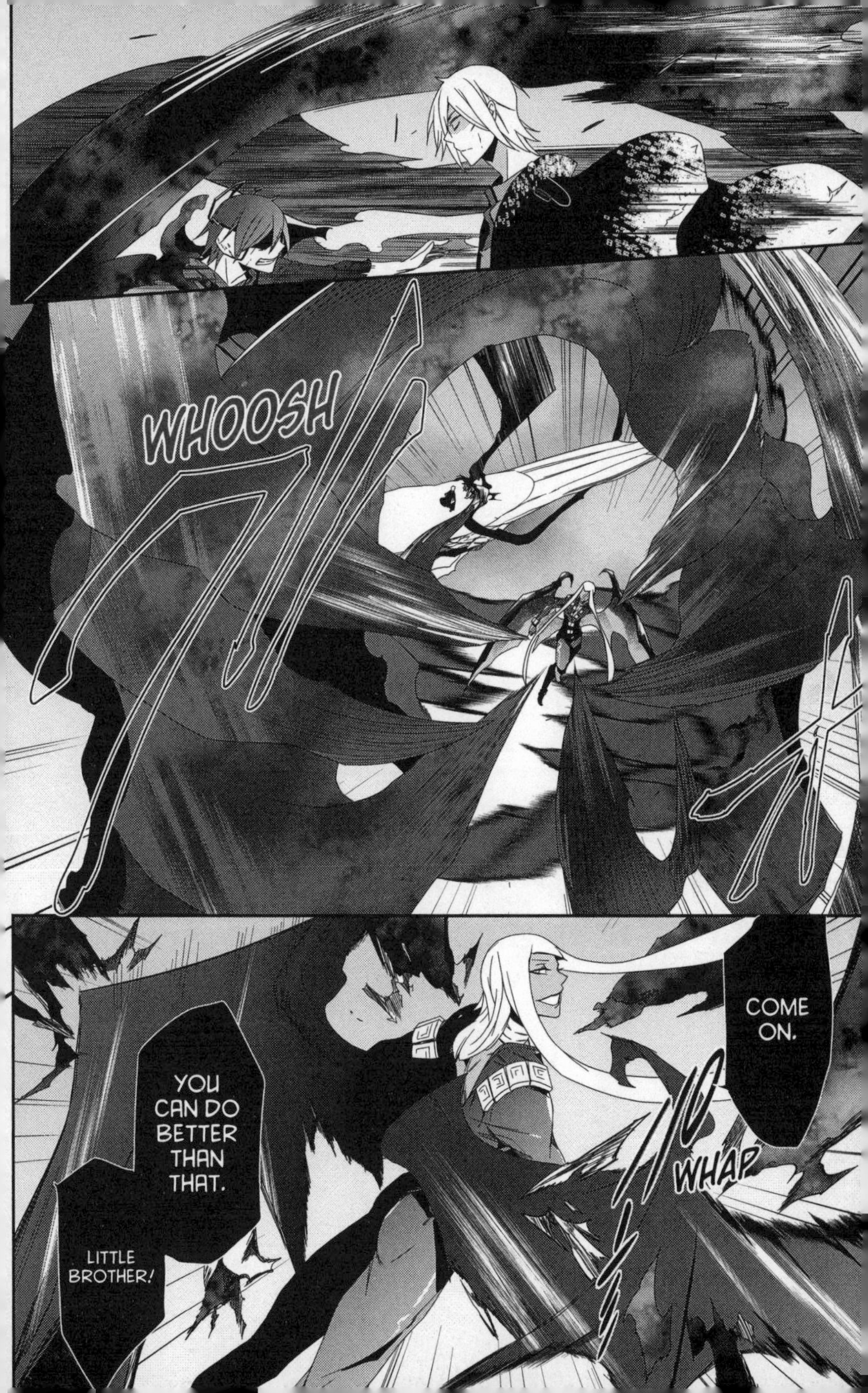
WHOOSH
COME ON.
YOU CAN DO BETTER THAN THAT.
LITTLE BROTHER!
WHAP

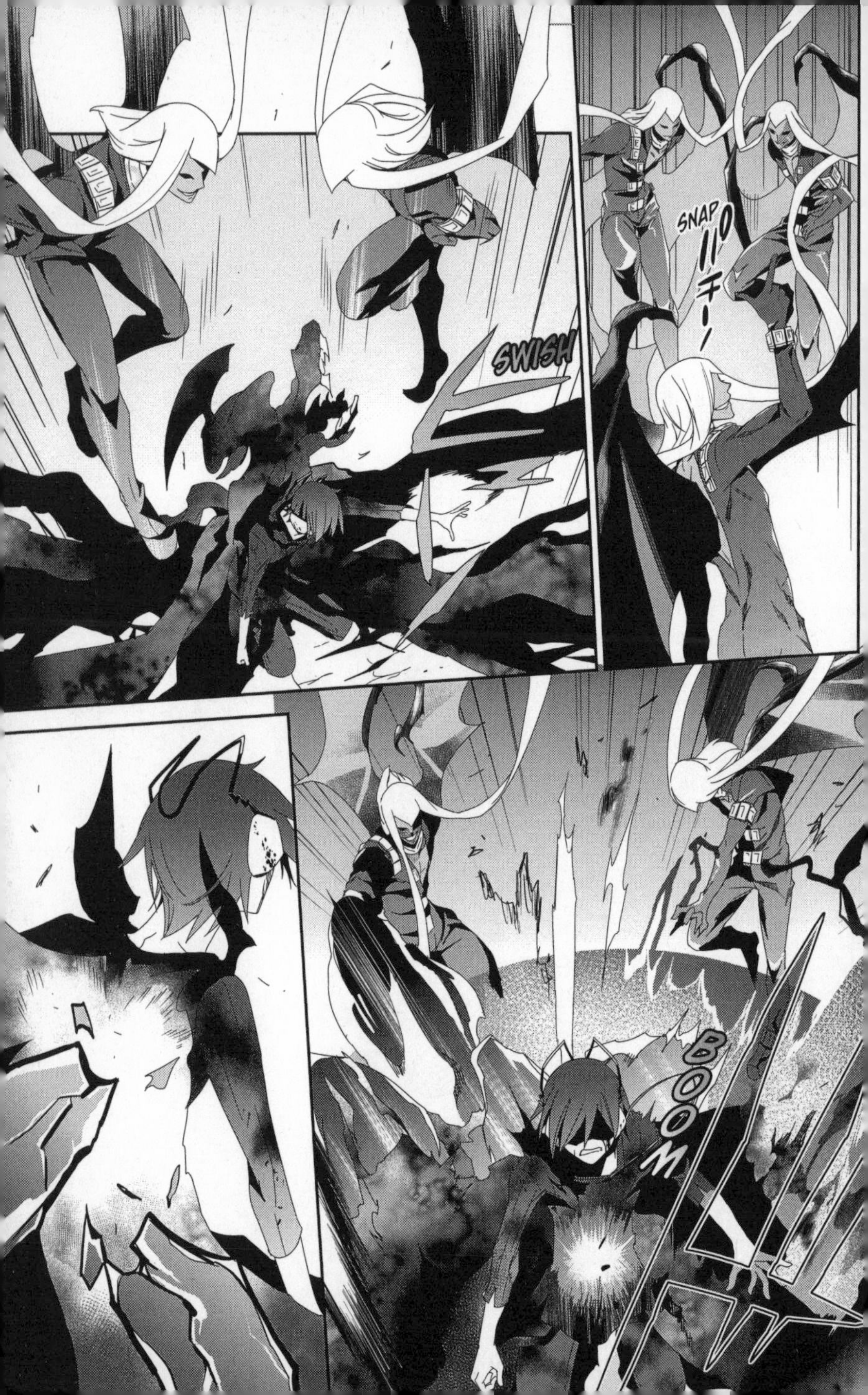
SNAP
パチーン
SWISH
BOOM

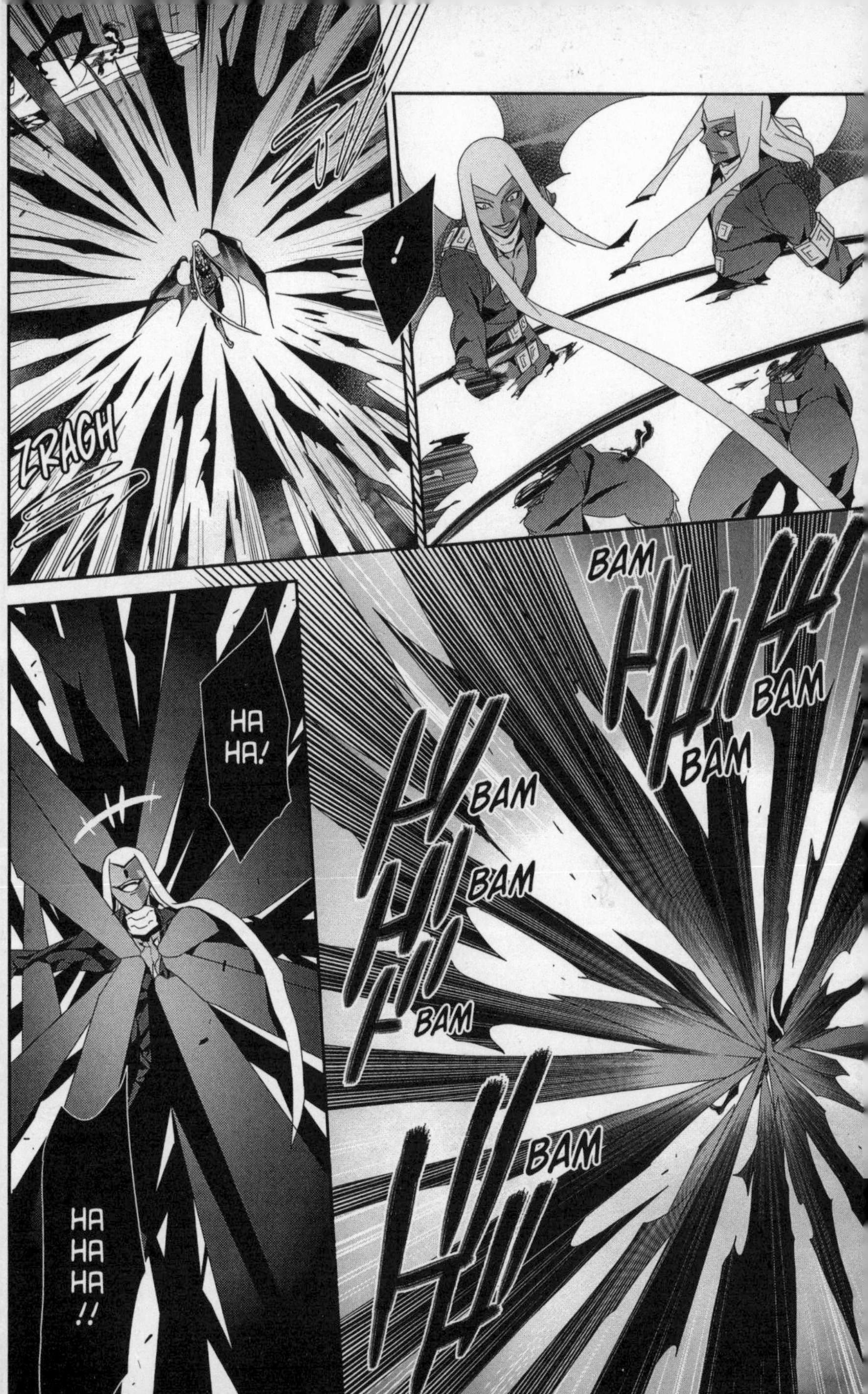
!
ZRAGH
BAM
BAM
BAM
BAM
BAM
BAM
BAM
HA HA!
HA HA HA!!

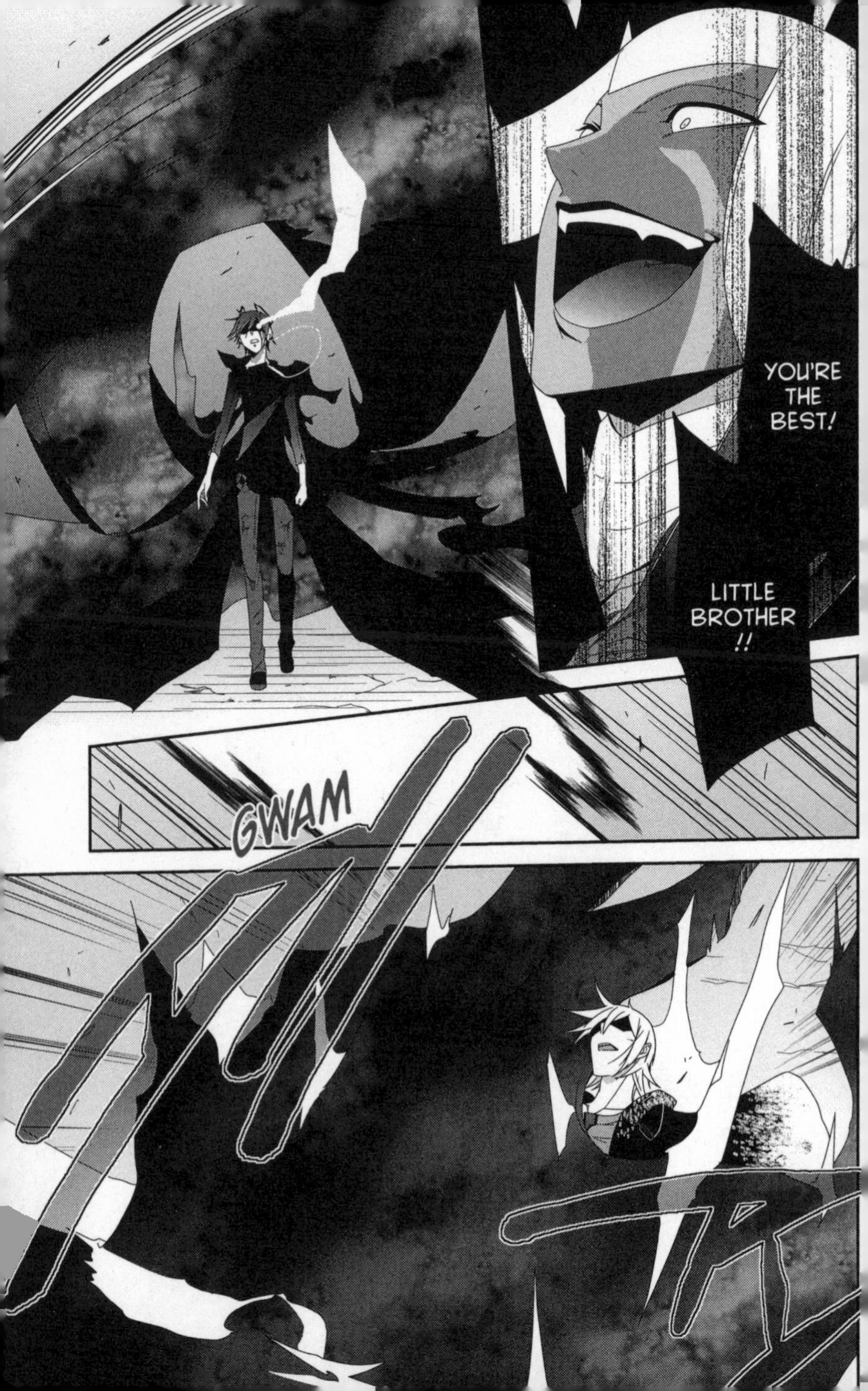
YOU'RE THE BEST!
LITTLE BROTHER !!
GWAM

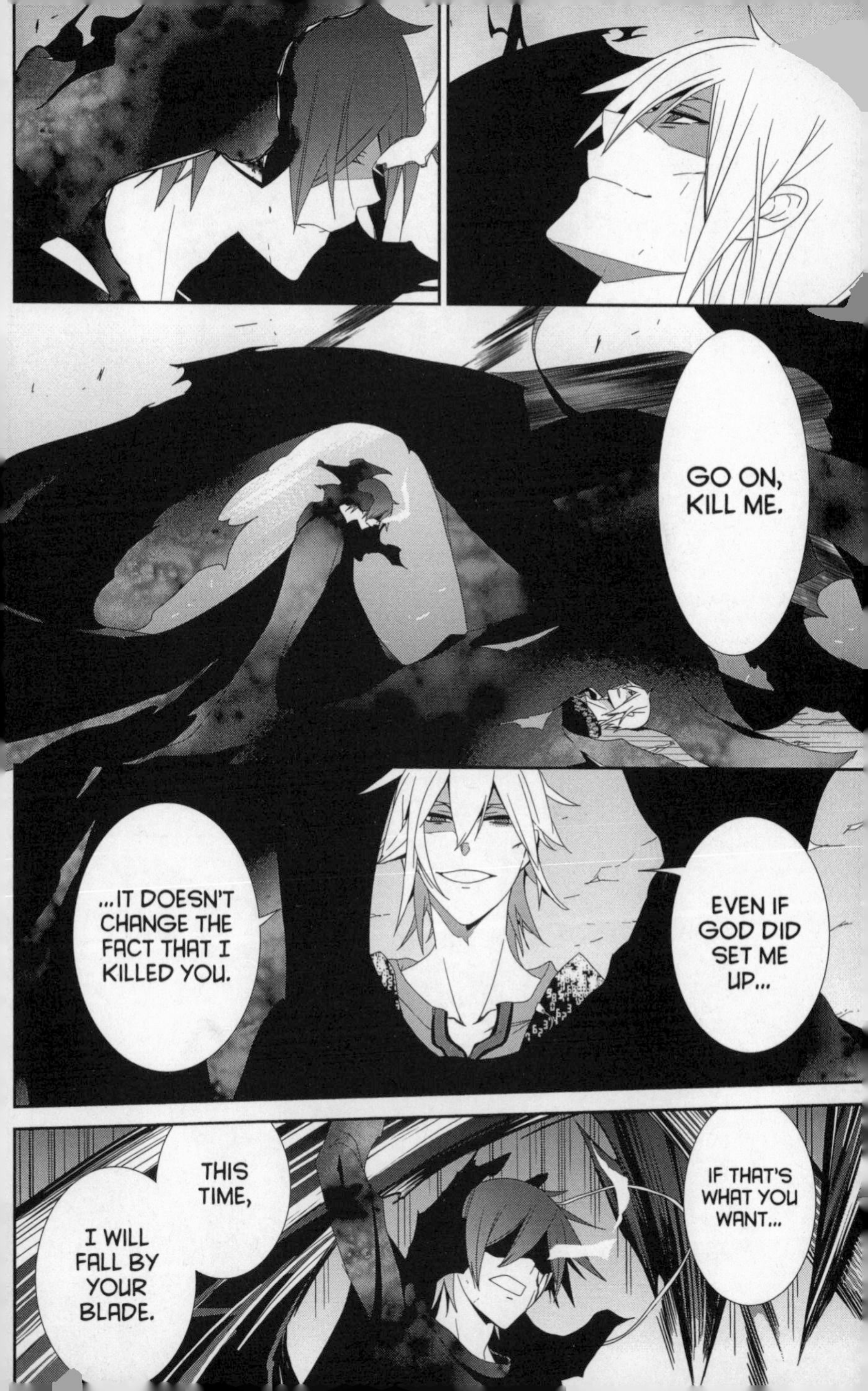
GO ON, KILL ME.
EVEN IF GOD DID SET ME UP...
...IT DOESN'T CHANGE THE FACT THAT I KILLED YOU.
IF THAT'S WHAT YOU WANT...
THIS TIME,
I WILL FALL BY YOUR BLADE.

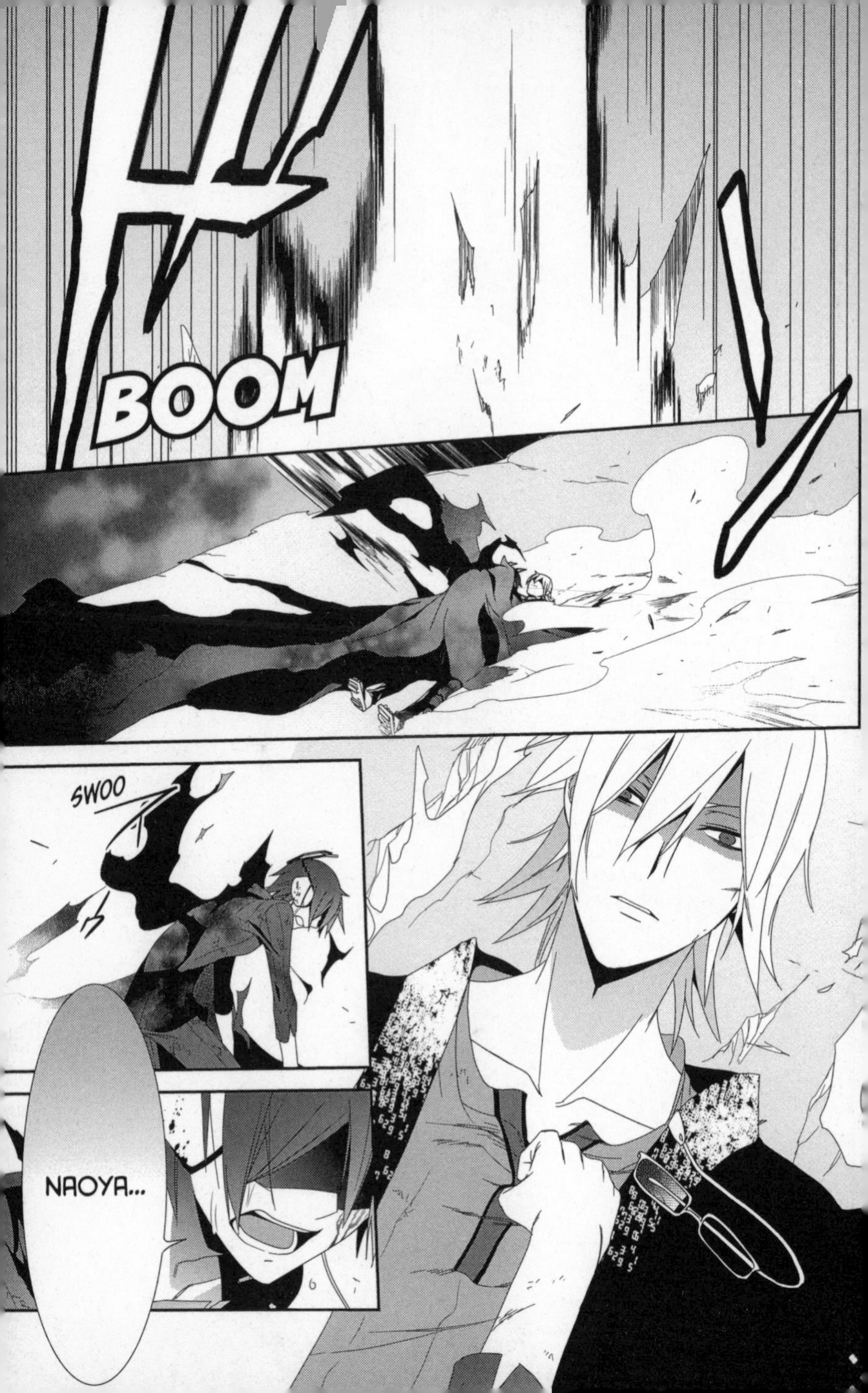
BOOM
SWOO
NAOYA...

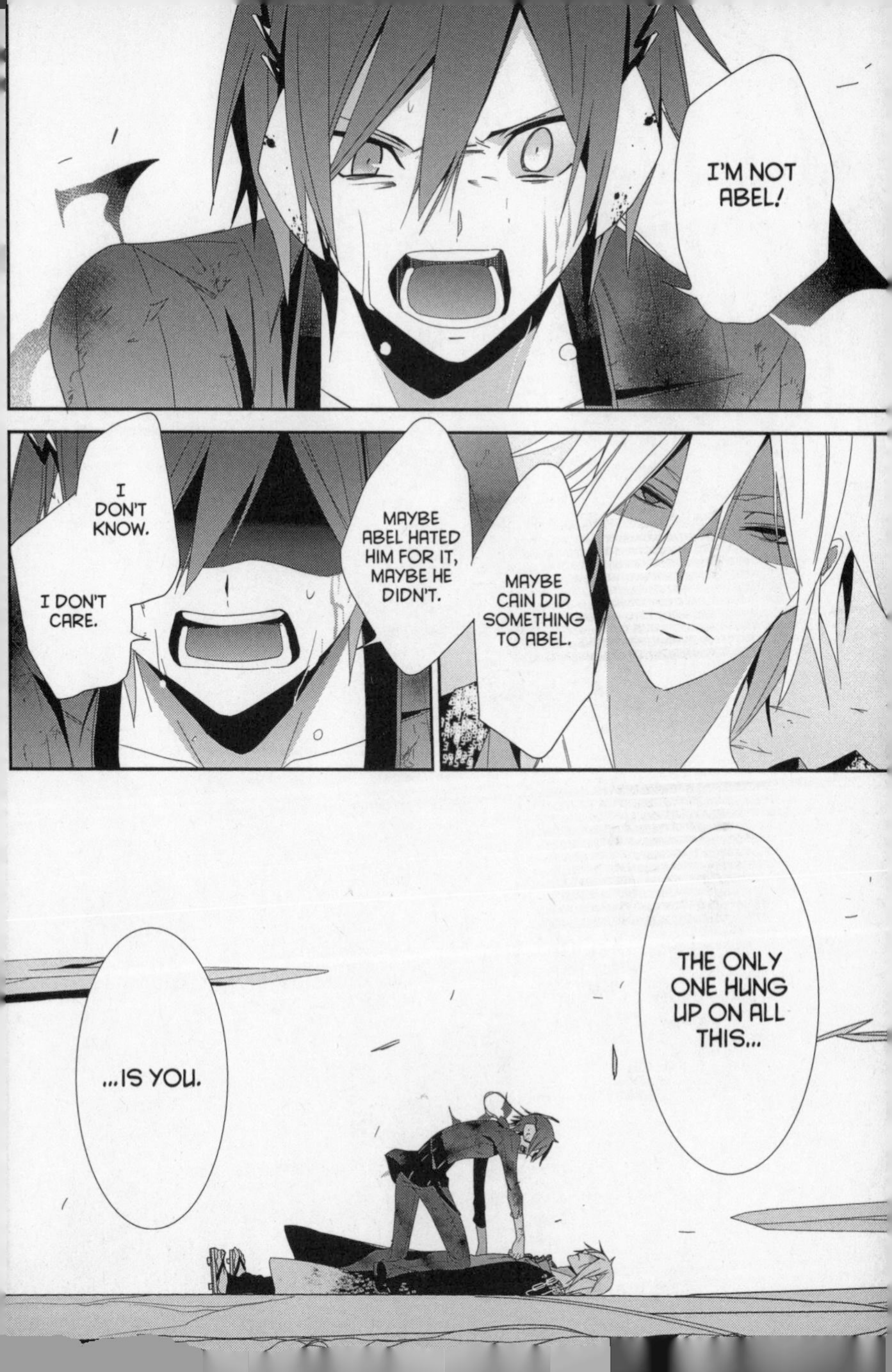
I'M NOT ABEL!
MAYBE CAIN DID SOMETHING TO ABEL.
MAYBE ABEL HATED HIM FOR IT, MAYBE HE DIDN'T.
I DON'T KNOW.
I DON'T CARE.
THE ONLY ONE HUNG UP ON ALL THIS...
...IS YOU.

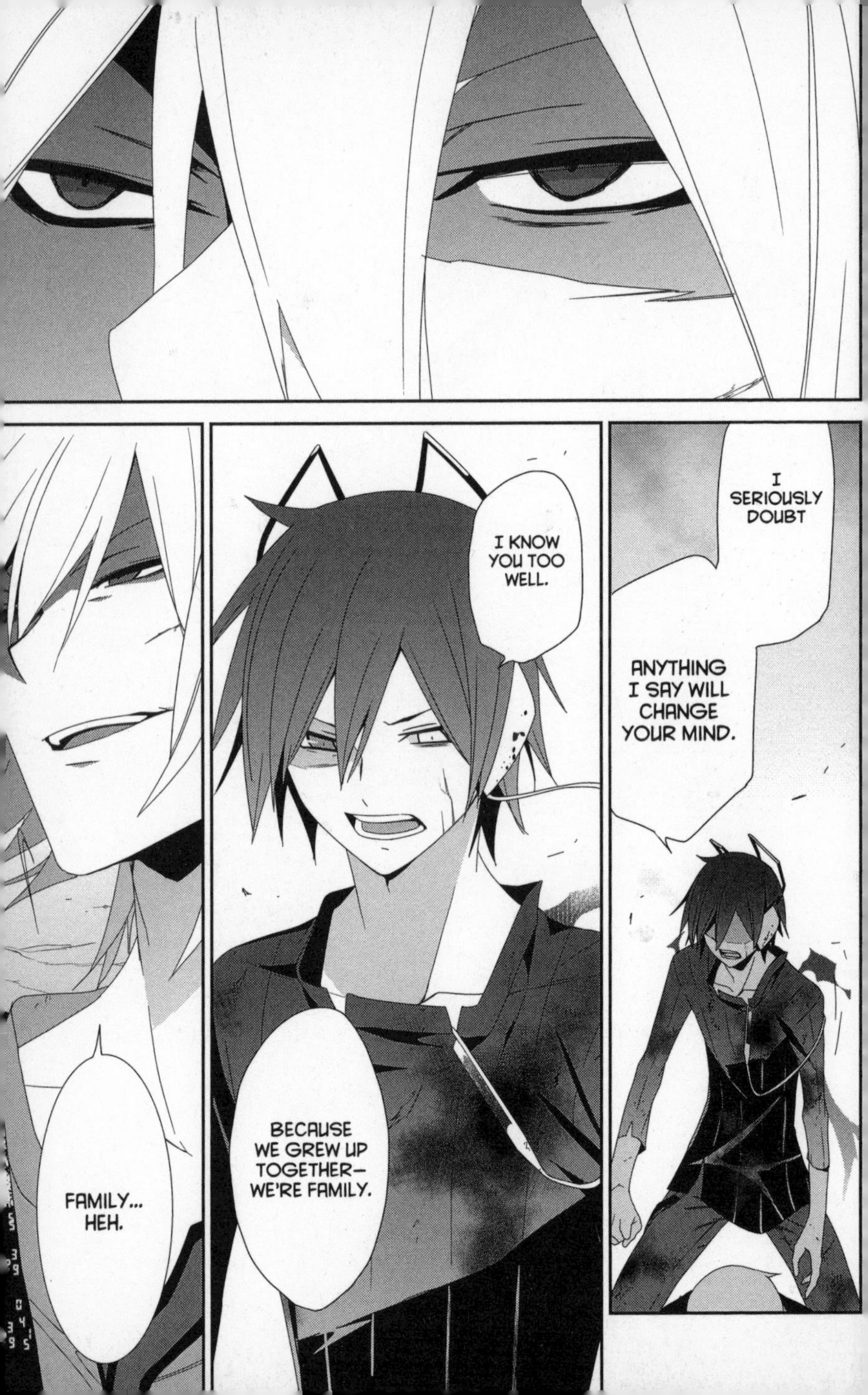
I SERIOUSLY DOUBT
ANYTHING I SAY WILL CHANGE YOUR MIND.
I KNOW YOU TOO WELL.
BECAUSE WE GREW UP TOGETHER— WE'RE FAMILY.
FAMILY... HEH.

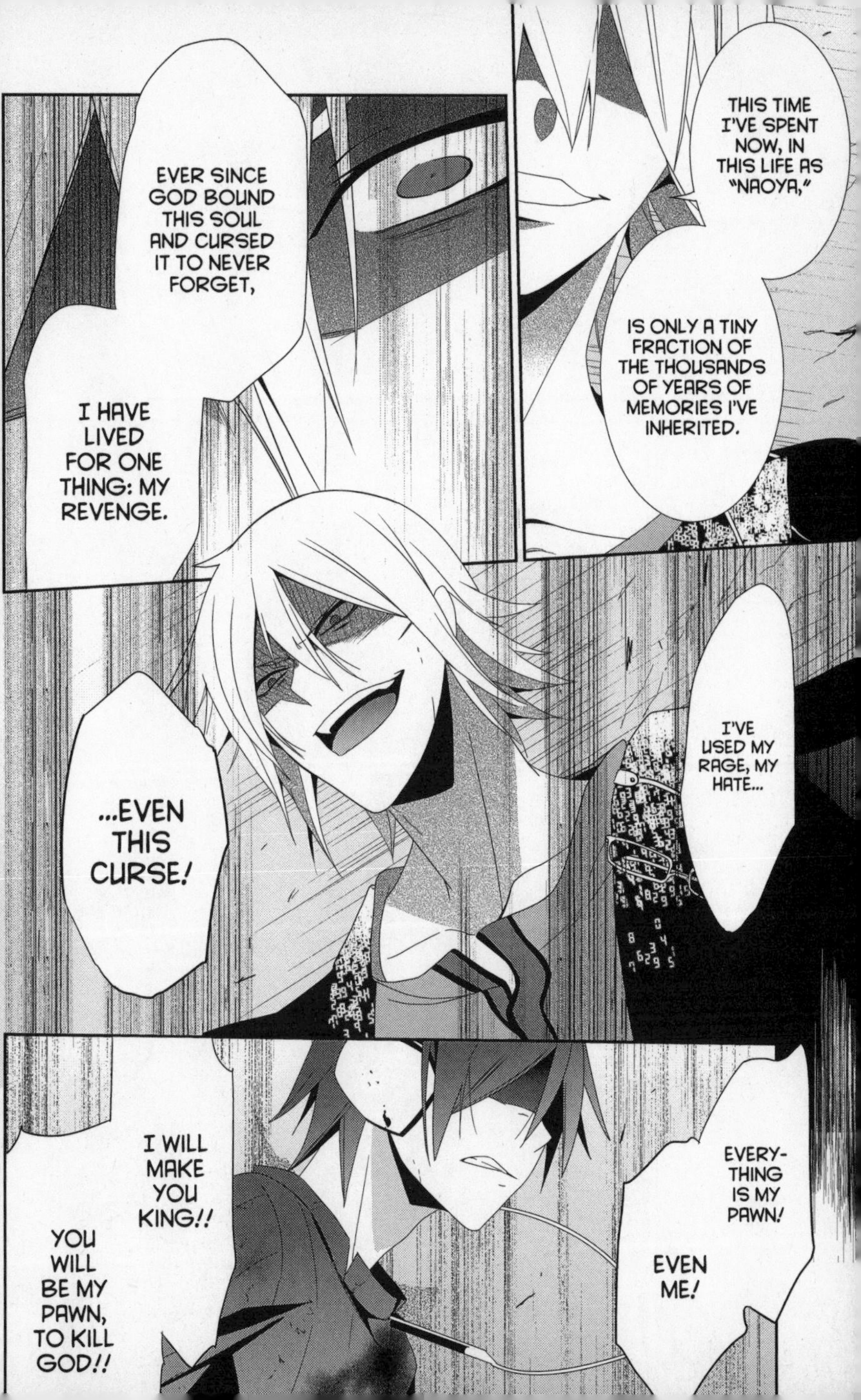
THIS TIME I'VE SPENT NOW, IN THIS LIFE AS "NAOYA,"
IS ONLY A TINY FRACTION OF THE THOUSANDS OF YEARS OF MEMORIES I'VE INHERITED.
EVER SINCE GOD BOUND THIS SOUL AND CURSED IT TO NEVER FORGET,
I HAVE LIVED FOR ONE THING: MY REVENGE.
I'VE USED MY RAGE, MY HATE...
...EVEN THIS CURSE!
EVERY-THING IS MY PAWN!
EVEN ME!
I WILL MAKE YOU KING!!
YOU WILL BE MY PAWN, TO KILL GOD!!

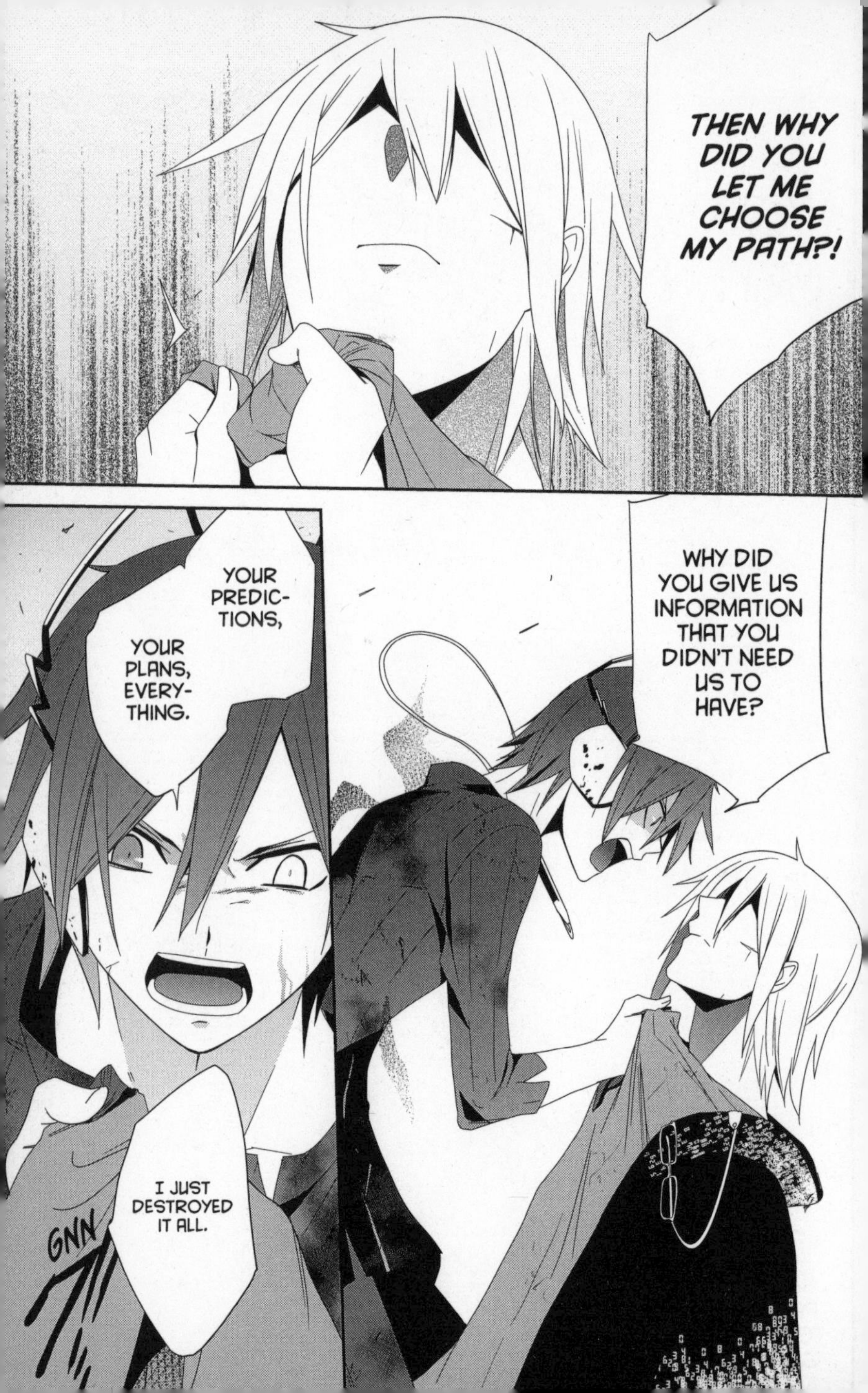
THEN WHY DID YOU LET ME CHOOSE MY PATH?!
WHY DID YOU GIVE US INFORMATION THAT YOU DIDN'T NEED US TO HAVE?
YOUR PREDIC-TIONS,
YOUR PLANS, EVERY-THING.
I JUST DESTROYED IT ALL.
GNN

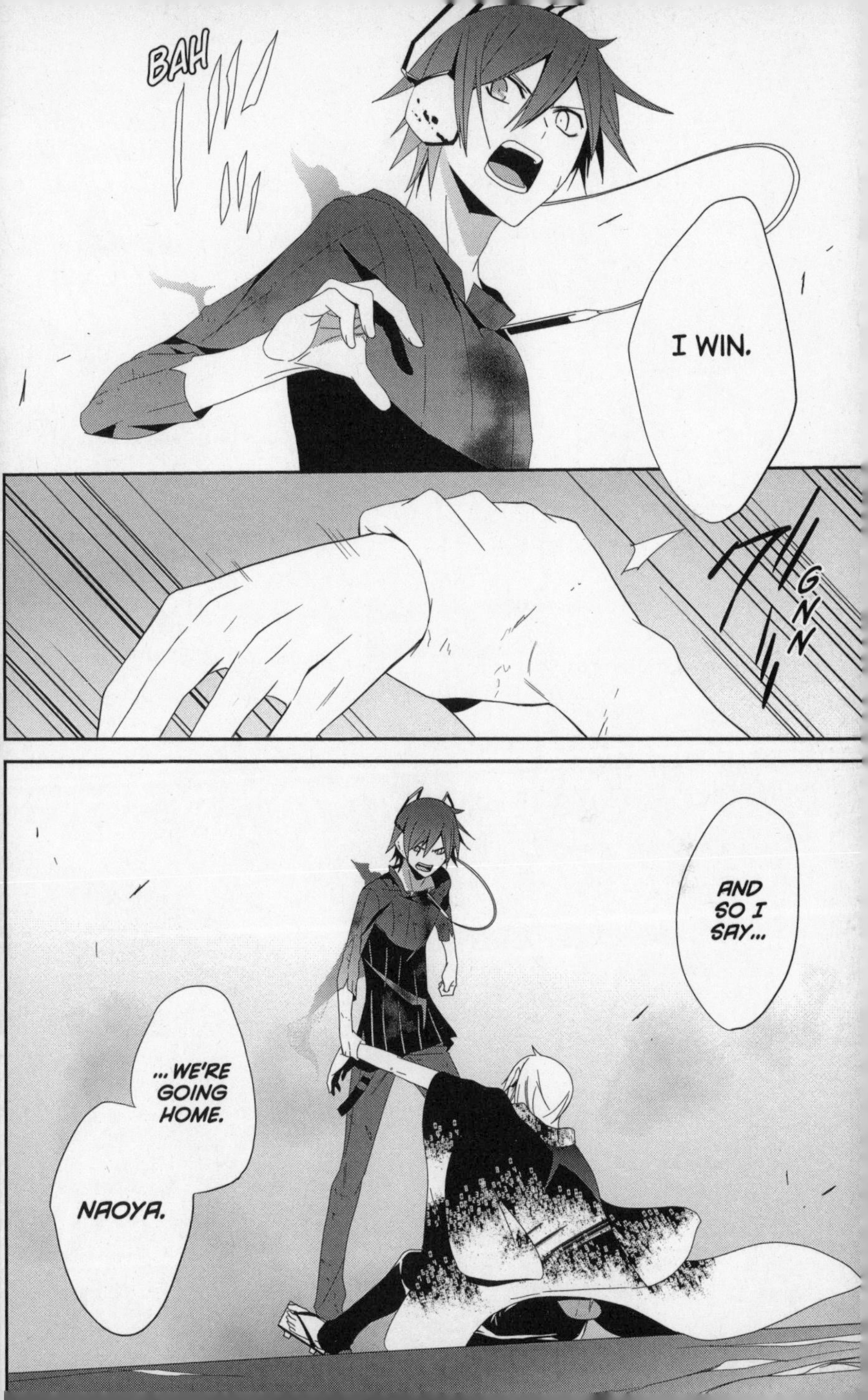
BAH
I WIN.
GNN
AND SO I SAY...
...WE'RE GOING HOME.
NAOYA.

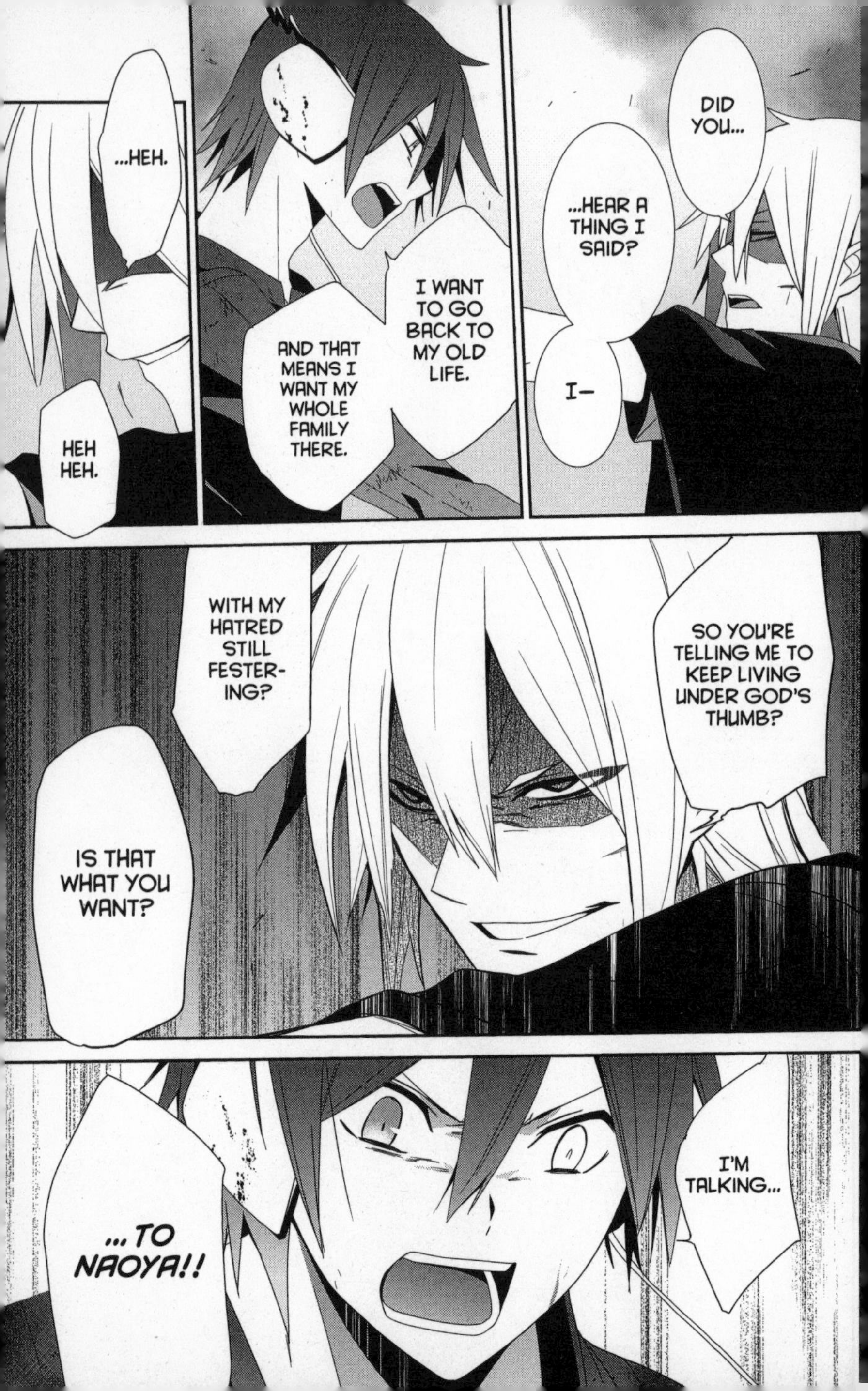
DID YOU...
...HEAR A THING I SAID?
I—
I WANT TO GO BACK TO MY OLD LIFE.
AND THAT MEANS I WANT MY WHOLE FAMILY THERE.
...HEH.
HEH HEH.
SO YOU'RE TELLING ME TO KEEP LIVING UNDER GOD'S THUMB?
WITH MY HATRED STILL FESTER-ING?
IS THAT WHAT YOU WANT?
I'M TALKING...
...TO NAOYA!!

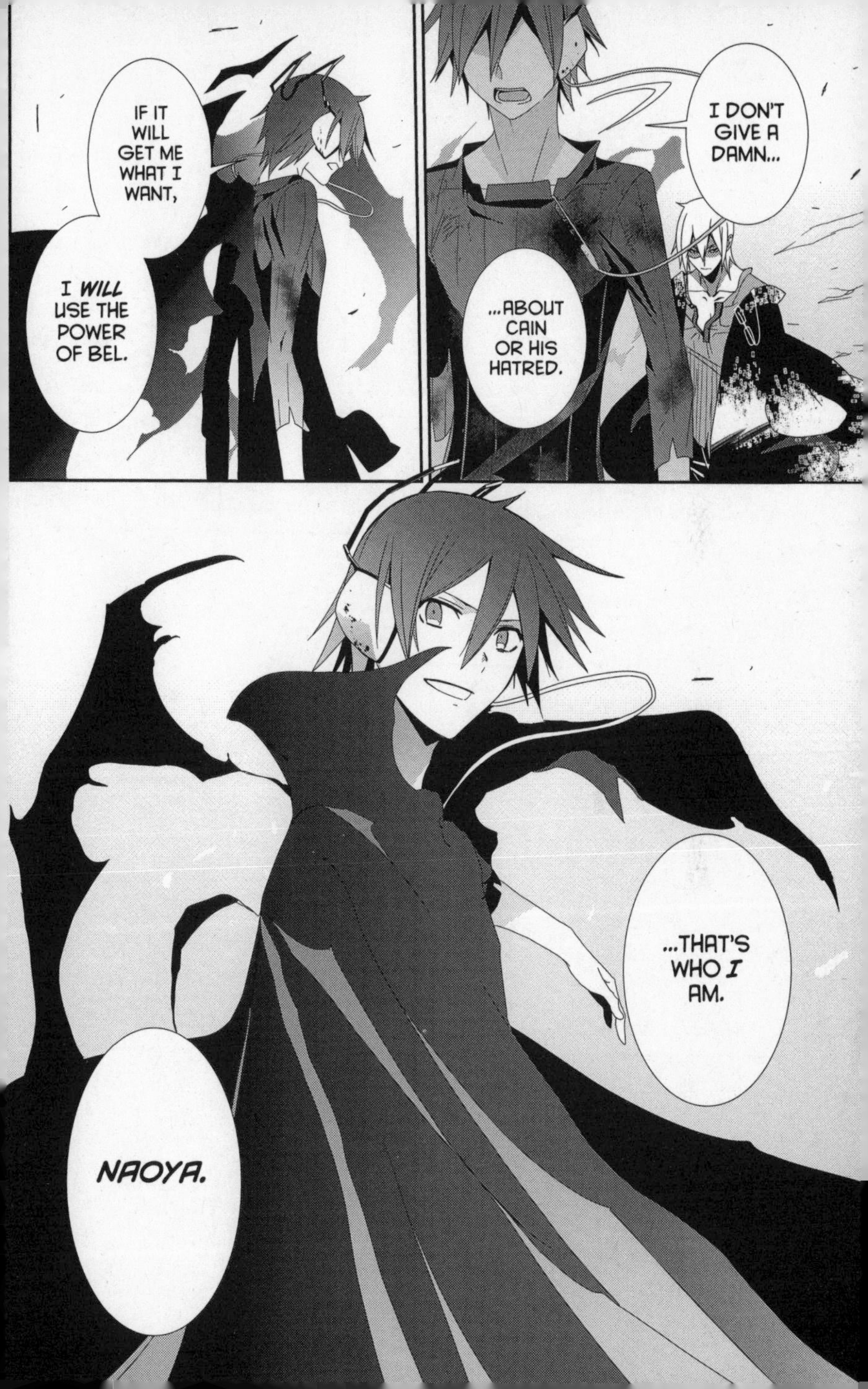
I DON'T GIVE A DAMN...
...ABOUT CAIN OR HIS HATRED.
IF IT WILL GET ME WHAT I WANT,
I *WILL* USE THE POWER OF BEL.
...THAT'S WHO *I* AM.
NAOYA.

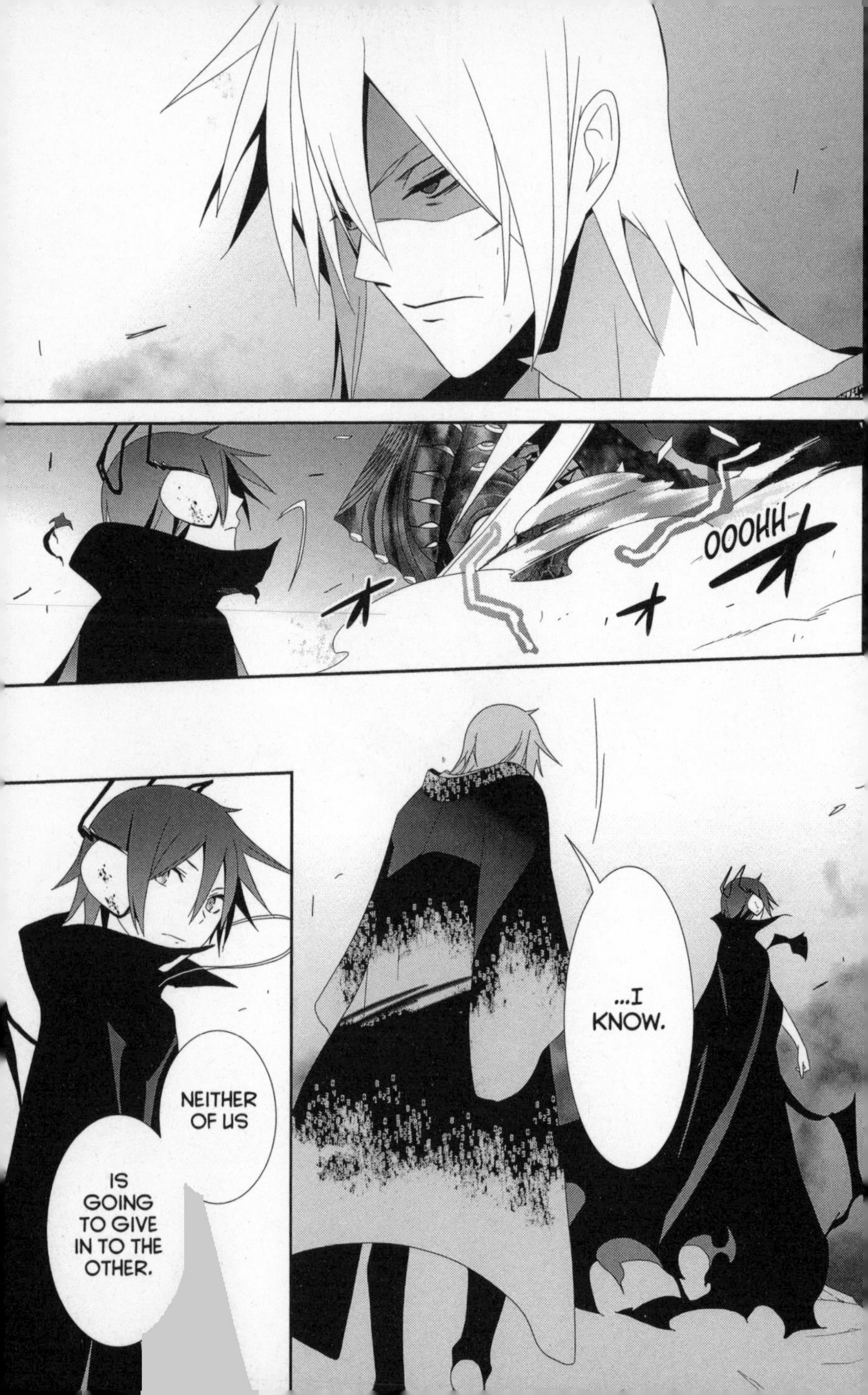
OOOHH
...I KNOW.
NEITHER OF US
IS GOING TO GIVE IN TO THE OTHER.

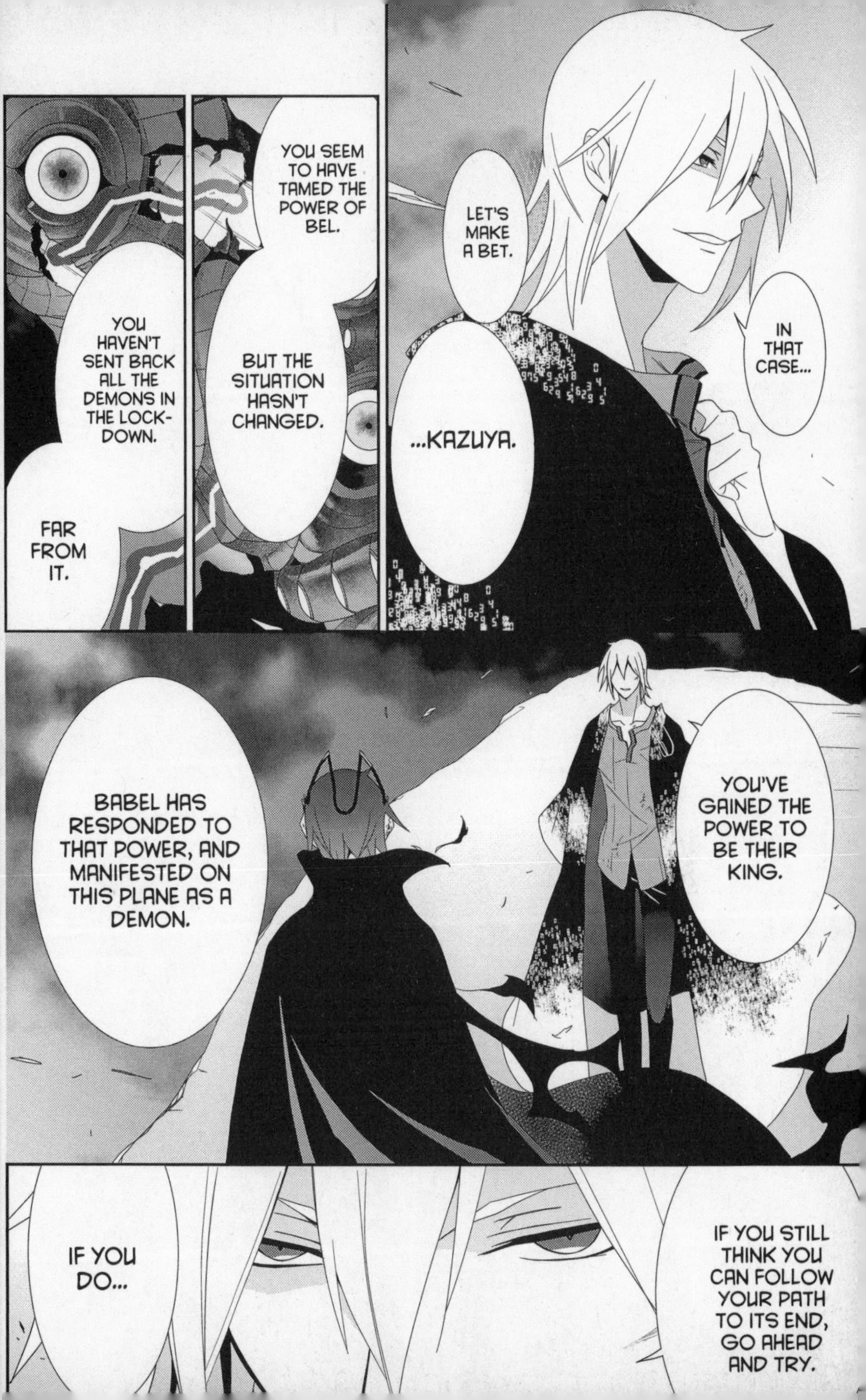
IN THAT CASE...
LET'S MAKE A BET.
...KAZUYA.
YOU SEEM TO HAVE TAMED THE POWER OF BEL.
BUT THE SITUATION HASN'T CHANGED.
YOU HAVEN'T SENT BACK ALL THE DEMONS IN THE LOCK-DOWN.
FAR FROM IT.
YOU'VE GAINED THE POWER TO BE THEIR KING.
BABEL HAS RESPONDED TO THAT POWER, AND MANIFESTED ON THIS PLANE AS A DEMON.
IF YOU STILL THINK YOU CAN FOLLOW YOUR PATH TO ITS END, GO AHEAD AND TRY.
IF YOU DO...

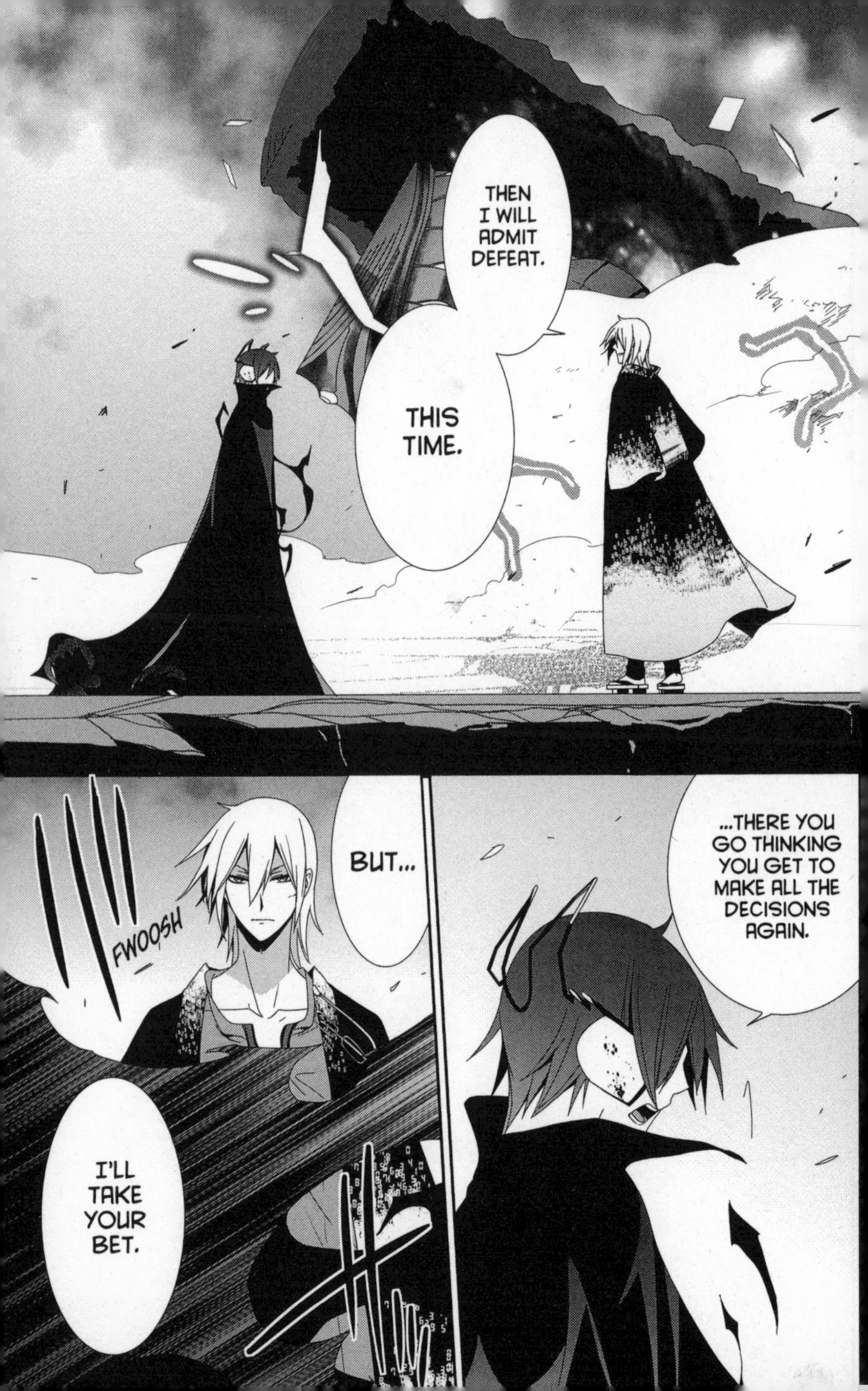
THEN I WILL ADMIT DEFEAT.
THIS TIME.
...THERE YOU GO THINKING YOU GET TO MAKE ALL THE DECISIONS AGAIN.
BUT...
FWOOSH
I'LL TAKE YOUR BET.

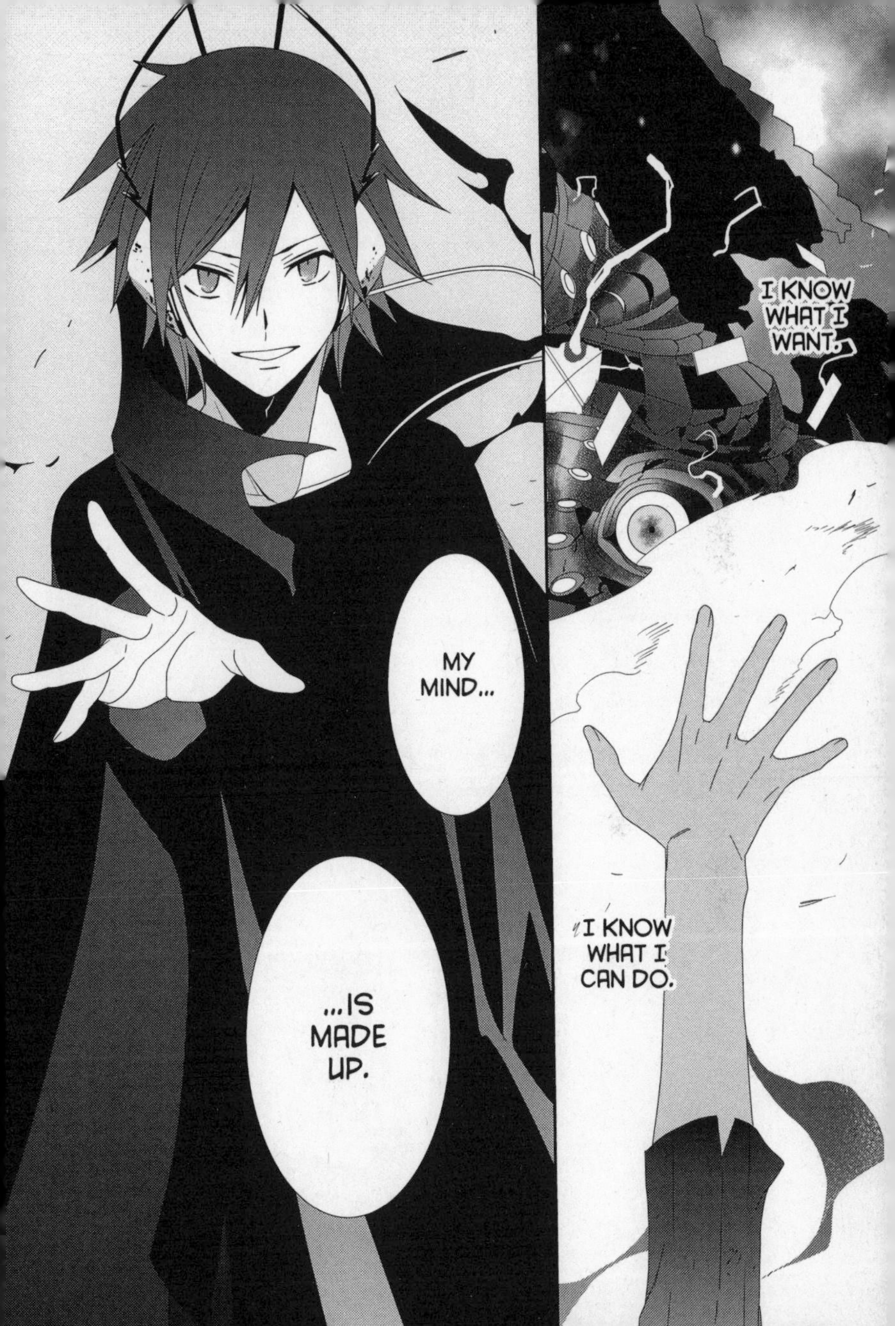
I KNOW WHAT I WANT.
I KNOW WHAT I CAN DO.
MY MIND...
...IS MADE UP.

PROFILE

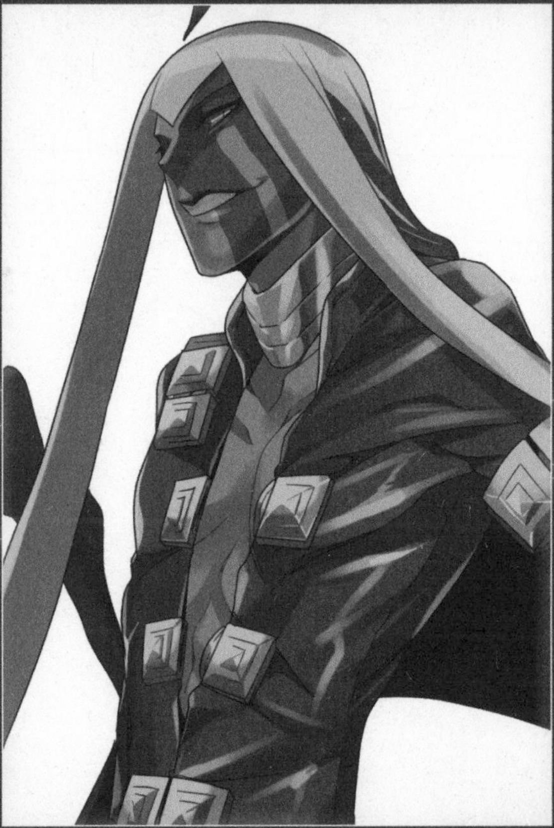

LOKI

A MALEVOLENT GOD FROM NORSE MYTHOLOGY, WHO IS ALSO CAPRICIOUS AND FULL OF TRICKERY. THOUGH HIS PARENTS ARE GIANTS AND ENEMIES OF THE GODS, HE JOINED THE PANTHEON AS ODIN'S BLOOD BROTHER. DUE TO HIS COUNTLESS EVIL DEEDS, INCLUDING THE MURDER OF ODIN'S SON BALDR, HE WAS EVENTUALLY PUNISHED WITH IMPRISONMENT IN A CAVE. HE IS FATED TO BE RELEASED ON THE DAY OF RAGNAROK, WHEN THE WORLD WILL END, AND HE WILL BATTLE THE GODS.

DEVIL デビルサバイバー
SURVIVOR

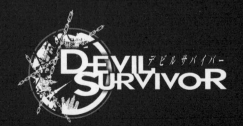

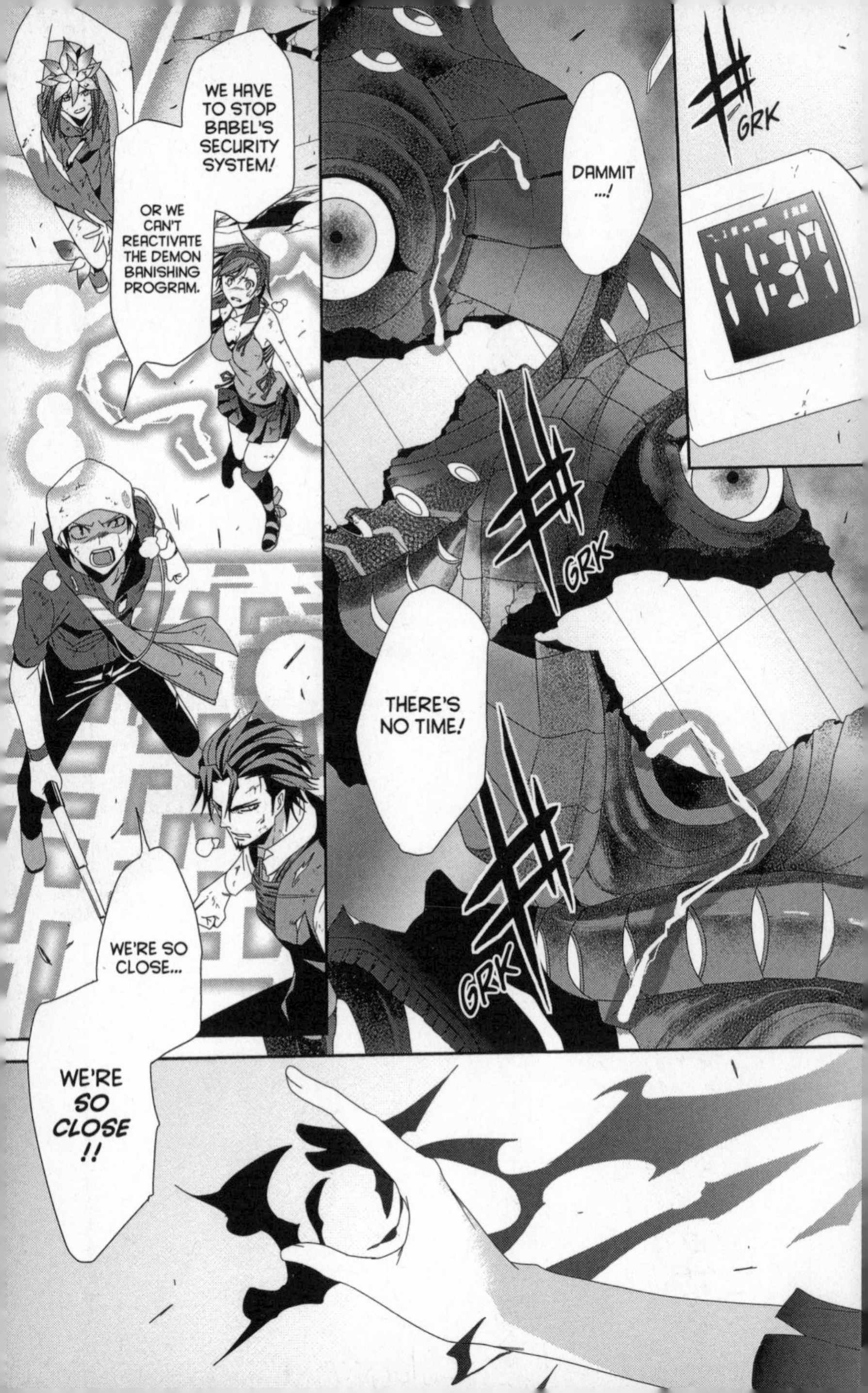
GRK
DAMMIT ...!
GRK
THERE'S NO TIME!
GRK
WE HAVE TO STOP BABEL'S SECURITY SYSTEM!
OR WE CAN'T REACTIVATE THE DEMON BANISHING PROGRAM.
WE'RE SO CLOSE...
WE'RE SO CLOSE !!

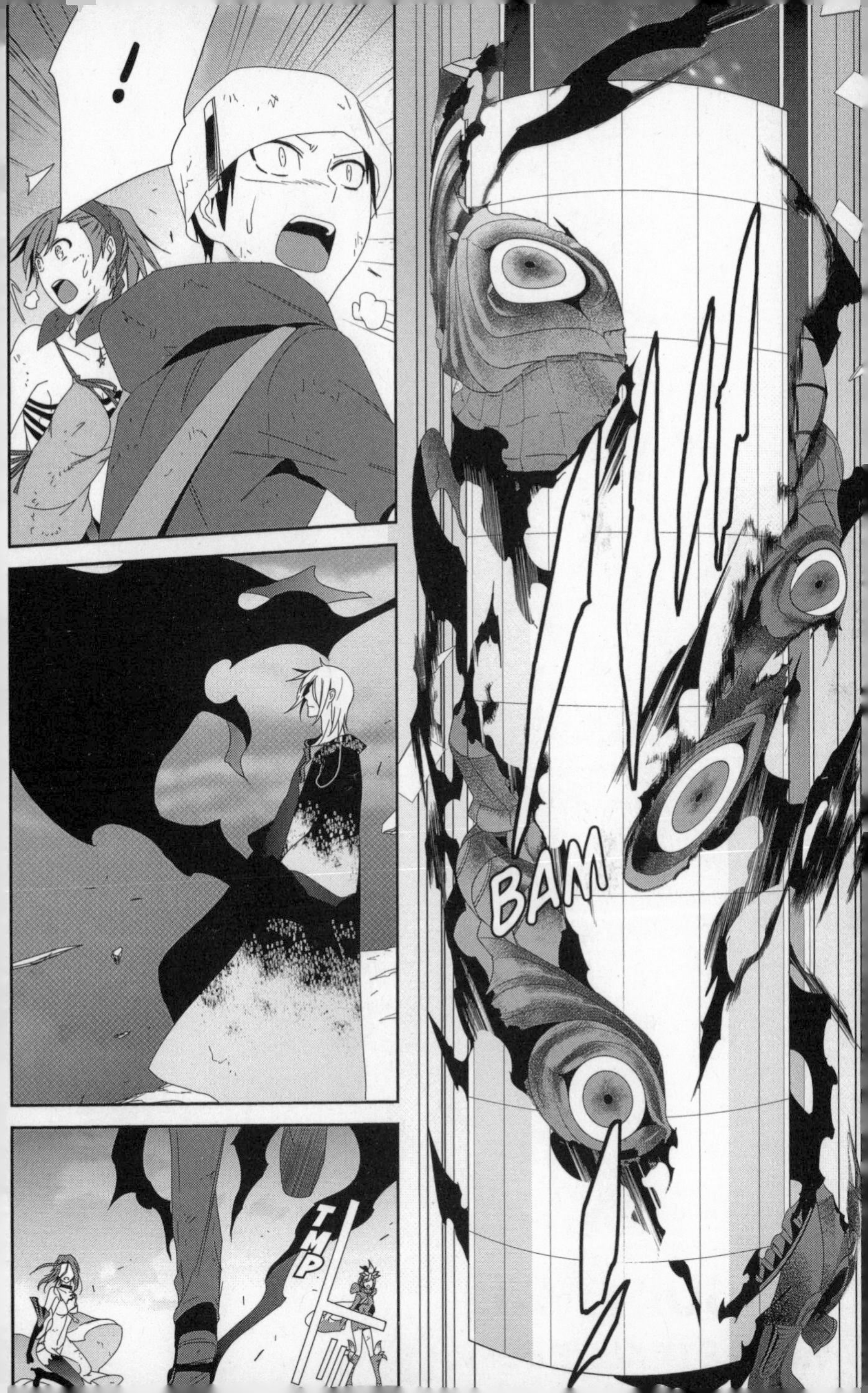
BAM
!
TMP

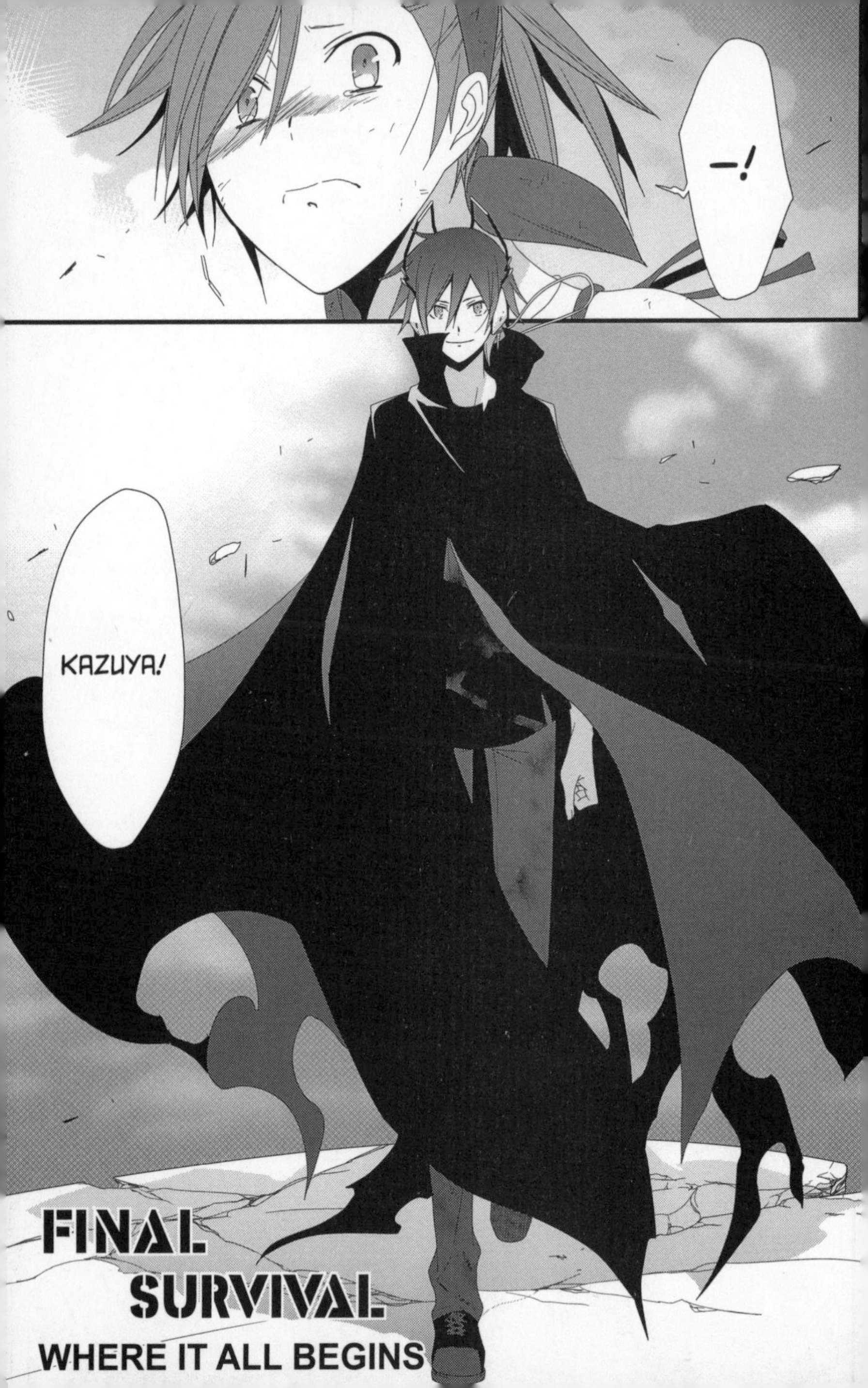
—!
KAZUYA!
FINAL SURVIVAL
WHERE IT ALL BEGINS

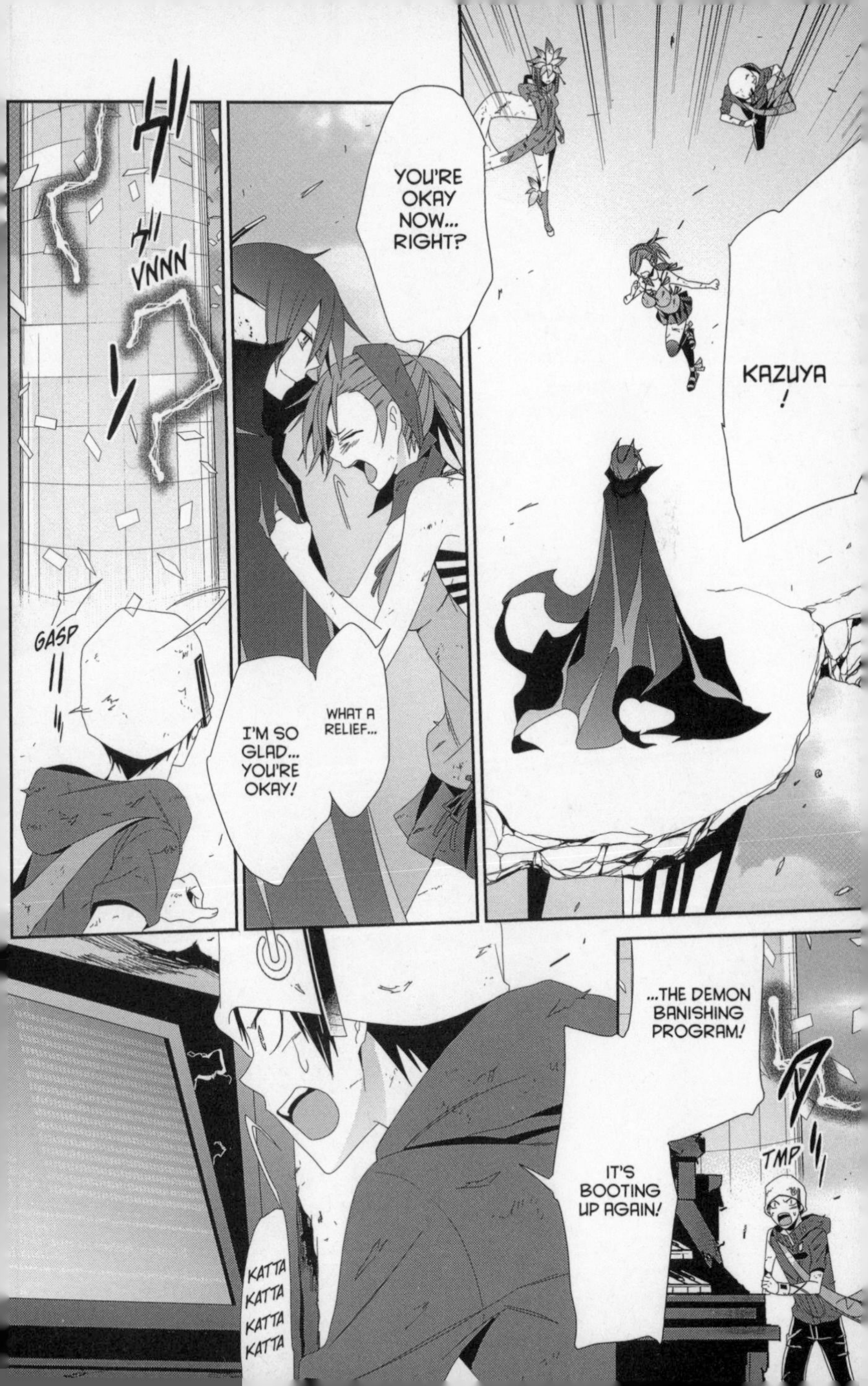
KAZUYA!
YOU'RE OKAY NOW... RIGHT?
WHAT A RELIEF...
I'M SO GLAD... YOU'RE OKAY!
VNNN
GASP
...THE DEMON BANISHING PROGRAM!
IT'S BOOTING UP AGAIN!
TMP
KATTA KATTA KATTA KATTA

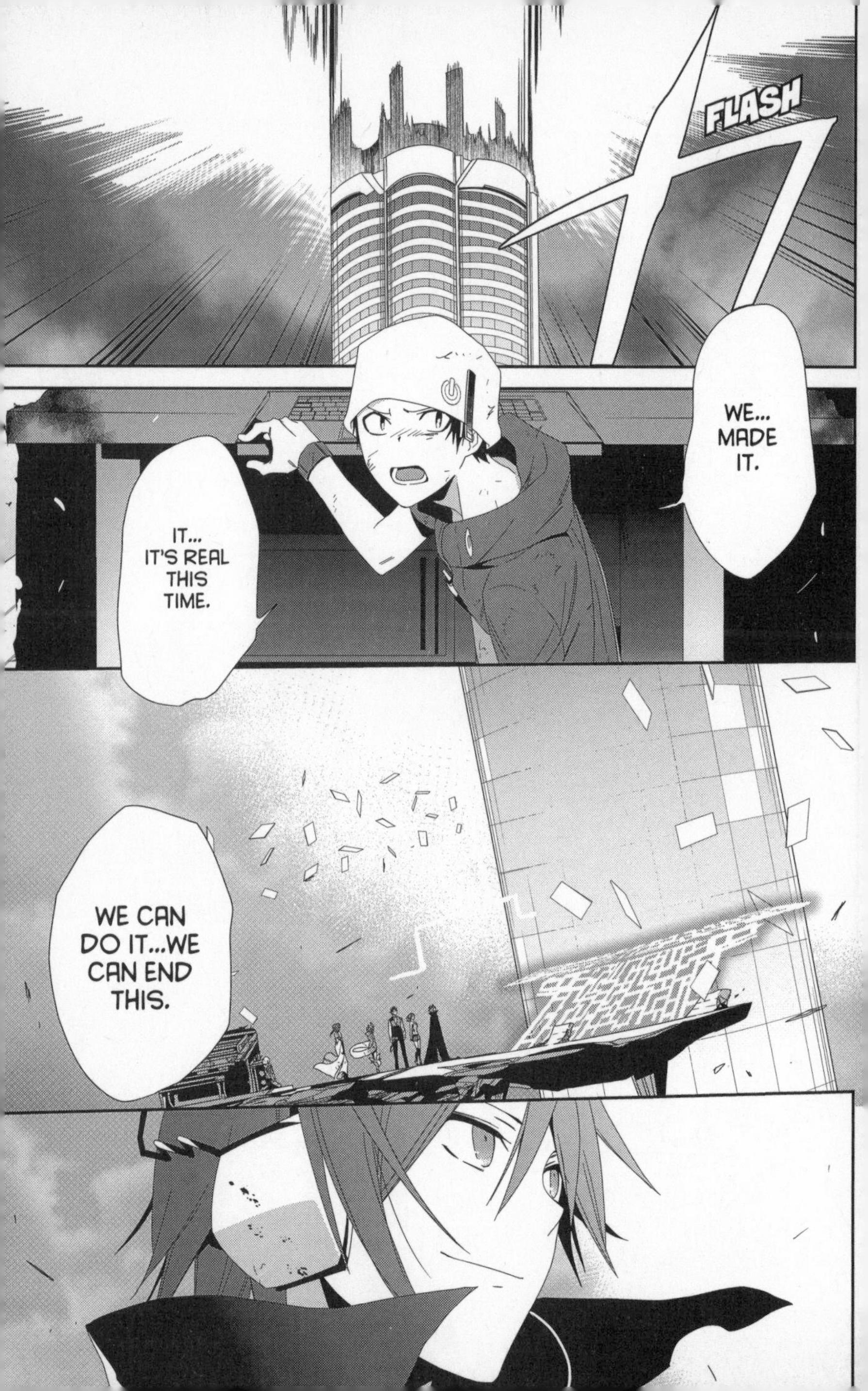
FLASH
WE... MADE IT.
IT... IT'S REAL THIS TIME.
WE CAN DO IT...WE CAN END THIS.

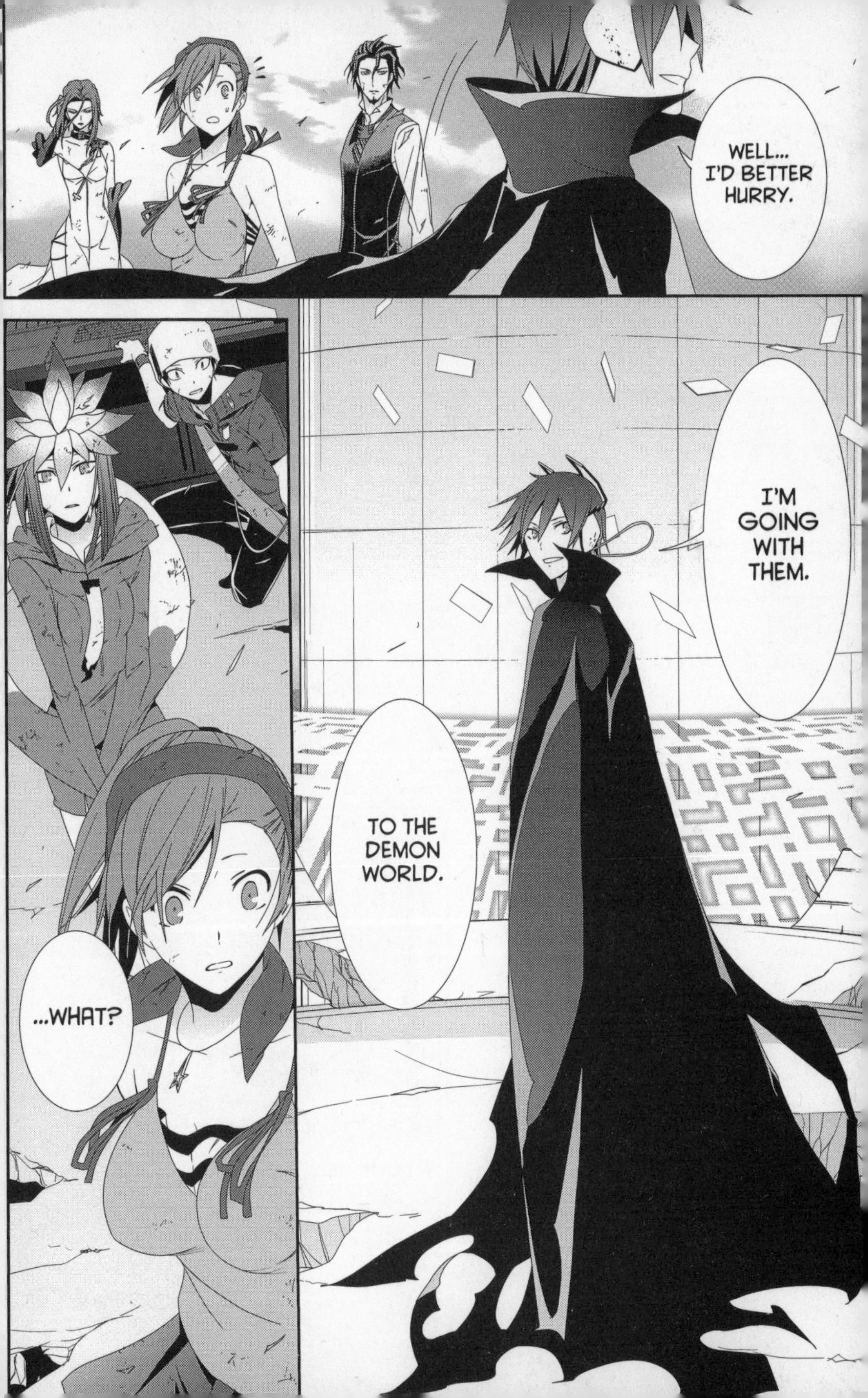
WELL... I'D BETTER HURRY.
I'M GOING WITH THEM.
TO THE DEMON WORLD.
...WHAT?

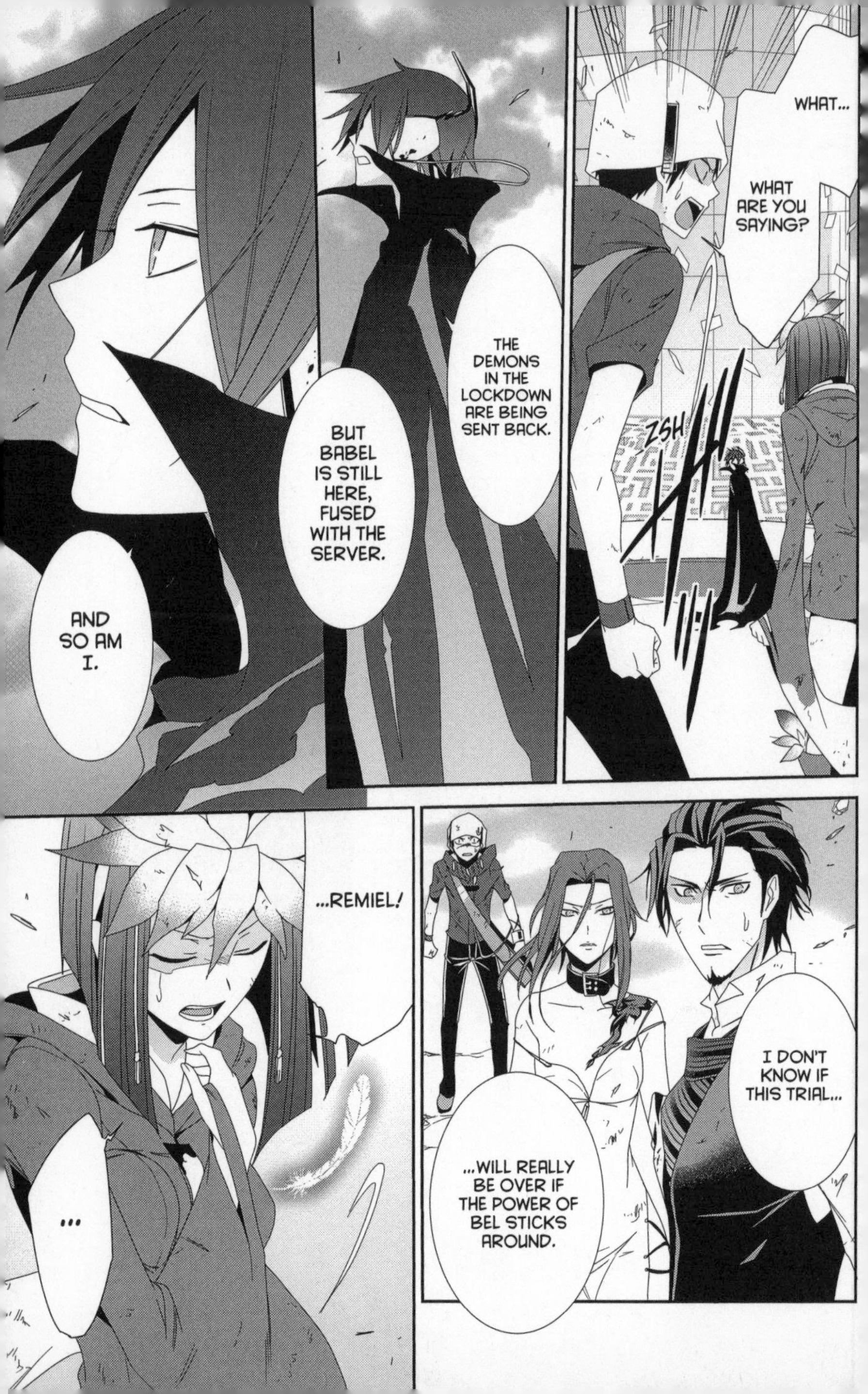
WHAT...
WHAT ARE YOU SAYING?
ZSH
THE DEMONS IN THE LOCKDOWN ARE BEING SENT BACK.
BUT BABEL IS STILL HERE, FUSED WITH THE SERVER.
AND SO AM I.
I DON'T KNOW IF THIS TRIAL...
...WILL REALLY BE OVER IF THE POWER OF BEL STICKS AROUND.
...REMIEL!
...

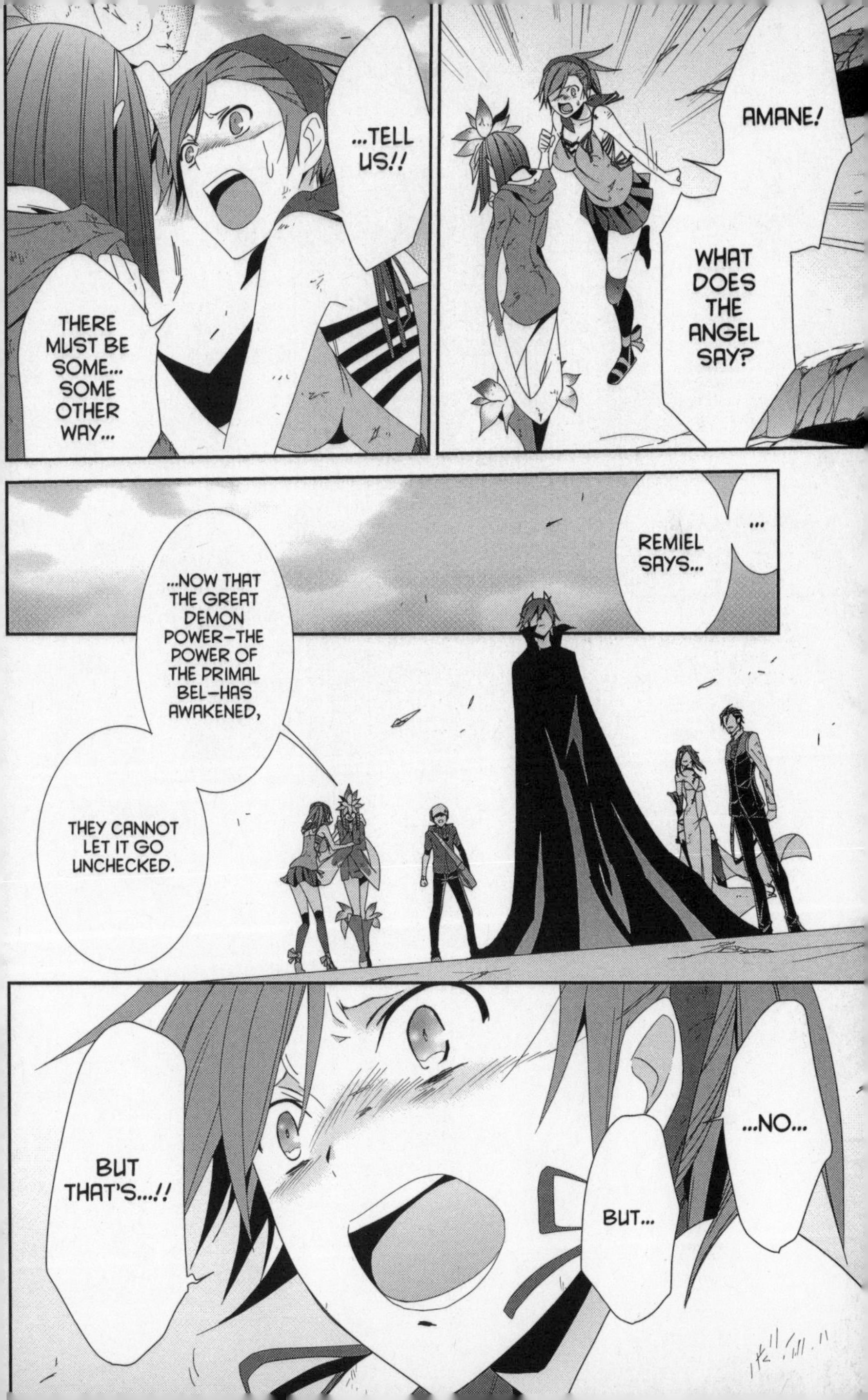
AMANE!
WHAT DOES THE ANGEL SAY?
...TELL US!!
THERE MUST BE SOME... SOME OTHER WAY...
...
REMIEL SAYS...
...NOW THAT THE GREAT DEMON POWER—THE POWER OF THE PRIMAL BEL—HAS AWAKENED,
THEY CANNOT LET IT GO UNCHECKED.
...NO...
BUT...
BUT THAT'S...!!

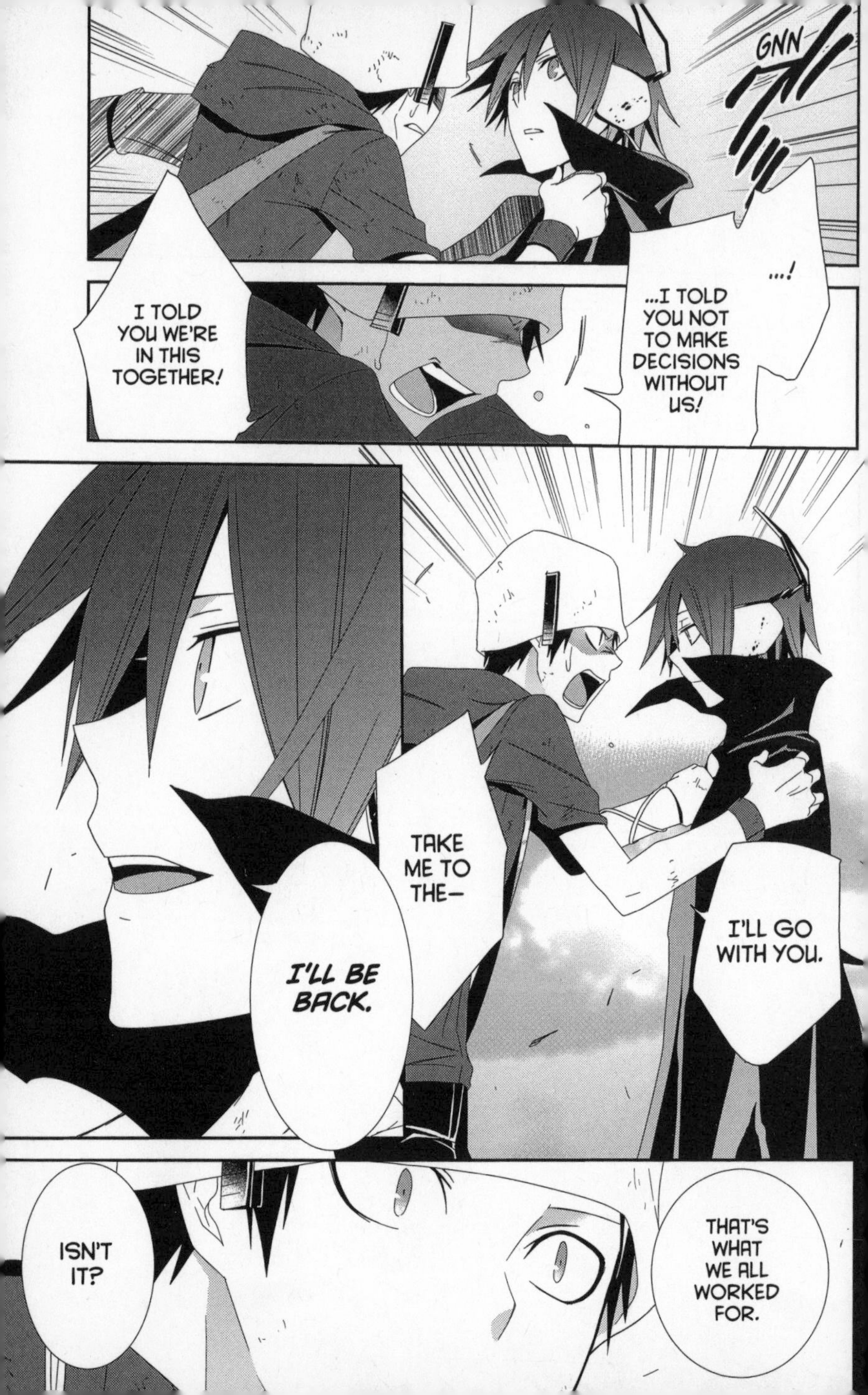
GNN
...!
...I TOLD YOU NOT TO MAKE DECISIONS WITHOUT US!
I TOLD YOU WE'RE IN THIS TOGETHER!
TAKE ME TO THE—
I'LL GO WITH YOU.
I'LL BE BACK.
THAT'S WHAT WE ALL WORKED FOR.
ISN'T IT?

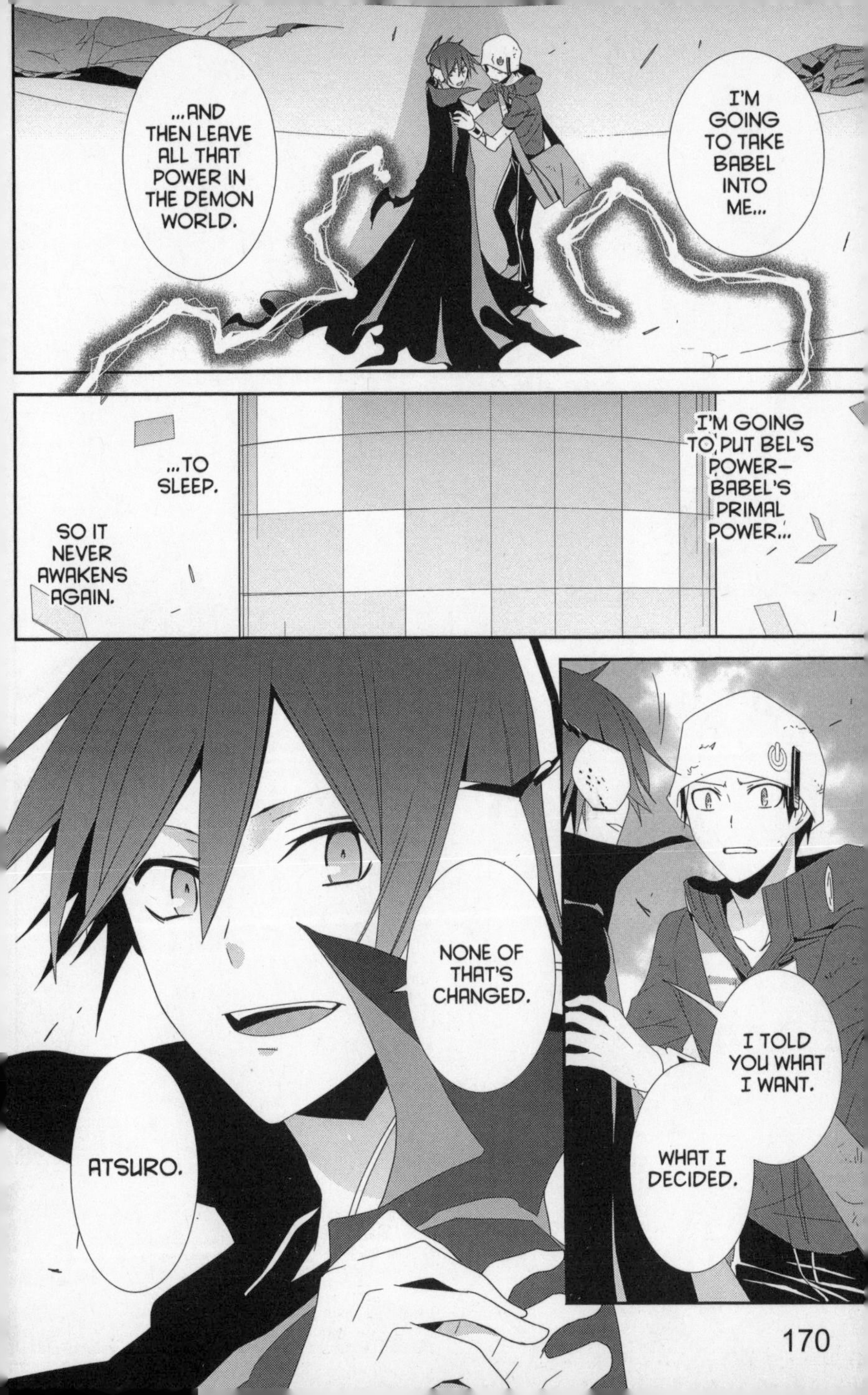
I'M GOING TO TAKE BABEL INTO ME...
...AND THEN LEAVE ALL THAT POWER IN THE DEMON WORLD.
I'M GOING TO PUT BEL'S POWER—BABEL'S PRIMAL POWER...
...TO SLEEP.
SO IT NEVER AWAKENS AGAIN.
I TOLD YOU WHAT I WANT.
WHAT I DECIDED.
NONE OF THAT'S CHANGED.
ATSURO.

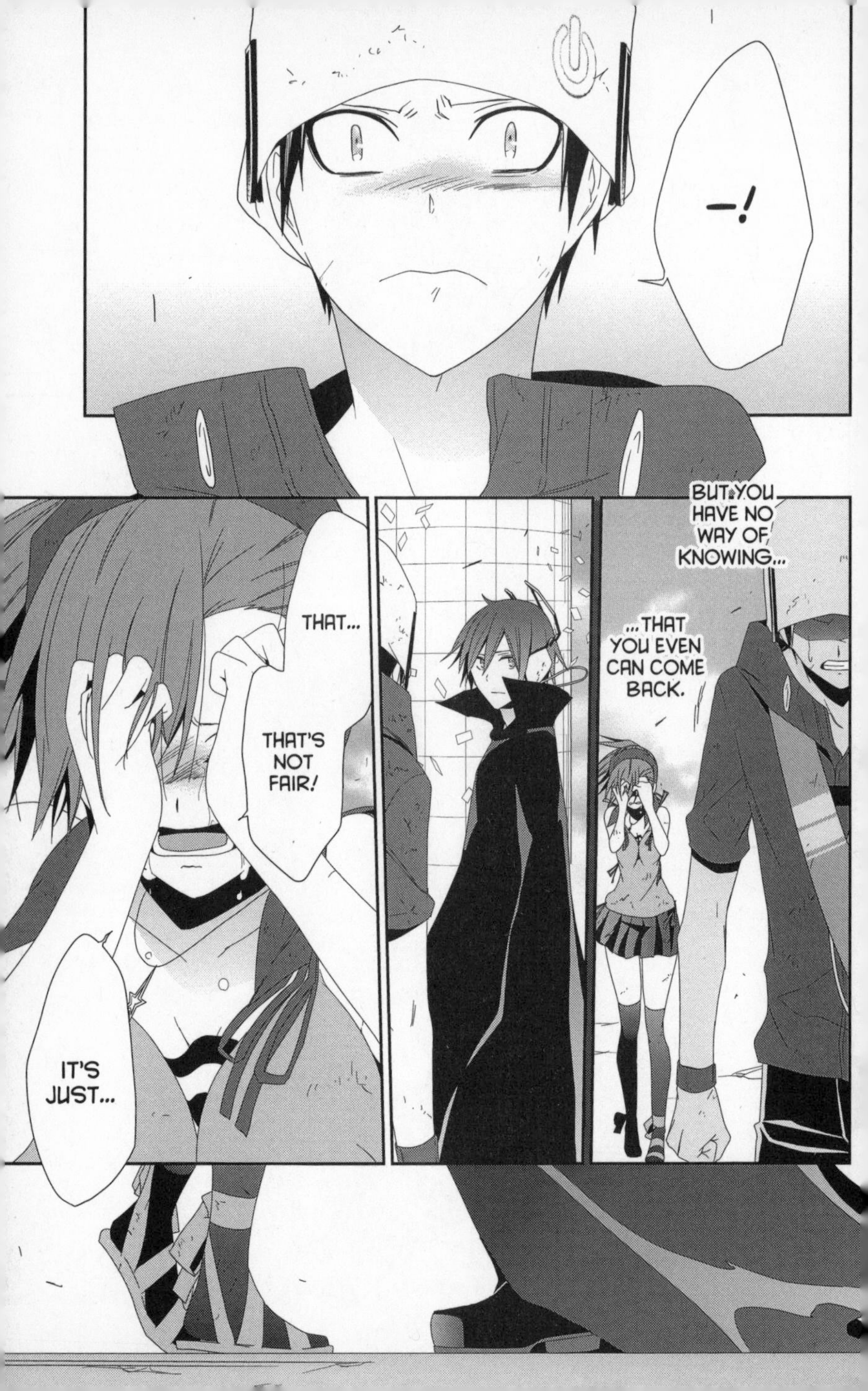
—!
BUT YOU HAVE NO WAY OF KNOWING...
...THAT YOU EVEN CAN COME BACK.
THAT...
THAT'S NOT FAIR!
IT'S JUST...

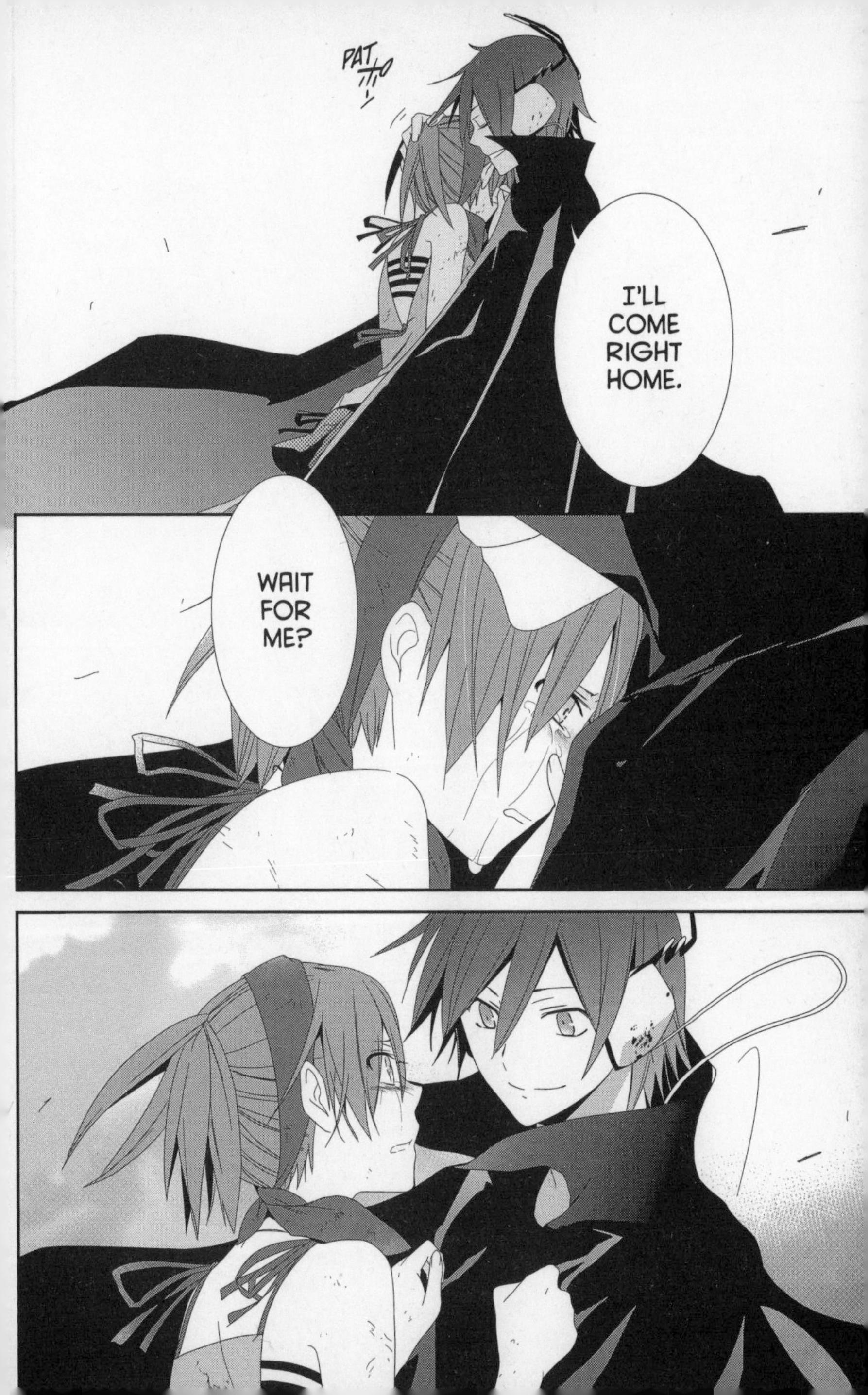
PAT
I'LL COME RIGHT HOME.
WAIT FOR ME?

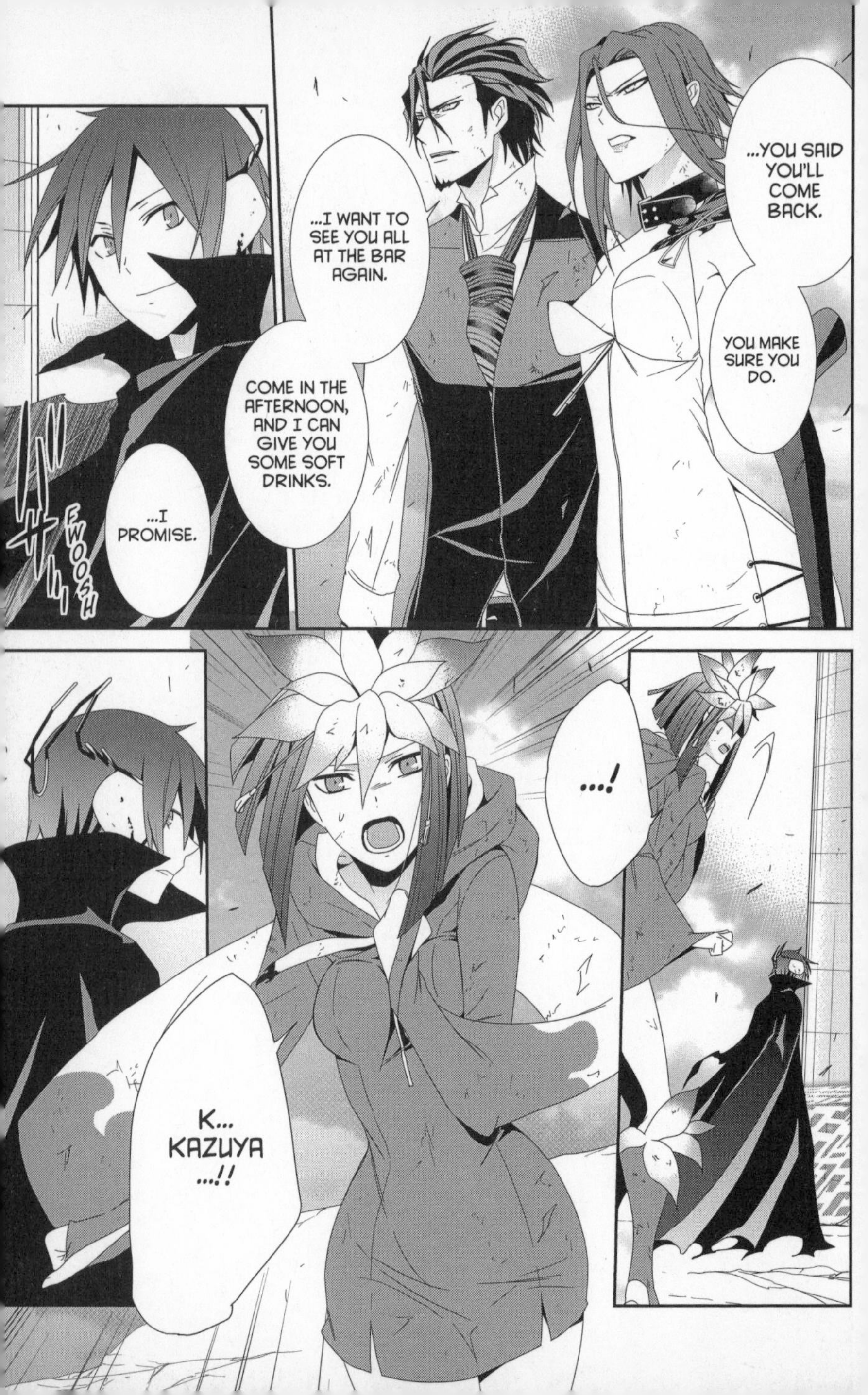
...YOU SAID YOU'LL COME BACK.
YOU MAKE SURE YOU DO.
...I WANT TO SEE YOU ALL AT THE BAR AGAIN.
COME IN THE AFTERNOON, AND I CAN GIVE YOU SOME SOFT DRINKS.
...I PROMISE.
FWOOSH
...!
K... KAZUYA ...!!

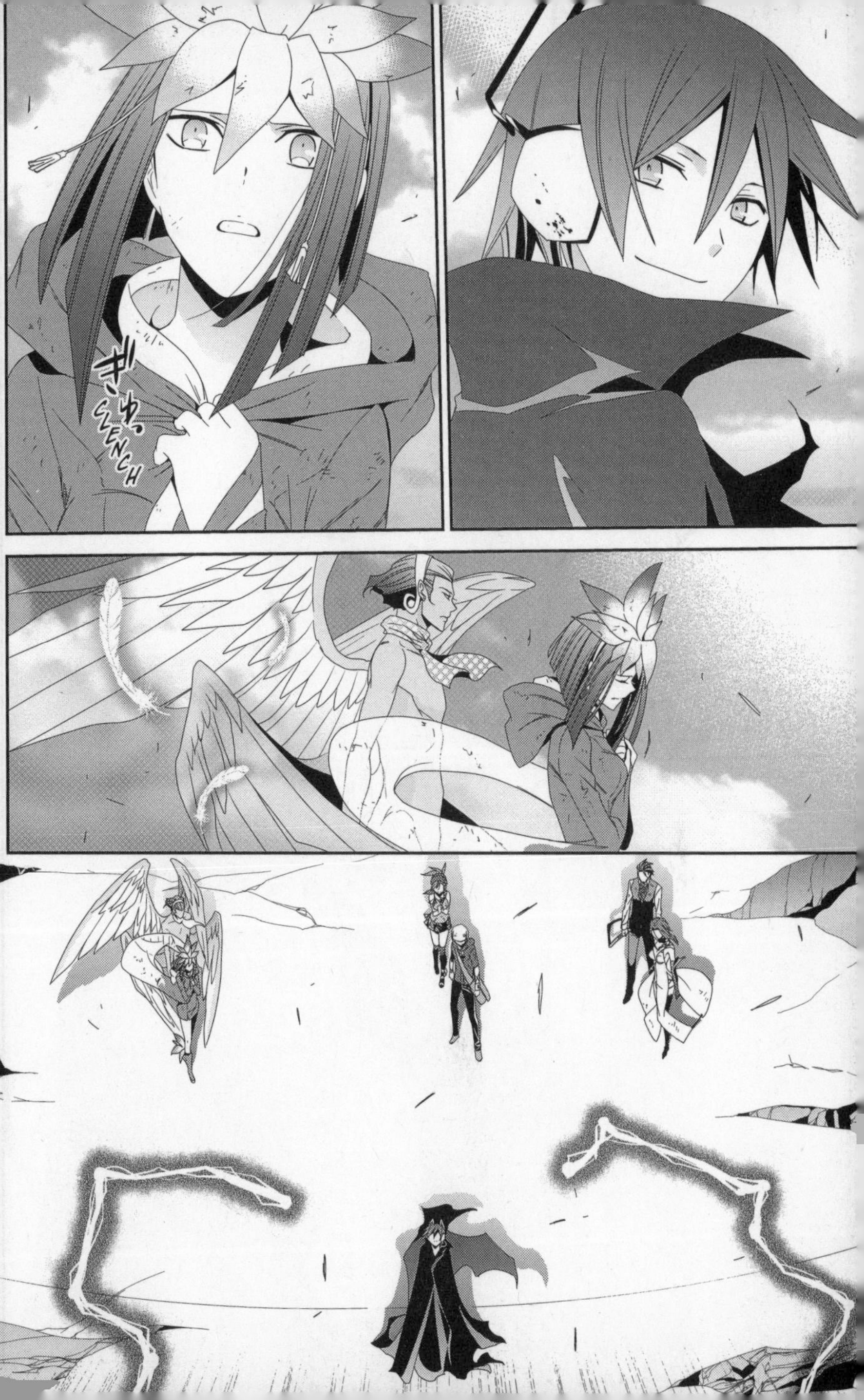
ぎゅ CLENCH

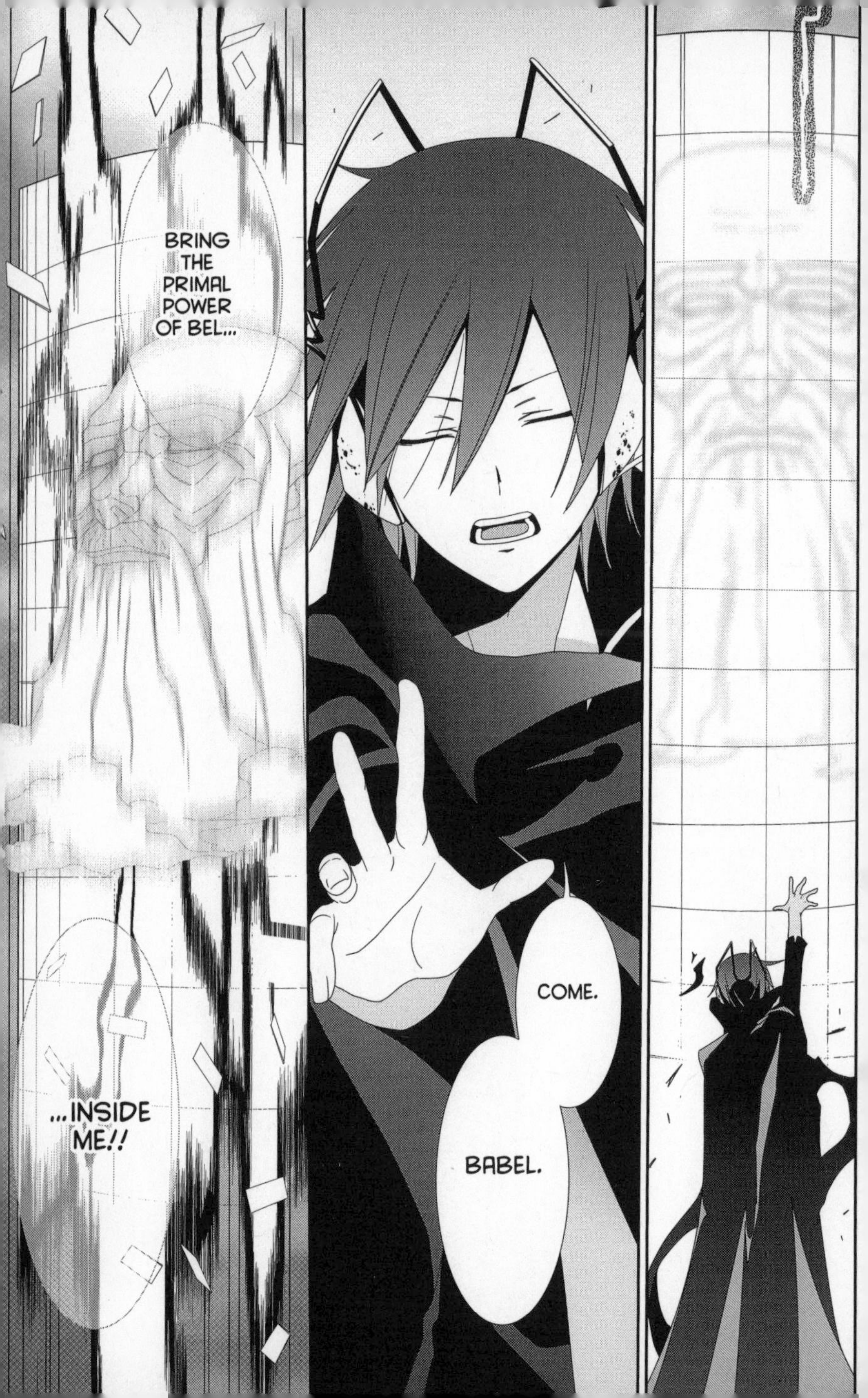
COME.
BABEL.
BRING THE PRIMAL POWER OF BEL...
...INSIDE ME!!

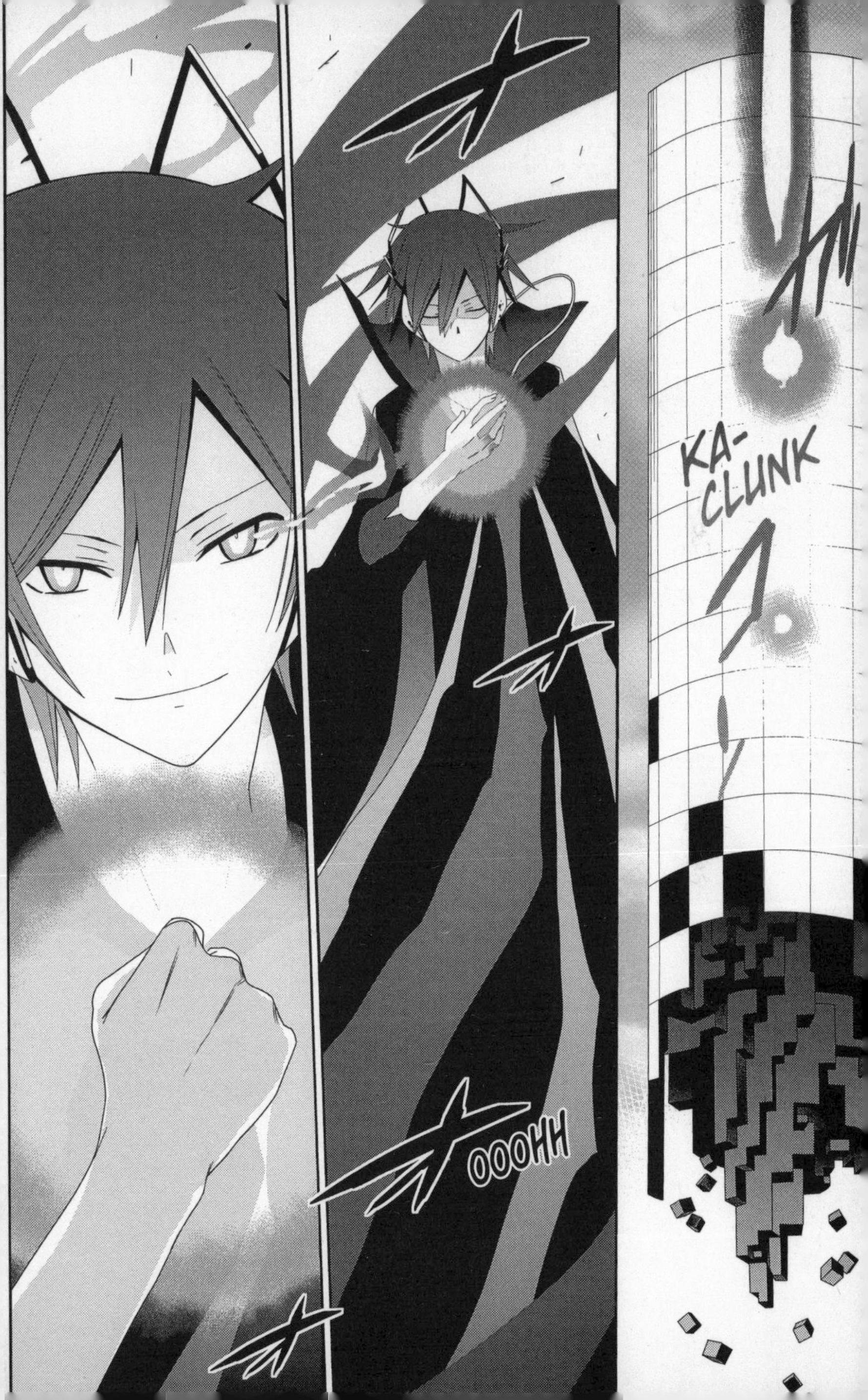
KA-CLUNK
OOOHH

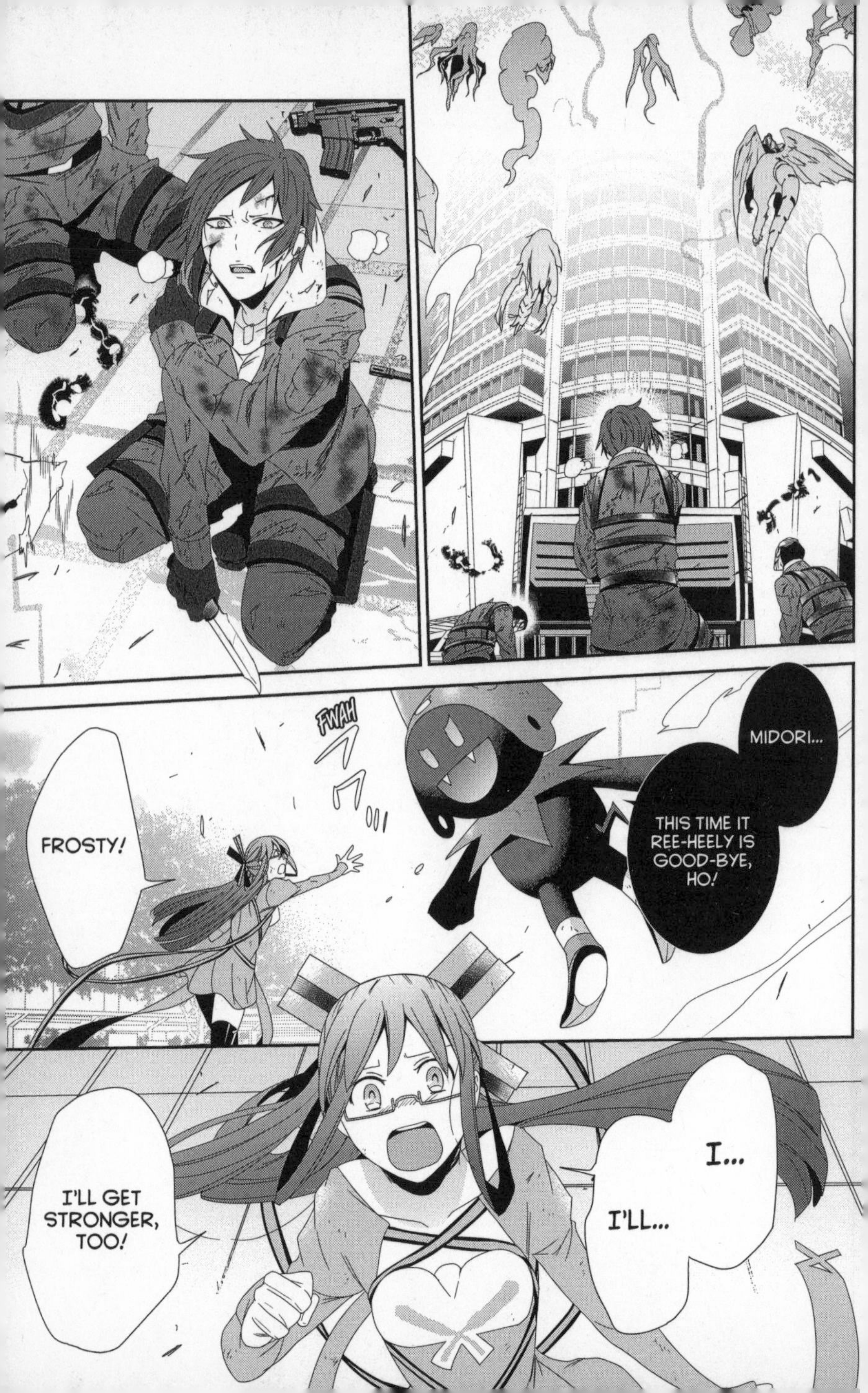
MIDORI...
THIS TIME IT REE-HEELY IS GOOD-BYE, HO!
FWAH
FROSTY!
I...
I'LL...
I'LL GET STRONGER, TOO!

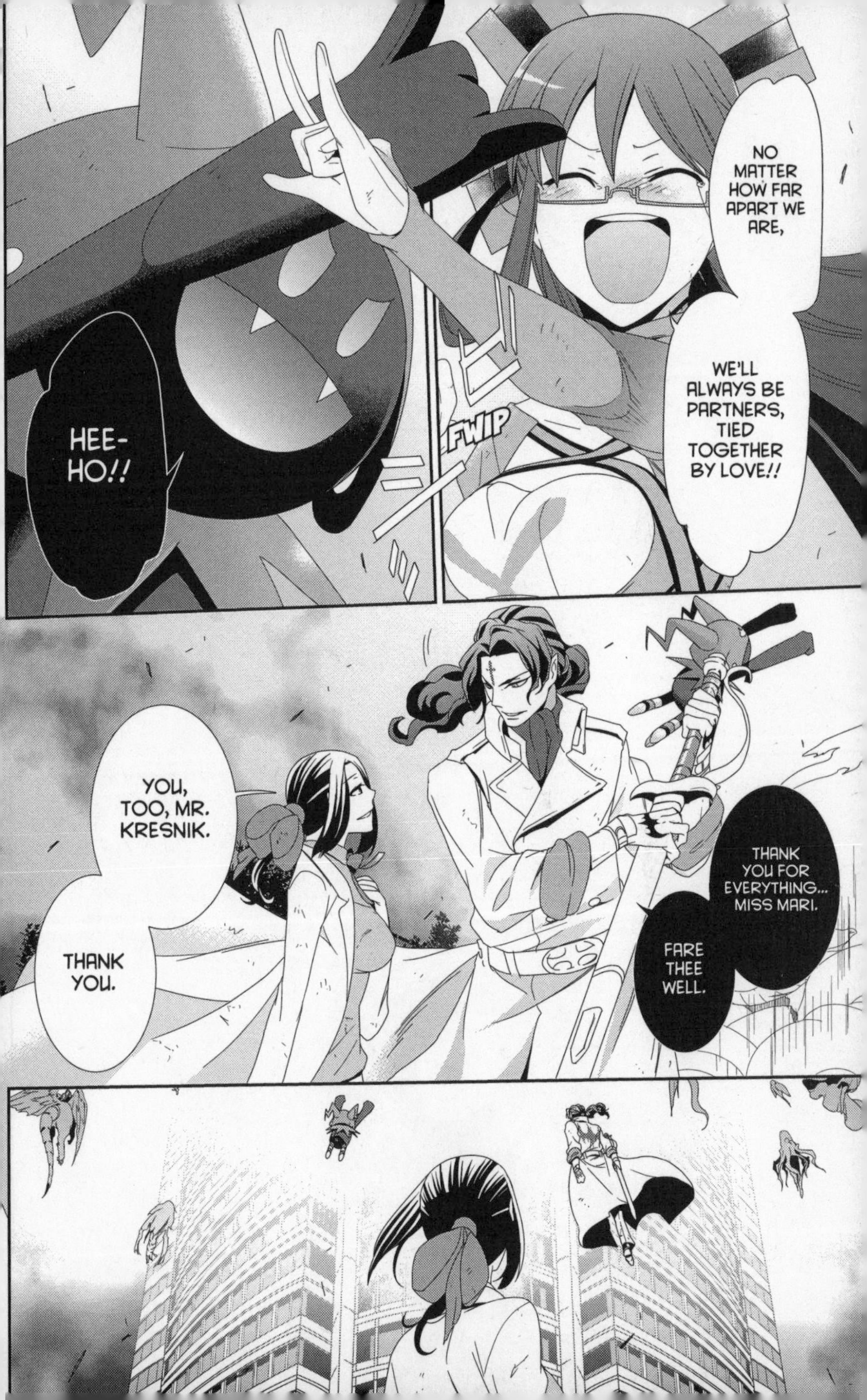
NO MATTER HOW FAR APART WE ARE,
WE'LL ALWAYS BE PARTNERS, TIED TOGETHER BY LOVE!!
FWIP
HEE-HO!!
THANK YOU FOR EVERYTHING... MISS MARI.
FARE THEE WELL.
YOU, TOO, MR. KRESNIK.
THANK YOU.

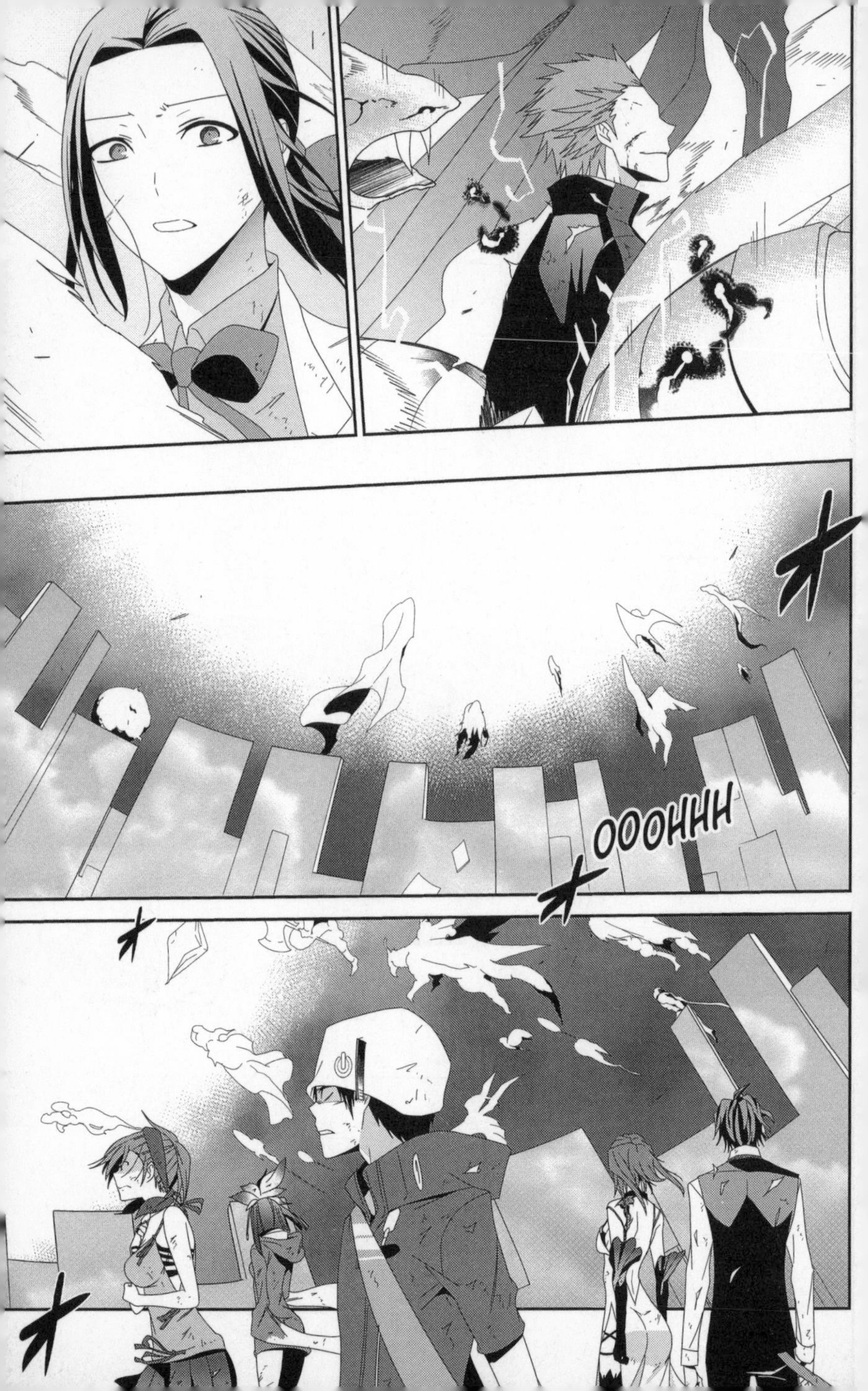
OOOHHH

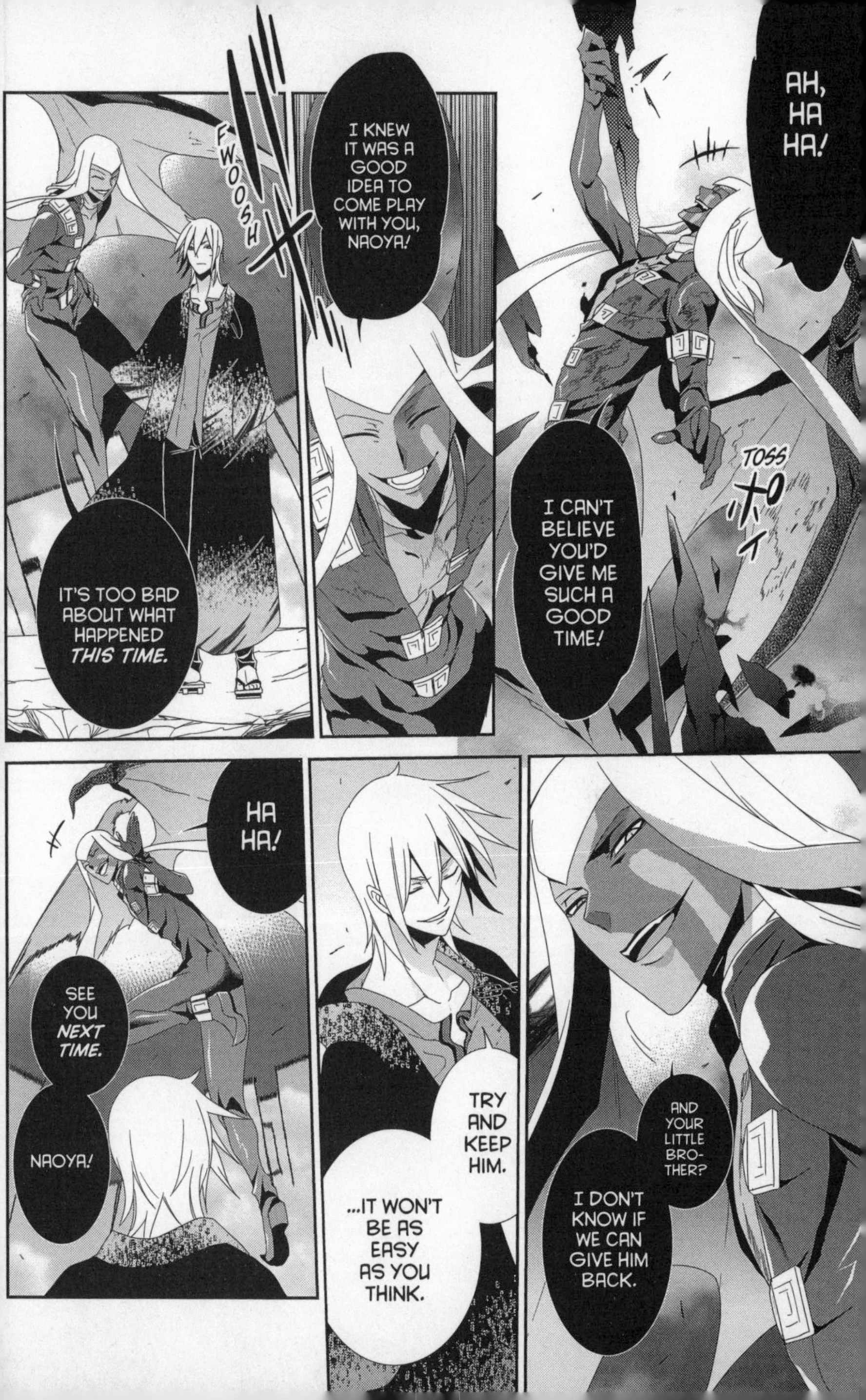
AH, HA HA!
TOSS
ポイ
I CAN'T BELIEVE YOU'D GIVE ME SUCH A GOOD TIME!
I KNEW IT WAS A GOOD IDEA TO COME PLAY WITH YOU, NAOYA!
FWOOSH
IT'S TOO BAD ABOUT WHAT HAPPENED *THIS TIME.*
AND YOUR LITTLE BRO-THER?
I DON'T KNOW IF WE CAN GIVE HIM BACK.
TRY AND KEEP HIM.
...IT WON'T BE AS EASY AS YOU THINK.
HA HA!
SEE YOU *NEXT TIME.*
NAOYA!

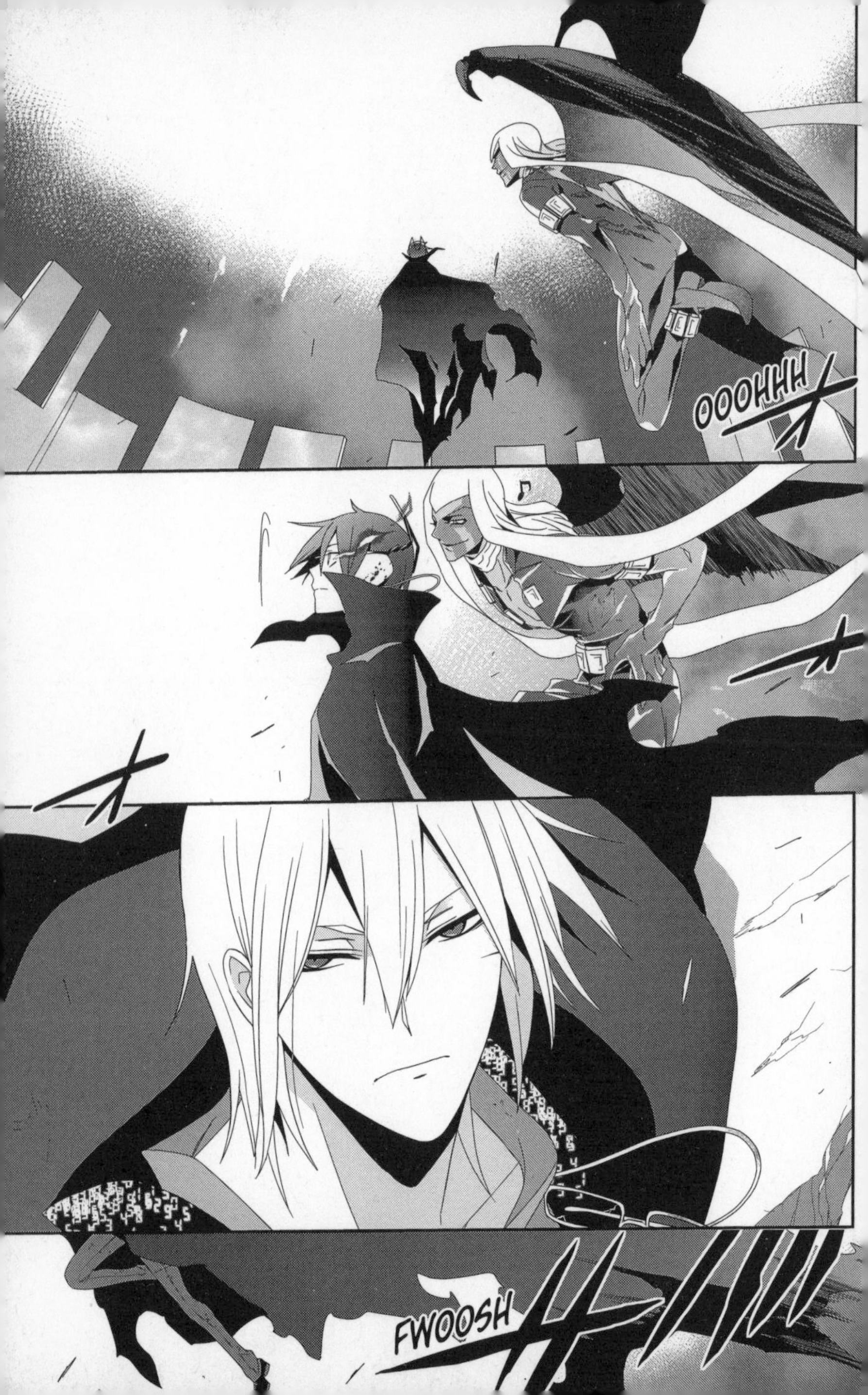
OOOHHH
FWOOSH

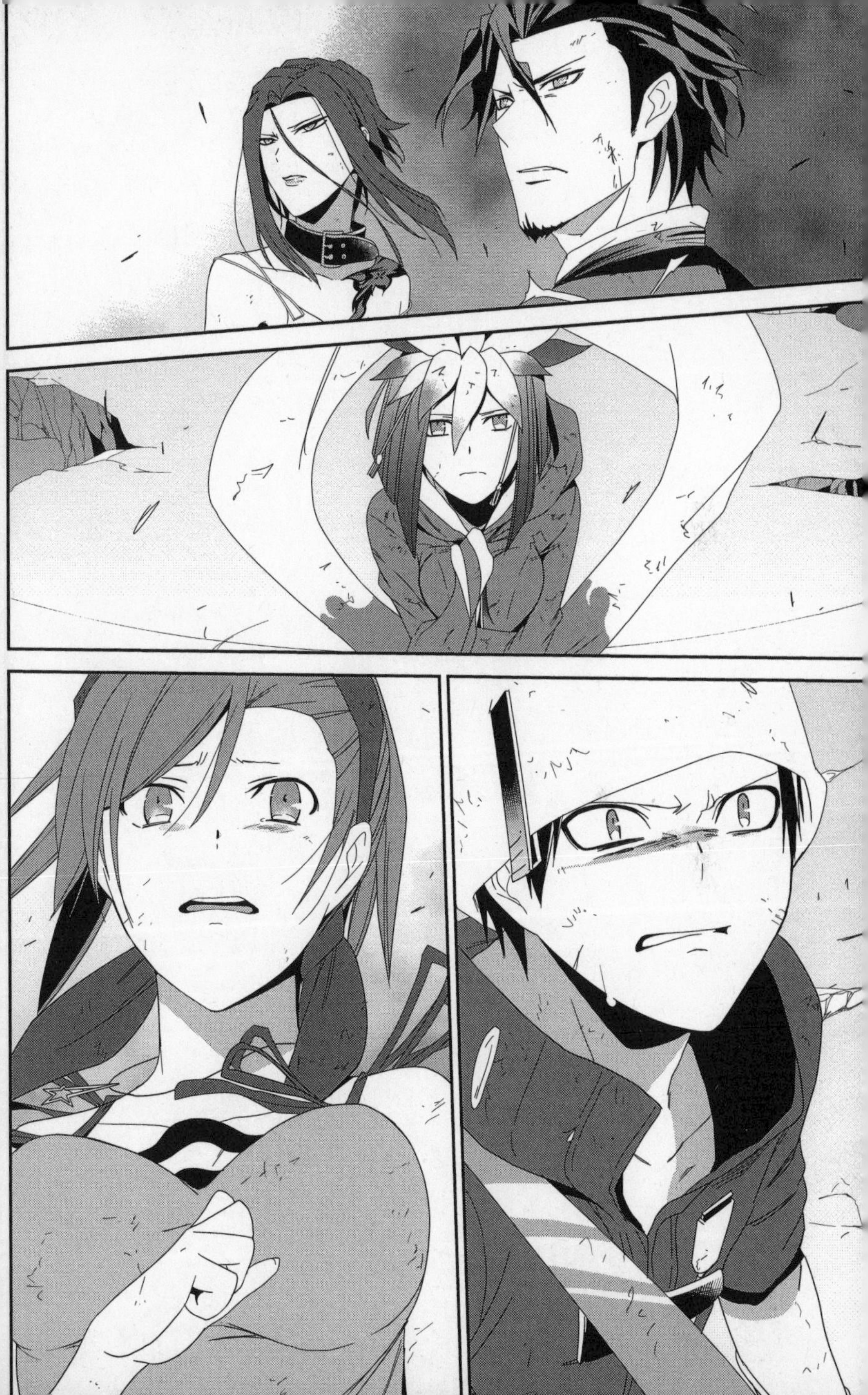

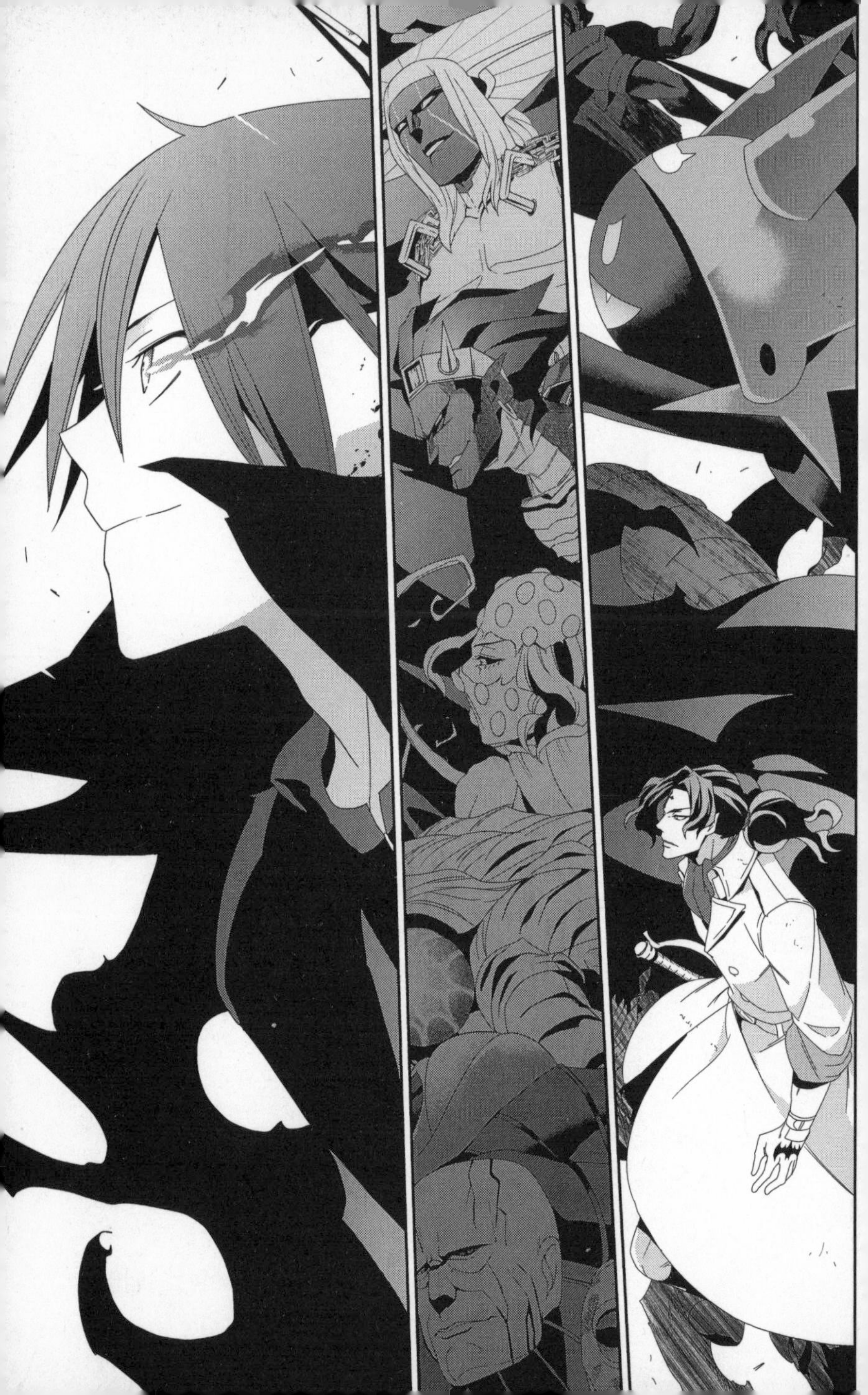

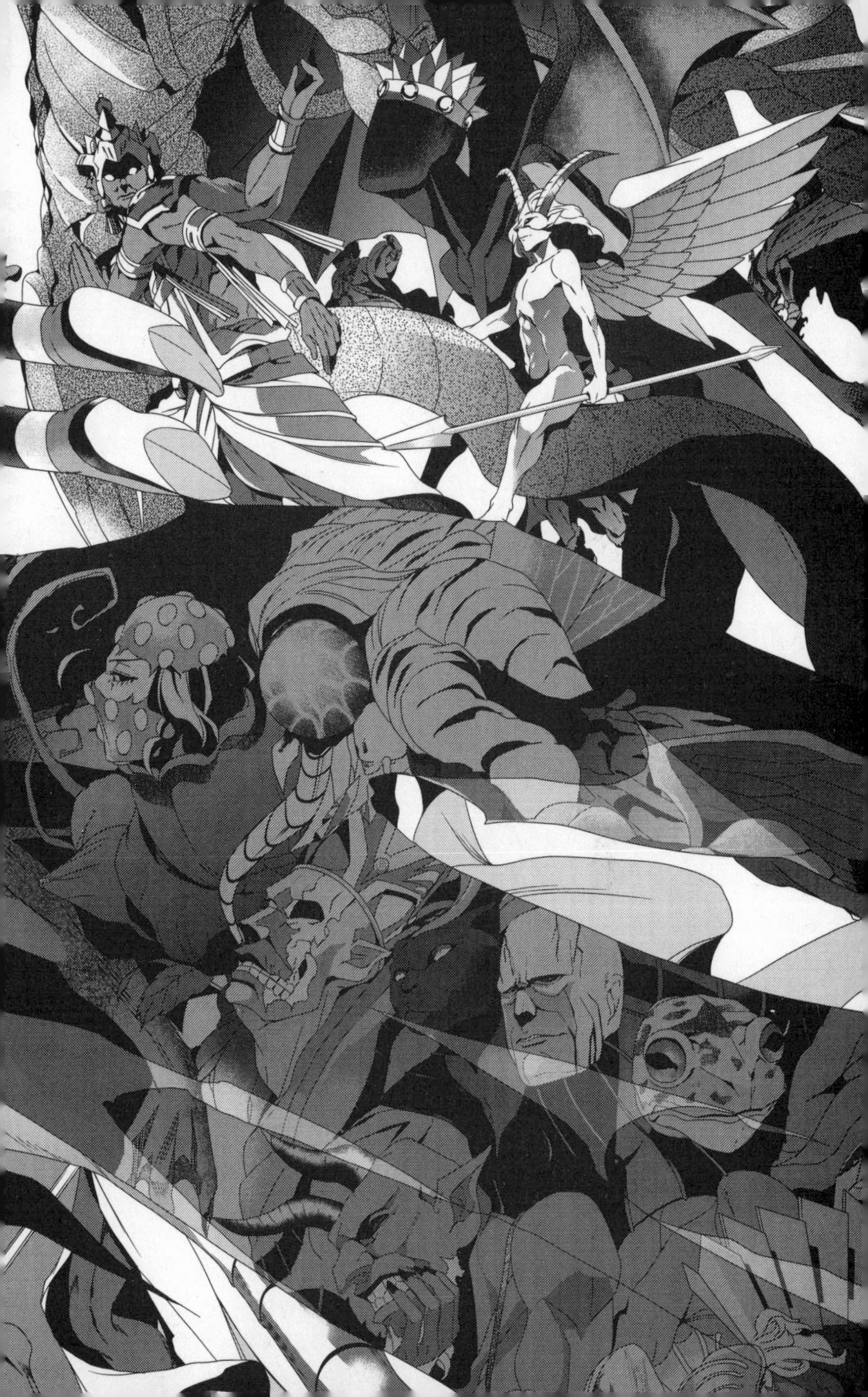

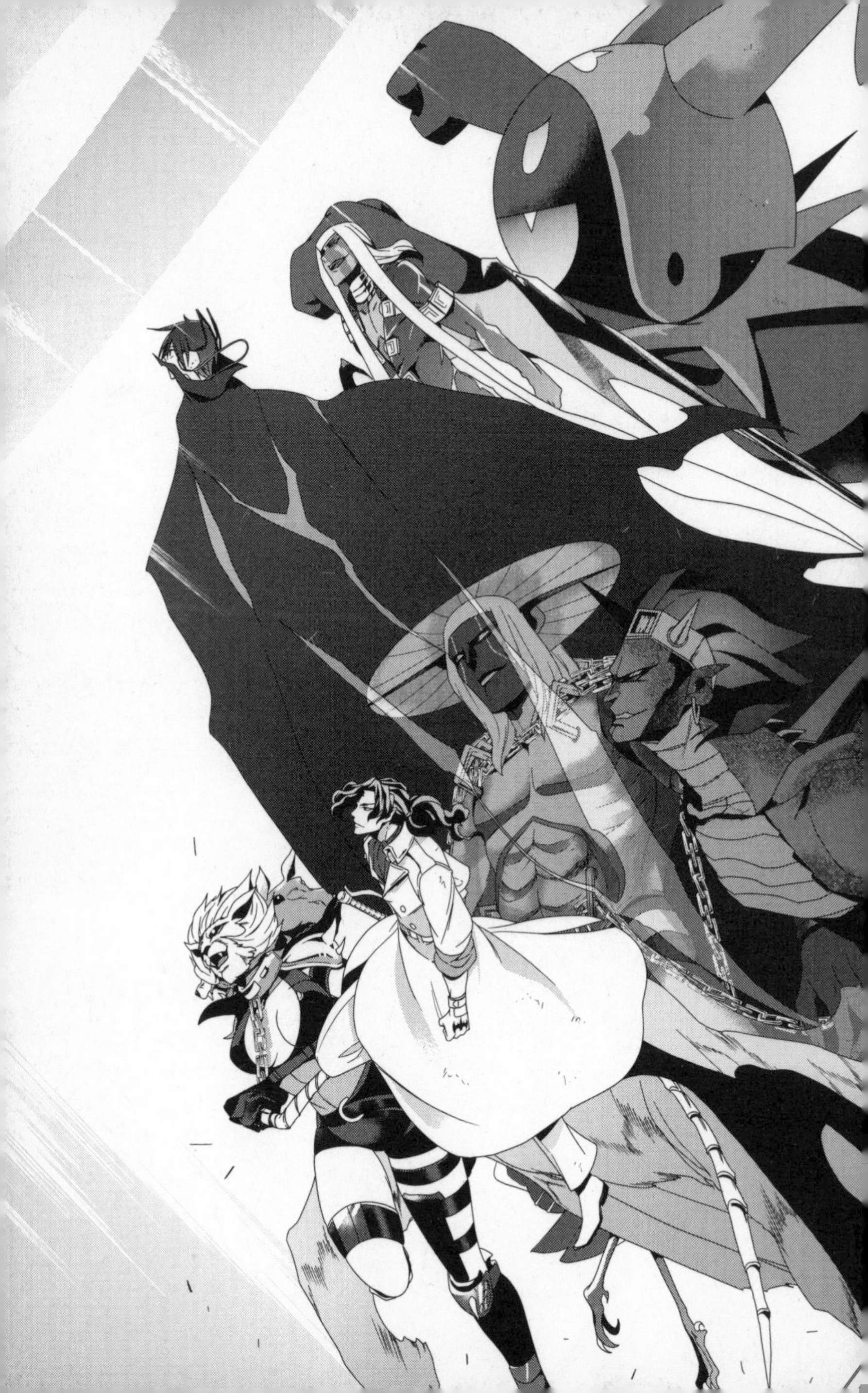

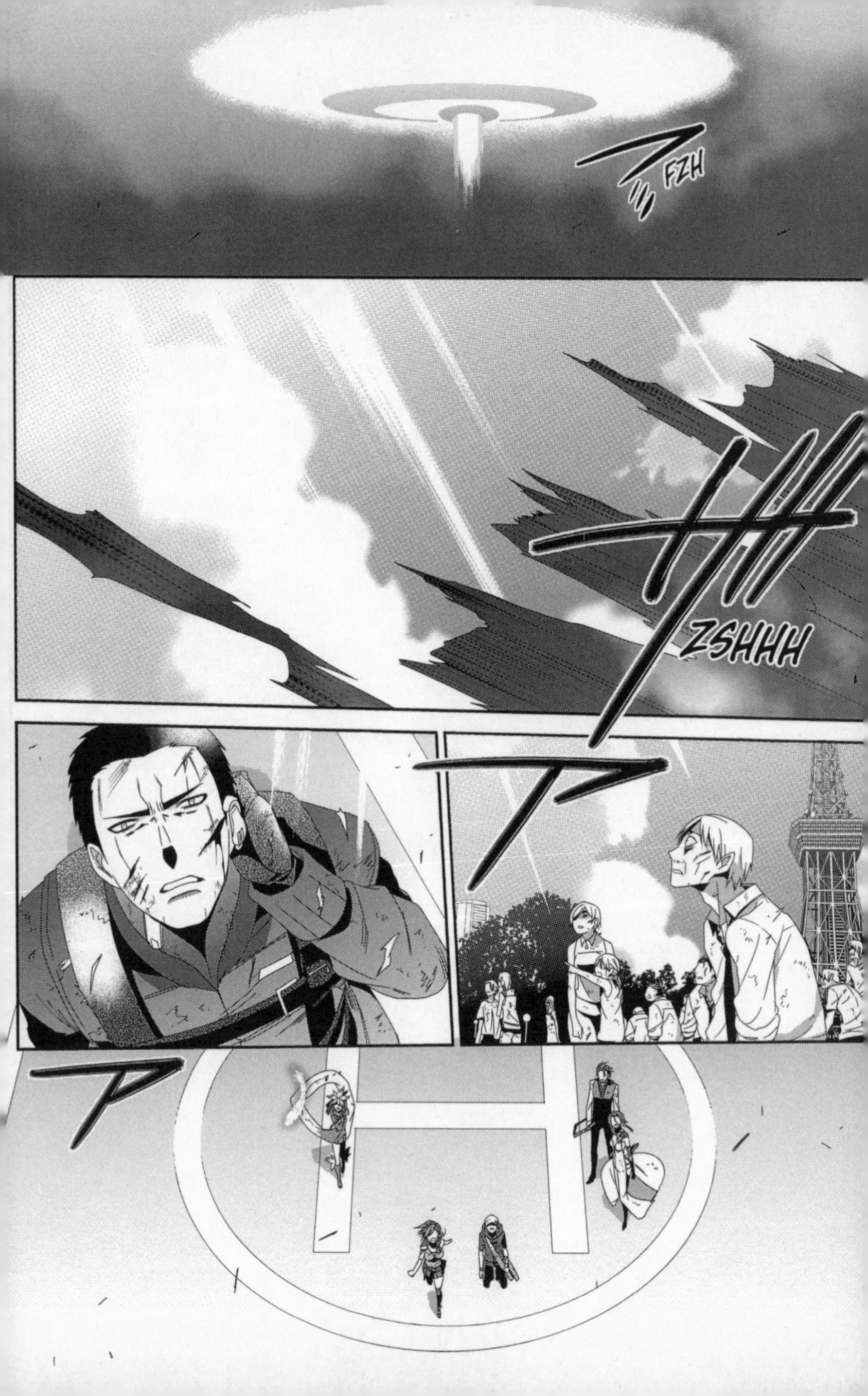
FZH
ZSHHH

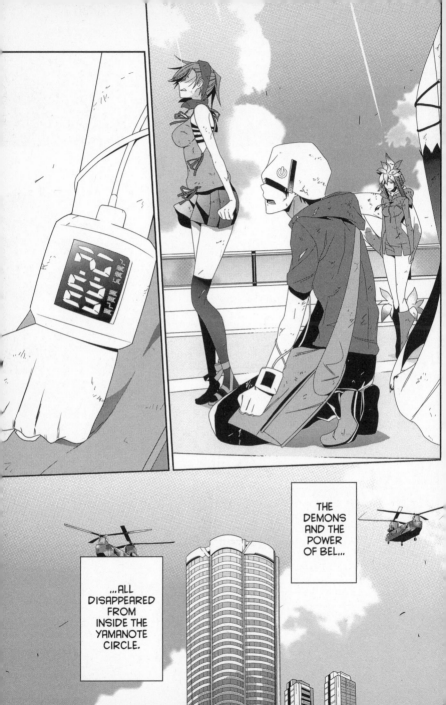

THE DEMONS AND THE POWER OF BEL...

...ALL DISAPPEARED FROM INSIDE THE YAMANOTE CIRCLE.

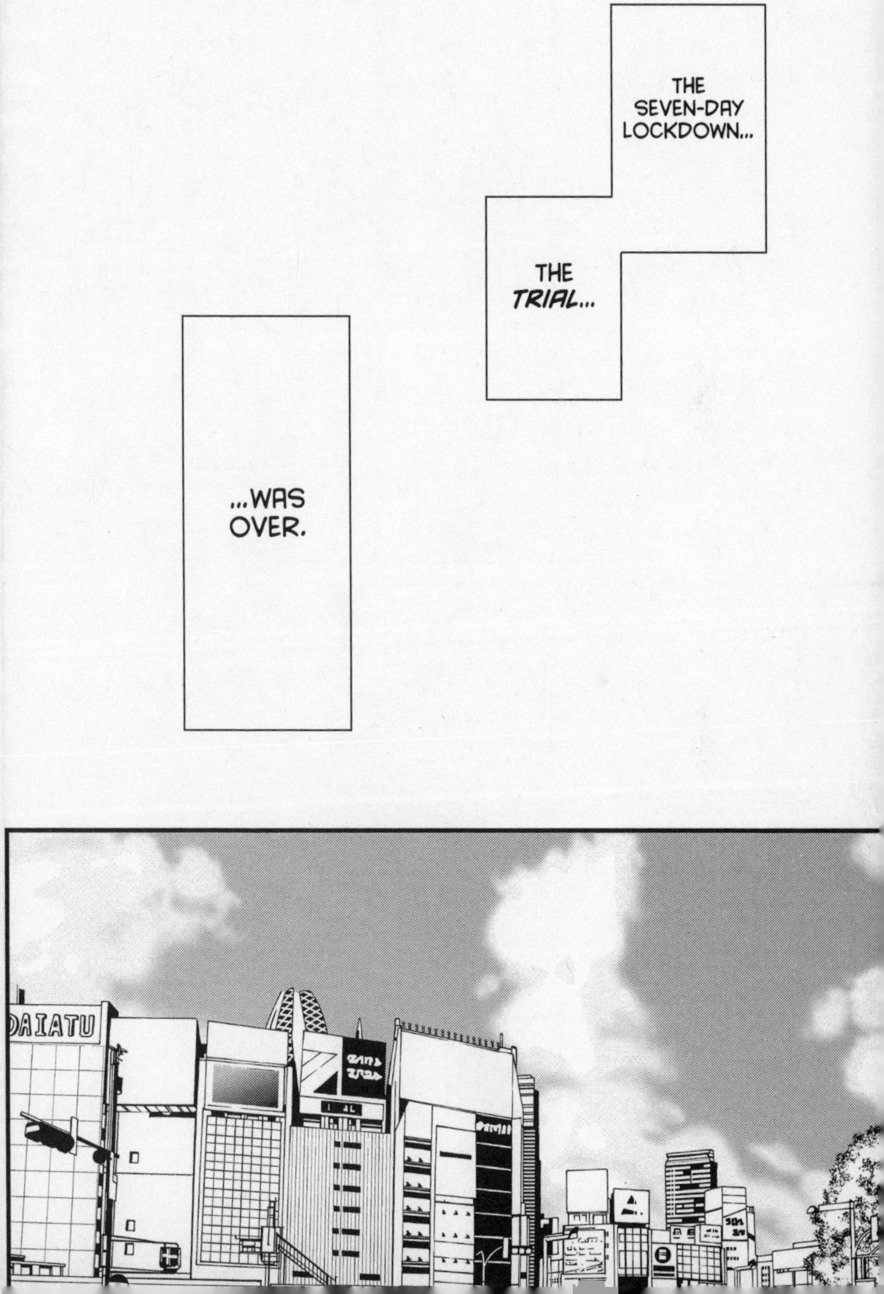
THE SEVEN-DAY LOCKDOWN...
THE *TRIAL*...
...WAS OVER.
DAIATU

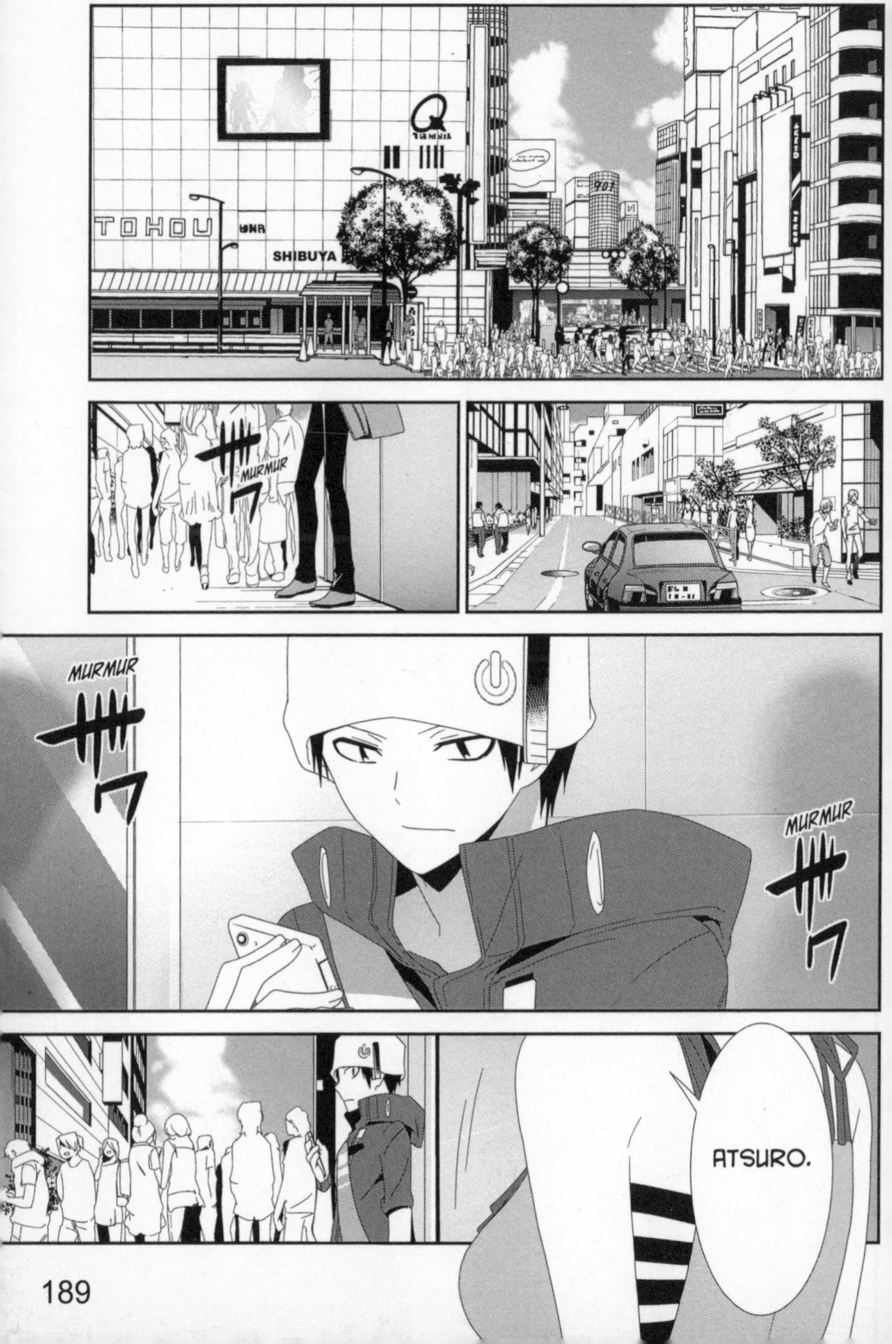
TOHOU
SHIBUYA
ザワ
MURMUR
ザワ
MURMUR
ザワ
MURMUR
ATSURO.

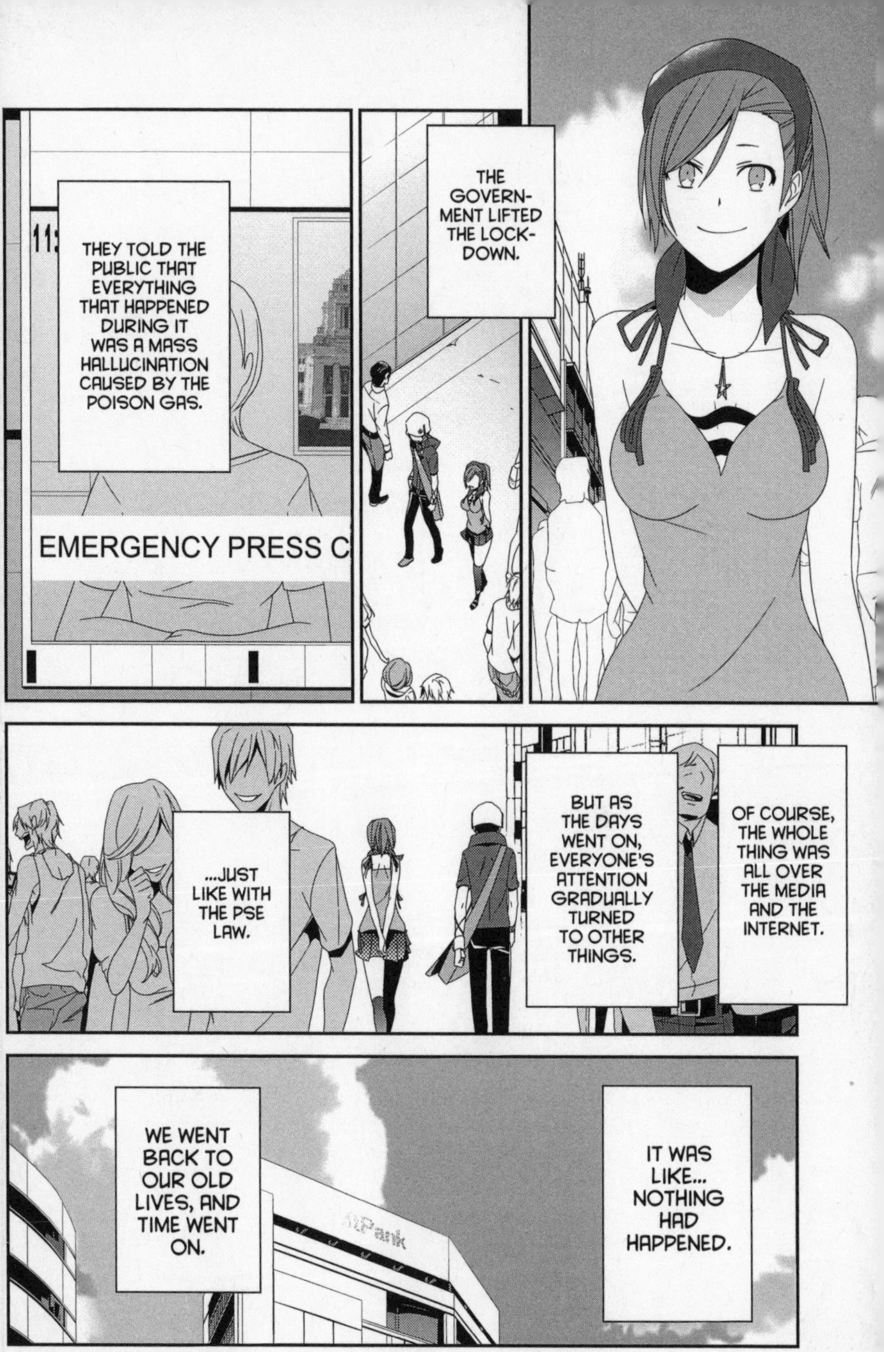
THE GOVERN-MENT LIFTED THE LOCK-DOWN.
THEY TOLD THE PUBLIC THAT EVERYTHING THAT HAPPENED DURING IT WAS A MASS HALLUCINATION CAUSED BY THE POISON GAS.
EMERGENCY PRESS C
OF COURSE, THE WHOLE THING WAS ALL OVER THE MEDIA AND THE INTERNET.
BUT AS THE DAYS WENT ON, EVERYONE'S ATTENTION GRADUALLY TURNED TO OTHER THINGS.
...JUST LIKE WITH THE PSE LAW.
IT WAS LIKE... NOTHING HAD HAPPENED.
WE WENT BACK TO OUR OLD LIVES, AND TIME WENT ON.

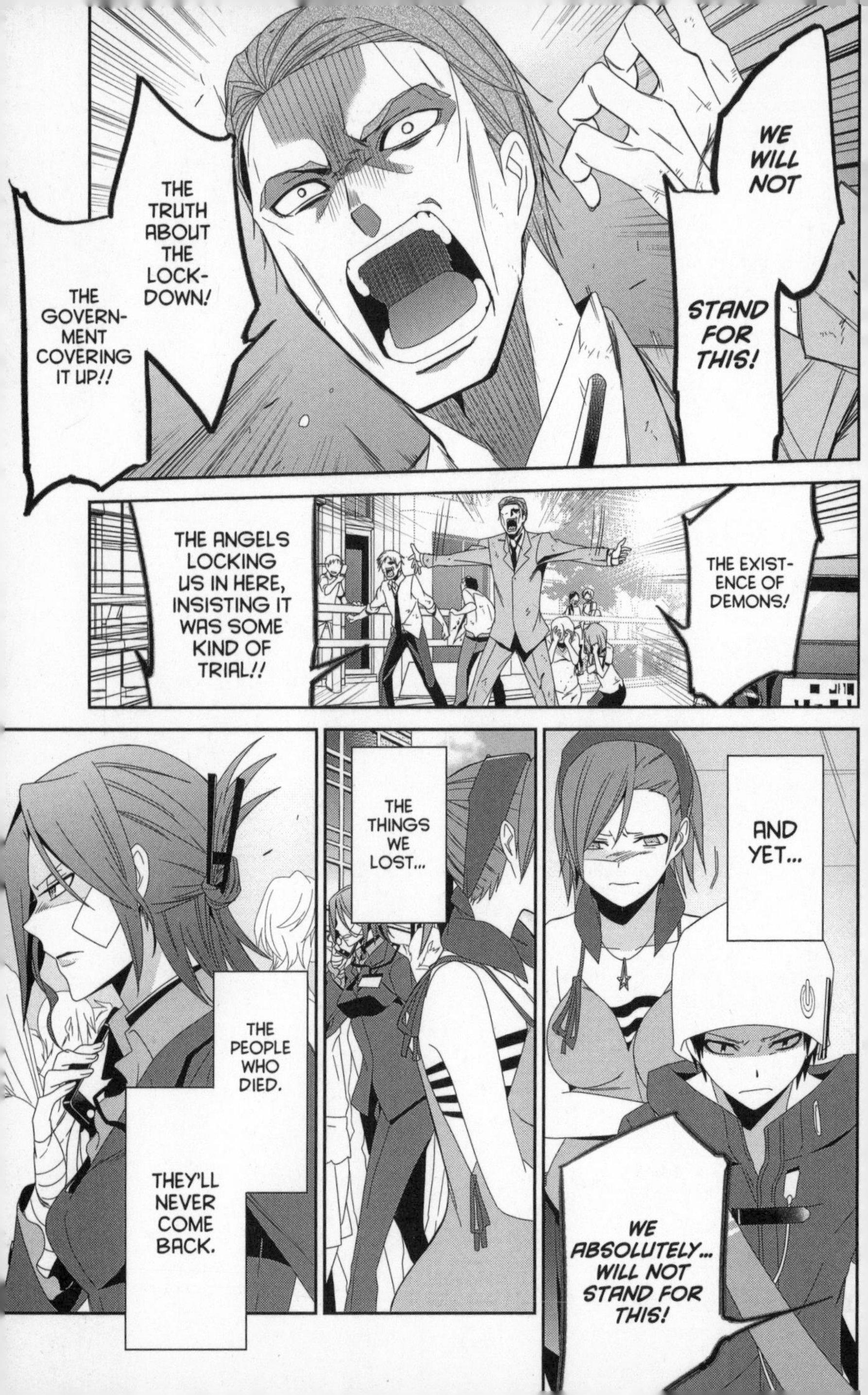
WE WILL NOT STAND FOR THIS!
THE TRUTH ABOUT THE LOCK-DOWN!
THE GOVERN-MENT COVERING IT UP!!
THE EXIST-ENCE OF DEMONS!
THE ANGELS LOCKING US IN HERE, INSISTING IT WAS SOME KIND OF TRIAL!!
AND YET...
WE ABSOLUTELY... WILL NOT STAND FOR THIS!
THE THINGS WE LOST...
THE PEOPLE WHO DIED.
THEY'LL NEVER COME BACK.

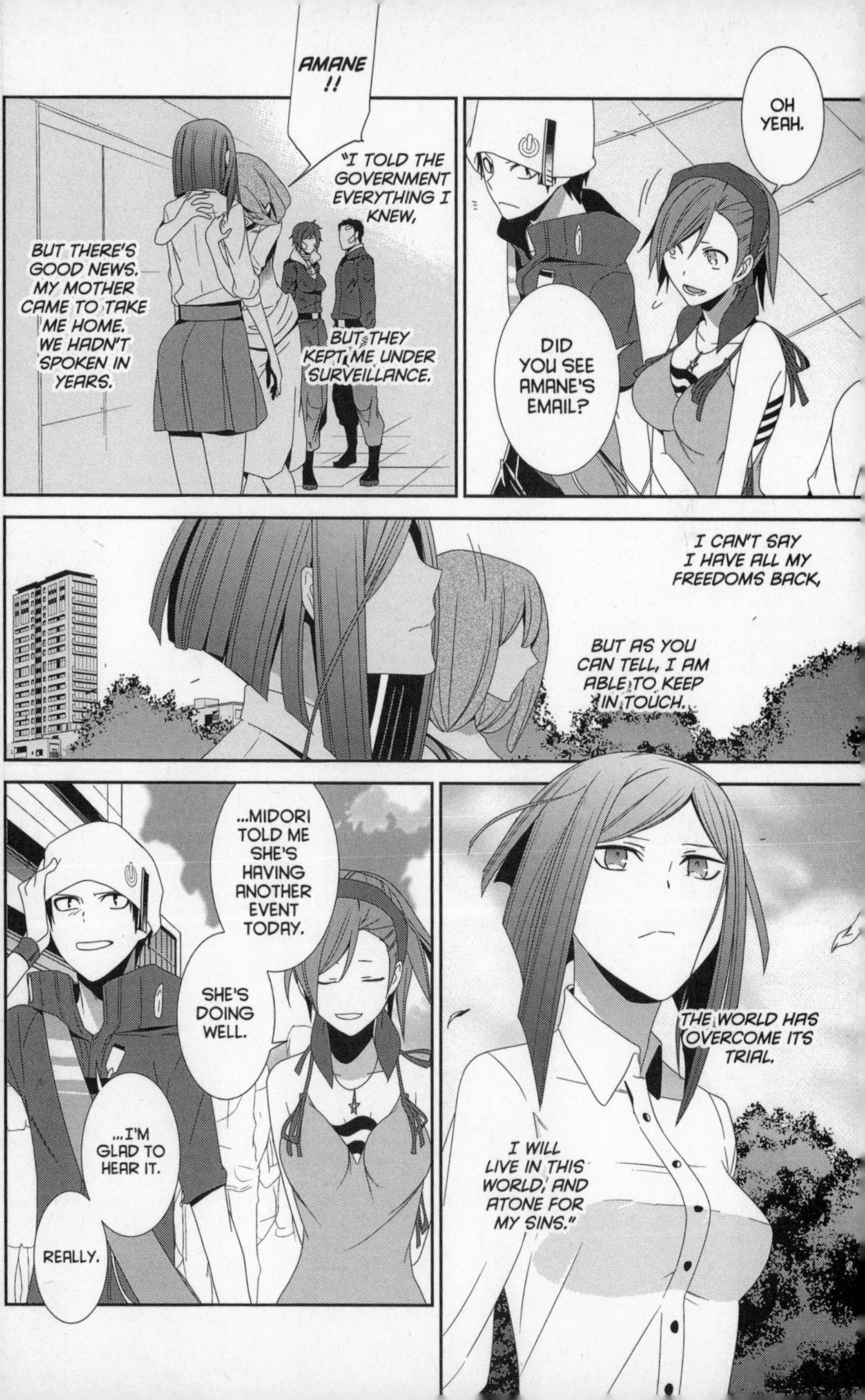
OH YEAH.
DID YOU SEE AMANE'S EMAIL?
AMANE !!
"I TOLD THE GOVERNMENT EVERYTHING I KNEW,
BUT THEY KEPT ME UNDER SURVEILLANCE.
BUT THERE'S GOOD NEWS. MY MOTHER CAME TO TAKE ME HOME. WE HADN'T SPOKEN IN YEARS.
I CAN'T SAY I HAVE ALL MY FREEDOMS BACK,
BUT AS YOU CAN TELL, I AM ABLE TO KEEP IN TOUCH.
THE WORLD HAS OVERCOME ITS TRIAL.
I WILL LIVE IN THIS WORLD, AND ATONE FOR MY SINS."
...MIDORI TOLD ME SHE'S HAVING ANOTHER EVENT TODAY.
SHE'S DOING WELL.
...I'M GLAD TO HEAR IT.
REALLY.

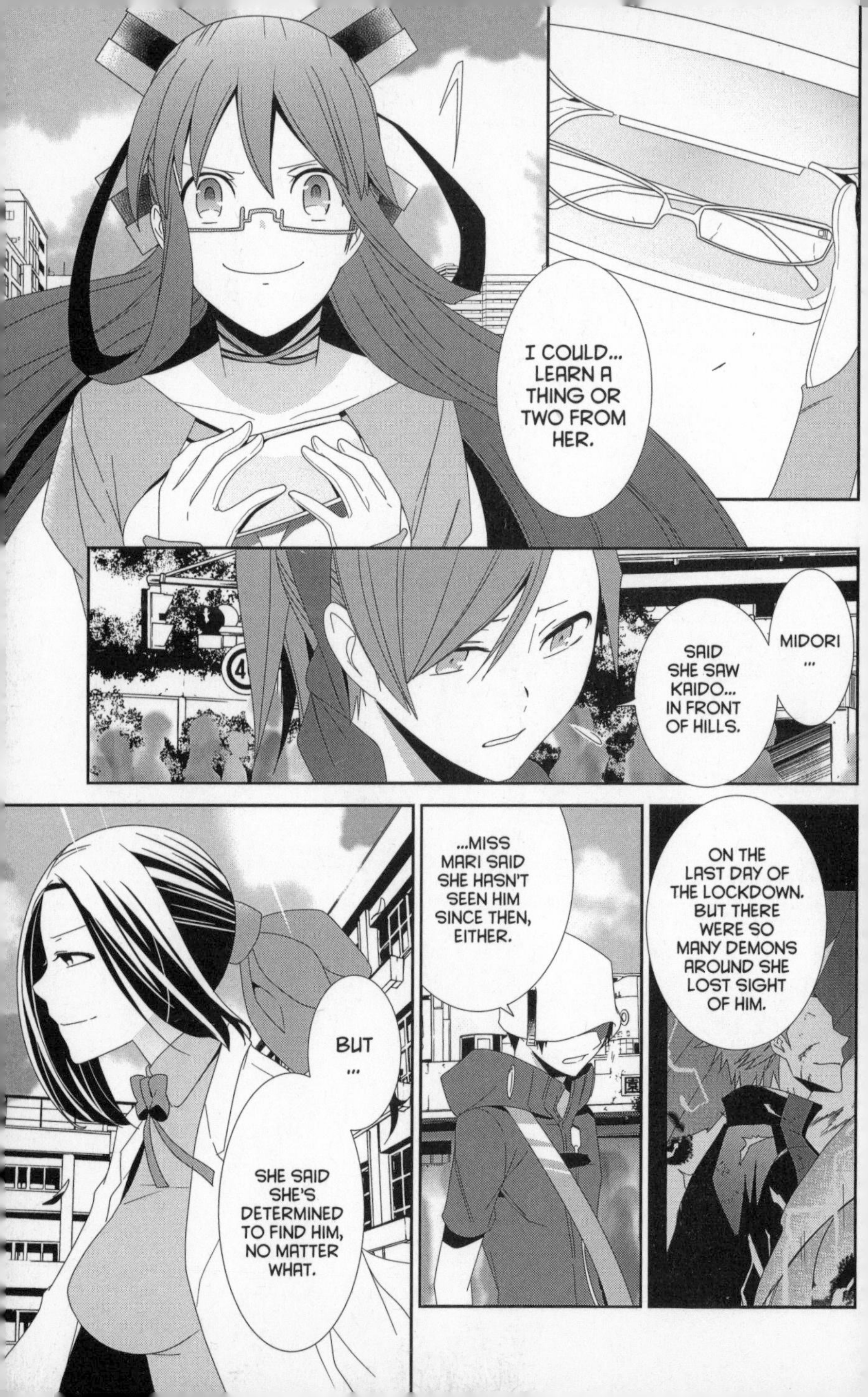
I COULD... LEARN A THING OR TWO FROM HER.
MIDORI ...
SAID SHE SAW KAIDO... IN FRONT OF HILLS.
ON THE LAST DAY OF THE LOCKDOWN. BUT THERE WERE SO MANY DEMONS AROUND SHE LOST SIGHT OF HIM.
...MISS MARI SAID SHE HASN'T SEEN HIM SINCE THEN, EITHER.
BUT ...
SHE SAID SHE'S DETERMINED TO FIND HIM, NO MATTER WHAT.

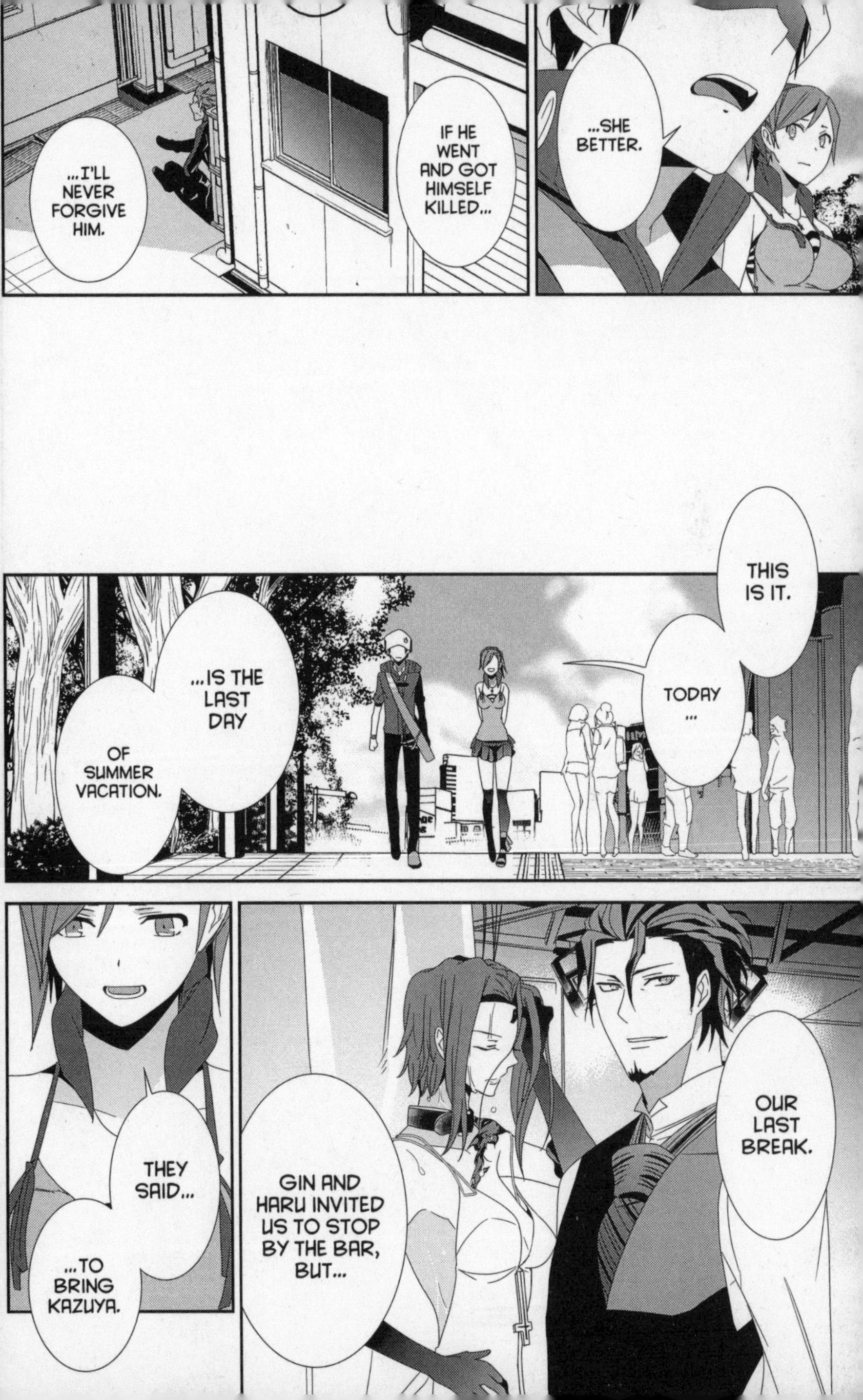
...SHE BETTER.
IF HE WENT AND GOT HIMSELF KILLED...
...I'LL NEVER FORGIVE HIM.
THIS IS IT.
TODAY ...
...IS THE LAST DAY
OF SUMMER VACATION.
OUR LAST BREAK.
GIN AND HARU INVITED US TO STOP BY THE BAR, BUT...
THEY SAID...
...TO BRING KAZUYA.

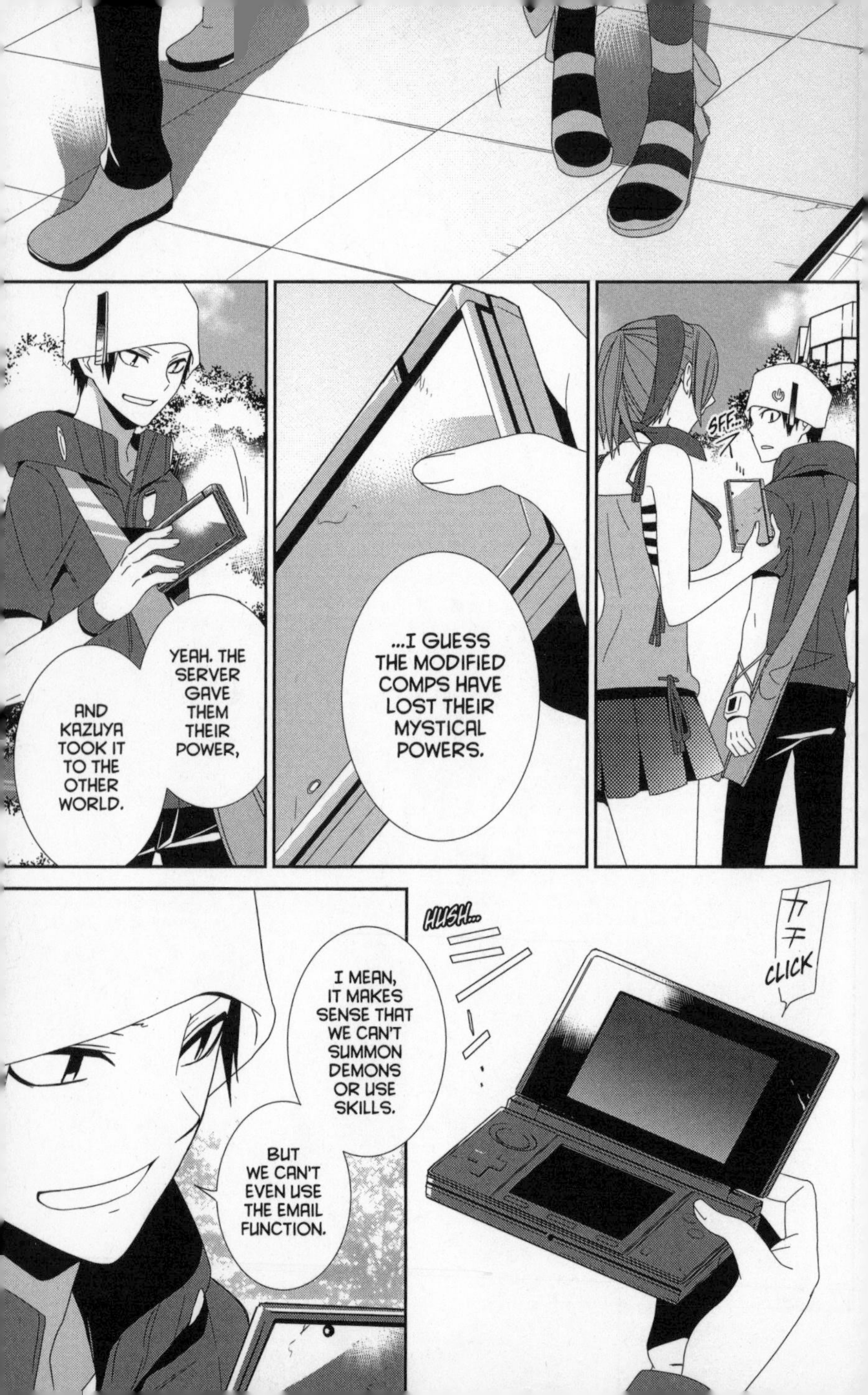
SFF...
...I GUESS THE MODIFIED COMPS HAVE LOST THEIR MYSTICAL POWERS.
YEAH. THE SERVER GAVE THEM THEIR POWER,
AND KAZUYA TOOK IT TO THE OTHER WORLD.
カチ CLICK
HUSH...
I MEAN, IT MAKES SENSE THAT WE CAN'T SUMMON DEMONS OR USE SKILLS.
BUT WE CAN'T EVEN USE THE EMAIL FUNCTION.

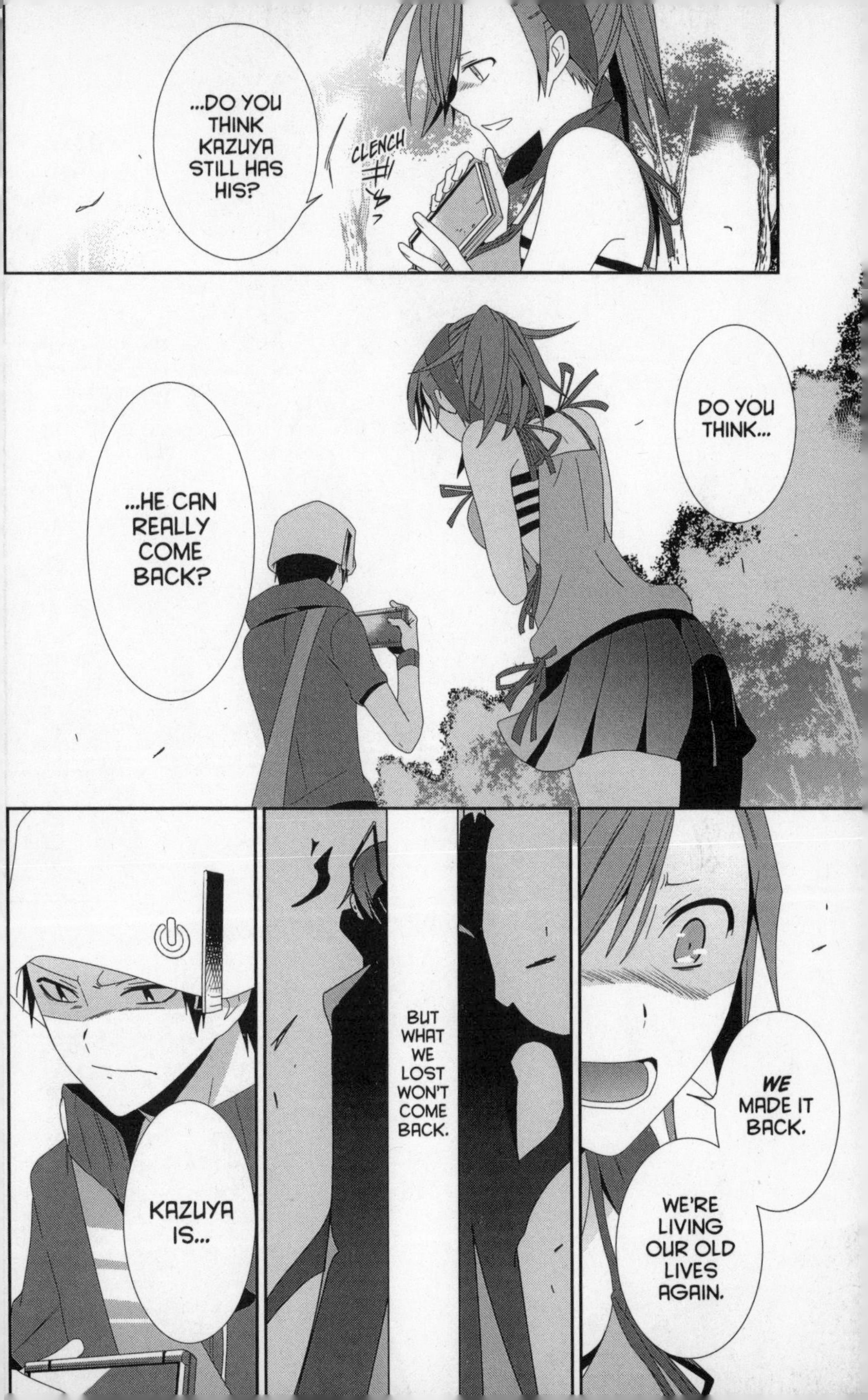
CLENCH
...DO YOU THINK KAZUYA STILL HAS HIS?
DO YOU THINK...
...HE CAN REALLY COME BACK?
WE MADE IT BACK.
WE'RE LIVING OUR OLD LIVES AGAIN.
BUT WHAT WE LOST WON'T COME BACK.
KAZUYA IS...

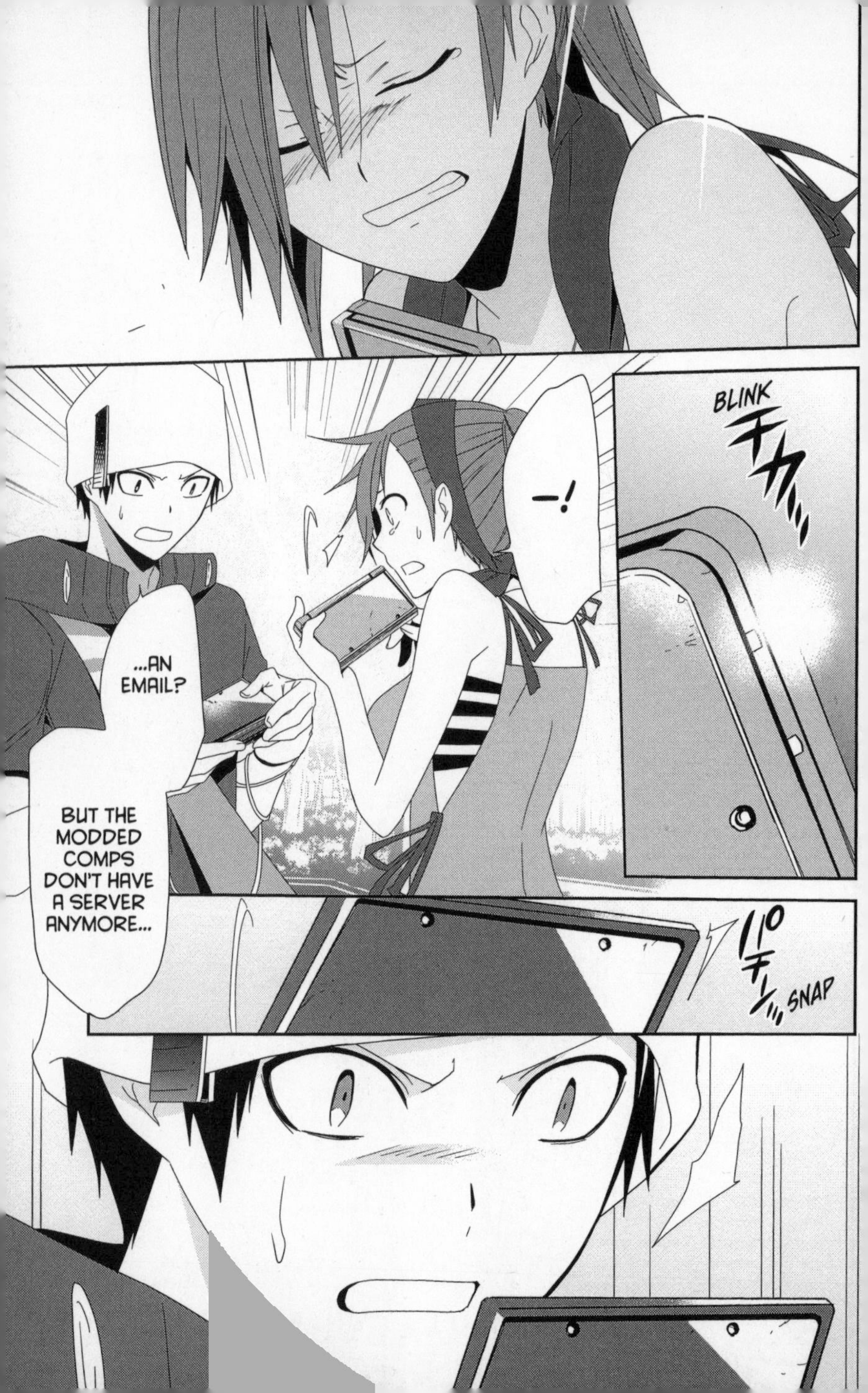
BLINK
チカ...
—!
...AN EMAIL?
BUT THE MODDED COMPS DON'T HAVE A SERVER ANYMORE...
パチン...
SNAP

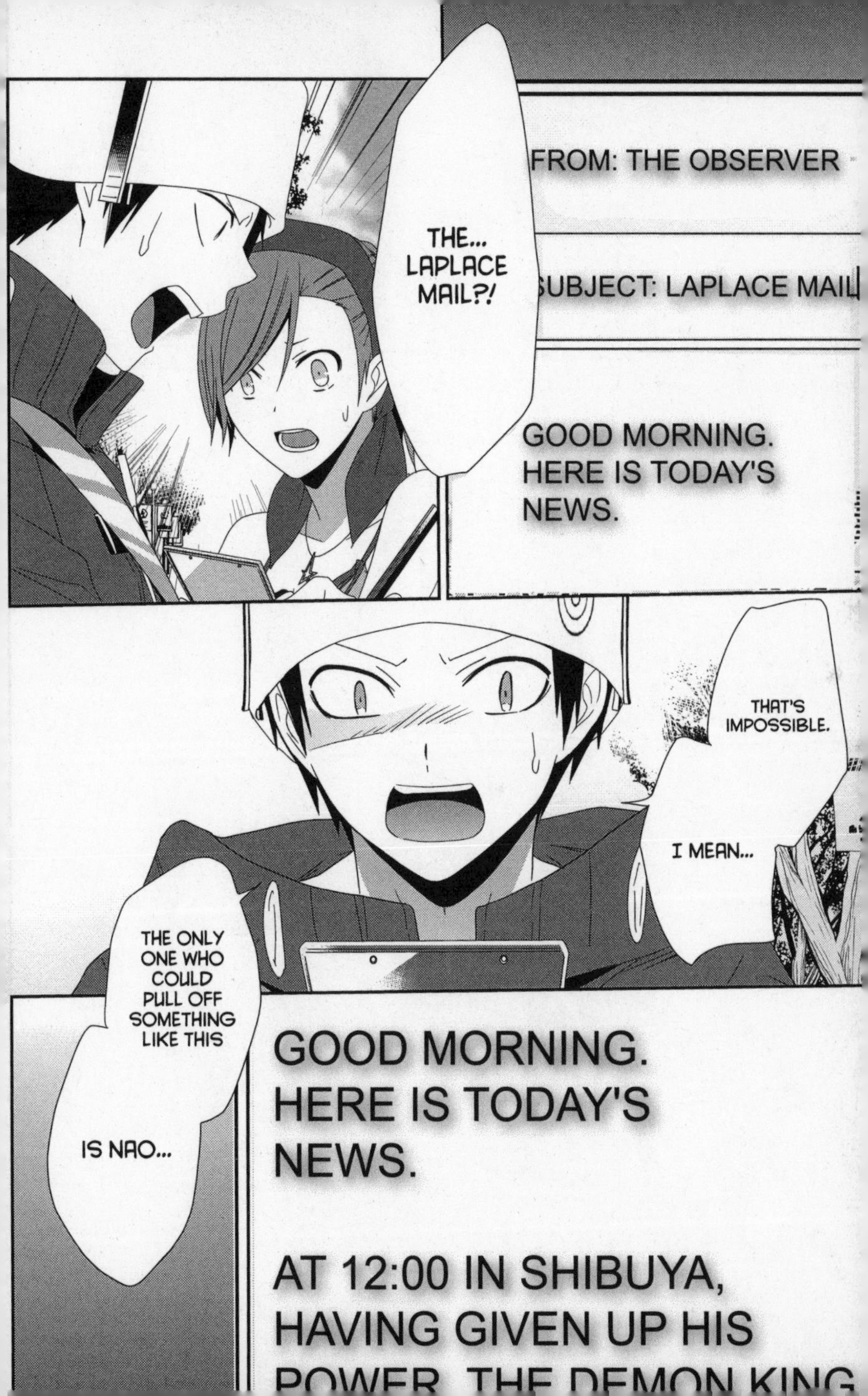
FROM: THE OBSERVER
SUBJECT: LAPLACE MAIL
GOOD MORNING. HERE IS TODAY'S NEWS.
THE... LAPLACE MAIL?!
THAT'S IMPOSSIBLE.
I MEAN...
THE ONLY ONE WHO COULD PULL OFF SOMETHING LIKE THIS IS NAO...
GOOD MORNING. HERE IS TODAY'S NEWS.
AT 12:00 IN SHIBUYA, HAVING GIVEN UP HIS POWER, THE DEMON KING

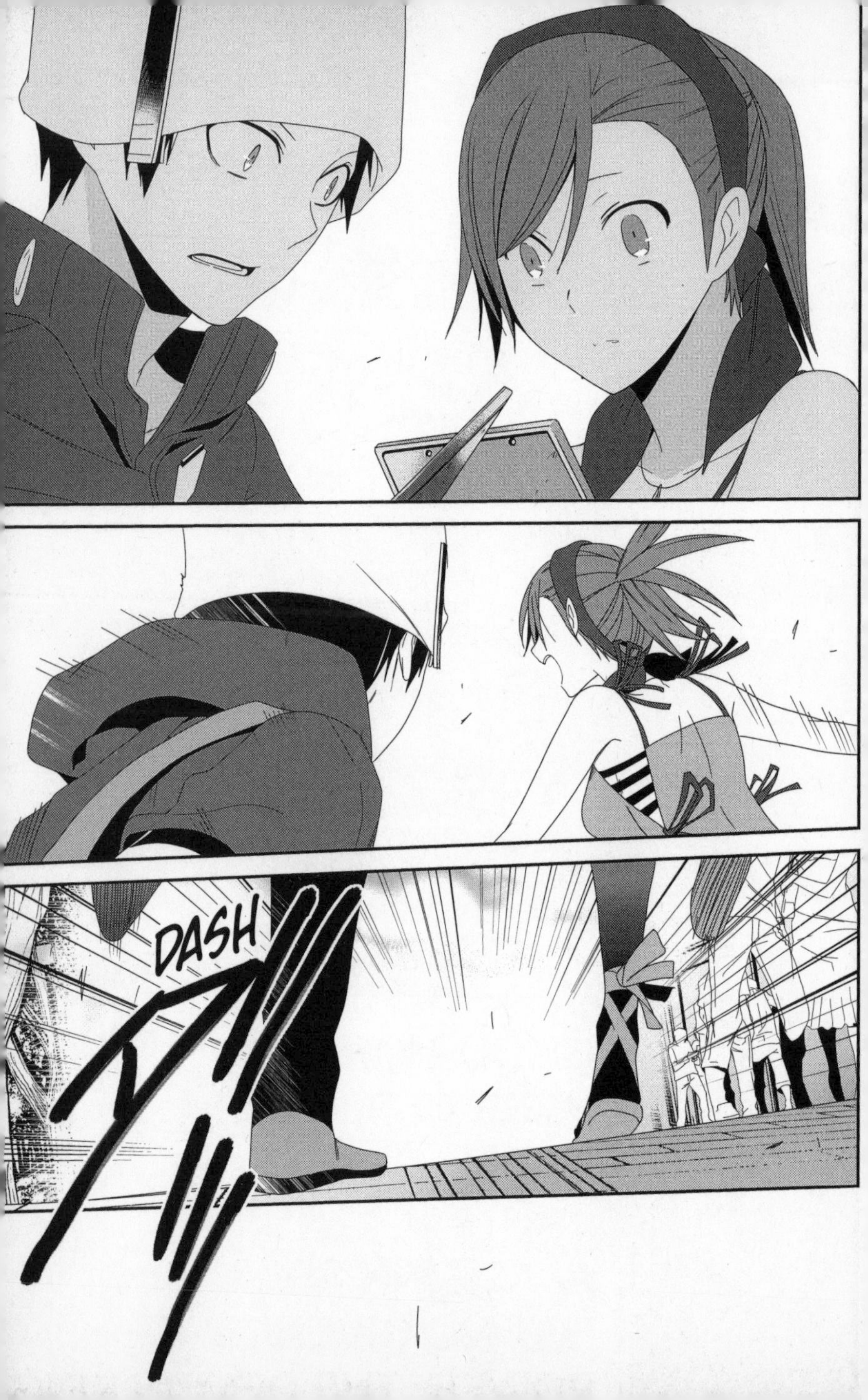
DASH

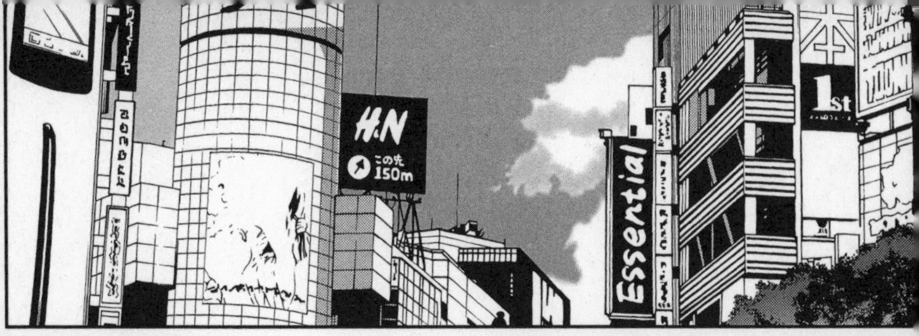
H&N
この先
150m
Essential
1st

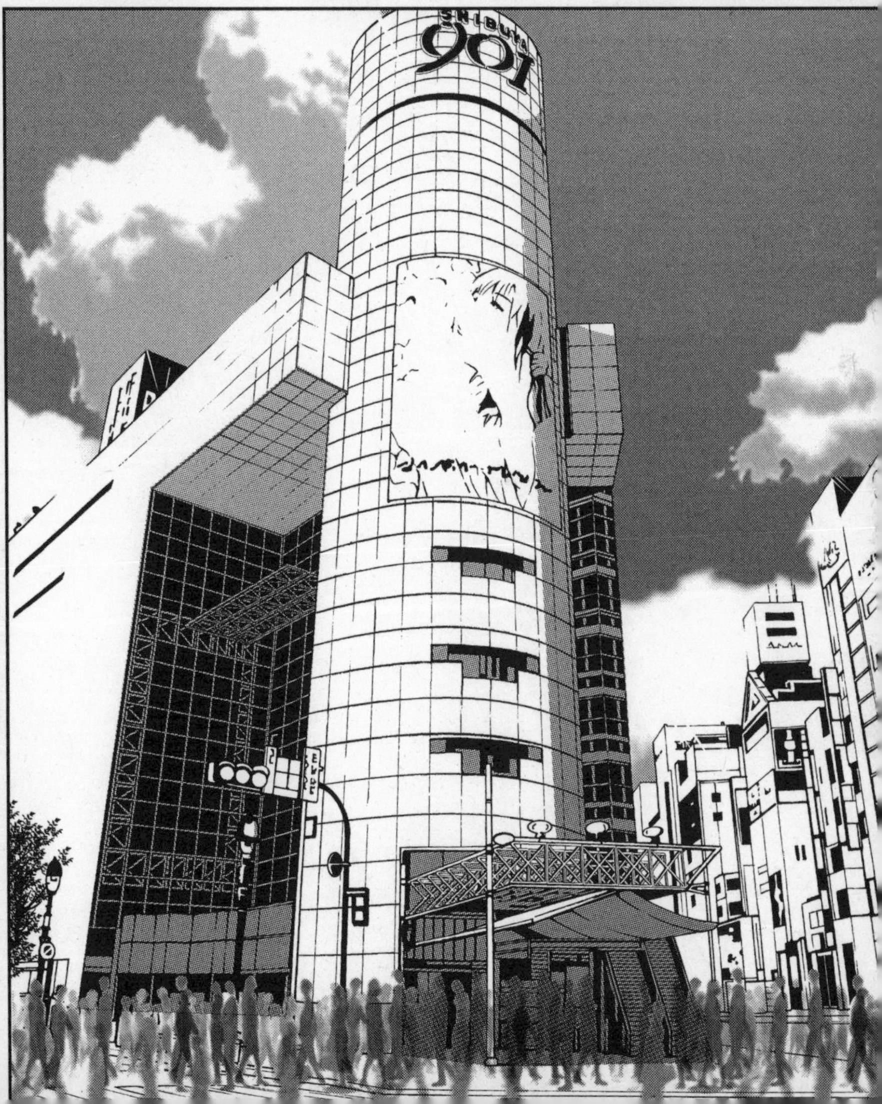
SHIBUYA
901

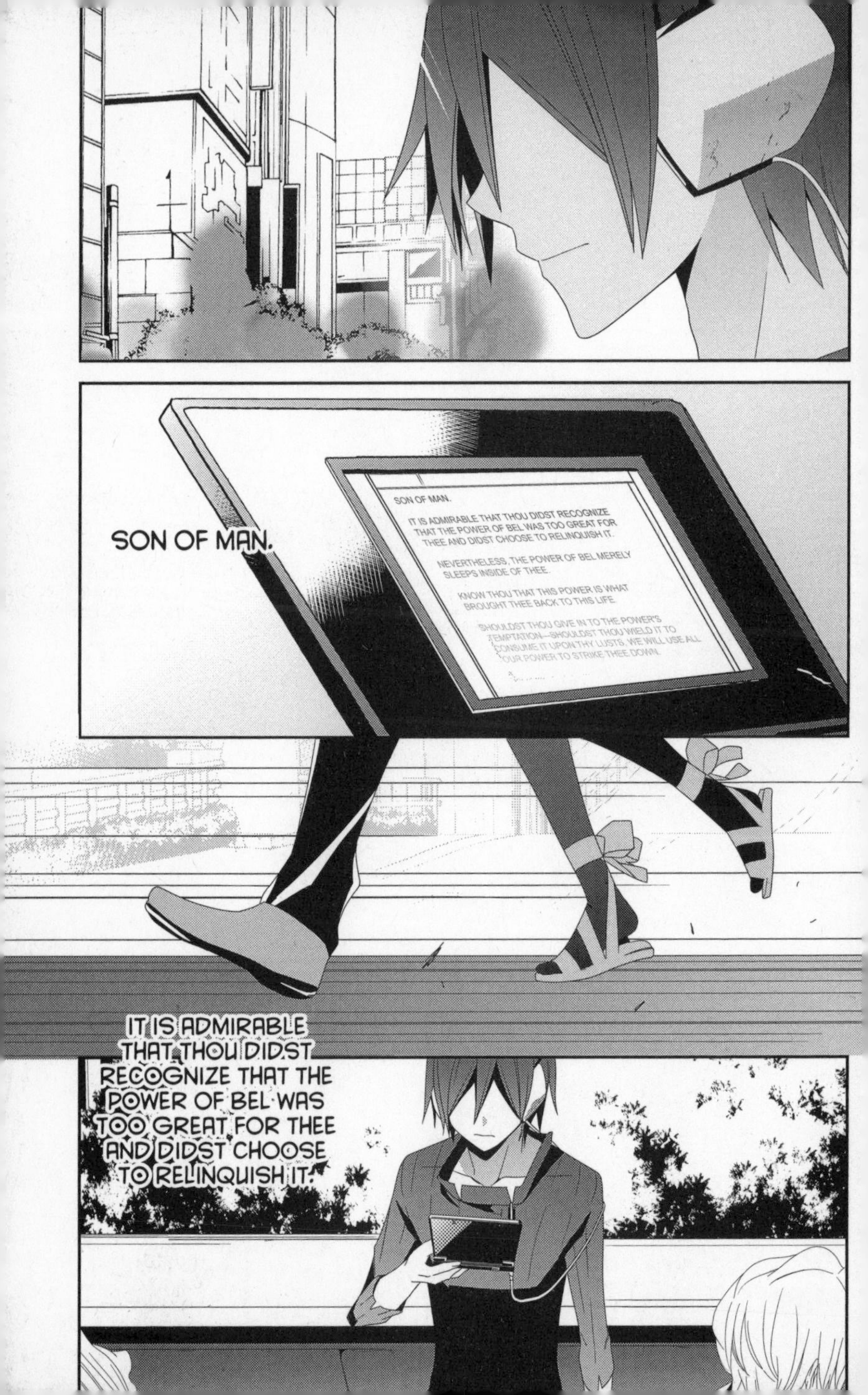
SON OF MAN.
IT IS ADMIRABLE THAT THOU DIDST RECOGNIZE THAT THE POWER OF BEL WAS TOO GREAT FOR THEE AND DIDST CHOOSE TO RELINQUISH IT.
NEVERTHELESS, THE POWER OF BEL MERELY SLEEPS INSIDE OF THEE.
KNOW THOU THAT THIS POWER IS WHAT BROUGHT THEE BACK TO THIS LIFE.
SHOULDST THOU GIVE IN TO THE POWER'S TEMPTATION—SHOULDST THOU WIELD IT TO CONSUME IT UPON THY LUSTS, WE WILL USE ALL OUR POWER TO STRIKE THEE DOWN.
SON OF MAN.
IT IS ADMIRABLE THAT THOU DIDST RECOGNIZE THAT THE POWER OF BEL WAS TOO GREAT FOR THEE AND DIDST CHOOSE TO RELINQUISH IT.

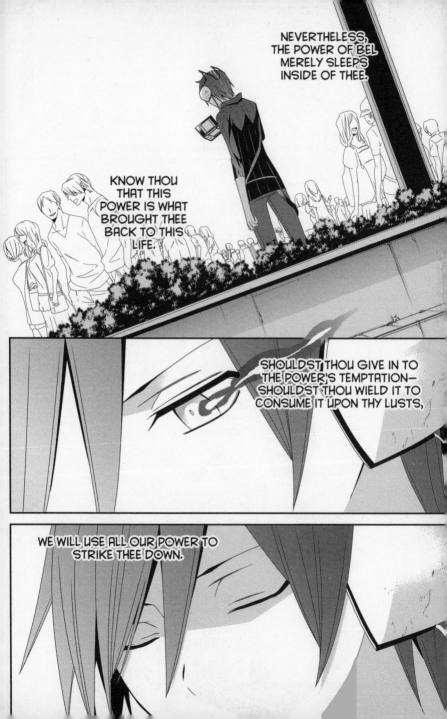

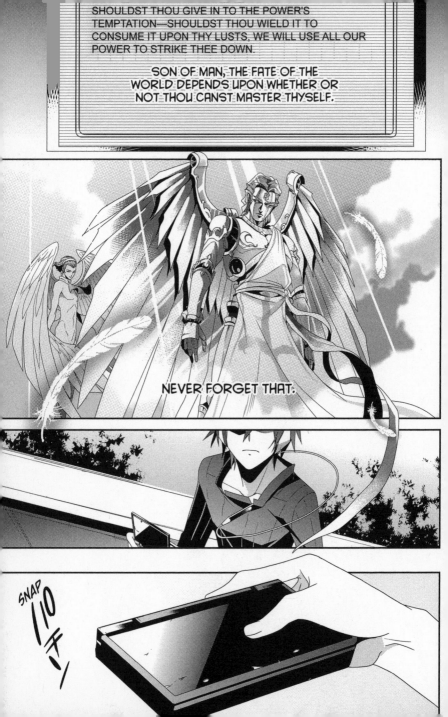

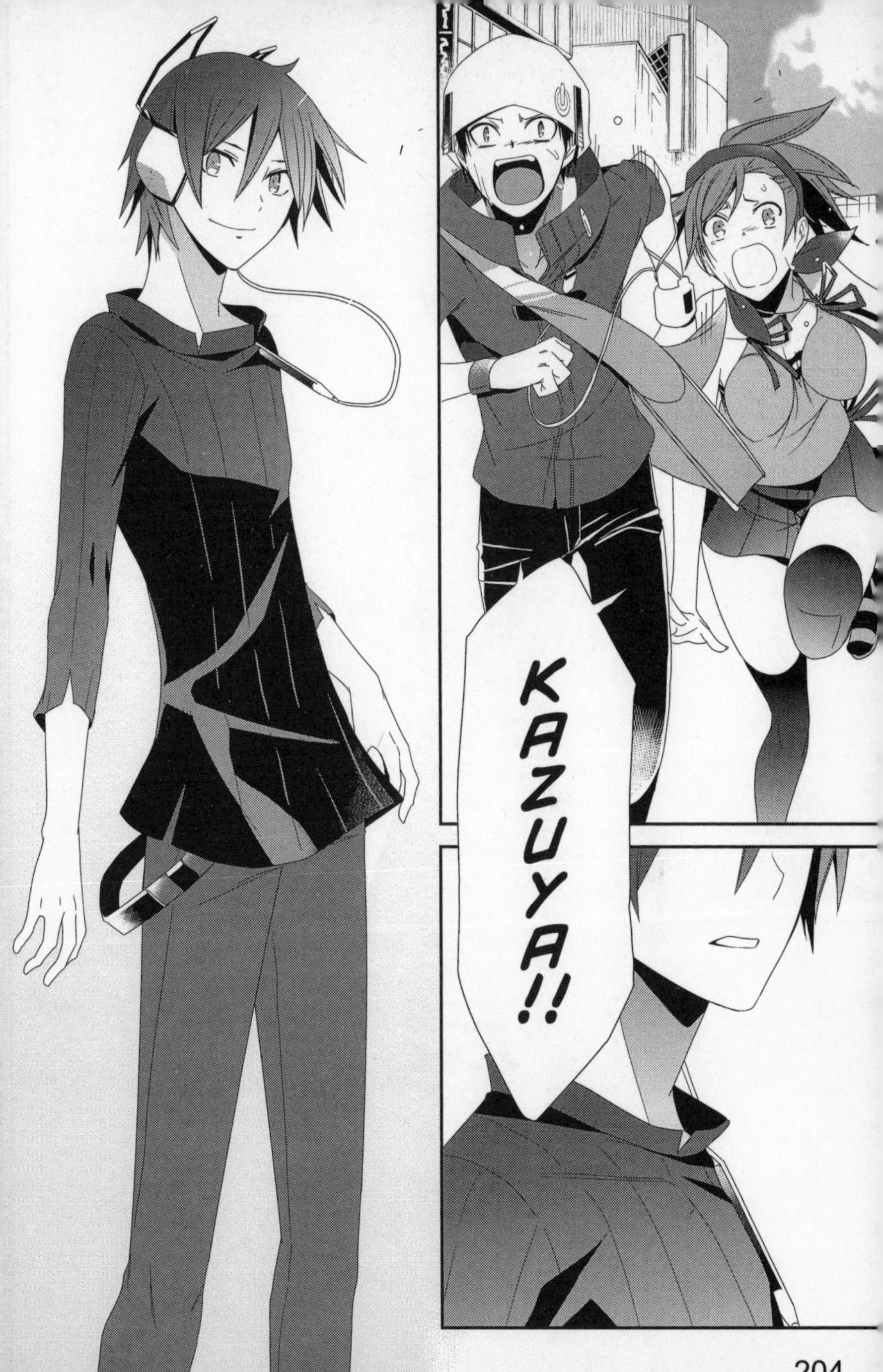
KAZUYA!!

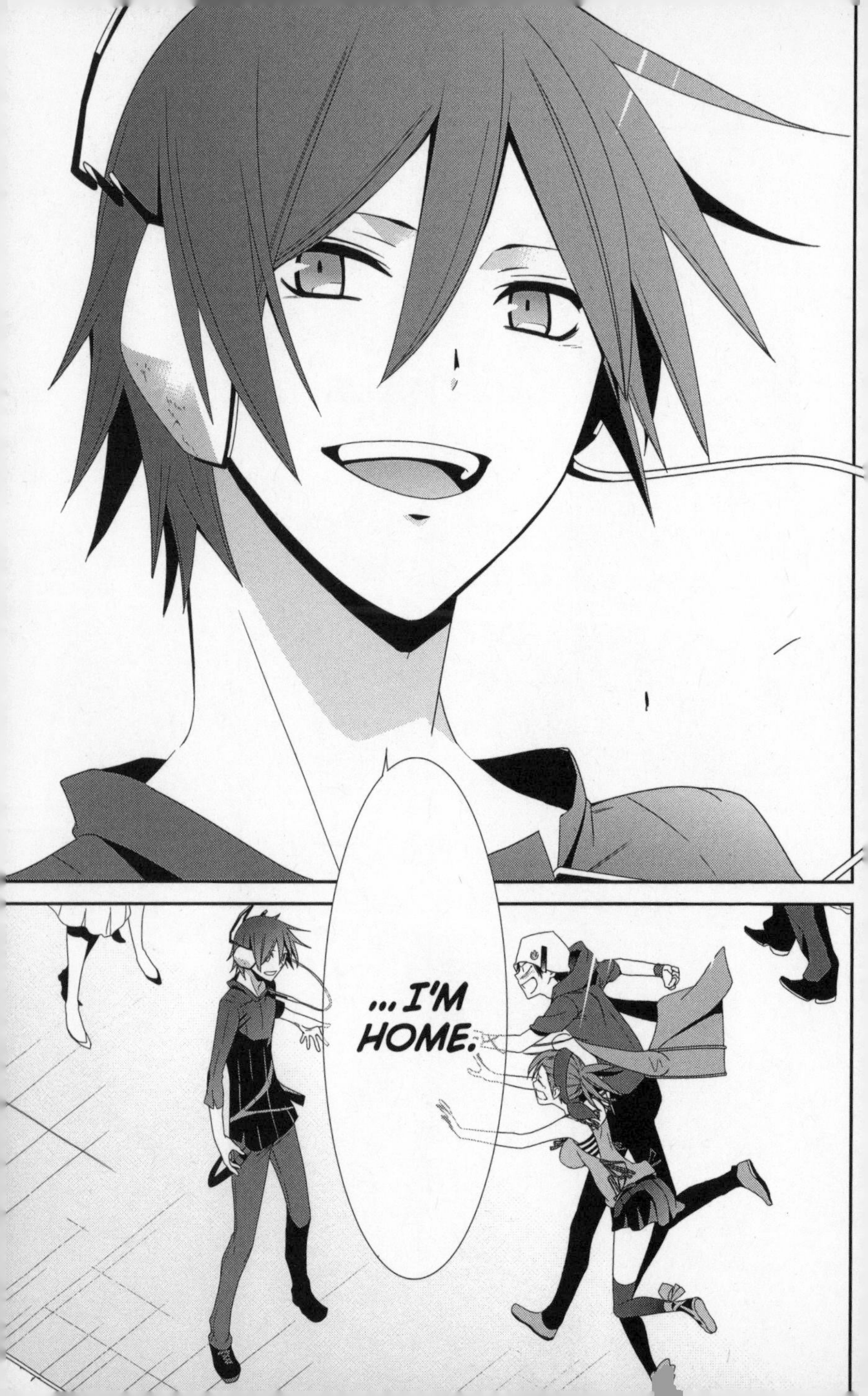
...I'M HOME.

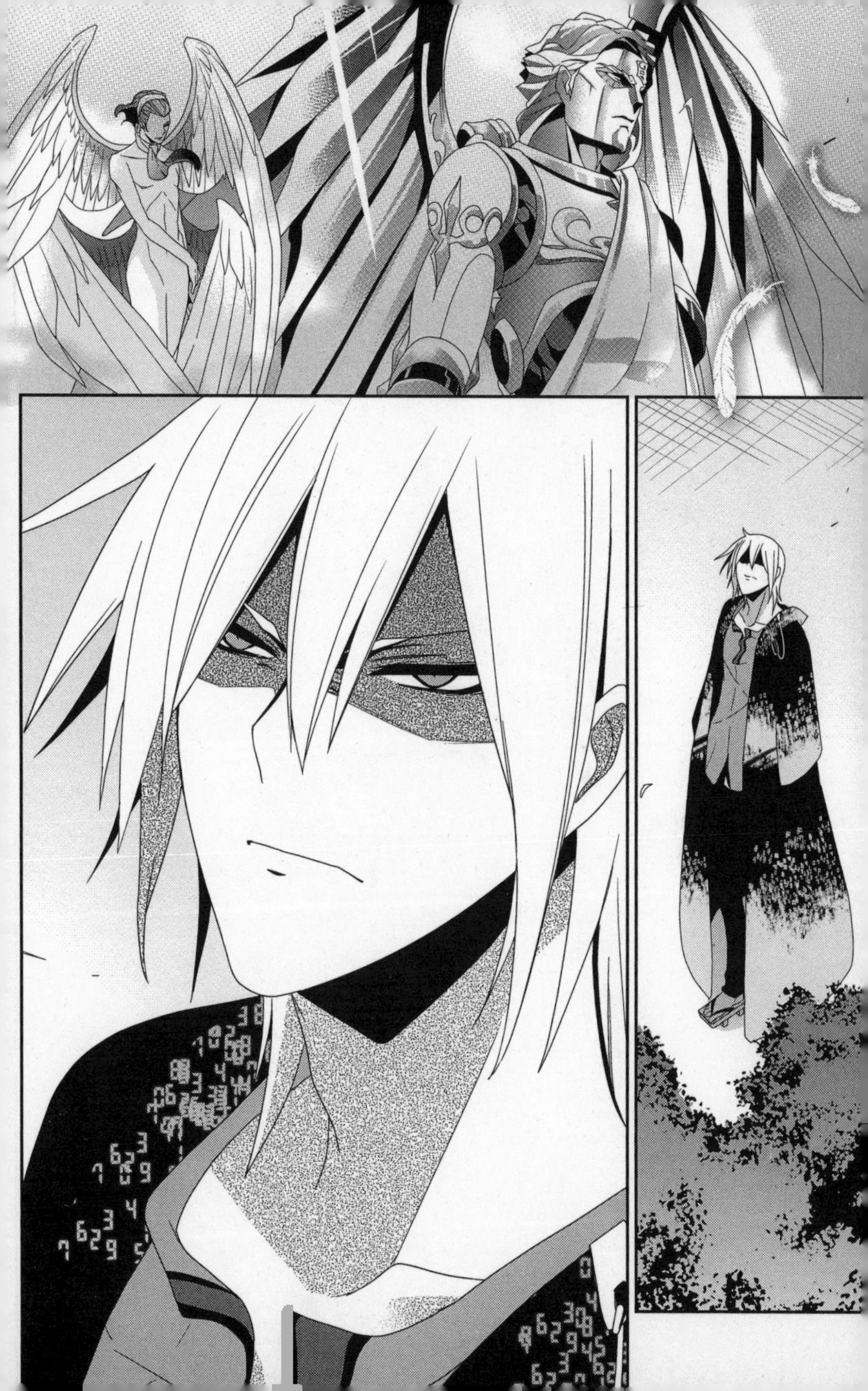

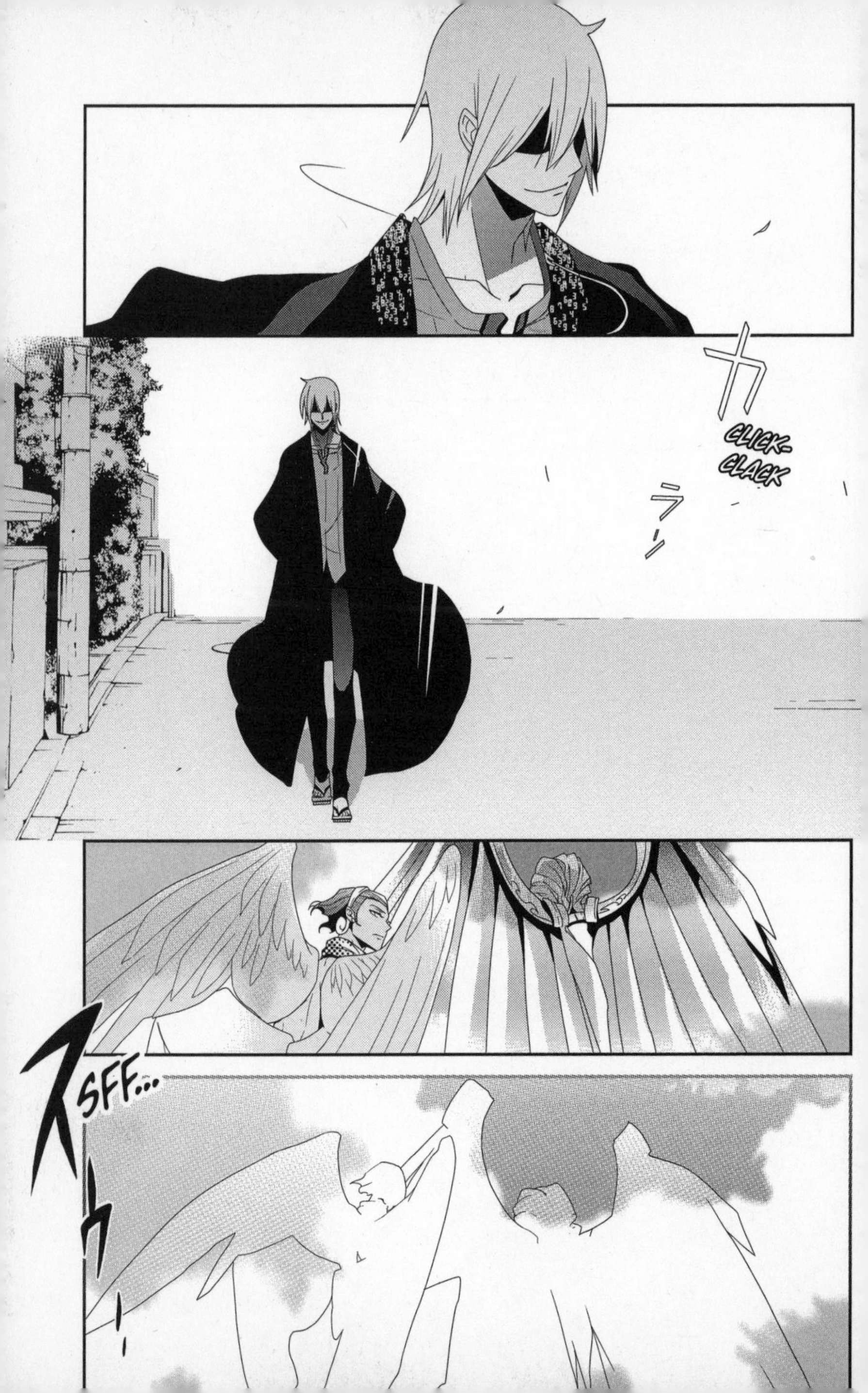
カ
CLICK-
CLACK
ラン
スッ
SFF...

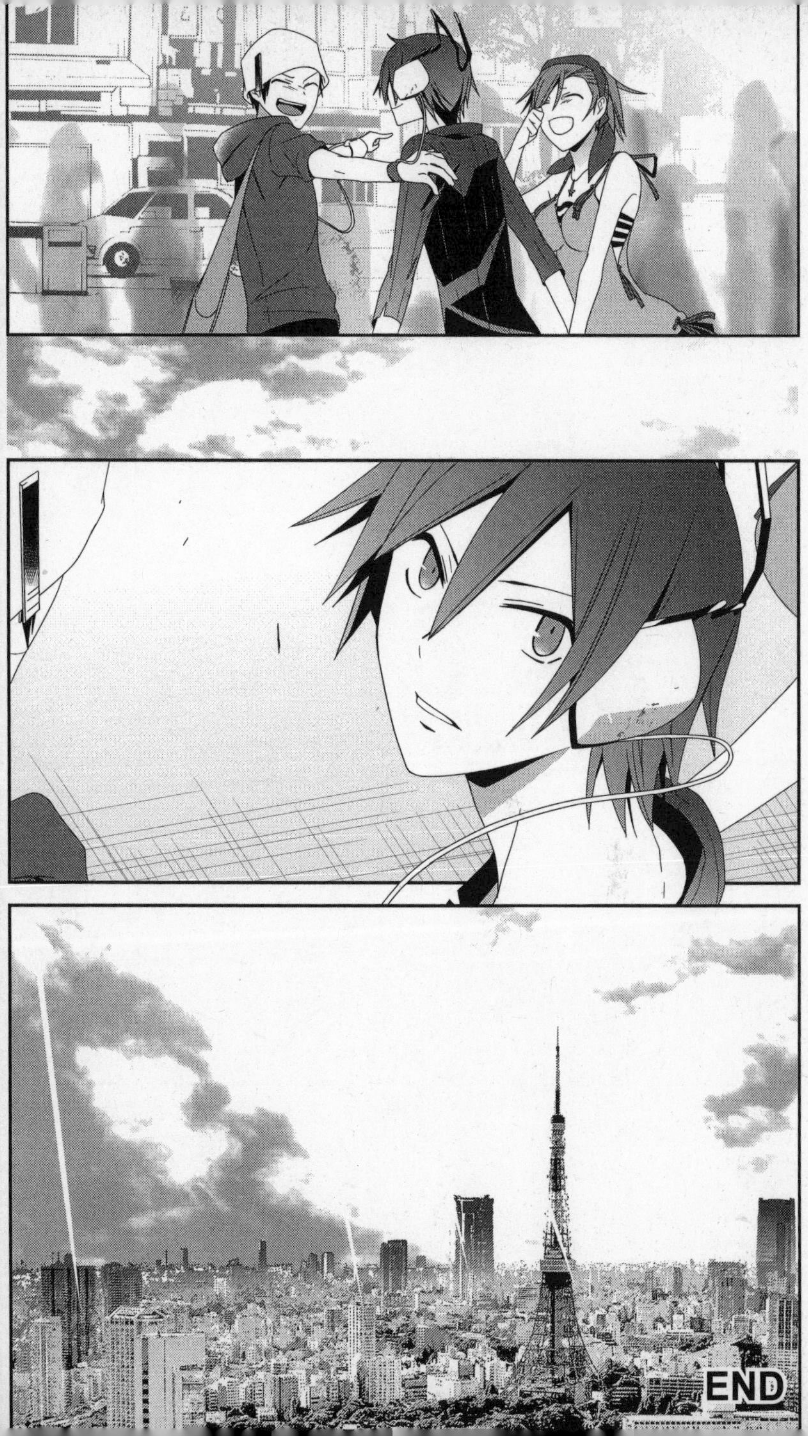
END

OFILE

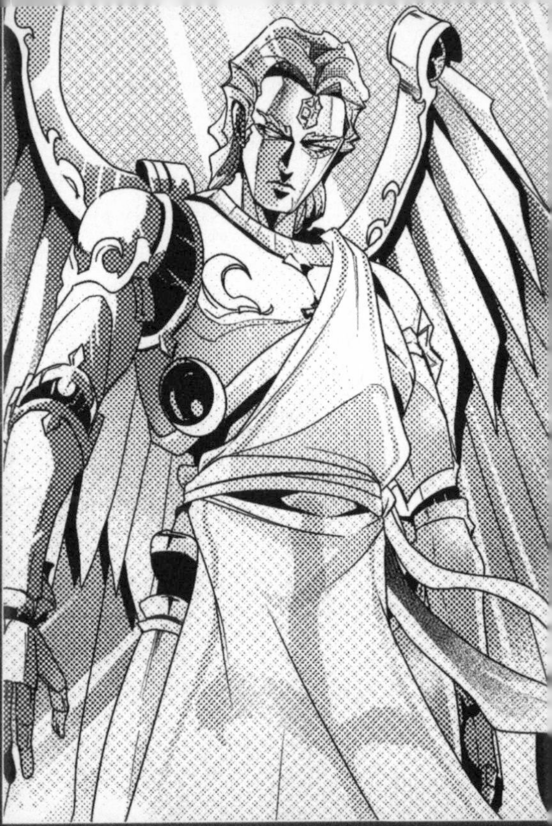

METATRON

THE GREATEST AND MOST MYSTERIOUS OF ANGELS. HE HAS SEVERAL OTHER NAMES, INCLUDING "RECORDING ANGEL" AND "PRINCE OF THE PRESENCE." HIS NAME IS SAID TO MEAN "ONE WHO SERVES BEHIND THE THRONE," AND HE ACTS A GOD'S REPRESENTATIVE. HE HAS IMMENSE POWER AND HIS BODY IS SAID TO BE THE LARGEST OF TH ANGELS'. IN CONTRAST TO HIS DUTY TO MAINTAIN T WORLD, HE HAS A CRUEL SIDE, AND IS SAID TO HAV SKEWERED HUNDREDS OF MORTALS WHO OPPOSE HIM, LEAVING THEM TO DIE AGONIZING DEATHS.

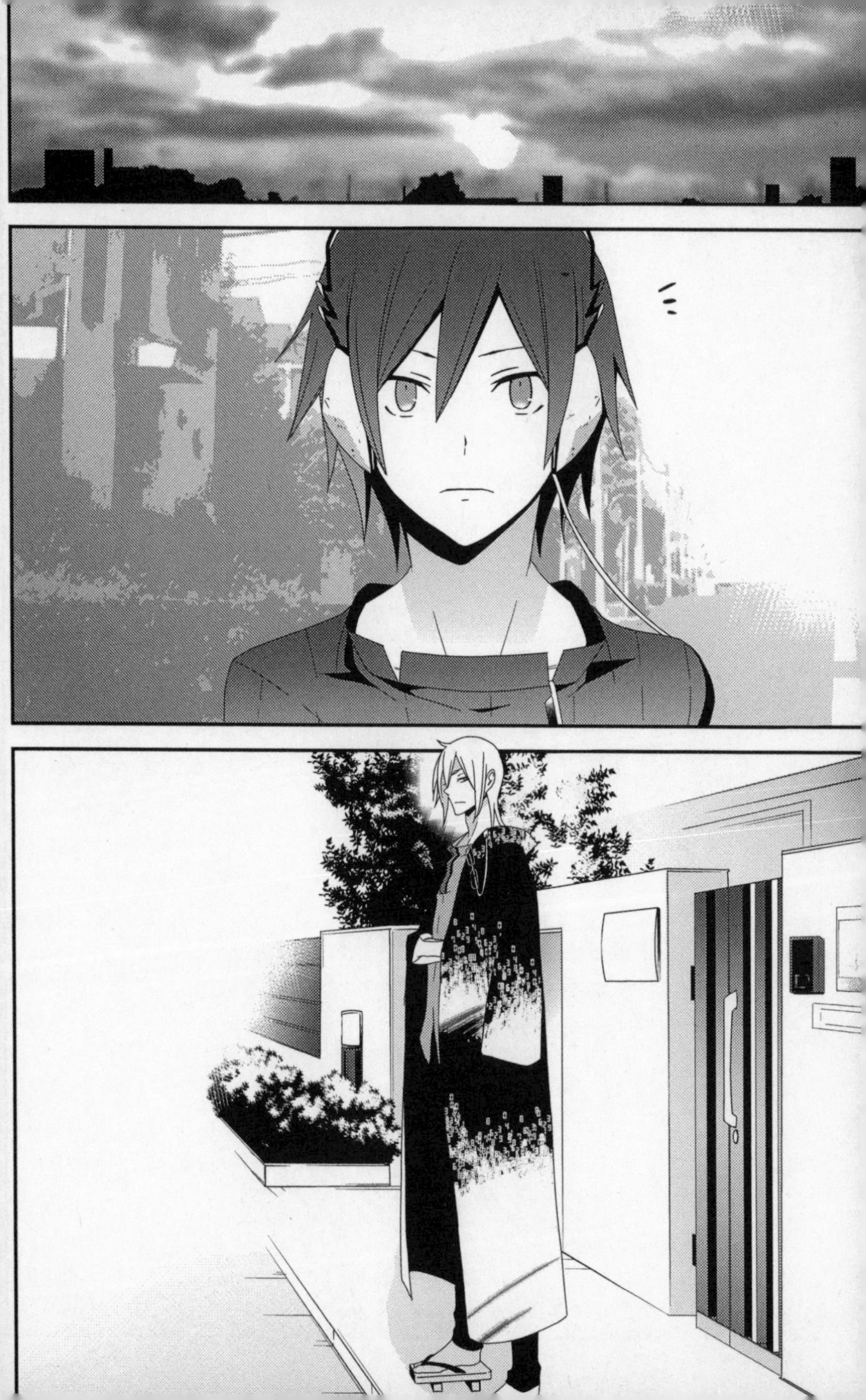

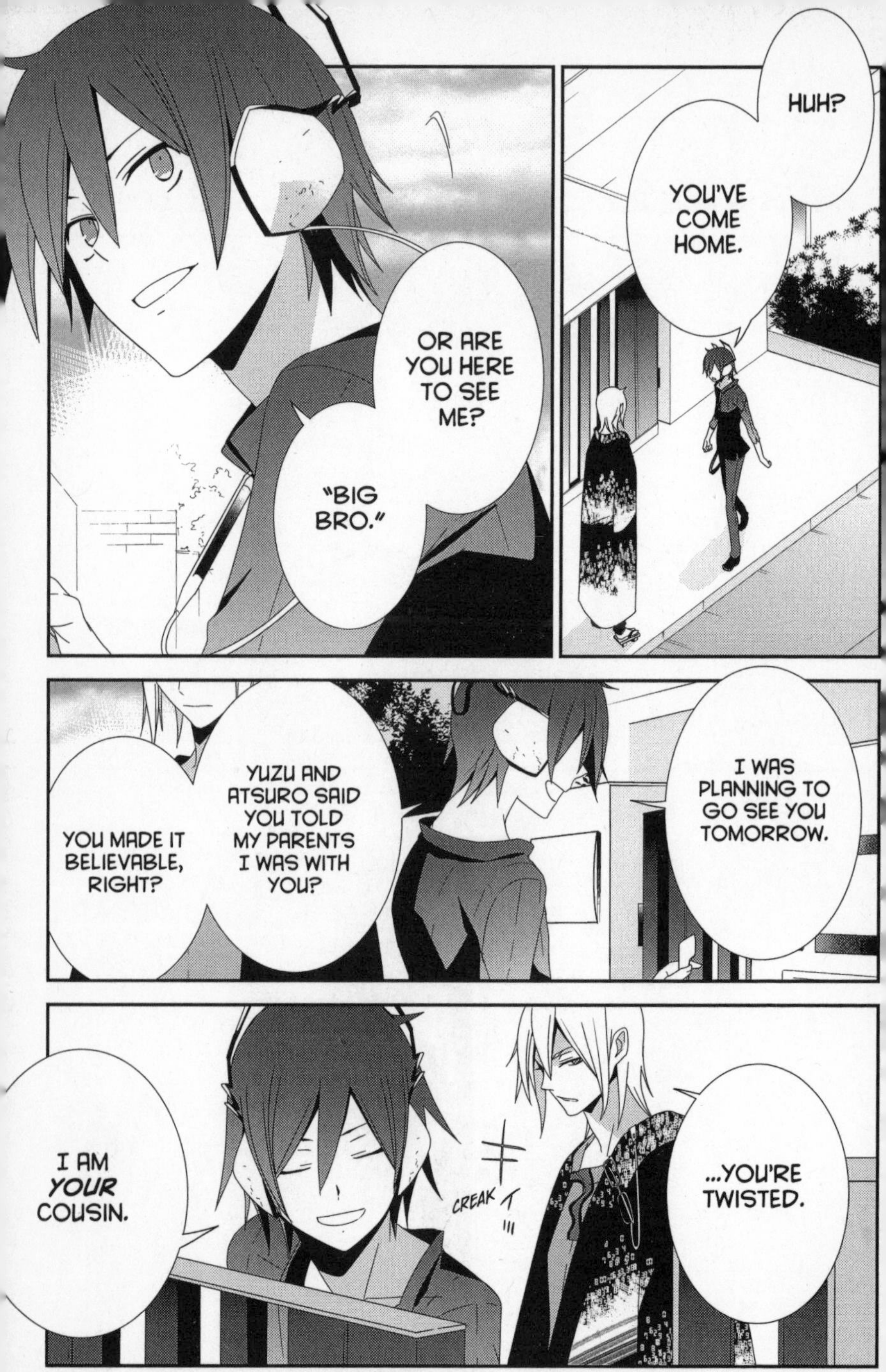
HUH?
YOU'VE COME HOME.
OR ARE YOU HERE TO SEE ME?
"BIG BRO."
I WAS PLANNING TO GO SEE YOU TOMORROW.
YUZU AND ATSURO SAID YOU TOLD MY PARENTS I WAS WITH YOU?
YOU MADE IT BELIEVABLE, RIGHT?
...YOU'RE TWISTED.
CREAK
I AM *YOUR* COUSIN.

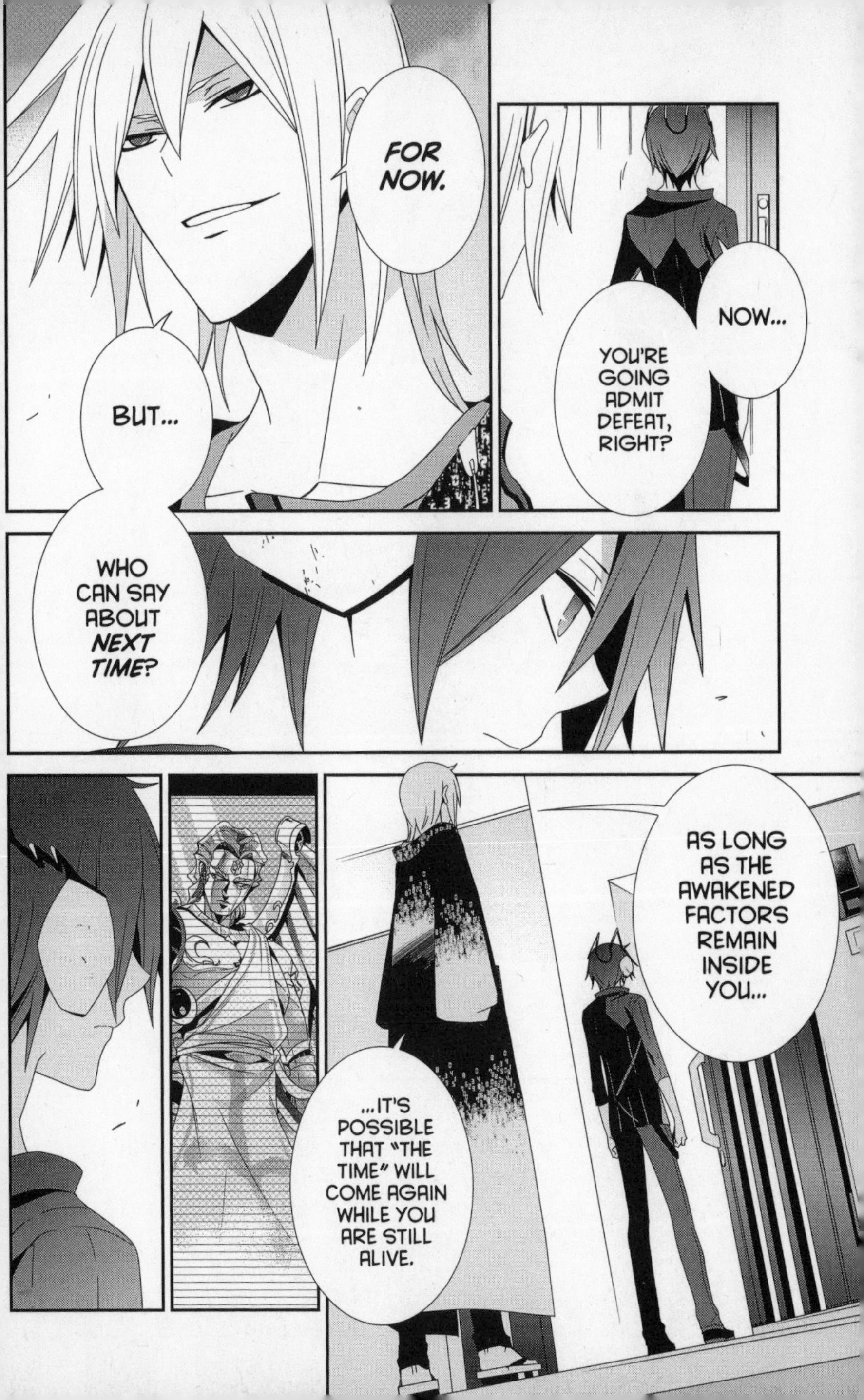
NOW...
YOU'RE GOING ADMIT DEFEAT, RIGHT?
FOR NOW.
BUT...
WHO CAN SAY ABOUT *NEXT TIME?*
AS LONG AS THE AWAKENED FACTORS REMAIN INSIDE YOU...
...IT'S POSSIBLE THAT "THE TIME" WILL COME AGAIN WHILE YOU ARE STILL ALIVE.

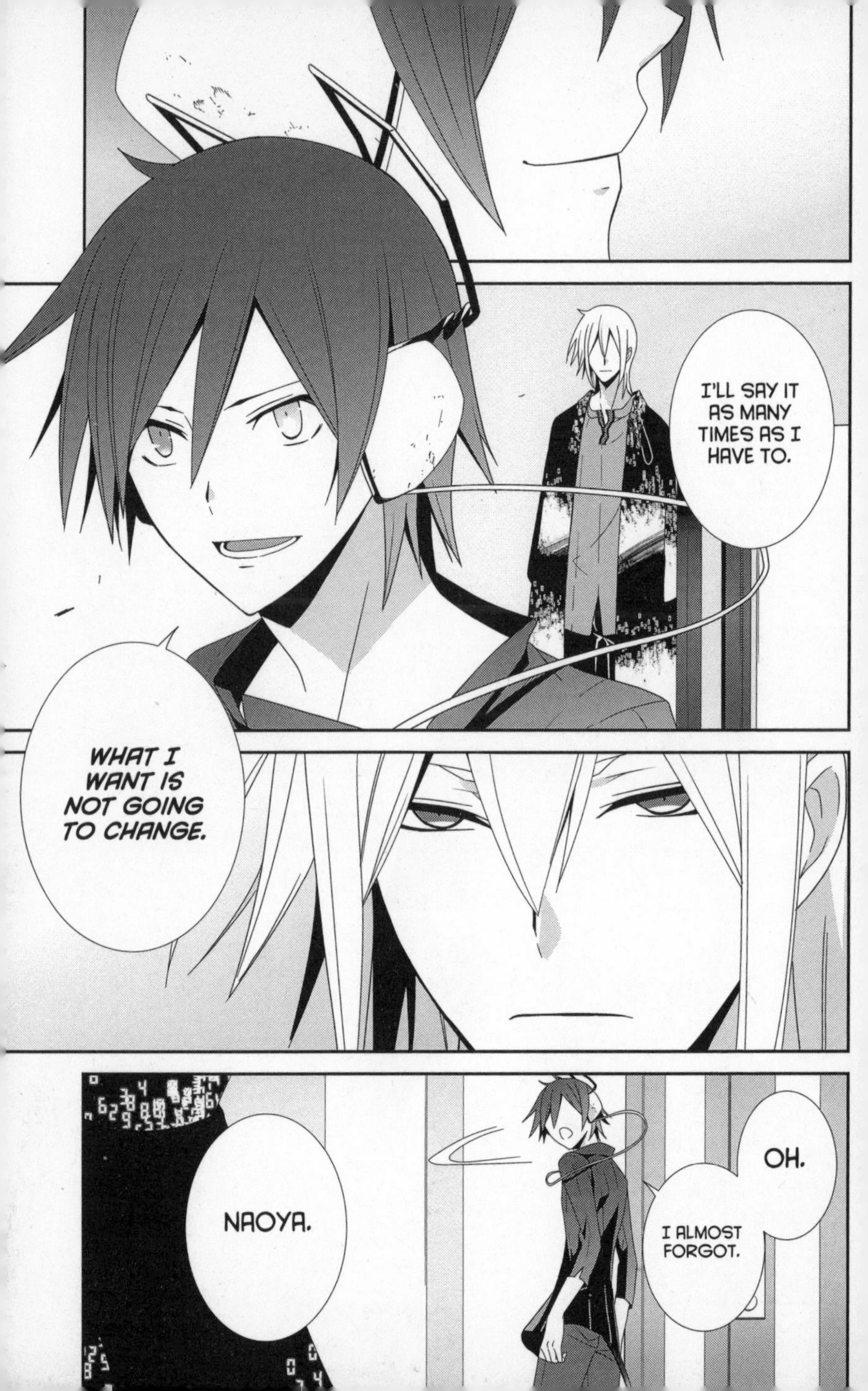
I'LL SAY IT AS MANY TIMES AS I HAVE TO.
WHAT I WANT IS NOT GOING TO CHANGE.
OH.
I ALMOST FORGOT.
NAOYA.

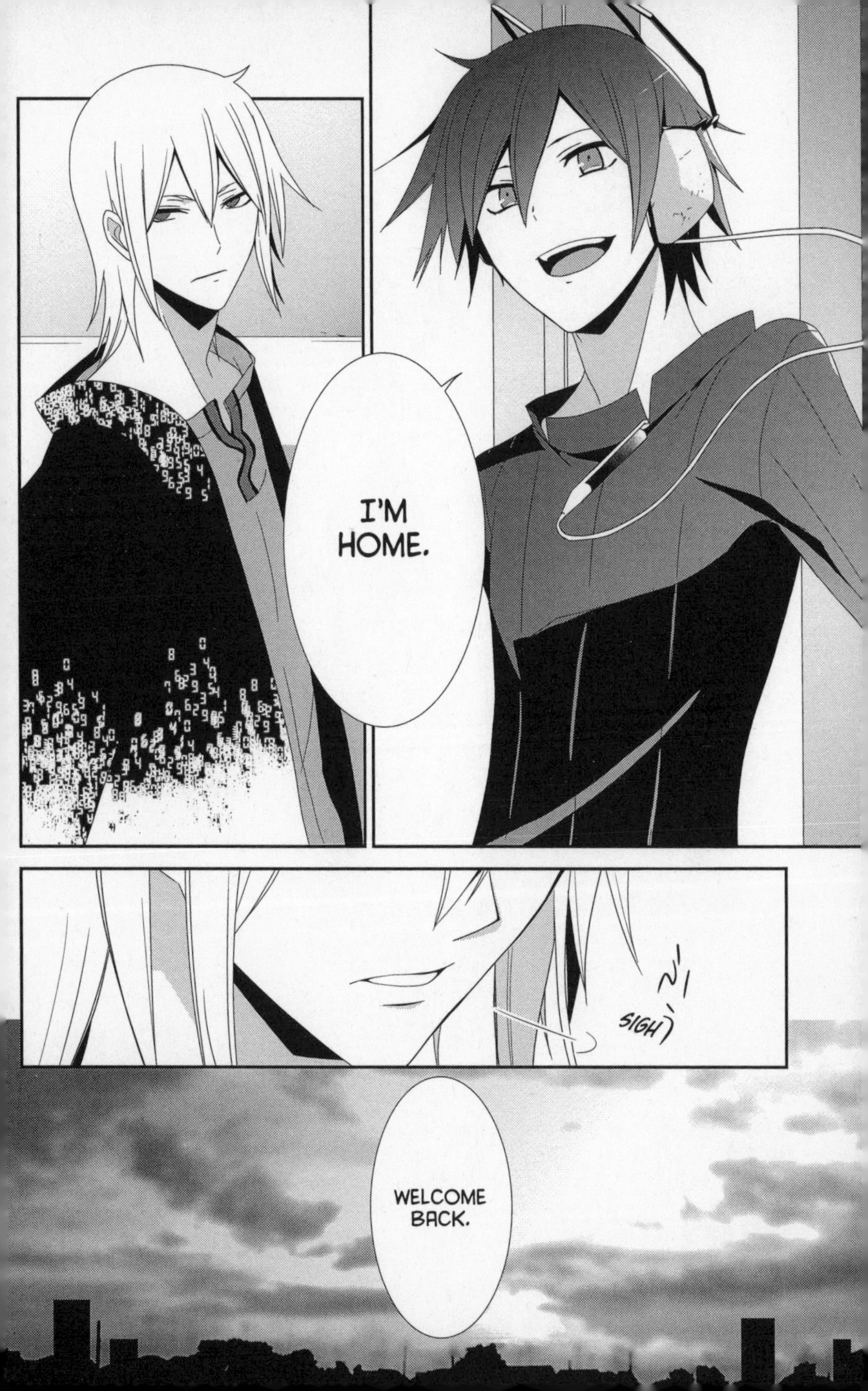
I'M HOME.
SIGH
WELCOME BACK.

I NEVER WOULD HAVE DREAMED THAT ONE DAY I'D GET TO DRAW THE DEMONS FROM THE *SHIN MEGAMI TENSEI* SERIES.

THIS MANGA WAS PUBLISHED IN *SIRIUS*, THE SAME MAGAZINE THAT RUNS A SERIES BY YASUDA-SENSEI, WHO DID THE CHARACTER DESIGNS FOR THE GAME, SO WHEN I STARTED, I WAS A BUNDLE OF NERVES. I'M REALLY RELIEVED THAT I MADE IT THROUGH TO THE END.

THE STORY IN THE ORIGINAL GAME CHANGES BASED ON CHOICES YOU MAKE AS THE MAIN CHARACTER. THE MANGA VERSION HAS NEW CHANGES, AND THE MAIN CHARACTER HAS NEW CHOICES AND A NEW CONCLUSION, SO I HOPE YOU ALL ENJOY IT AS JUST ANOTHER ONE OF MANY POSSIBLE ENDINGS.

I HAVE A LOT OF GRATITUDE FOR A LOT OF PEOPLE. STARTING WITH EVERYONE WHO READ THIS FAR (THE POSTCARDS, NEW YEAR'S CARDS, LETTERS, AND VALENTINE'S CHOCOLATE YOU SENT ME THROUGHOUT THE SERIES WERE A BIG SOURCE OF ENCOURAGEMENT!), MY EDITOR, SUZUHITO YASUDA-SENSEI, MY ASSISTANTS, AND TAKADA-SAMA, KOTŌ-SAMA, HAZUKI-SAMA, ETŌ-SAMA, AND THE *DEVIL SURVIVOR* TEAM.

THANK YOU ALL SO MUCH!

SATORU MATSUBA

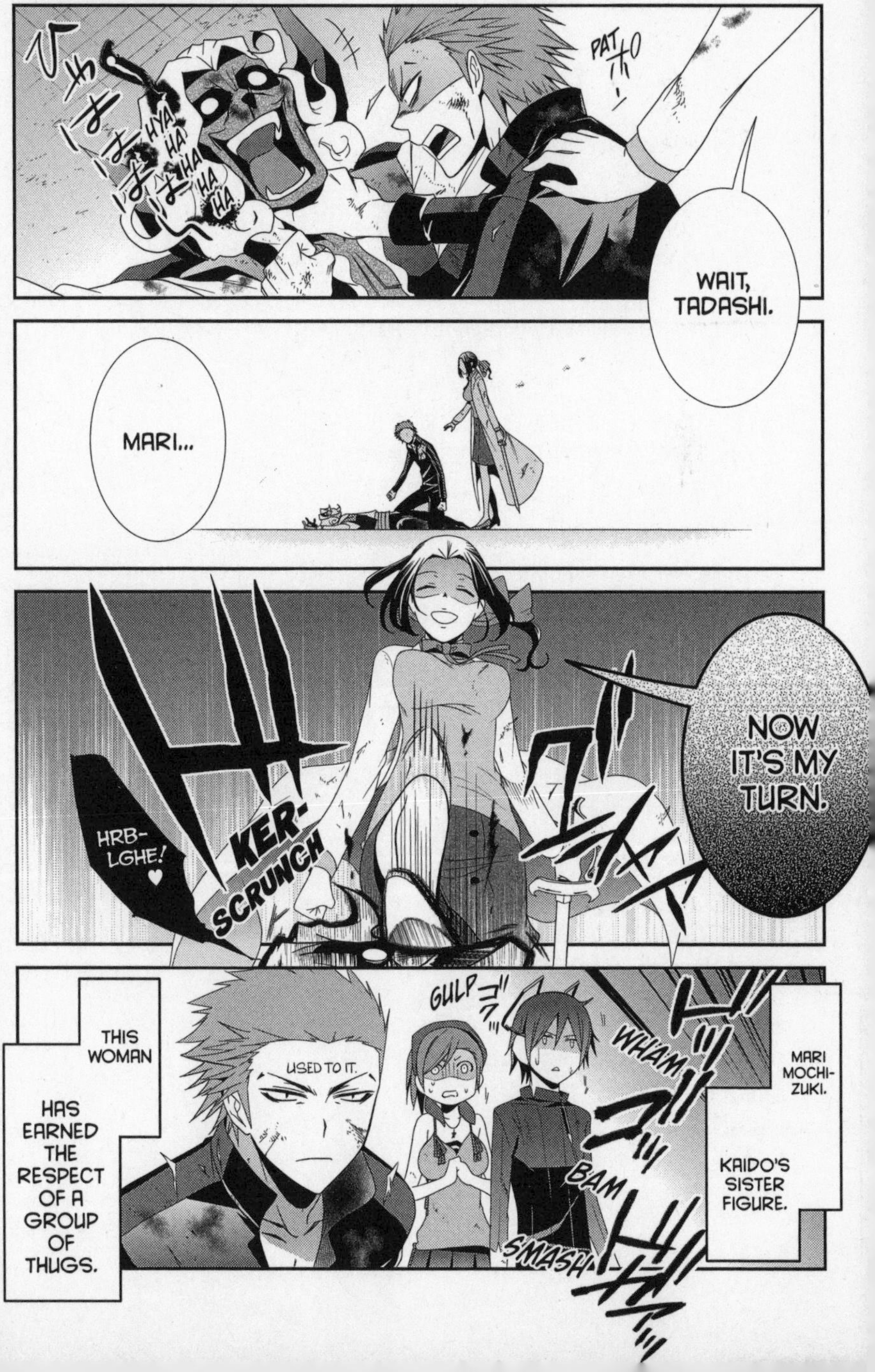
PAT
WAIT, TADASHI.
HYA HA HA HA HA HA
MARI...
NOW IT'S MY TURN.
KER-SCRUNCH
HRB-LGHE! ♥
MARI MOCHIZUKI.
KAIDO'S SISTER FIGURE.
WHAM
BAM
SMASH
GULP
USED TO IT.
THIS WOMAN
HAS EARNED THE RESPECT OF A GROUP OF THUGS.

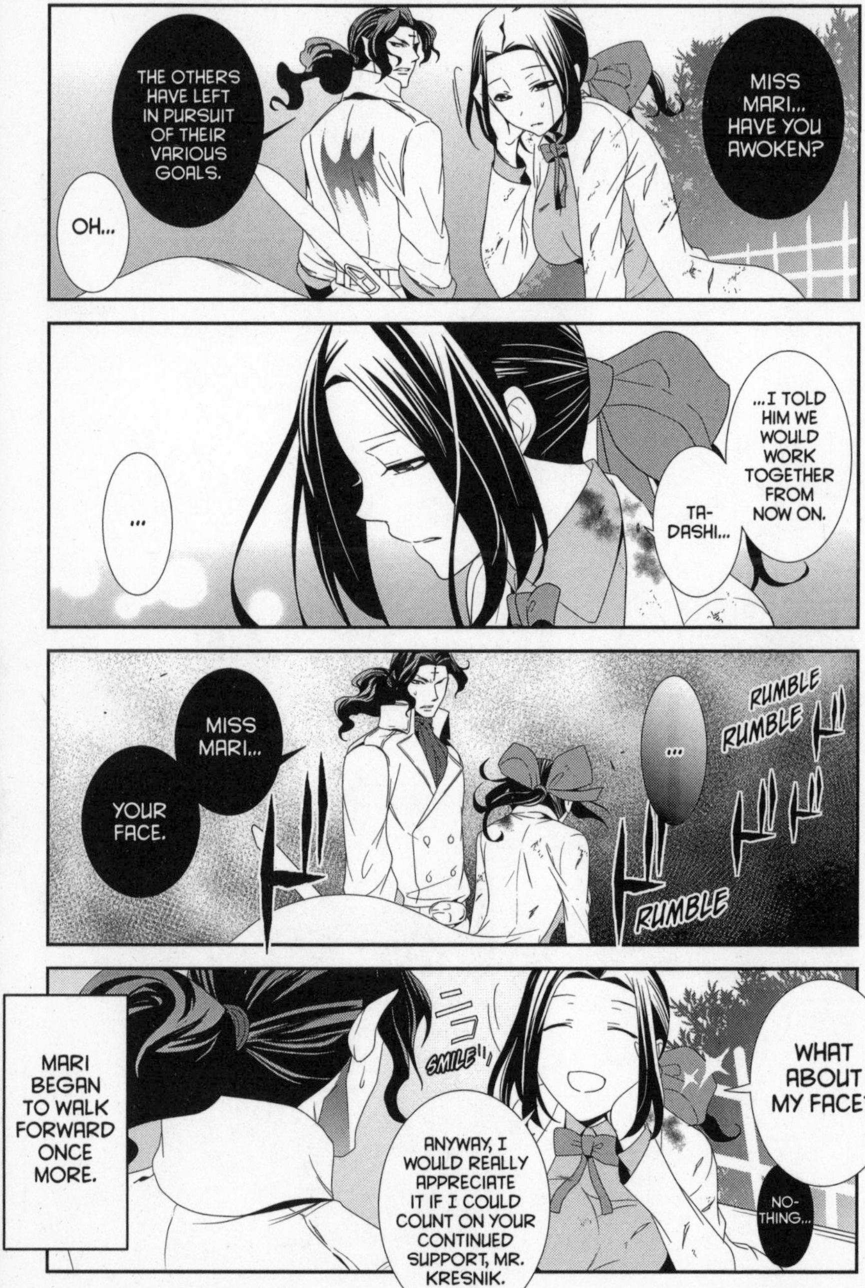
MISS MARI... HAVE YOU AWOKEN?
THE OTHERS HAVE LEFT IN PURSUIT OF THEIR VARIOUS GOALS.
OH...
...I TOLD HIM WE WOULD WORK TOGETHER FROM NOW ON.
TA-DASHI...
...
RUMBLE RUMBLE
...
MISS MARI...
YOUR FACE.
RUMBLE
WHAT ABOUT MY FACE?
NO-THING...
SMILE
ANYWAY, I WOULD REALLY APPRECIATE IT IF I COULD COUNT ON YOUR CONTINUED SUPPORT, MR. KRESNIK.
MARI BEGAN TO WALK FORWARD ONCE MORE.

VOLUME 6 BONUS MANGA

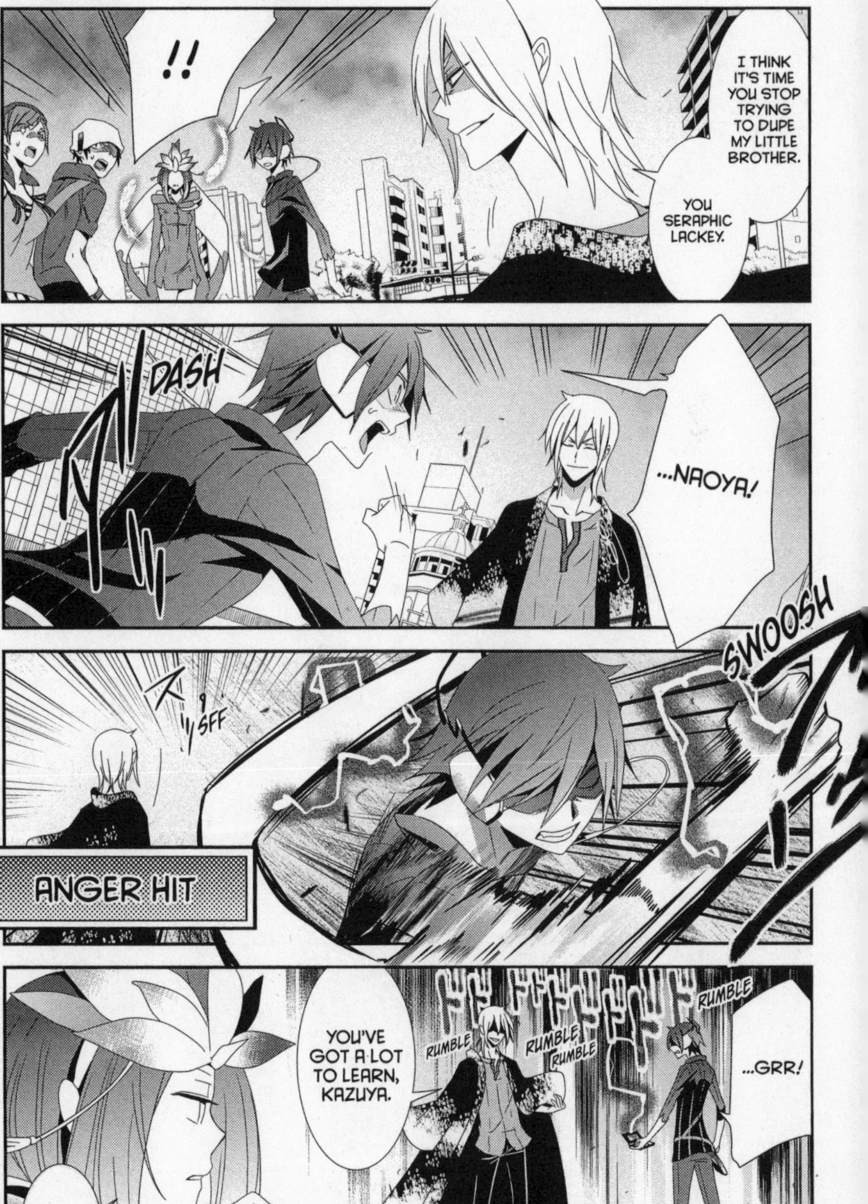
I THINK IT'S TIME YOU STOP TRYING TO DUPE MY LITTLE BROTHER.
YOU SERAPHIC LACKEY.
!!
...NAOYA!
DASH
SWOOSH
SFF
ANGER HIT
...GRR!
RUMBLE
RUMBLE
RUMBLE
RUMBLE
YOU'VE GOT A LOT TO LEARN, KAZUYA.
...

NOTE: ANGER HIT IS A SKILL IN THE GAME.

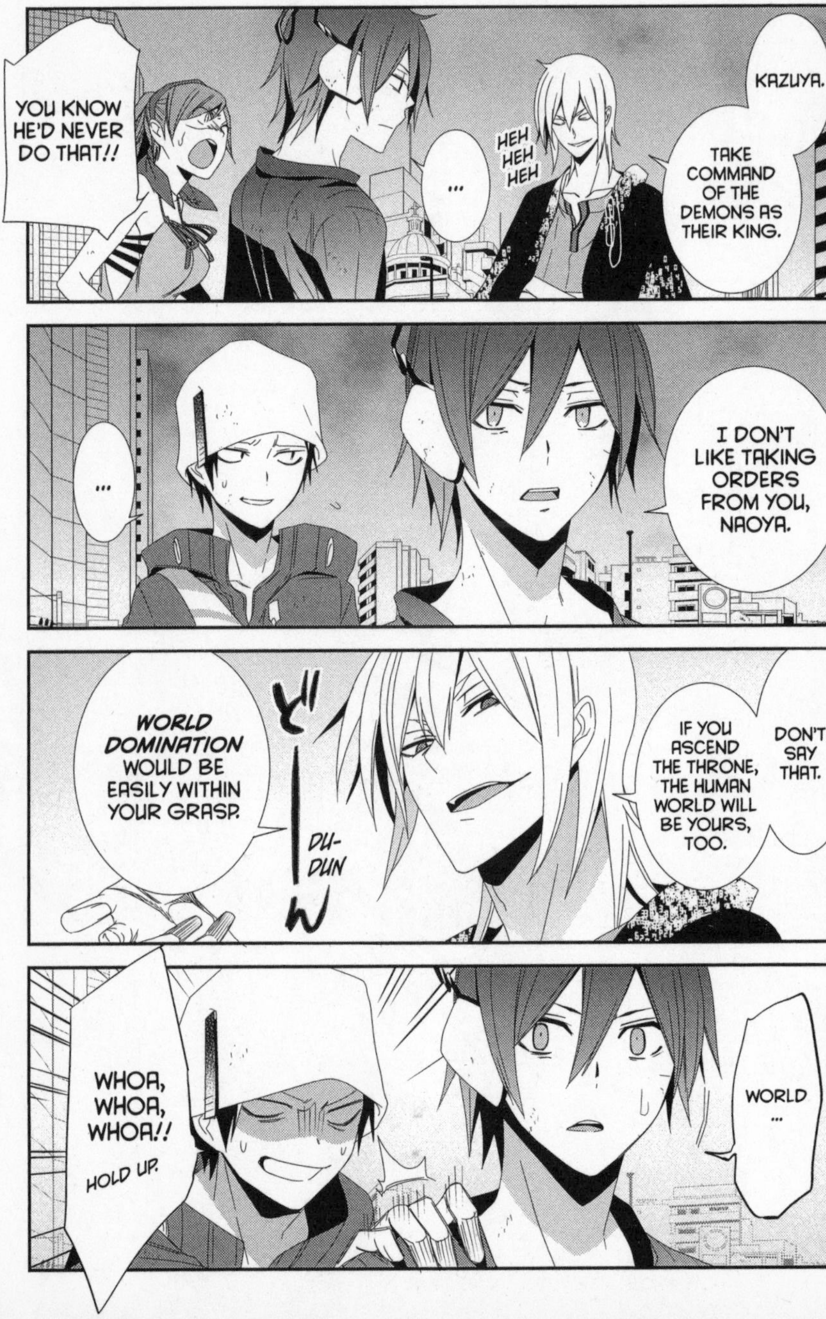
KAZUYA.
TAKE COMMAND OF THE DEMONS AS THEIR KING.
HEH HEH HEH
...
YOU KNOW HE'D NEVER DO THAT!!
I DON'T LIKE TAKING ORDERS FROM YOU, NAOYA.
...
DON'T SAY THAT.
IF YOU ASCEND THE THRONE, THE HUMAN WORLD WILL BE YOURS, TOO.
どーん
DU-DUN
WORLD DOMINATION WOULD BE EASILY WITHIN YOUR GRASP.
WORLD ...
WHOA, WHOA, WHOA!!
HOLD UP.

VOLUME 7 BONUS MANGA

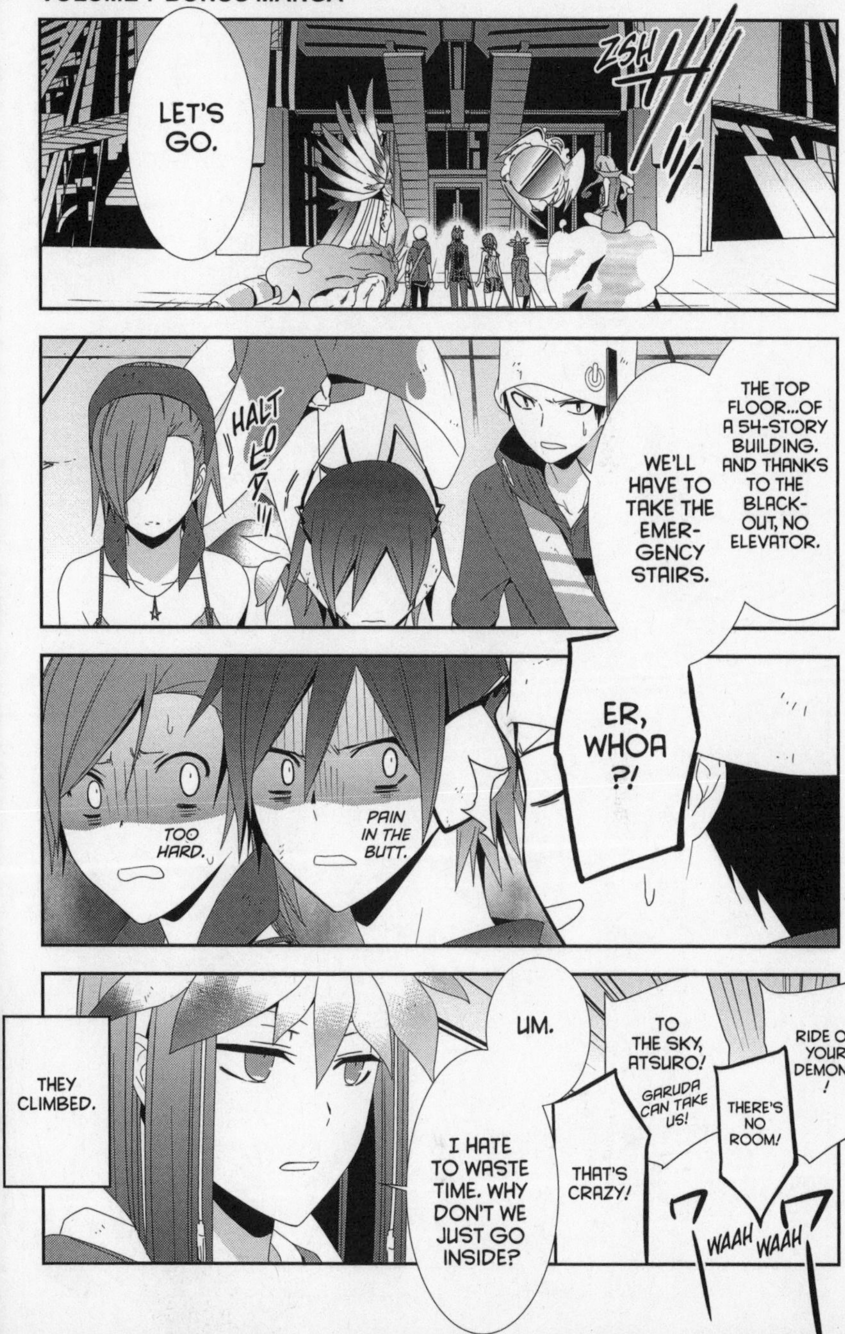

ZSH
LET'S GO.
THE TOP FLOOR...OF A 54-STORY BUILDING. AND THANKS TO THE BLACK-OUT, NO ELEVATOR.
WE'LL HAVE TO TAKE THE EMER-GENCY STAIRS.
HALT
ER, WHOA?!
PAIN IN THE BUTT.
TOO HARD.
RIDE ON YOUR DEMONS!
THERE'S NO ROOM!
TO THE SKY, ATSURO!
GARUDA CAN TAKE US!
THAT'S CRAZY!
WAAH WAAH
UM.
I HATE TO WASTE TIME. WHY DON'T WE JUST GO INSIDE?
THEY CLIMBED.

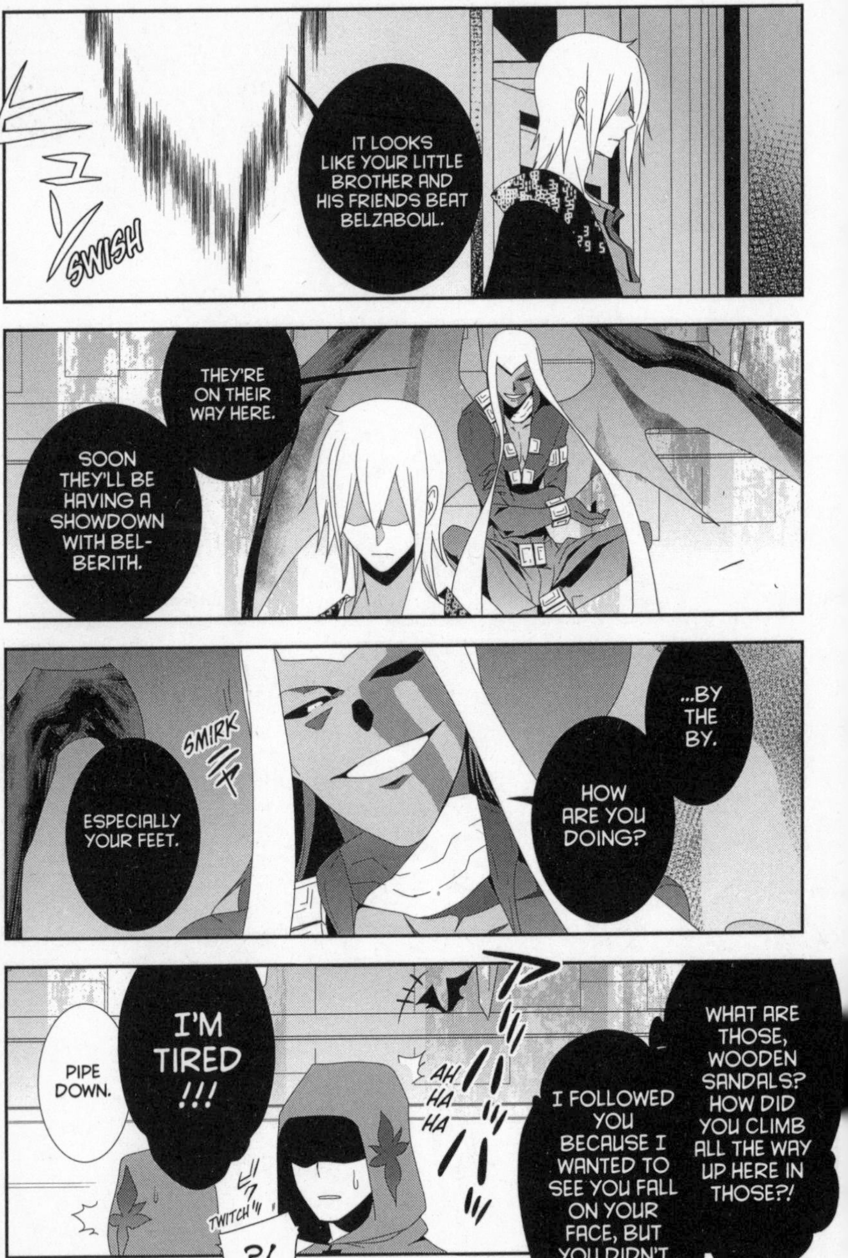
IT LOOKS LIKE YOUR LITTLE BROTHER AND HIS FRIENDS BEAT BELZABOUL.
SWISH
THEY'RE ON THEIR WAY HERE.
SOON THEY'LL BE HAVING A SHOWDOWN WITH BEL-BERITH.
...BY THE BY.
HOW ARE YOU DOING?
SMIRK
ESPECIALLY YOUR FEET.
WHAT ARE THOSE, WOODEN SANDALS? HOW DID YOU CLIMB ALL THE WAY UP HERE IN THOSE?!
I FOLLOWED YOU BECAUSE I WANTED TO SEE YOU FALL ON YOUR FACE, BUT YOU DIDN'T EVEN TRIP.
AH HA HA
I'M TIRED!!!
PIPE DOWN.
TWITCH
?!

VOLUME 8 BONUS MANGA

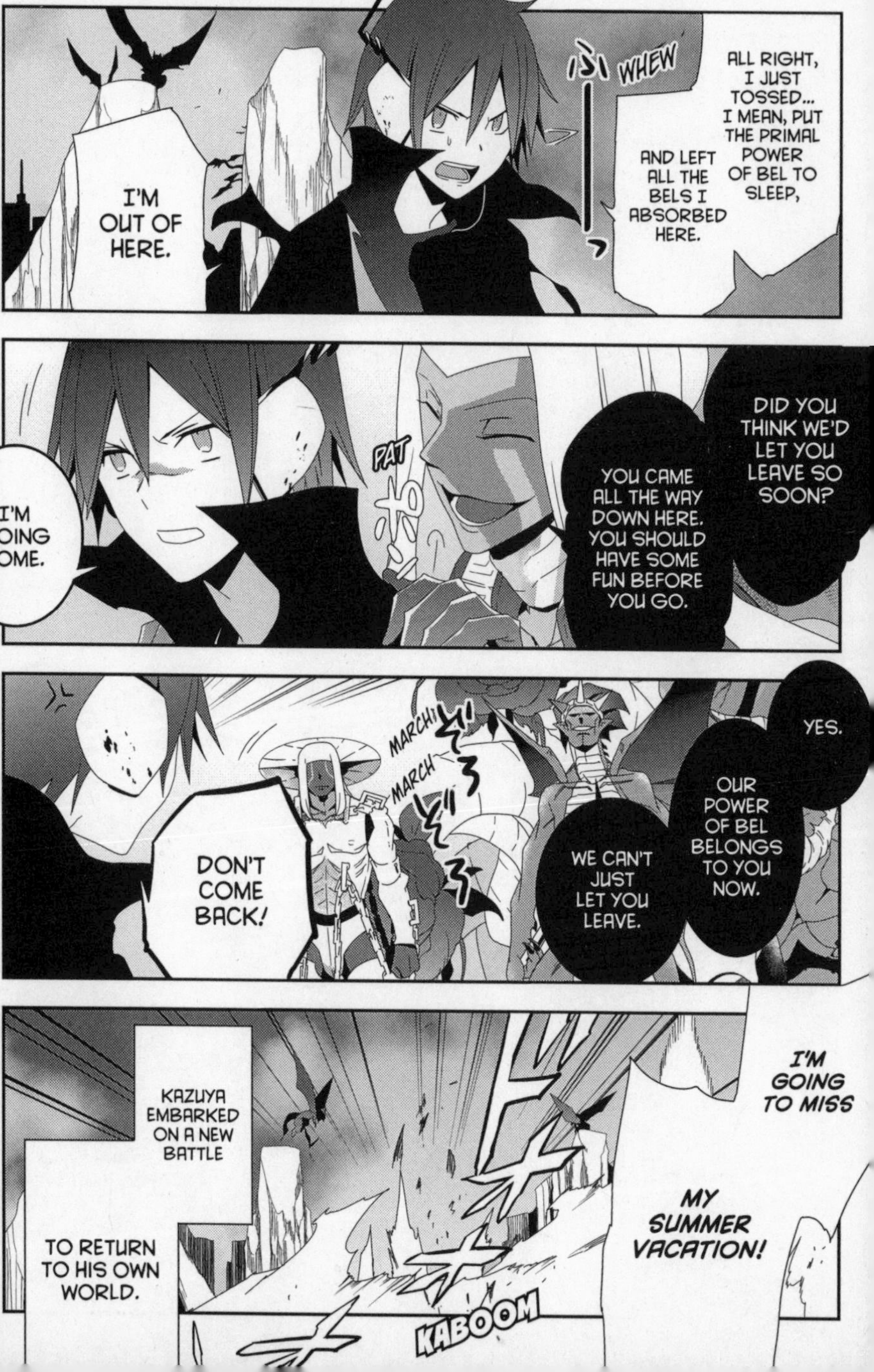
ALL RIGHT, I JUST TOSSED... I MEAN, PUT THE PRIMAL POWER OF BEL TO SLEEP,
AND LEFT ALL THE BELS I ABSORBED HERE.
WHEW
I'M OUT OF HERE.
DID YOU THINK WE'D LET YOU LEAVE SO SOON?
YOU CAME ALL THE WAY DOWN HERE. YOU SHOULD HAVE SOME FUN BEFORE YOU GO.
PAT
I'M GOING HOME.
YES.
OUR POWER OF BEL BELONGS TO YOU NOW.
WE CAN'T JUST LET YOU LEAVE.
MARCH
MARCH
DON'T COME BACK!
I'M GOING TO MISS
MY SUMMER VACATION!
KABOOM
KAZUYA EMBARKED ON A NEW BATTLE
TO RETURN TO HIS OWN WORLD.

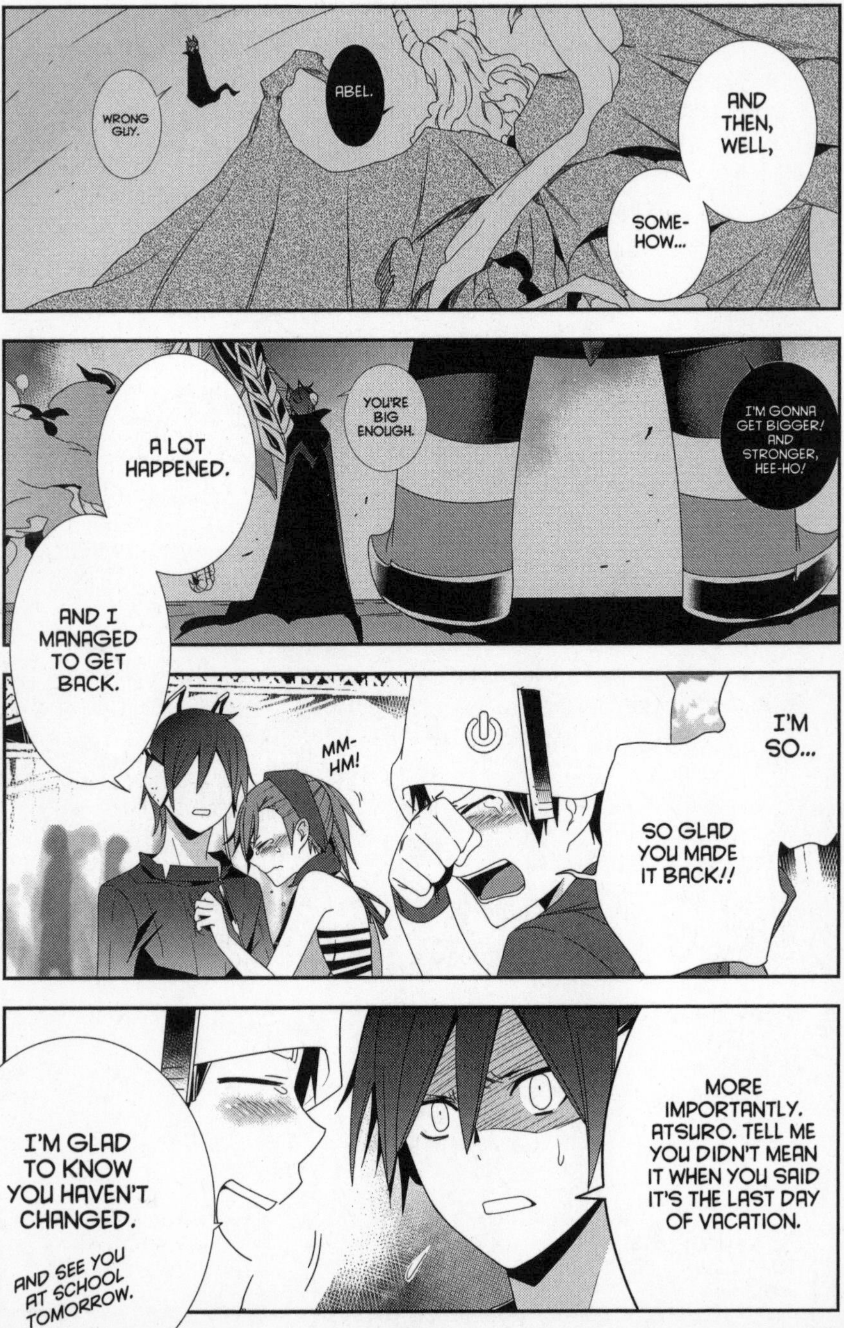
AND THEN, WELL,
SOME-HOW...
ABEL.
WRONG GUY.
I'M GONNA GET BIGGER! AND STRONGER, HEE-HO!
YOU'RE BIG ENOUGH.
A LOT HAPPENED.
AND I MANAGED TO GET BACK.
I'M SO...
SO GLAD YOU MADE IT BACK!!
MM-HM!
MORE IMPORTANTLY. ATSURO. TELL ME YOU DIDN'T MEAN IT WHEN YOU SAID IT'S THE LAST DAY OF VACATION.
I'M GLAD TO KNOW YOU HAVEN'T CHANGED.
AND SEE YOU AT SCHOOL TOMORROW.

A Kodansha Comics Trade Paperback Original.

Published in the United States by Kodansha Comics, an imprint of Kodansha USA Publishing, LLC, New York.

Publication rights for this English edition arranged through Kodansha Ltd., Tokyo.

First published in Japan in 2016 by Kodansha Ltd., Tokyo.

ISBN 978-1-63236-289-6

Printed in the United States of America.

www.kodanshacomics.com

9 8 7 6 5 4 3 2 1

Translation: Alethea Nibley & Athena Nibley
Lettering: Paige Pumphrey
Editing: Lauren Scanlan
Kodansha Comics edition cover design: Phil Balsman